FREE ENTERPRISE

FREE OR LOW COST TECHNIQUES TO START YOUR BUSINESS, IDEA, INVENTION OR, DOUBLE YOUR EXISTING BUSINESS

HOWARD F. BRONSON, MSJ

Copyright © 2009 Howard F. Bronson, MSJ

The Free Market Institute Press

All rights reserved. No part of this book may be transmitted nor reproduced in any form, in any country by any means mechanical, manual, electronic, including, photocopy, digitization, recording, or by any information retrieval or storage system in existence or that comes into existence at a future date, except as may be permitted by the 1976 Copyright Act or, in writing from the author, except in case of reviews or situations where singular quotes or paragraphs are utilized in a classroom setting.

Permission for use, interview, speaking engagements, quantity sales or consultation inquiries should be emailed to fairnessinc@hotmail.com

PRINTED IN THE UNITED STATES OF AMERICA

First Edition March 2009

Library of Congress Cataloging-in-Publication Data

Bronson, Howard F., 1953-

Free Enterprise/ Howard F. Bronson - The Free Market Institute Press ed.
p. cm.

ISBN: 1-4392-2818-3

TABLE OF CONTENTS

I. Dedication	1
II. Foreword	3
III. The Science and Power behind This Book	17
IV. Disclaimer	22
V. MAXIMIZING THE ACTIVATOR AND POWERPOINTER SEGMENTS	23

CHAPTER ONE — 39
FINDING YOUR MOST POWERFUL IDEA
Discovering The True Entrepreneur Within

CHAPTER TWO — 65
ADVANCING YOUR CONCEPT
The Process of Self-Assessment

CHAPTER THREE — 92
ASSESSMENT
How To Test Your Ideas and Business Concepts for Free

CHAPTER FOUR — 123
DO-IT-YOURSELF R&D
Create a Model and Protect It

CHAPTER FIVE — 147
FIRST STEPS TO MARKET
Materializing Your Concept

CHAPTER SIX — 179
TESTING THE MARKET
Listening With Logic vs. Emotion

CHAPTER SEVEN — 201
INITIAL SALES
"Hello Out There. What Do You Think?"

CHAPTER EIGHT — 227
PRICING, SALES and DISTRIBUTION
Converting Dreams to Dollars

CHAPTER NINE   253
CREDIBLE, MOSTLY-FREE ADVERTISING THAT WORKS
"Hey boss, look at this."

CHAPTER TEN   299
CREDIBLE, NO-RISK PAID ADVERTISING
Maximizing 'Return On Investment'

CHAPTER ELEVEN   335
PUBLICITY
Developing Good Sales 'Karma'

CHAPTER TWELVE   353
CONVENTIONAL ADVERTISING
If It Doesn't Pay, You Don't Play

CHAPTER THIRTEEN   377
MOVING GOODS & SERVICES TO MARKET
The Joy of Demand

CHAPTER FOURTEEN   389
THE INTERNET 'WORKS' SYSTEM
How to Become a 'PAMPS' Champ

CHAPTER FIFTEEN   399
BUSINESS SUCCESS
The Elements of Sustained Profitability

AFTERWORD   409
Overcoming Any Business Challenge

INDEX   433

DEDICATION

My new bride often chides me for working late hours, even at this stage of my life. So she came up with this clever idea of planting my desk in the corner of the living room. Sounded like a good idea at first; it was a large place to allow me to spend the usual 2 hours of nightly catch-up. In the beginning, it worked out just fine, until I felt this little tug at my pant-leg. It was my baby daughter Gabriella. She wanted to play and dance and sing. "Not now, Daddy has to work to make money to take care of the family." But after some time, and considerable tugging and whining, her message got through.

For my two oldest daughters now full grown, I often chased them out of my home office and spent many late hours there. Yes, I made decent money as a result but I lost those moments with them forever. And all that money? It came and went.

Money is vital for a comfortable American life. Money is also replaceable. But moments are precious. So don't forget the value of those irreplaceable moments with your own children.

This book is dedicated to all of those moments...climbing Haystack Mountain in Vermont with Ashley and Rachel, attending virtually everyone of their ballet recitals from ages three to seventeen, dancing each night with little Gabriella, watching Ari fill the room with joy with his smile, watching Joel mature into a young man of integrity and love, every drop of laughter shared, seeing my bride and I celebrate the moments together and realizing their value.

***

Moments. When it comes to money and moments, one serves the other. Always remember which serves which.

FOREWORD

We Live In Challenging Times to say the least, and there is more work to be done than ever before in history. Yet, unemployment is up, bankruptcies are at a record level, foreclosures are through the roof, oil is proving to be both an environmentally and economically impractical means of fuel, (even if the inflated oil industry likely collapses under its own greed), food prices around the world promise to lead to a new outbreak of disease, famine, food wars and riots like we've never seen. 'Bailout', 'ridiculously low interest rates' and "We'll just print more money" seem to be the rallying cries but not the substantive solutions.

There's even tougher news than this: We do in fact, have the solutions to each of these problems right now. The technology, intelligence and political knowledge already exist. But what relevance does our business or idea have to do with all of this?

Because deep down inside, we know full well that the solutions are within each of us.

Right now, there is man who is making a full compliment of foods and deserts all from readily available beans, a farmer accidentally figured out how to grow wheat on almost half as much water, a single mother created a modest chocolate-chip cookie business in her small town, another created safe-plastic and lead-free toys two years before the lead scare sent millions of toys and baby bottles into the trash. A man figured out to make a plastic that heals itself, another created a system for keeping bullet wound and other trauma victims alive for an hour instead of just moments so life-saving treatment could be rendered, a former communications buff revisited the cold fusion process and created the basis for a system that could safely take us off of oil dependency forever.

And my favorite: People just like you are running national Multi-Million Dollar television advertising campaigns that promote and sell their idea for virtually no money. I could fill this entire book with truly amazing success stories; some as simple as a good recipe or simple service concept offered out of your own home, all the way to concepts that will solve the world hunger and green-house problems in less than three years. You'll read about all of the best and systems to advance your idea and most of them are either free or, cost very little money.

So why aren't all of these great inventions and solution-centered businesses happening right now? Why is the cost of oil out of control, why do the very promising solutions always seem to get buried, why did they really kill the electric car? The answer:

Componential Politics.

Now before you put this book down, believing it's all above your head, at least allow me to define *componential politics*. The succinct definition is you. How can that be, how you embrace a concept you've never even heard of? Most importantly, what if you have a very basic product or service that you simply want to develop profitably? Well,

Tough times inspire us to become more creative, inventive and self–reliant.

FREE ENTERPRISE

please don't disappear. Whether your concept is modest and you just want to learn all of the new free avenues available to make a few thousand or, even a few hundred extra dollars, this book will show in very plain language and in just a few weeks, you'll see the promised results. Or, if you've held an endless energy source in your hands (as I have) that could heat and cool your home for years without fossil fuels, this book will help you to advance your concept and bring it to life.

Whatever your concept or service is, from low tech to high tech, you will be amazed at how effectively you will be able to make your idea happen. The only real condition that I have is your dedication to making your idea into the best it can be. When you do that, you create a new *component* that helps make things better. Whether a low-fat chocolate-chip cookie or, a local lawnmower shop that can help customers gain 10% more gas performance from your lawnmower (multiply that by 80 million lawnmowers), your best work becomes a component of *Yankee Engineering* 3000, which all helps to improve things. So the reason a lot of these great ideas aren't happening yet is because you haven't put them out there yet.

Then there the second word: Componential *Politics*. Politics is not just whom we vote for, it's also the social efforts to allow us to work together more effectively. How many readers ever lost a job due to office politics? Politics have been defined as the art of the possible. Politics can also render the necessary and promising, impossible. Ever had a health-insurance dispute where you knew you were in the right but, became overwhelmed in the fight to receive the coverage you were already entitled to in the first place? Congratulations, you know what real politics are.

The living rooms, garages, basements, home offices, home laboratories, office or free University- incubators and back yards are abundant with every solution to make our world better. A young mechanic in Northern California created a whole new cost-effective means to generate electricity from wave-power. This is not a new concept but the way he did it, using old engine fly-wheels was. His venture could have provided electricity to five-million Californians with a home-power generation unit. It never got off the ground.

A dedicated man in the Midwest built a personal flight craft using old motorcycle engines. He will succeed. What's the difference?

One surrendered and one didn't. Which one are you willing to be? If you allow me to help you advance the right idea that works for you, that idea will drive your success. The key is in learning the simple and often free steps available to you to build an ever-strengthening bridge between your concept and cash-flow.

Are tough times getting to you? Do you suddenly need an extra $900. each month or a few thousand dollars each month? Is the great river of money passing you by? Did you know that you could connect to that river stream and make the money you need if you are willing and able to do something about it?

Real political solutions begin with you and the work you do.

FOREWORD

Do you feel a bit overwhelmed or discouraged? Well, guess what, there are millions in the same situation that you're in. No, it isn't as easy as so many of the schemes and scams promise because if it were, everyone would be rich by now. But if you are willing to follow some very workable and pragmatic steps, you can make real and substantive improvements in your personal economy.

This is quite simply a book about trust and results that lead to money. Each section has a stated goal and specific steps. The goal of the intro is to tell you that if you use this book properly, it will improve your life and you will make more money with your very own idea or business just by following the steps outlined in this book. Are the steps hard to understand and use? Absolutely not. Will money just drop into your lap without any effort? Absolutely not and do not believe for a second that anyone can deliver on that mythology you see advertised everywhere, everyday.

If you follow the clear steps in this book relevant to your idea, steps which are generally similar to following a recipe, your idea will advance. In this book, you'll find every real possibility for helping to advance your idea in a real and measurable way.

And the more effort you put into it, the more results you will see and the more money you will make. I can easily guarantee that. And I guarantee that you will save thousands of dollars in development, marketing and promotion of your idea, business; any enterprise you're endeavoring to build.

When you see things improve either for your existing business or, your brand new enterprise, only then will you say to yourself, "Hey, that was a lot easier than working twice as hard and wasting all that money like before." Or you may say something a bit more severe to your advertising or marketing consultants.

For me personally, my primary goal is to see far more ideas from people like you come to life and survive as a sustainable business than is presently the case, and to show you how easy it can be to survive and thrive with your idea by using the techniques in this book Ventures are in fact adventures. They can rekindle hope and drive in the spirit. And when they make some money, you become inspired to build from there. All you need are the simple steps that nobody told you about, at least not yet.

So what's so special about the techniques outlined in this book? Quite simply, most of them will deliver exactly what you need to develop a successful concept, business, organization, for little or no money. All you need to do is spend some time putting these free resources to work. You may be familiar with several of the basic techniques but certainly not all of them. What is not familiar to most of you is that these powerful techniques, the same ones that people are presently spending billions of dollars to enact, are now generally free or very close to it. That's good news for a host of reasons because at present, well over 90% of all great ideas and great business concepts go to the grave with their creators un-realized. And more than half of all new endeavors will waste in

You are just steps away from your own success.

FREE ENTERPRISE

excess of 70% of their initial expenditures and will fade away as a result. Those remaining often give up because they fall under the false impression that they need a lot of money to develop their idea.

I am here to tell you that 90% of you have been severely misguided and it's no surprise. Most entrepreneurial books, programs or sales programs begin in one of three ways:

1) They promise you untold riches from whatever idea is in your head. Then they basically tell you that all you have to do is believe in yourself and pay them lots of money.

2) They promise you untold riches for whatever idea is in their head. In other words, only if you employ their system (for an added substantial fee, of course), will you join the lucky one to three percent who succeed with their program. By the way, my system when used properly has over a 90% success-rate.

Compare that to any invention submission organization, many of whom have a documented success-rate of less than one percent! And they charge anywhere from $700. to $2,500. to allow their customers the privilege of enjoying that 99% failure-rate.

3) They promise you untold riches but only if you sell their product.

In reality, the untold riches are untold because they don't happen so they can't be told. They cannot happen, at least to you from these programs and they're not designed to enrich you but to enrich them. Don't believe it? Go to www.ftc.gov and read the slew of warnings and the billions of dollars that hopeful dreamers, inventors and entrepreneurs throw away, along with their hopes, to large, professional-sounding submission organizations.

In the next six months, no matter what I say, no matter what the FTC does, almost 20% of all great dreamers will spend an average of $2,000. each and will get nothing but discouraged from making their great idea happen.

We have to work together to stop this because at present, the situation has become so severe that society as a whole is being deprived of important advances in business and innovation. Because of greed and deceit the invention and small business industry are suffering from their own version of a global warming-type crisis.

You'll learn more about those simple protective measures later and then one-by-one, we can work together to soundly and simply reverse these discouraging trends by simply putting the power of media and development in <u>your</u> hands. All you have to do is open those hands and I will give you everything you need. But why should you trust me?

The answer is quite simple: You should trust whomever really delivers measurable results, not those who simply deliver you slick promises.

Most of what you will need to do to develop your idea will cost you little or no money, just a little time.

FOREWORD

You should trust the guy who is willing to prove his results for virtually no money and who is willing to refund your money if you don't see results. $29.95 with guaranteed results vs. $2,000. to as much as $20,000. (you know who you are), which makes more sense to you?

If you are willing to use this book to learn how to make use of the tens of thousands of dollars of solid free advertising and development media readily available to you, I will promise you:

1) Better-than-expected results for your best ideas.
2) Greatly reduced or, eliminated advertising and all development expenses.
3) Faster or enhanced profitability.

Most importantly, I promise you a more fulfilling life. All you need to do is give this book a chance to change your life and a willingness to believe that the success of your idea is not just your natural birthright but your destiny and that there is no excuse for you not to claim your success.

Many who buy this book are just starting out but even if you're well on your way, there are so many techniques you can use to reduce costs and increase profits that you'll quickly see a substantial R.O.I. (Return on Investment).

This book is a business booster that you'll refer to over and over again and if you already have an ongoing enterprise that you simply want to enhance in development, manufacturing, advertising or publicity, simply jump right to that section and follow the directions in that section and if you do, I promise you that in a matter of a few short hours, you will pay for the cost of this book many times over.

Now if you are in fact starting out and find yourself saying "I'm not creative," "I can't build a business." or, I love this one: "My dad says that all I have to do is work hard," well, stop that. First of all, we are all creative one way or another.

Think of the single mother of two who wants to start her own business but laments that she's so busy figuring out how to get her children to school, how to survive on her meager salary, pay her rent and make a hundred other things happen just to get through the month. Can you imagine someone like this who has to invent and create 100 new ways to survive every month actually saying she isn't creative?

And what about our hard worker? I've met many successful self-made millionaires and billionaires who slaved day and night to get their first business off the ground. But the same is not true about their second or third ventures.

So it stands to reason that if you can save 90% of the time, expenses and frustration to bring your idea to a profitable state simply by learning from those who slaved away, why wouldn't you learn their proven shortcuts? As the expression goes, be a smart worker, not simply a hard worker.

Your money: Limited. Your ability to dream: UNLIMITED

FREE ENTERPRISE

People hesitate to pursue their great ideas not because they don't believe the ideas could be highly successful. They know the ideas are good. They don't engage in creative endeavors because they don't know where to begin. They have it in them, they just don't know how to get it out of them and share it profitably. Then if they finally muster up the courage to begin, they quickly become discouraged.

What if somebody steals their brilliant idea, what if they go bankrupt? Well then, we have to wonder about the millions of businesses large and small that operate successfully today on some level. From the street vendor to the creator of a plastic that heals itself, what sets them apart from you? Could it be you are worrying about the wrong things? Do you think that the successful street vendor in Calcutta or, the inventor of the cryogenic process that extends survival for trauma victims (yes, it's true) worry like you do or, do they even have time to worry?

Could it be that you're not getting anywhere because you're worrying about worrying instead of taking solid action to make your idea a reality? And since the solutions and methods to grow your idea are so easy to adapt, isn't it time to admit that the success you want is waiting for you if you really want it? Do you really want it, more importantly, do you need it?

Wanting to succeed is a noble characteristic. Needing to succeed is a far greater driving force. But you need money, don't you? Like the two famous electronics vendors. One was dirt poor; the other was given a $100,000 gift to help him get started.

Ten years later, the 'gifted' one ended up working for the guy who started with nothing. What's right with this picture? Wanting to succeed is simply not enough. Needing to succeed from the core of your being, needing to feed your family, get your kids through college, needing to improve the world in some way; what better combination of reasons are there?

I am inspired. I have been knocked down, broke, betrayed, and disappointed, Yet, I am inspired. I have often stood up for the right thing only to be accused of doing the wrong thing. I have saved companies and organizations from themselves only to be vilified.

Yet I am inspired. I fall forward, I fail upward. I learn from my mistakes but do not let my mistakes control or discourage me or, keep me from a destiny to serve. And because I let nothing stop me, I keep learning and growing. And because I need to succeed, I succeed in filling a need and get better at it all the time because you teach me.

Every entrepreneurial, psychological and spiritual writer I know says the same old thing. What is your purpose, what is your plan? They insist that you must have both but they're missing the bigger point for most which is that for the most part, most of us already know our purpose if we simply want to take a moment to look at ourselves. So the more important question is: What took you away from your dream?

Your good idea can make that extra money you need if you follow the numerous success options in this book. Be sure to check out the 'Core Strategies and Tactics' for some of the most impactful basics you can easily do for little or no money.

FOREWORD

For most of us the short answer is 'life' 'happenstance', kids, a promising job; all the right reasons but ultimately, the human mind has an amazing mechanism that reveals itself as that nagging sense of sadness and emptiness that we struggle to cover over because we know there's something better inside of us. But we're afraid, unless we have to succeed. In that case, when we have to overcome or crash through any barriers in our way, we invent solutions.

So it is a commitment to succeed that makes us reach deep inside ourselves to awaken the great inventors or entrepreneurs at happens because we are willing to solve any problems. That's what this book is all about: solutions, solutions, solutions. Shortcuts that work better than the long version, free development and media access that often works better than the paid versions.

You'll learn how to access all of them and you'll learn how and why the free systems are growing all the time and how and why these free systems if utilized properly, can often yield superior results.

The other thing we fear is the process of self-discovery. In the last paragraph, I suggested that we already know our purpose *for the most part.*

We cannot know it completely until we try and unfortunately, for many who do try, discouragement comes quickly and they rush back to their boring old secure life with less danger but an irrepressible boredom. Then they can say, "Hey, we tried and real success just isn't in the cards for me." This book is for you because it will allow you to keep trying by taking more well-insulated risks until you find the concept that really excites and motivates you each day. Risks with virtually no consequence.

You Tube, My Space, Blogging, Twitter, e-bay, Text Messaging podcasting, and a host of others not even heard of by most people just a short blip ago – what do they all mean, what is happening to media? Three things actually:

1) Media is in the hands of the people like you and me, more than ever before.
2) Media can reach from you to a precisely targeted individual like never before.
3) Most of the formerly protected and exclusive media is now free and effective if you're willing to learn the simple steps and, take the time to make it happen.

Welcome to the free media revolution and its literally millions of free opportunities. It's the biggest thing that's ever hit the free world and you're going to learn how to make it work for your ideas. The free media revolution began nearly thirty years ago. Back then, I showed readers how to access a handful of free media systems and every few years, I would update the process. Today, the free systems that have become available just in the past year are more plentiful and powerful than anything available over the past three decades and once you learn these systems, you will always be able to keep up with the changes and new free trends on your own.

Determine what success means to you and then, commit to that success.

FREE ENTERPRISE

What this also means is that ideas or business prospects that used to cost thousands or hundreds of thousands of dollars to test, establish, rent retail space for, incorporate, advertise - you can now test for little or no money at all.

Testing out a venture today is like having a money-back guarantee because you don't have to spend the money you used to have to spend and, you can often do it all for free. Can you see all the old excuses evaporating? And can you see all those consultants evaporating as well as the power and capabilities come easily into your hands.

You know that there is work to be done, things to improve and you've had several ideas in the past but you never knew what to do to make them happen. Unless you feel your world is perfect and there is nothing you can do to make a difference, use this book to give your good ideas a real fighting chance. You really can make a positive difference in this world and, in your bottom line with minimal risk. Low risk and high profit are the keys.

Books promise but systems deliver. The best comments I used to receive about my earlier books were that the pages became torn and tattered from overuse.

Now here's a book with three times the volume and content and 1,000 times the value. Use these systems well, wear out these pages and together, we will make your idea the success it deserves to be. Now let's get to it.

How to Eliminate EXCUSES

Because I want each of you to succeed, I've carefully studied the things that might cause you to fail. The biggest reasons are the self-invented excuses for not moving forward that we tend to disguise as logical explanations. Use this list and pointers to help eliminate these unnecessary barriers:

Here are the top ten reasons concepts fail and, what you can do to overcome these obstacles. You'll note there are many fears and doubts listed; concerns that used to seem real and foreboding. You'll also see how this book is designed to help you eliminate these concerns.

1) **Lack of Confidence**. You just don't believe that you have what it takes to make your concept work so you never really give it the energy it deserves. As a result, you defeat yourself from the beginning. The book will help anyone to learn as they go and as you become an expert in your field and the money starts flowing, so does the confidence.

How will a shift in your thinking enhance your approach?

_____

_____

You can make your idea successful simply by joining the 'free media revolution.'

FOREWORD

2) **Lack of Money**. You think you need money to become productive but in truth, it is productivity that makes money. Think of the thing you ca right now to build value for your concept and do them. Each step will bring you closer to positive revenue.

How will a shift in your thinking enhance your approach?

---

3) **Fear of Having Your Concept Stolen**. People spend far too much time worrying about putting a lot of effort into a concept only to see someone come along and just take it. If this were a commonplace event, how would so many of the millions of the businesses large and small survive? In addition, as you progress, you should expect competition. Use that competition to keep improving your product. Also, the more effective you are in your marketing, the larger your markets share. So this excuse doesn't work either.

How will a shift in your thinking here enhance your approach?

---

4) **Fear of Making Mistakes**. This is a legitimate fear but that's why we've revealed so many ways to test and develop your idea for free or, for very little money, so your mistakes won't be costly and you can learn from them and, move forward. Accept mistakes as a pathway to your success.

How will a shift in your thinking enhance your approach?

---

5) **Fear of Not Being Able To Build a Trusted Team**. This can admittedly be a trial and error process so in the beginning, don't be too anxious to give away shares or interests until you know that each member of your team can pull their weight. Also, do you really need a team? Do not bring on people you don't need. Instead, first learn the simple systems in the book and you may discover that the book will eliminate the need for excessive team-building.

How will a shift in your thinking enhance your approach?

My 'Litmus Test' will allow you to test your big or small ideas for little or no money.

FREE ENTERPRISE

6) **Not Being Able to Come Up With a Concept That Best Suits You.** The book will show you how to evolve your best concept and test it risk-free. Dare yourself to try out your capabilities and you'll be pleasantly surprised at how your ideas will start to take on a life on their own.

How will a shift in your thinking enhance your approach?

_____

_____

7) **Doubts about Being Able to Successfully Reach Your Customers or End-Users.** You'll learn how to identify prospects and develop a profile of their habits and patterns. Then, you' learn about all of the best media to effectively reach them. Best of all, you'll learn how to test the media for free or very little money.

How will a shift in your thinking enhance your approach?

_____

_____

8) **Professionals Are Advising You That These Systems Won't Work.** Invariably, some expert in media will insist that you have to pay a professional to do everything. In the meantime, thousands of people are using the easy-to-follow systems in this book that prove the professionals wrong. Sometimes, people don't want to admit that these systems work because it takes business away from them.

How will a shift in your thinking enhance your approach?

_____

_____

9) **Fear of Business Headaches.** Yes, business can have its frustrations but weigh that against not trying to improve your life. How will the bills get paid then? In addition, you will learn how to make most of your business headache-free, especially as your develop your customer service.

How will a shift in your thinking enhance your approach?

_____

_____

What is the value of an excuse whose only purpose is to excuse you from succeeding?

FOREWORD

10) Fear of Not Having the Time To Build Your Dream. You'll learn how to find more time for your daily life than you presently have, even with your new venture. A successful business can make life easier and happier on so many levels because you will have earned yourself more freedom to choose the life you truly want.

How will a shift in your thinking enhance your approach?

Personal Challenges

What have you learned about your idea today and what are the next steps you need to make it functional and profitable?

What is interfering with your progress and what steps are you taking to overcome those barriers? Who else is really going to do it for you? If you are not willing to inspire yourself, who else will but if you get excited about your idea, you will attract all kinds of positive elements. Momentum begets momentum.

I have dedicated my life to working with the entrepreneur and small business venturer. For the past three decades, I have either followed or developed all the key free or low-cost resources.

Every year, some new resource crops up; some new invention for marketing or communicating to the world about your venture. But the past year has been the exception or I should say, exceptional.

Free resource opportunities have increased not by three or four-fold or even a hundred but by a thousand-fold and just in the past year alone!

That means that the free media and business-revolution has now created more opportunities for inventors and small businesspeople than ever in history. And all of it is available to you for free or very low cost. That means you can do more than ever before but with minimal risk.

This book reflects the finest thinking of foremost experts in concept development and is dedicated to encouraging inventors, dreamers and anyone with a business they want to grow, throughout the globe.

This wealth of knowledge is in demand by top-line corporations and small-time inventors alike. The corporations spend billions each year to access what is now basically free media. Why do they do this? Because they don't know any better. For just the small price you paid for this book, you have very similar access that they have; free top-level resources that on a personal basis could cost you thousands of dollars. In essence, simply by purchasing this book, you are saying "I've hired you to help make the best out of the

Through this book, you will learn how to build a business around your dreams. Exercise your right to free enterprise and all of the amazing free resources to get there.

FREE ENTERPRISE

best of my idea!" or more specifically, you invested in our ability to help you profit from your ideas.

This book reflects years of frustration and discouragement that you'll never have to go through. It all began with a book entitled, Good Idea! Now What? With virtually no money or publishing experience, that small book sold 50,000 books before Time-Warner bought it. That book was the direct result of years of hard-knocks, learning in the trenches.

Succeeding with that first book was essential to prove to people like yourself that it could be done; that major marketing and development techniques could be adapted for the reader's personal use; that $50,000 marketing and advertising campaigns could often be achieved with better results, for far less, and that effective results-getting marketing-concepts could be customized to suit your own particular needs.

And now, this all new-creation is more information-packed than any book in its field, with literally thousands of resources and specific techniques, new production and marketing breakthroughs; each designed to help you bring your idea closer to reality.

This book is a dream-preserver and nurturer of ideas, large and small, laid out in a step-by-step fashion, complete with areas for you to notate and track your progress. It will become your own custom marketing guide engineered by you, just for you.

And don't forget when you need concise and specific guidelines, just contact my organization and we'll get you moving forward again with minimal cost.

This book also shows how money was being wasted by people who just didn't realize that much of their marketing and development could be done for little or no money, people who were formerly spending ten or twenty thousand dollars for a limited radio or TV tour or for various print publicity campaigns that never produced results. Now those same people are achieving much better results while investing far less to receive a real return on their investment, and of course that deeply satisfying positive return on their dreams.

Through this book, we are going to work together first to cultivate the best idea for you to work with and then take it step by vital step until it successfully reaches the end-user; the customer.

To have that essential economic edge in these uncertain economic times, you have to find the most practical way to build your dreams. It's our job to give your dream strength and integrity while helping you prove to yourself that your most sensible marketing paths are often the least expensive. We also want to work together and do everything possible to protect your dreams and ensure your success.

There are so many things that you can do to bring your idea to life. Don't let it die—you have no excuses now. This book is your marketing conditioner. Be patient and flexible be persistent.

In truth, we can always do what we really want to do.

FOREWORD

Yes we live in challenging times but that only means that we are each challenged to rise to the times and as you read this book, you'll discover that the simple and often no-cost systems available to you, are in fact an evolution of the intention of our founding fathers.

FREE ENTERPRISE. It's waiting for you.

**

It's not the wolves beneath your bed that ever you will need to dread. It's just the wolves inside your head.

FREE ENTERPRISE

Start with a Promise to Yourself

...first, not with a fancy or even a simple plan as many might try to convince you. As you'll see when you're finished, this book will become your master-planner research & development marketing guide. You must begin by making the following commitment contract with yourself.

I, _____, have purchased this book to help make a positive difference in my life by helping me to bring my idea(s) to fruition and/or to increase revenue to my existing business. I realize that while there are no substitutions for hard work, it is time-wasted to simply work hard at the wrong using the wrong outdated techniques. These new systems are usually better, quicker and either free of charge or, far less expensive ways in which to channel my valuable time.

I recognize that no failure is a waste of my resources if I have learned to use that failure as a stepping stone and then found a way to move ahead — and that it's better to make a thousand mistakes on a small scale than one mistake on a larger scale. To this end, I shall temper my zealousness with good listening and positive and ongoing self re-evaluation.

I am keenly aware that while I may have a limited or even highly limited operating budget, I can still generate an unlimited amount of dedication, enthusiasm and wisdom to discover new opportunities every day. And I will be my own light; I will connect my own dots and find the right path to my success.

_____   _____
Signature   Date

These free resources which have evolved over the past 30 years, are yours for the taking and, the providers of these free resources compete aggressively to get you to use their free service.

THE SCIENCE AND POWER BEHIND THIS BOOK

A successful marketing book requires meticulous planning and research. Most importantly, it requires the right mix of author, editor, publisher, sales force and proper media exposure.

I have seen too many of my friends being held hostage to employment situations where the predominant goal was to make money at the expense of family, friends, integrity and community. I've known far too many people who have had enough of this "me" behavior but were too afraid to stand up and make a change, and become their own 'hero'.

In this endless super-webbed world, how do you find the elements that embrace these ideals and link up just the right team? I have dedicated my life working to answer those questions so that you may have the power of productivity and success and that dream became the book you now hold in your hands.

My background consists mostly of creating simple and effective marketing strategies; hundreds of them to apply to any idea or venture. I also spent most of my career identifying the barriers to success and the means to overcome those barriers. One of those key barriers was cost and I have worked tirelessly to help spawn a free or sponsored services 'war' where key media and develop services are lining up by the Thousands to offer free media and development avenues to you.

How fast is it growing? As one small example, a few years ago, if you googled *free press release distribution*, there were just a few hundred-thousand listings. For those of you who have been paying thousands monthly for press releases or advertising, take a moment to google this topic right now to see for yourself.

Even if you eliminate 80% of all the google results for this topic as either irrelevant or duplicated, you will discover several Million free media resources. And this is just one small example of what has become available just in the last year alone! Revolution? You bet, so take advantage of it because you are the primary beneficiary and this book will show you how to access all of it.

Technique vs. Technology

Instantly, within moments after word about this book first started to get around, I started to receive hundreds of inquiries, offers and demonstrations from every technology imaginable and unimaginable.

Each one promised to deliver or manage media or, produce a more effective use of all the systems mentioned in this book. In fact, weeks before this book went into its first printing, I not only knew these products existed, I knew that new ones were cropping up

As you're reading this, keep saying to yourself, "I can do this. I can really make that extra money I need and I will make it happen."

sometimes every hour and that one would have to research ongoing to review and present each one.

To me, this is a very good thing. Certainly, I couldn't keep adding each new technology to the book, nor would that ever be my intention. It's critical to note two things here:

1) This book is about technique vs. technology. Technology is advancing by the moment and no book or single website could ever completely keep up. If however, you take the time to learn the many basics in this book, you can apply them to any technologies you choose.

2) This book is designed to affect the way you think about your possibilities. As you learn that the Free Media Revolution belongs to you, you will discover that you can find solutions and ways to move forward that you never knew were previously available. That will involve a measure of determination, imagination, strategic thinking (none of which are hard to do and all in this book) and technologies as you choose to apply them.

Every new technology that flashes across your email seems to promise something new and better. Some are helpful, some are not but if you work with this book, you will learn how to advance your idea to its best chances of developing revenue.

Being true to your gifts helps

I also discovered that a 'well examined life' will also lead to the most spiritually and financially successful life, but I could not find any books out there with the right and substantive balance of effective inspiration with sufficient instruction on how to benefit financially from that inspiration. So I set out to build upon my original theories stemming from the original books I wrote on the topic *Good Idea! Now What?* And the *'Great Idea!'* series to create a friendly directory that has never existed before but that every business, large and small really needs.

This book is designed to help move the reader through the fear of change, by making something better far more attainable. It serves as a step-by-step guide for creating new business opportunity, by helping you to understand the importance of how a flexible business plan (flexplan) produces an optimal physical and spiritual state as well. Never before have individuals faced so many challenges and opportunities at the same time. This book seeks to help you to think in new ways to open your eyes to the many new opportunities available to you.

Our ability to keep up with such demand has taken a toll on us, creating conflict between our true nature and how we see ourselves. In other words, most of us are not doing the work that they know they were born to do.

Fear and anxiety are not unfounded but they can and will easily be overcome with some simple action steps. These feelings are very real to those who have chosen to

There is nothing more powerful than a motivated promise to ourselves.

THE SCIENCE AND POWER BEHIND THIS BOOK

believe in what the world around them has determined to be true. Media bombarding us from every angle has filled our lives with so many mixed messages that we are not able to decipher the essence in our lives anymore. Many of us, especially, our youth are deluded into thinking that their wants are in reality, their needs. Unless self-actualization becomes a great video game or hot download, most don't care.

In first grade, I sat there with my mom and teacher and learned that I was dyslexic. I was to repeat first grade, and was told that I might never really be able to read nor write. Well, what you're holding in your hand is my eleventh book, very well reviewed and one of the top idea-development books in the world, written by me, the dyslexic kid branded to go nowhere.

I defied gravity to reach my dreams. My dyslexia forced me to become creative just to survive, and I've applied that creativity to every sales and marketing challenge we face today.

My handicap was the only thing that allowed me to discover who I really was and what I discovered is that we are all far more than we think we are.

Any of us at anytime can readily defy our own odds simply by first making the choice to do so and then, by connecting with the appropriate army as resources to not just rise far above any challenges but to become our best selves specifically because we worked to overcome those challenges.

Your success, your fulfillment, all your rewards are waiting for you. Don't tell me you can't do the same thing that I have done, don't tell me you can't defy gravity. Read this book and learn every method necessary to reach in and discover the best of yourself. I know you can do this because I started with far less than you and look at me today. I could write a book about it!

How to Discover and Spark Your Creative Edge

Conventional wisdom dictates that inspiration and education will give you the creative edge you need to succeed on your own but don't downplay hardship and struggle. As with physical pain, your financial and emotional pain are trying to tell you something and if you want to move away from that hurt, you will need to inspire your inventive creativity or, business savvy.

The world has all of the self-appointed gurus that it could ever need and they will tell you that you simply need to believe in yourself but that advice on its own will never help you to become all that you can be.

Fear is generally the great paralyzer that stops us from taking any real leaps of faith but if we shift our perspective for a moment and look at fear as a kind of pin that keeps jabbing us, that fear can be transformed into an energy that propels us forward.

Suddenly, instead of wanting to succeed, that pin-prick reminds us that we need to succeed. Skip Morrow is one of my favorite cartoonists and illustrators on the planet and

Just to get a small idea of how effective this book will be for you, stop for a moment and google 'free press release distribution'. And that's just one of the endless free pathways for developing your idea.

since he's a very kind and humble soul, I'm sure he would not want me to mention him in this book so I won't...much. But a few summers ago, while riding my old bicycle up a rather large hill near his home, I thought I was going to die from exhaustion. It was a hot and humid day, this was a tough hill and I had already ridden about nine hilly miles.

As a challenge, I thought I'd try to see if I could still muster the strength to make this last great hill but alas, I had run out of steam; there was nothing left so halfway up, my legs could not make even one more rotation. I knew I had to stop. And just as I did, the meanest, largest most frothy-mouthed, snarling large killer-dog came out of nowhere and opened its maw large enough to swallow me and my bicycle. The speed that I pedaled the remainder of that hill has to be a world record. The exact speed was precisely three inches ahead of that animal's determined fangs. I made it right to the top and that killer dog ran out of steam.

When I use my fear and doubts this way, I make an extra effort to move as far away from that pain as I possibly can. I compel myself to think a bit more rationally, strategize just a little more effectively and, I move forward because backwards would take me right into the dog's mouth.

I know my readers well. I know their hopes and struggles. I know that hundreds of thousands of people purchased this book to help them gain a badly needed financial edge. They are relying on the systems and techniques within it to take them to a higher financial plain because their current financial plain just won't sustain anymore and the dog is getting closer. I take that responsibility very seriously and my goal is to ensure that this is the best marketing investment you've ever made.

How to Change Direction without Beating Yourself Up

You know you have great ideas and great business potential and perhaps in the past, it has taken you to exciting places. Perhaps not. In any case, if you ask most people if they are where they expected to be financially, especially nowadays, the majority will give you a resounding *no*. Whether it be health finances, career or personal life, for most people nothing seems to go as they wish it would and believe it or not, that's often a good thing.

If you're reading this right now, you're smart and capable because you're being proactive. When life seems to go off course, people take a course, in school, that is. They learn something new; a technique, a new behavior, a new hobby or vocation. And as we take on newer healthier habits, we generally don't have time for the old bad ones.

So what happens if not just some, but all of your plans crash and you have to start right from the beginning? That's why many people bought this book either to help them enter a new and exciting phase or, to begin it all again. In any case, it's all new again and there's an automatic air of enthusiasm and rebirth when we have to start again.

When you overcome that which you think you cannot overcome, you become stronger and virtually unstoppable.

THE SCIENCE AND POWER BEHIND THIS BOOK

My divorce was one of the most painful experiences I ever had to go through. Forget the financial devastation and the nightmarish legal battles (they just come with the territory), I felt such a great wave of disappointment that I let so many people down, especially, my children, who turned out just great, by the way.

It had not yet dawned on me that losing was also a vital aspect of eventually winning. In today's economy, the vast majority define security as having the means to live comfortably for a reasonable period of time.

Unfortunately, that time-frame is generally six months. So most families feel that if they can stay ahead of the storm for six months and avoid any disasters during that time, then they're doing okay. But one tip of the scale; illness, loss or reduction of income and it could all collapse.

At the same time, these families fear that losing everything will spell the absolute end of their world but they only have six months of breathing room and for most families, that is in reality; survival mode as opposed to thrive mode.

As crazy as it sounds, for most people if they have to begin again, they have really only lost about six months vs. the loss of some great fortune so starting over and learning how to get more from a chosen venture, could afford far greater security. Going back to the starting line is not so far away.

One of the breakthrough elements of this book is that it allows you to test the feasibility of any idea without spending any significant money. While some poor bloke spends $100,000. to develop a business around an idea, build a prototype and mold and then, manufacture the product, you could test a similar idea with a few press releases and virtual drawings.

I've worked very hard to ensure that you don't risk what you already have while allow you to test any number of ideas. And I've seen simple press releases generate purchase orders even before the business or product was created. Nearly 25% of you who purchased this book read about it through one of my many press releases and each one of those press releases didn't cost a dime.

The notion of starting over can seem like a foreboding and defeating prospect. But there are people who do it constantly. They float ideas until something catches on and they make a very good living at it. That is the life of every salesperson in this country and those people are the backbone of the world of commerce.

If you life isn't going according plan, then it's time to adjust the plan and that's what this book is designed to do for you. There is always a new way to do it better. If the wolves are at your door, start a zoo, if you're at the end of your rope, swing over to another rope. All that's required is a willingness to step out of defeatist thinking and take a chance and you're learning how to do that with minimal risk.

You can create a far more self-reliant financial security for yourself, starting today.

DISCLAIMER

You will hopefully find this book both inspiring and instructional and you'll find countless ways to grow and protect your idea. We also need to protect ourselves with a disclaimer even though we've never encountered any problems as a result of Mr. Bronson's many books.

The prospect of developing an idea, business or any enterprise can evoke wonder and great success. It can also evoke fear and frustration. Ideas are delicate and, if properly nurtured, can transform a mere notion into an industry.

Then why do some dreams fail; why do so many great ideas never get the chance they should? The primary reason is that most people are not aware of the many common-sense steps available to turn an idea into something viable.

Most of these common-sense steps and techniques are either free or cost very little money. The intention of this book is to advance as many ideas as possible by guiding people in cost-effective directions; ideas that people used to think they could not afford to develop.

In designing this book, I attempted to prevent you from spending your money or energies in the wrong direction. Still there are no guarantees for success. Some readers might make a lot of money or realize even loftier goals. Others may not. No book, seminar or program can responsibly guarantee your success. We cannot, but perhaps we can our very best efforts in assisting you in your quest for advancement. The real success of your venture is up to you!

It's never the good idea that fails; it's all in the choices the dreamer makes. An idea only outlives you if you never let it die.

MAXIMIZING THE ACTIVATOR, POWERPOINTER AND **CORE STRATEGY AND TACTIC** SEGMENTS
How to Get Inspired and Get Moving

The bookshelves including your own, I am sure, are packed with books telling you what to do but most marketing books simply either assume you know the 'how to' elements or they can't really explain how to put their great marketing or inspirational ideas into action. So you're left with theory without proof or strategy without tactics to engage those strategies.

Life definitely gets better with a brighter attitude but to keep building that positive momentum, you must also have specific techniques at your disposal. Without real techniques that you can use to specifically grow your venture, general advice then becomes nothing more than theory, meaning it is unproven or untested. What differs with this book is that you will be able to see that the steps work.

Having written many successful advice books, I realized that for my books to be valid and true to their words, I had to provide clear and workable instructions for everything I discussed so that the reader could prove to themselves that my concepts really worked.

They would do this by following the simple recipe-like instructions and then by, observing the positive results that they create. So for each chapter I wrote, I created *ACTIVATOR*, *POWERPOINTER* and the extremely vital **Core strategies** and Tactics Segments , all of which are designed to work synergistic ally to help readers to immediately put their concepts into practice both with instructional know-how (Activators), logical inspiration (Powerpointers) and specific recipes for making your business profitable (**Core strategies and Tactics**). Readers learn not only how to become inspired to do things, they learn that they can indeed achieve those things with a vast a full compliment of the core systems to make it all work.

This creation of these respective segments to supplement each of the fifteen core chapters proved to be wildly successful and greatly broadened my following. For those who required education about the latest marketing or concept development techniques, they would carefully read through the first part of each chapter.

For those who already understand the core principals and merely want to employ the direct techniques on an immediate basis, they could just skip to the 'Activator' segment, somewhat like the guy who doesn't want to read the instructions but just wants to try to put it all together in spite of himself. In that case, you'll find 76 of my **Core strategies** and Tactics interspersed at the end of each powerful chapter. Don't just stop there; there are also hundreds of additional techniques and tips throughout the entire

Declare that Now is the time to stop non-productive thinking and re- direct your life.

FREE ENTERPRISE

book. One or two of the right tactics can make all the difference between success and failure for your idea so don't miss any of them!

This book is designed to provide you with a victory realized by the achievement of the various steps of your idea. These two complimentary segments serve to ensure that success will be achieved. The activator segments following each core chapter are engineered to get your concept moving; that means *working, operating, making money* or simply, achieving your goal for your venture. There is no greater joy than achievement, especially when that achievement comes from first taking a deep look at what you have to contribute, finding a way to make it no matter the odds and then, turning your idea into a profitable business.

Thirty years ago when I was a copywriter for American Express right out of college, I was constantly amazed that anyone would pay me money to craft cleverly-worded ads. Big money. I still can't believe it simply because writing is a natural gift and people actually were giving me money me for what came naturally. That's the joy you deserve to have with whatever idea suits you.

So often we wonder how we might make either a supplemental income or a strong income stream without realizing that we have the tools to do it ourselves. As the good witch said to Dorothy, "You've had the power all along." You do indeed have the power. All I am doing is helping you communicate that power and earnings potential.

But you thought this kind of achievement was beyond your reach. Making it was for someone else. Somebody told you it would require a lot of money just to secure a space to start a business. Somebody told you it would cost hundreds or even thousands of dollars to protect your idea, even more to advertise. Someone snapped "Get a real job" when you tried to get your book or song published, or your invention or organization started. And you don't have the money, drive or capability to make it happen for you or your family.

Those somebody's, though generally full of good intention, were often very wrong and instead of helping you to make your idea happen, in reality, they were in the way and were reinforcing the most negative feelings about yourself.

The evidence in your favor to succeed is everywhere: Most enterprises started with nothing and became something. How? The first citizens of the United States had nothing and not only survived, but *thrived*. Why? The answer is simple and should not be any big secret, but it is:

You will see that theme repeatedly throughout this book. It is a prime foundation. But you've been taught to be afraid. And that's the second key element for success: *Survival;* being forced to succeed, as we alluded to earlier.

There was a time when the expression. "Either you eat the bear or the bear eats you", was an actual warning and not just a figure of speech. Sometime the best way to choose to survive, thrive and success is having no choice but to succeed.

Maximizing Your Internal and External Natural Resources

I have high and low-tech clients everywhere. One of my favorite clients is Rustic Mountain Furniture in Orderville, Utah. Created over a decade ago by Clayton Cox, he lived in an economically-challenged town with few revenue options aside from basic tourist-services. Clayton has a growing family and had to find a way to thrive. So what did he do?

He looked within and, he looked around. He had one real talent: he could render some interesting furniture from large pieces of scrap Aspen and Pine logs he found in the nearby Cedar Breaks forest. He had been doing this as a hobby for friends since High School. Then he realized that people really loved his work and would pay him well for it. Over a decade later, he has a thriving business where he makes over 80 natural Aspen or Pine items and ships all over the world. Talk about maximizing assets.

What your best internal and external resource and are you applying that fully to your venture so that this venture becomes your greatest *Innoventure*? We're going to take you from where you are, to success, not by simply cheering you on but by giving you all of the right specific recipes to bring your particular idea into a profitable reality. By recipes, I mean specific *strategies* (plans to advance your idea) and tactics (the actual steps to achieve those strategies).

You will find countless ways to develop your idea. Most cost little or nothing to use. You will learn how to choose the ones that will most effectively advance your idea. You will not find expensive hidden surprises or charges. No one is going to try to push you into spending even hundreds of dollars. Instead, you will learn that *you* can produce consistent quality results on very well-managed budget.

You can build your team. You can build your dream and as you progress, you'll realize that all those things that used to hold you back will not hold you back any longer. If you have the right idea and a determined attitude, success is just a matter of using the correct strategies and tactics.

Hundreds of millions of people around the globe have found a way to create enterprise and survive and thrive. All I have done in this book is take the best and most workable systems that they used, and put them all here in clear and understandable form. And I don't make them sound difficult or fancy so I can then turn around and charge huge consulting fees. They are clear, easy to understand and highly effective.

They are here and they are *clear* and cost either very little to initiate or, nothing at all and there are new ones cropping up every day. My readers let me know on a constant basis and I am grateful to them for enhancing my work.

There is no one simple system that works for everyone. So if you've heard that, exercise caution. Everyone is different and different concepts require different approaches. You will learn how to select the most effective approaches for your particular

FREE ENTERPRISE

venture. The Activator, Powerpointer and Core Strategies segments are designed to treat every individual as someone with something unique to offer, if only they knew how simple it was.

That's the goal: to show you the simplest way to make your venture successful and profitable. All you need to add is the sincere effort and willingness to make it work.

Those little one-liners at the bottom of the page

Ever notice how you can read some books for page after page and wonder if you're gaining anything new. These days, books must not simply compete with the Internet, text messaging and Hundreds of Thousands of interactive websites, they must integrate with them. That is achieved in two ways: The first is that books must have fluidity with the Internet, referring to specific websites as needed. And they must enable the reader to personalize the reading experience as much as possible.

That's why you'll find sections in this book where you answer vital questions essential to the evolution of your idea. That way, this book becomes your very own personalized business and marketing plan action plan. In essence, a book is no longer just a book; it is a multimedia venture whose information creates neural networks that are virtually that endeavor to reach every end user who can benefit in some way or another.

The next essential element is efficiency of information. Every page must have a take-away; something specific that you learn from that specific page. Those take-aways, in broadest terms, are summarized at the bottom of each page, serving two purposes:

1) To help you summarize and appreciate the point of that particular page or segment and
2) To tickle or refresh your memory regarding any point of the progression of your idea.

Some of you may be intimidated by the length and size of this book but I assure you, you will never get lost nor overwhelmed. This book is designed to guide your for the life of your venture and, provide you as much guidance for every step. If you seek certain support for a particular point, just go to that point in the book.

This is everything that I've learned in over a half-century of living. It's me and all the hours or research and invention for evolving ideas. So when you need a piece of me, the book will always be there and in a highly comprehensive manner.

It's not enough to be inspired if you don't turn that inspiration into something real and tangible. Words are empty if not acted upon with real action steps leading to your goals.

Who Are You?

Do Any of The Following Describe You?

*Frustrated Inventor with high hopes but limited sales

*Aspiring Writer or Musician and you just need a break

*Accomplished Inventor looking for a ways to launch or expand your product into real and profitable markets

*Dedicated Fundraiser who wants to expand your reach to prospects

*Hopeful Entrepreneur looking for that most promising business venture

*Starving Artist seeking both the steps and courage to turn your talent into a self-supporting career, or supplemental income source.

*Promising Baker or Restaurateur

*Problem solver seeking the right people to work with

*Brilliant and/or Curious Researcher

*Electronic Genius or Imaginative Mechanic

*Household Tinkerer

*Entrepreneur of any type looking to connect with those people who can make your idea possible.

Do you want to open a small store, workshop, or studio, or build a home-based business? Do you offer a particular service? Do you dream of becoming one of these things? You can.

Are you sitting there reading this, worrying that you don't fit into any of the above categories, wondering if you'll ever find a way of taking your life to a higher and more profitable place? Did you know that your feelings and worries are shared with the accomplished inventor and small businessperson struggling to supercharge their concept?

It's productivity and dedication that make money, not the other way around.

FREE ENTERPRISE

There is always a way to create the life and business that you want and that will bring you fulfillment in each day. Do you want to build a home-based business, open a small store or, offer a particular service? Do you have a world-changing technical innovation that is trapped in politics and egos?

I've seen them all and have come to discover that no idea is ever any better than its creator's drive to make it work. Do you dream of becoming what you can become? You can. You can create the life and business that you want that will bring you some challenge and fulfillment in each day.

The purpose of this book is to help you turn your idea or business into something profitable; to get it made, functional and presented to the right industry, backers or, to the general public for sale. ***To put money in your pocket.*** Some of you will be starting right at the beginning. Many of you clients already have ideas and some are ready to sell but they don't really know how to sell them. For the sales challenge alone, you'll learn over fifty simple ways to do that.

As you go through the simple process of responding to the crystal-clear steps, this segment of the book becomes your personal business and marketing plan. It works for any venture that you want to build a business around. It works equally for men, women, groups and families. It works for the tinkerer and the rocket scientist. Why? Because the seemingly sophisticated steps towards building any business are not rocket science. And because you make this guide what it needs to be for your purposes, it becomes a guide that you will understand, with all kinds of marketing power boosters along the way.

And don't say you're not creative or you don't have what it takes to create a business. We each have something inventive, imaginative and playful that gets us through even the most routine of days. All you need are clear steps that really work for you, steps that will take you to exactly where you want to go. These steps and charts will show you clearly how to build a profitable business around your idea. All you have to do is follow them. Inventing is fun, the idea of building a business can be very exciting, but what's most exciting is turning your concept into something that makes money so the fun isn't interspersed with financial panic.

If you think you're not creative, you're not alone. The people who will most tell you that they lack creativity are in fact, creative people because their creative machinery is working overtime.

Creativity and originality are not just for some people; everyone has it within them and with creativity comes the dreaming of unlimited possibilities and a growing hope for a better future. Even if you are planning to create a typical everyday enterprise, you will still place your creative mark on it.

Some people will tell you that creative people, like musicians and artists, are simply born thinking differently but at some point, they had to pick up a paintbrush or guitar and you can bet that in the beginning, it was not a pleasant experience.

Cheers and inspiration that take you up without real instructions on how to keep climbing, quickly collapse in discouragement and confusion.

My neighbor's daughter was what you would call a problem child. Her worst trait: She would argue about everything. They could not get her to do anything in the family without arguing. Everything became an unnecessary and embellished issue. This odious trait remained a strong part of her personality throughout college where at first, her arguments with teachers reflected in poor grades. As time, went on, the contrariness morphed into rational debates and today before the age of thirty, she made partner in a law firm.

You have a combination of characteristics and talents that are unique to you. You also have the ability to become the dedicated expert in your field and as you become an expert, your personal economy will grow as well.

FIRST ACTIVATOR
How to Jump-Start Your Creativity

We each have something that we can do well but we can't always see it. Discovering our creativity requires some self-examination and experimentation. It's there; we just need to spark it.

Here are Eleven ideas for sparking yours:

1) **Wake up at an odd hour and write down the first thoughts that pop into your head.**
2 **Travel to a new place and where you feel inspired, note what you're inspired about.**
3) **Visit old friends or family you haven't seen in a long time. Often they can help you to remember things about yourself that will inspire your creative process.**
4) **Take one day to study everything you possibly can about your idea then, forget about it for a couple of days and observe how your new knowledge affects your creativity.**
5) **See a beautifully-produced movie or show. Or visit an inspiring attraction. These experiences can help to bring out the best in ourselves.**
6) **Take a long walk in a new place, if you can, in the woods or a park. This can help to calm the mind and allow for the good ideas to flow.**
7) **Give up a bad habit (especially smoking, drinking or poor diet). This helps to clarify the mind and inspire hopeful thoughts.**
8) **Imagine how you want your lifestyle and finances to be. Picture yourself there already and all the things you had to do to get there.**
9) **Pledge to expect more from yourself. If you persist, you will find something within. Practice using fear and frustration as fuel for hope and vision.**

Time to get activated and pointed in the right and powerful direction!

FREE ENTERPRISE

10) **Choose three successful mentors in or related to your field and try to learn what they did to get inspired.**
11) **Attend a seminar, gathering or any meeting that is totally alien to you. This may help you to pick up ideas you never even considered.**

There are many time-tested assays like Myers Briggs or Jung personality-typing tests. For some of you, these tests may prove helpful and can be readily found online. I opted not to use these methodologies for the simple reason that while they may help with identifying proclivities, they miss the mark on personal passion and conviction.

Should you know your shortcomings? Of course but in the interest of exploring your own self-reliance, I believe you need to find a way to fill those gaps and not orient away from them.

I prefer the concept of reframing and retraining your brain. Some people recant the tire phrase "thinking outside the box.' But then, you could be in a box outside the box. So just throw all the boxes away and imaging instead that your brain is a vast array of wires and you need to grow new ones. Thinking about how to make your concept fly will help you achieve that.

As you're exploring, explore carefully, virtually, cerebrally and vicariously. I encourage courage but I also advocate caution so you don't become discouraged about your best ideas. That's why, very early on, I have provided the following to help protect your dreams and aims.

Let Me Introduce Yourself to Yourself

We have a problem in this country and the world, for that matter: People don't generally know what they want or they become very competent and comfortable at something they really don't want to do. Then they have to convince themselves that they are not living up to their true purpose because they have other obligations and responsibilities. Noble sacrifice except that a bigger sacrifice would be to explore and pursue those things that you were truly born to do.

Do you know what real talents you have already or, is this a question you trivialized long ago? I sure wish I could have because life would have been a lot more comfortable. As a dyslexic, it was often difficult for me to get up to speed with various tasks. I had the intellect and, often tested at the genius level but those same tests suggested serious problems with basic comprehension skills. It often came out backwards to me.

As a result, often academic and career opportunities passed me by, not because I wasn't capable or even over-qualified, but because often when teachers or superiors were speaking to me, it often sounded like a foreign language. How frustrating for them!

Just as you learn something every single day, no matter how blah the day, you should learn some useful thing from every page of this book.

Since every problem somewhere means an opportunity elsewhere, I settled into the unsettled fields of both journalism and marketing. That way, I could hop from concept to concept with minimal frustration, at least in the short-term. My ideas, counsel and approaches were generally well-received because they were generally unique since I looked at things with a broader and more creative perspective. But aside from my loyalty to my loved-ones, animals and my writing, it was difficult for me to find my place.

Then years into my career a funny thing happened: I began to hear from a number of my friends and observed that an increasing number of my friends, colleagues and associates were facing and somewhat paralyzing depression issues as they neared the end of their primary careers.

Most were now in their fifties, financially-comfortable and somewhat lost. At first, I didn't think anything of this, figuring it must simply be mid-life. But when some of my more brilliant or even genius-level friends were clearly expressing their fear and unhappiness, I began to investigate.

I discovered five primary issues that have created a new decade of quiet desperation:

1) They often stumbled into a career without really thinking about what they wanted to do.
2) They became very competent, well compensated and, highly-praised for their work. They might not have been all that happy but their egos certainly were.
3) They determined that the process of self-understanding and true self-acquaintance to be a waste of time and, a potential interference with cash-flow and their general obligations.
4) Most of my friends and colleagues were bright, graduated at the top of their class and companies tripped over each other to 'capture' them. Naturally, these high-achievers were so good at their jobs, they remained there, praised, supported and secure until years of life flew by.
5) Even for the rest of us who were not exactly at the top of their class, security became the guiding issue in lieu of self-identity.

Who had time to figure what they really wanted to do? I had a very accomplished friend who worked on a top-secret government project. He was very well-paid and very highly praised. The specific government agency who hired him gave him a direct assignment which was a component of a much larger project. Without my friend's special genius, the project would fail or as the officials told him "The fate of the free world may hinge upon your accomplishments."

He did his job extremely well and after wards, went back to his regular work in aviation, never knowing what his work was going to be applied to. When he heard the

We all have something in us that can help us to make more money.

FREE ENTERPRISE

news on the radio that his work would allow the timing-relay to detonate the atomic bombs in Japan, he had a total nervous breakdown and was hospitalized for a year.

Pretty extreme but true story and a pain that he had to live with for his entire life: Working "blindfolded" on a project that would kill 100,000 human beings. Certainly your decisions or lack thereof are not as extreme as this but the lesson is clear:

We should take a hard and painful look at our lives instead of allowing flattery, money and security to entrap us in a career path that really doesn't challenge or fulfill us. Unfortunately, most of us don't go through this process because they think they can't afford to. But with this book showing all of the free ways to explore and test ideas, how can anyone afford not to?

I admire each of my five children but for the moment, I am going to shine the spotlight on my oldest daughter who at the tender age of 23, fell into a prestigious and secure job as a development executive for a renown rehabilitation hospital for seriously-injured children, war veterans and general accident victims. She is outstanding at her job and each time I speak with her, she is on a new project or mission, making great and influential friends all along the way.

How could a father be more proud? She could remain in the field for the rest of her life and become powerful and successful. I am certainly proud of all of my children at different times. I am proud of how my two oldest progress in their careers, I am proud that my two-year old already knows how to say 'please' and 'thank-you' and that she, along with my ten-month-old, have a clear reverence for living things.

But what I am most impressed with regarding my oldest daughter is her chief complaint that while she is totally dedicated to her job, she still "has no idea" about what she wants to do with her life. Even with all the accolades, stability, security, especially in these tough financial times, she is perceptive enough to know that her real happiness will come not from how here career shapes her life but how *she* designs and shapes her life.

Is this an easy thing to do? Yes and No. "Yes' in that it will lead you to a happier career-path, and no in that it is not always easy to know both your true good and true bad points. That said, the good points will generally take care of the bad ones. And you do run the risk of disappointing the ones who love and depend on you. But if you don't go though this struggle, at least cerebrally, you run the greater risk of disappointing yourself years down the road when purpose and substance will mean far more to you than ego-stroking and money.

I thank my lucky stars for my dyslexia because it prevented me from getting trapped in a career that wasn't really who I was. I had no choice but to find out who I was. Now I can tell you that disappointment is a teacher that most people foolishly struggle to avoid.

Instead, they should look at it, embrace it and learn from it without fear. And the sooner they do, the sooner they will start doing the things they love and my experience

What do you really want to do and why aren't you making time to do it?

is that people are happiest and most successful when they do those things that are most meaningful to them.

For those of you who are largely through your career lamenting "He's describing me. I'm guilty of getting lost in my own superficial success," don't fret; nobody is leaving you hanging here. The news for you is better than for most younger folk because not only can you use this book to redirect and own the next chapter in your life, you can often incorporate all of the practical skills, wisdom and contacts to ensure a very successful transition.

So what about those highly noble traits of responsibility and sacrifice? Anyone can argue that they gave up doing what they loved in order to do more for those they love. But think of what the entrepreneur sacrifices: security, dignity, sleep, business and personal relationships, pride.

In the end, it is the successful self-actualized entrepreneur who sleeps because they end doing far more for themselves, society and those they love. I have a favorite part of this book that is critical for readers to achieve so they can benefit for all the other elements here. It is wherever I ask you the three most important questions: Who are you? Who are you? Who are you?

SCAMGUARD
How to Protect Your Right to Fulfill Your Dreams

"Life, Liberty and The Pursuit of Happiness" What does that mean to you? Are you living the life you truly want to live? Are you actively engaged in your own pursuit of your happiness? When you are engaged in the work that you love, you are indeed pursuing your happiness. But if your work seems more like drudgery and excessive sacrifice, you're not abiding by a basic constitutional right. Our founding fathers knew that for a free country to thrive, each individual had to thrive and for an individual to thrive, they had to pursue their happiness in their work.

The intention of this book is to not only show you that you worthy and relevant dreams are attainable but that you have to learn how to nurture and protect them. Most readers will quickly adapt the systems in this book to nurture their idea but far too many people feel that protection means patents and copyrights.

Though I devote a section to general concept protection, you will learn that for most people, these documents are merely pieces of paper if you do not take steps to market your idea as your truest protection is effective marketing or communication of your concept.

What I'm more concerned about is not seeing my readers ripped off from phony invention submission companies or consultants who charge you are hefty retainer for simple tactics you may engage yourself with little or no money and some earnest

Don't you dare give up on your dreams but instead dare to dream. It could be why you were put here in the first place.

effort. Billions of dollars are wasted by well-intentioned dreamers. Together, we can bring that number down to near zero. We have to; we can't afford to be scammed anymore.

As we work together to activate your concept(s) and we strive to tip the balance from doubt and fear to hope, there are some sensible precautions that you would be wise to follow. That said; do not be ashamed if you fell for any of the aggressive or predatory scams out there. I hear at least 100 new stories each day. Ten years ago in earlier Internet days, that number was just a handful. Still, as the scam artists have become more sophisticated and widespread, so have the simple defenses. The basic principal is the same: Do Not Spend A Lot of Money to Develop and Test Your Idea. If you follow that primary guidepost, you'll generally protect your concept. There are ways to protect yourself and your wallet and most importantly, the spirit of your dreams.

Here are some important warnings to protect you as you develop your idea:

Do NOT respond to Inventions Wanted etc. ads you see on TV or in small print ads that promise free offers or evaluations. Their aim is to get as much money from you as possible while doing little or nothing useful in return.

Do NOT trust invention companies who call you and tell you how wonderful your idea is, and then try to secure a sum of money from you (usually $700. to $2,000).

Do NOT pay anyone to present your product to industry or distributors.

While some companies do not accept presentations from anyone due to liability issues many of these doors, more large companies are opening their doors to the public once again, often through some excellent contests, competitions and, via a general submission process.

DO Explore smaller and mid-sized manufacturers, many of who are actively seeking a competitive edge. The only thing you would pay is a commission to a company that creates a sales avenue for you that produces real revenue.

Do NOT pay anyone for a patent search that you can easily do on your own online through the USPTO (United Patent and Trademark Office) website.

Do NOT pay anyone other than the USPTO additional fees for filing a provisional or patent pending on your idea. These cost about $100 directly from the USPTO. (You will notice that we include all of those documents for free in your kit.)

You can grow and make more money anytime you choose. But you have to work at it.

Do NOT rush to invest in costly prototypes before attempting to make far cheaper (but functional) models on your own.

Do NOT spend any more money than you have to on the patent process, as the real secret for most successes is setting up sales opportunities.

Do NOT trust anyone who seems to emphasize your weaknesses as that can make you vulnerable to spending money for coaching you do not need.

My Invention "Refugees"

In the corner of my office sits an ever-growing stack of very neat business folders from inventors of all types who signed on with Invention Submission, Help, or Technical companies that often advertise on television. You've seen their ads on television and would-be inventors waste up to $3 Billion annually on these companies. The companies themselves recently revealed that 99% of the ideas they "work with" go nowhere. They get their clients by simply telling each caller that they have a great idea with tremendous potential. Clients then spend anywhere from about $700 up to thousands of dollars for which they receive those handsome folders with their invention inserted.

There's so much information out there about how to build a business; so many ridiculous promises on the Internet that everyone starts to sound like a sales huckster and then, all promises sound diluted.

When you see promises like that stuffed in your email, you know they can't all be true and realize that most aren't true. They're just after as much of your money as they can get a hold of. So it starts to appear like an overwhelming process and you feel like you'll never get the personal and special support that your special venture requires.
NOTE: If you have already engaged an unscrupulous source, who took your money and did nothing, remember that they cannot take your creative spirit. Use the free or low-cost techniques in this book to regain your footing. And to help compensate you for your losses, you may apply for a 50% discount off of any of Mr. Bronson's follow-up services above the one-month trial. All you need to do is provide substantiation of your negative experience.

Even if you're building a rocket, this is not rocket science. But amidst all of the extra over-promises that scream at you from every direction, there are in fact, specific and logical steps that will lead to your success; Step-by-step interactive instructions that become your daily action plan referred to earlier.

In addition, there are some highly effective, easy-to use business secrets included that will give your idea that extra edge for success. This guidebook is the final booster that will assist you in building your concept from one strong platform to the next.

FREE ENTERPRISE

Never written a business plan? It doesn't matter. This system focuses more on the doing than the talking. Just respond as thoughtfully as you can with the processes in this book and it will help you to take your idea from any stage, and into a profit-making form.

This proven program helps you to think in terms of daily and weekly steps and inspires and directs you to real progress. And if you've ever built a business around an idea you know that getting through the steps successfully and imaginatively can be all that matters at times. You also know that there are numerous times when you wanted to give up but you found a way through. This book contains all of those shortcuts and more.

You'll notice that the steps are broken down into a total of fifteen primary chapters. The length of time required will depend upon the progress that you make and you will be able to gage that clearly by virtue of the results your achieve.

All the chapters will build upon one another and are designed to ensure that you don't suddenly stop simply because you don't know what to do next.

The ACTIVATOR and POWERPOINTER tips are clearly noted and explained. They will help to build or enhance any kind of business venture, from building a model or business model, to over 50 separate approaches for marketing your business.

All you have to do is select those items that will work best for you. Read each step carefully and take all the time you need to answer as honestly as you can. Sometimes, you'll need to walk away from the process, to reflect, evaluate, and just to keep your answers fresh.

There are some elements of this system that where you will need to refer to your drawings, designs, blueprints, recipes, whatever. When you need to do that, note on that section SEE BLUEPRINTS, SEE PHOTOS, ETC, so you can refer to the needed item. Also, whenever you list a name or any resource, be sure to identify clearly who they are, and include a phone number and email address.

You'll notice that I provide you with just a limited amount of pages of blank lines after each question. I have found that this helps the reader to remain more focused. When you use this system, keep all answers right to the point. Answer as many as you can with clear and concise lists. This is not an exercise in literacy; it is a system that becomes your business development plan. So what you write need to be clear and concise instructions.

Save Your Questions

As you find you way through this system and watch your concept take shape, you will build upon your idea. You will also encounter problems and challenges that will be unique to your venture. When you encounter any of those barriers, write down the clearest question you can think of to overcome the challenges at hand.

When you have them all coordinated, keep them on a readily available list. Then, as you follow the steps in this book, keep looking at those questions and observe how you are able to find the answers as you develop your idea.

MAXIMIZING THE ACTIVATOR, POWERPOINTER

Many people are used to calling a help-line when they run into a complicated problem, like when a website presents a problem. Most of the time, you'll be amazed at how much you will be able to achieve on your own. But if you have a specialized challenge, there are ways to engage Mr. Bronson's and his staff and the end of this book.

In these pages, you will find clear headings relating to the status or progress of your particular idea. So, as you see yourself in that particular place or steps, that's where you will begin. If your idea isn't exactly reflecting what you had hoped, then you should start at the beginning to ensure you are heading in the right direction. Now let's begin the process of putting real action and results to your dream.

As Andy said in The Shawshank Redemption: "Hope is a good thing" But results leading to a real and measurable success are a better thing.

CHAPTER ONE

FINDING YOUR MOST POWERFUL IDEA

Discovering the True Entrepreneur within "We are what we think. All that we are arises with our thoughts. With our thoughts we make the world."

Siddhartha Gautama – the Buddha

Overview

Are you where you want to be, really? Is this what you envisioned for your life, family, or have there been many shocks and surprises, twists and turns, perhaps too many? Are you on your way to being the best that you are? Too many of us often stumble into careers, families and general lifestyles, which even if secure and financially remunerative, may take us from a truer and far more profitable direction.

Do you want to direct and act upon your life, or simply react to it? And why do that when there's a dreamer; a truer self within each of us, just bustin' to break out and make your life far more rewarding, not just financially, but in so many other ways as well.

Activator Steps for this Chapter
1) Perform self-assessment of current direction.
2) Explore new potential directions.
3) Formulate a more fulfilling, and more profitable, venture.
Perform Self-Assessment of Current Direction

Don't Resist It!

No life goes exactly as planned. That would be pretty boring. Mistakes and surprises shape and strengthen us, and best of all, test us and reveal to us, capabilities we never dreamt we had. So as we begin by getting you fixed and focused on where you really want to be, we have to first make sure you have a sense who you are and what you were wired for.

That way, we can sync up where you want to be with where you really ought to be. What is your purpose here? That's our first and most important task.

"I have a great idea!" light bulb flashing over your head, eyes as big as tomatoes. Everyone's had some kind of inspiration in their lives but the trick is to keep that light bulb burning bright. And there is no greater voltage to keep that bulb burning brightly as those concepts that come from the very core of who you are.

Trust your instincts and gut to lead you away from those things that are not meant for you and, towards your specialness. And view the roadblocks as simply part of the process.

FREE ENTERPRISE

But also, often prior to this, these dreams come from panic, fear or despair. Of the thousands of emails I receive, so many speak of not having enough money in general, or as expected, by a certain point in their lives. Pity, whether to ourselves or others, is paralyzing.

We have to take stock and get to work now. Whether the wolves are at the gate, or whether you're simply looking for a way to supercharge your existing venture, make the commitment to get through this entire book. Absorb all of the basic steps.. Paste them on your ceiling right over your bed and learn everything you can about creating a flow of your best ideas.

The key to moving from your challenges to a better place is realized by following through on the correct strategies. That is where the best ideas come from. Many of your new insights come from some of the more difficult challenges you've come through. And remember to turn to the POWERPOINTERS through the book to give you more specifics on conquering worry by engaging real businesses steps to drive you forward.

For the earliest man and woman, danger and survival were daily issues. One wrong turn and you could be some prehistoric beast's Happy Meal but if you learned to either 'fight or flight', more succinctly put: If you learned how to strategize, you might survive to overcome new challenges.

We owe our lives to those first 'Happy Meal Survivors' whose very existence was contingent upon their ability to invent new ways to survive and even thrive and enjoy some degree of peace and comfort.

In the challenging times we face today, the prehistoric beast is represented by fear of scarcity, lack of money and/or of family security. The *unplanned.* . Prior to this age of declining income for so many, we were fairly comfortable. But the beast is lurking amidst those who seem too comfortable.

So we face a situation where we have to rediscover our courage and reinvent ourselves, to get back into the world more than before, and to share more than before. Today's fight or flight, often forces us into the most productive, most lucrative, happiest times of our lives.

So many people tell us that they feel so afraid, lost or left behind in these uncertain times. But these are times when we have to create that supplemental income. We don't have the luxury to be lost and in despair and we never have to be lost if we are willing to discover our-selves.

So, Step One: ***Don't resist the true direction that life is taking you.***

See more than just a faint shadow of who you are.

How To Look in New Directions

Creativity is the exploration of possibilities. It's the mental exercise of suspending and transcending your existing guidelines, walls and rules so you can consider brand new possibilities without harm. You have to learn to play a game of "what-ifs" and play it to the max. If you're not willing to take the simple mental risk of astounding and shocking your- self, you run the risk of never really surprising, delighting or amazing yourself, never growing and never profiting financially. Creativity is the exploration of you. And that means being willing to explore without fear of failure, humiliation or embarrassment, no matter where it comes from.

There are many books that will attempt to offer you specific categories and systems to help you define your talents. This is a horribly limiting practice. You must refuse to be categorized in order to truly choose your own path. "What's new?" is one of the greatest colloquial expressions of all time. What is new about you that you need to test and explore?

One of our greatest reasons for our successes is that we never let anyone corral us into just one specific area. We get nervous when we hear people use the words 'should' or 'must' excessively. Do your best to ensure that your thoughts are truly your own. That's where your deepest enthusiasm will come from.

We have earned a certain degree of freedom and control over our lives and you can have the same privilege as you learn to celebrate your personal potential and initiative.

It doesn't matter if you're originating something from the center of your heart and mind, or using your unique wisdom and common-sense enterprising skills to improve upon an existing product. You — and you alone — hold the key to your truest success and your most fulfilling path.

If your idea doesn't begin to gel after the first chapter, keep reading. Because as you understand the creative and developmental process, your degree of possibility thinking will also grow. Your creative muscle will strengthen. That may take a few days or months. The delay makes no difference unless you're under a severe time constraint.

Begin carrying a little notebook around and make notes about any ideas you may want to pursue. Or you may prefer to use a PDA or personal recorder. What are the dreams and wishes that make sense to your lifestyle? And you know those thoughts that breeze in and out of your head? Write them down. Every spark counts when you are in the selection process.

The creative process plays games with us. It seems to throw fragments your way as if from nowhere, and you find yourself almost automatically saying, "Nah, that's crazy." And then you forget about the whole concept. How many times have you only

It is the drive, and every living being's basic right and nature, to build something that is their very own.

FREE ENTERPRISE

remembered that you've forgotten an idea without recalling the actual idea? Isn't that maddening!

That happens for two reasons: The first is that we are conditioned to forget. We're taught to think in a grown-up way and to lose our childlike sense of wonder. But should you have to sacrifice one for the other? Who made that law?

The second reason is a fascinating component of our own evolution. There exists a mechanism that cancels out our short-term memory of things. That's very frustrating. And most living creatures abhor frustration. Since we already know that frustration is the true mother of invention, that inspired humankind to learn to record events from the very beginning, first with stones to count or mark property.

So your fragments are not really fragments - they may in fact be the roadmap to our evolution and progress - clues and puzzle pieces. You have to put those puzzle pieces together. A fragment can be a single word, an illustration, a question. It's always a willingness to learn and explore the clues you have subconsciously left for yourself.

You have to re-train your daydream process. From now on when any of these notions whiz by, stop them in their tracks and write them down. Never say 'nah' because these are the puzzle pieces that you must have to complete the picture.

Your fragments matter because your constructive, beneficial thoughts matter. You matter. Just hold onto those thoughts in writing and you'll soon see what we mean.

Every week or so, dump these precious fragments on a table and try to see if some of these fragments are beginning to suggest an overall picture of what your venture may be. You'll begin to see your mental jigsaw puzzle come to life.

Don't make copious notes. Excessive rambling is more a sign of anxiety than creativity. There should be very little anxiety involved. Think like a caveman. What will make your cave or surrounding territory easier to deal with? You don't need to have anxiety about this. Have fun with this process. Learning is a great high, especially when you can see how it will directly shape your future.

Don't fear your creativity. Welcome it and let it take you wherever it takes you. It's who you are. Just gently plant a few seeds here and there, and keep checking for patterns. Look and listen in your own style. You're aiming to grow with something that's going to be an important part of where you really want to be.

Don't limit yourself just because you think a problem or goal seem a bit large in scope. Writing this book seemed scary to us until we began attacking it page by page, and one day we found ourselves with a book.

For many, this is also a process of creating a more realistic relationship with one's truer self - your heart - your soul - whatever you want to label it without feeling too uncool. As the brilliant empowerment author Marianne Williamson would say in her presentations, as she places her hand on her heart: "You know…in here…You know."

ACTIVATOR TWO
How Do You Get There?

For many people, "getting there" is defined by the term *Invention* but the majority of people also mistakenly believe that inventors are these eccentric folk who hole themselves up in their kitchens or garages making weird stuff.

Where are your clues taking you?

The truth is we are all inventors and must take every step to design and invent the life we truly are born for' whether it's a business, or any other project. We have to invent it. Some of us are born to lead; others have a natural flair for baking or electronics, art, writing, organizing for safer neighborhoods or better schools.

The key rule for identifying your best idea is: *Your idea will take you where you want to go, and allow you to learn who you really are.* Your identity is who were born to be, your best idea should take you there. So without further delay, let's start making it happen.

Don't say "I can't, I'm just not ready"

In over thirty years of counseling people and helping each to see their own creative potential, this is one of the barriers that many people come up with to prevent themselves for becoming who they always wanted to be. This is not an acceptable reason but in fact, an excuse for not being more truthful about your personal potential. If you're feeling a bit stuck right now, that is not a valid reason to stop this process. Getting stuck only happens when we don't know what steps to take.

The truth is, what prevents people from progressing in their lives is not a lack of potential or attainability of the goal, but a long-hardened resistance to learning what you need to learn. We all like safety but growth and better security require some degree of emotional risk and sacrifice, *but not a great deal of financial risk.*

So throw out the excuses and long-winded stories about why it hasn't happened. Now you have the clear steps to follow, to take you where you can and will go. The risks are minimal and the potential gains could enhance your life forever.

Ever notice how those people who repeat the same old complaints, aren't trying to make a real difference in their lives? Don't end up like that when a series of small efforts could change everything for you.

If you already have your heart set on an idea, let's take a closer look at it to ensure you'll want to stay with it. If you don't have an idea in mind yet, that's fine. Don't panic, do not berate yourself with negative self-talk like, "oh, I'm not an idea person," or "I've never been creative." Just relax and take a more composed and deeper look at yourself.

In truth, we are each born creative. We ourselves are created.

Do not spend a lot of money on anyone no matter what they promise, unless they have proven they can deliver.

FREE ENTERPRISE

And the more we endeavor to create what we were meant to create, the more complete our lives will be. And those "complete" people are the ones who have all the success they can handle because they experience that inherent joy of seeing their best and most contributive ideas come to life. So for those of you still seeking out their creative side, don't worry, it's already there. All we have to do is help you to identify it and have fun with it. Because true success is a true joy.

We'll take a closer look at how we develop ideas and open ourselves up to the process. All you have to focus on at this point, is how to activate the creative process within you. And once you do, that will positively affect everything you do in your life forever.

From the beginning, you must promise never to limit your imagination. And saying that you have no imagination is not an acceptable excuse. If you have a brain and a heart, you can imagine and you can learn how to reveal it to yourself. Maybe you've had a few brainstorms in your life. Maybe not and at this point you really don't know if you have anything you can really develop and market. You need to first start by changing nothing except your willingness to use your imagination far more effectively.

The truth is you do have something, some concept, service or product. Everyone does. And that self-definition has best been revealed to you by means of the challenges you overcame or, are overcoming.

Often if we take a second look, we learn in the oddest places and situations, not merely how calamitous life can be, but who we are and what we are made of. Accidental discovery, compelled by unexpected or evolved need, is precisely how we survived and evolved since the beginning of time.

You are already by nature, an inventor. That is how you made it to this point. And to carry that to the next level, we all have some gift that we can market successfully. Is it that special cake or little tool you make for neighbors? It could be that new battery you've been tinkering with in your garage, the one powered by your own stomach acid, to run a new artificial heart, or that newsletter you've been cooking up in your basement, which reflects your special knowledge about something. Or the next level of chocolate chip cookie (call me).

Maybe it's your talent for solving conflicts or an idea to make your community a better place in which to live. It's there and this book will guide you to it, but you have to give us your full cooperation and willingness.

It's not such a foreboding process. You'll actually begin by discovering what you've always had, and then build on that with the processes outlined in the next two chapters.

Whatever your gift, or whatever the outcome of any exploration, the ultimate discoveries are realized by action; perhaps by trying to go in one direction only to stumble along the way and discover a new direction. But you have to try to some degree to truly know.

Everyday people achieve success with these systems everyday. Now it's your turn. This day is yours.

First, you have to do one thing. Let's borrow this exercise from the late and great Norman Vincent Peale. Put the book down for a moment, walk over to the nearest open window and throw all you self-doubts and 'I can't do it' talk out the window. And do it right now. What have you learned today?

It's your will to succeed, to learn and build from your mistakes, challenges and adverse circumstances. It's that childlike joy about greeting each new day, anxious to find what joy the world has in store. To listen to those who know more than you do. To calmly listen to yourself and learn without resistance. And to persist on making your dream into what it was always meant to be.

The greatest joy of this experience is that you'll discover that so has trapped your creative process for so very long. It's about taking enough time to assess the best of who you are and use it to do the most beneficial best that you can. And guess what? That's where the money is as well.

This process will happen with your idea. As your thoughts develop, you begin to get a strong sense of ideas that relate best to who you are. Often people come up with ventures that outwardly seem to have no relevancy to their lives.

Real wishes are often breakaway hidden loves that need to be properly guided. And ultimately, you will have a true relationship with your idea in a fashion similar to the relationship you're beginning to cultivate with your truer self. That's because your idea reflects your truer self. ("Oh, now it makes sense.")

Too busy, lazy, sick? That makes no difference because the right idea will spark ample motivation. We progress not by mere capability but by a willingness to develop that capability. So hang up your hang-ups and take advantage of that incredible American gift of free thought and exploration.

We are a rare society by virtue of our extensive creative freedoms, even in this age of terrorism. That's what also makes us one of the most creative societies in history. And from creativity comes productivity and from productivity, the money you deserve to make.

Many readers have never allowed themselves to have a free thought in their lives. They fear it will lead to chaos and paralysis. But even chaos and decay are part of the foundation that feeds creativity so don't be afraid to explore this very positive and most promising aspect of your life. That's how to get out of your cave. Every person grows by finding those tiny sparks that self-inspire.

When you become truly inspired, nothing can stop you because all obstacles become temporary and all knock-downs never keep you down. So begin the road to self-inspiration. Let your mind wander. You can always come back. Go out and live your life as you normally do. Start off by simply thinking
about possibilities. In no time, you'll find that you have more ideas than you ever gave yourself credit for. That discovery generally comes as a refreshing and motivating surprise.

Get inspired about trying out some of your ideas. With the free systems in this book, you can try out many of them with little or no risk.

FREE ENTERPRISE

Keep at it until you have really found something that you will nurture and market, something that you can build that meaningful relationship with. Remember, if it is where you want to be, you'll find the wherewithal to stay on that challenging but ultimately rewarding path.

How To Formulate a More Fulfilling and Eventually, a More Profitable Venture

An important aspect of the success process involves learning how to make the right wish come true. To continue shaping your idea, you need to make a Three-Stage Wish. Real wishes usually come true but you have to know how to make a real wish.

STAGE 1 – HOPE / BELIEF

If asked most of you to make a wish, most of you would wish for lots of money. Most people are indeed stuck in the first stage, more than ever in our proud history. Too bad because reward follows the wish. So you can't wish for a pile of money, or to win the lottery or a jackpot in Vegas. Nothing against lotteries, in fact, maybe our income taxes should be replaced with mandatory lotteries. Perhaps that would serve as a better incentive. But "Lottery People" who hope that some freak remote chance will drape them in clover, rarely succeed because they tend to live their lives, waiting for something to happen, instead of taking those little steps each day that would give them a far greater prize, and the true character to appreciate what they're earned. The harder I work, the luckier you get. One must get past this childish first stage because hope alone cannot produce your success.

STAGE 2 – DESIRE / INTENTION

This stage of our wish is that thing we want to improve, that problem that we want to attack. What specific area of your world would you like to improve? Maybe you want to communicate better with your family or find a way to realize increased employee productivity? Maybe you want to develop a new or improved product or service?

What about a way to do your small part to make the world safer for children? Let's work with the "safer children" notion as STAGE 2 of our wish.

STAGE 3 – CREATION / ACTION

Following is an actual example of how one of my clients brought "safer children" to the third stage.

You have a talent that's waiting to make money for you.

A rather brilliant man presented his concept by first telling a story about a girl he knew who dove into a swimming pool and was instantly and horribly electrocuted due to a frayed wire in an underwater pool switch. He vowed that he would muster his gifts to make sure such a nightmare would never happen again.

He channeled his passion into the development of an underwater safety switch that eliminated electrical contact near the pool area. The product he created and I marketed represents the vital **STAGE 3** of our wish and that's what you want to head to. Be it a product or service, STAGE 3 represents your rough plan of attack. This is one of the most difficult and pivotal points in developing a viable concept essentially because you often have to violate one key rule about human-nature: your emotional safety. But this is the best time to risk all: when you are exploring the choice of the concept. It's safe because the risk is cerebral, and the better your self-exploration at this point, the better the chance for financial success, independence, and career fulfillment.

ACTIVATOR THREE
How To Create a Clear-Cut Goal

At the time of this writing, we lived beneath these spectacular thousand-foot red sandstone cliffs in an elegant development called La Estancia in Kanab, Utah. Everyday, my wife and I would take our then one-year old baby daughter for a walk beneath these sheer rock faces accompanied by our Olde English Sheep Dog who would bounce and prance her way around the development with us, never straying far from our little girl and never ever going near the loose rock-face of the surrounding cliffs.

Then one day, she spotted a flock of birds. She had never caught a bird before but always felt it would happen the next time. These birds were perched about a-third of the way up the cliffs, so imagine our amazement when our generally cautious dog made a bee-line straight up the cliff, seeming to defy gravity.

Of course, when she arrived at the perch, the birds were well on their way, laughing (if birds can do that), and then we carefully coaxed our dog down the cliff as she whimpered, quite unsure how she got up there in the first place.

Our dog defied gravity because her goal was so strong that not even gravity or her generally cautious nature could stop her. She wanted the goal far too much to be stopped.

How strong is your goal? How badly do you both want and need to succeed?

You need to make you concept and goals so strong, that nothing can stop you, even gravity and certainly, not a bunch of missteps or failures. That's just part of the process.

Creating Goals you really want to meet

A good vision requires focus and focus is the rudder that steers us to our goal. But what is a goal, really?

When you say "I can't", it usually means, "I won't."

FREE ENTERPRISE

A goal is more that just a target, it is a moving target. So, it's important not to be excessively rigid because as your concept develops, it will change and grow with all the new pieces of data that you collect.

As your concept evolves, you'll start to see your market more clearly, and you'll discover markets that didn't seem possible before. The viability of your ultimate result will be contingent upon your own ability to best incorporate the many discoveries you make along the way.

Your First Task

In just one sentence, write your goal in the simplest language possible. What are you trying to do? What do you see yourself achieving? Begin the sentence with the word 'To.' Underneath your statement, write the following: 'Subject to change - A Lot.'

To (your goal statement)
Subject to change - A Lot

Now, put it up on the wall where you work so you can see it every day and as you work through the book, you'll learn how to create a plan that's specific and workable. And flexible. It's called the *flex*plan.

When we create these goals, within a very short time, they look very worked over, with original statements modified over and over again.

If it helps, make a visual collage of your goals. Cut out pictures from magazines or do your own drawings. Paste them on a poster board along with your mission statement, and hang the whole thing on the wall. Surf the world, via the Internet. Observe everything.

The beauty of writing and visual graphics is that they aid us in sustaining our vision. So, get that mission statement on the wall.

Think all it takes is an Idea?

What's in an idea by itself? Absolutely nothing. What about a really good idea? Still nothing, nothing, nothing, until we act upon that idea. Wherever I go, from ten-year-olds to 90 year-olds, they line up to tell me about their great life-changing idea. I have to say that the majority of them are fairly impressive. From an after-market hybrid system that attaches to the back of a vehicle like a small trailer, to a private community-delivery system that cuts the cost of produce delivery by over 60%, it's amazing to hear what people think of.

Whenever I come to a small town, I always try to engage the local coffee klatch and it's not that I'm in search of anyone's ideas. It's fun and stimulating to talk with other people about other ideas. In fact, I don't think there's a more enjoyable conversation than when people talk and dream about ideas. This achieves several things:

Adversity makes you stronger but only if you are willing to become stronger from it.

1) It awakens our own sense of what's needed in our lives and, general society.
2) It challenges us to think about ourselves and our capabilities.
3) It helps us to not let our own thought become stale and stultified.
4) It can help us to either come up with new ideas or, keep out own ideas on track.
5) It can foment new and meaningful relationships in our lives.

There is a down-side to discussions about new ideas. Often people simply like to dream, complain or fantasize and it stops there.

People often don't act on their best ideas because…

1) They don't know what to do.
2) They're not truly passionate about the idea.
3) They're more focused on making money than on the intent of the idea.
4) They think they need money to make their idea a reality.

There is so much work to be done in this world. We need more ways to keep our children safe, keep families together, save energy, develop alternative energy, stretch our finances, stay healthier, happier. If you look around even in your own town, you'll be amazed at the problems that need to be solved. What can you do with the right team?

Inventors and entrepreneurs are not simply lonely hermits locked in their basements; they are the root of what makes American freedom so special. But it takes courage and listening. You have to really believe in your idea. And if you do and if you're willing to struggle forward, you'll be both amazed and delighted about what can be born from a single thought or a single conversation. You just have to find the right thought and, the right conversation.

Just start wondering about your own possibilities.

FREE ENTERPRISE

Summary

Many of our readers already have their ideas in mind and are simply using this book as a marketing reference, but our experience shows that the best marketing, even the most money, won't sustain a poorly shaped idea. This is your life. Give it the value you want it to have by paying attention to the true entrepreneur within.

Perform Self-Assessment of Current Direction.
- Think about your likes and dislikes.
Explore New Potential Directions.
- Make notes about your random and fragmented thoughts.
- Carry a little notebook or PDA. Don't underestimate the value of an old-fashioned note-pad. There is something very soothing to the creative spirit about writing without electronic support.
- Write it down!
- Periodically dump your ideas on the kitchen table and look for patterns in your thinking.
- Keep at it!
Formulate a more fulfilling, ultimately more profitable, venture.
- Make a Three-Stage Wish:
STAGE 1 – HOPE / BELIEF
- Get past just wishing for money, or to be a wealthy vegetable.
STAGE 2 – DESIRE / INTENTION
- Complete the following sentence: "I wish I could ..."
- Complete Connection #1 - Creating a Mission Statement
STAGE 3 – CREATION / ACTION
- Use this book to turn that passion into reality.

Potential Challenges and Solutions
Challenge: "I don't see myself as an 'idea person'."
Solution: This is the key problem. People have great ideas all the time but without means of implementation; at least that's what they think. If you think of your ideas as dreams, you can achieve a better understanding.
Dreams are the subconscious mind's way of digesting or processing old ideas and coming up with new ones. Listen to your dreams. They show us that we are all 'idea people.'
Challenge: "I don't feel I have what it takes to develop an idea."

A fragment of an idea isn't merely a fragment - it's proof that you as an individual matter in this world - that you are part of the connective evolution that advances humankind.

Solution: The world cries out for improvement at every level, be it survival, leisure, etc. - you name it. One must get out in the world and try on a few idea hats to see how they fit. In this initial phase, it costs you nothing to mentally shop around for ideas, and in doing so, you will learn how to develop you own idea selection process.

Before You Continue . . .
- Are you really taking a good look at what your real entrepreneurial center is?
- Are you showing sufficient courage to explore your possibilities?
- Are you open to the possibility that your original idea may not be what you'll end up with?

FIRST POWERPOINTER
How to Settle In on the Right Idea

To avoid putting all your eggs in one basket, choose three to five possibilities that make you curious, different directions that you can see yourself going in. Take your time to explore the viability of these directions. Do some preliminary exploration. Browse the Internet; make contact with someone in each field.

Use my litmus test to check out the feasibility of these ideas before you commit. Stay in touch with your contact and keep an arms length relationship until your instincts tell you to move in that direction. Remember, the more options you have, the better negotiating position you will be in to move in that direction. These kind of mental explorations cost you nothing. It's the daydreaming you've always done, just reawakened a bit.

Allow yourself to be open to moving in any one direction that starts to feel right for you. You might even find yourself moving in several directions at once. That's fine as long as you don't overwhelm yourself in the process.

Observe any subtle changes in your fields of choice. Notice how you feel if you are drawn in a particular direction. These changes may come in the form of a feeling, recurring positive visualization, or an inner voice that is pointing you in a direction. Do not disregard this sign as it has an intelligence that will guide you.

As always beware: Self-doubt may try to distract you from this guidance. In fact, you may be sick of hearing about your own cynicism. What does that tell you? It should suggest that you need to be a little bolder in your thinking. Begin training yourself to start thinking about possibilities, more than your self-doubts.

Once you have learned to quiet down and listen to those elements that will truly help you succeed, you will see that all positively directed people share the same thing in common. We all want to help make a better world; we just never knew it because were so caught up in believing we should be something we are not meant to be.

Learn what you have to offer then, simply learn how to take the simple steps to offer it.

FREE ENTERPRISE

In many cases, that has over-coated us with a sense of superficial need. This is not the natural state that human beings were meant to live as we were all born into innocence. We have only learned over time to become self serving through social conditioning created by a few self serving individuals who happen to have found a way to reach millions of people.

So clear your mental palate and begin creating. You have it within you!

ACTIVATOR FOUR
How To Grow The Right Idea or, Make the Most Out of an Existing Idea

Finding the right idea actually embraces three concepts: The first is to help you clearly identify an idea or business that best suits your needs. The second is having sufficient faith and confidence that you will take the proper steps (as described in these daily guidelines) to see your idea reach a functional and profitable place. What is different about this program is that you are not handed a grocery list of promising ventures that I seek to promote. This is about you and your ideas. Everyone is different and should not be limited by any list.

The third is assembling the right team and resources and, choosing them for the right reasons. We all need to work with others, no matter how much of a loner we think we are. Invention and innovation can compel healthy socialization.

"I don't have the money"

You will also notice that I absolutely do not emphasize raising money at this point. This is one of the major preconceptions that most budding entrepreneurs have. For the beginning stages, the reality is that raising or borrowing money can create more problems that it solves for two reasons: First of all, much of the beginning process is a self-test. Do you really want to pursue this path? The only way you will know is by trying these initial steps. Secondly, much of the initial process is free. They are simply exercises of self-identification. It is productivity that makes money, not the other way around. Once your momentum and level of commitment are established, you will learn about many resources for developing your idea. Money is only one option.

As noted earlier, many people buy this book with an idea already in progress and they just need to refine their production or sales. Those people will jump right into this and be able to move through the steps very quickly. But many of you are just getting

With fear and anger suspended and eventually subdued, a much larger universe opens to you. Take a good look at all the hopeful things about yourself.

started with either an idea that you want to examine, or no idea. For the first step, think about what you might want to do. Talk it over with, friends, family and colleagues.

Don't rush into the first idea that pops into your head. No idea ever turns out like we envision. There are usually several wrong turns that that turn out to make your venture more promising than you ever envisioned.

Developing a venture is not that difficult, but these questions will require thought and time to things you may not have previously looked at. Enjoy the process and the new adventure.

Once you have that team assembled, you move to the next level of challenges:

1) *An over-abundance of enthusiasm and good intention but, with limited direction.*
2) *Lack of Money*
3) *Lack of all or certain skills required for a real success.*
4) *Lack of utilization of the specific skill sets that your team possesses.*
5) *Lack of effective management top inspire and achieve the basic tasks at hand in order to build a platform for the next steps.*

Leadership Tips

So how do you lead a willing team to success? And how do you *keep* them willing with little or no money? The best way is to follow this simple guideline:

1) *Is this a practical and achievable concept for your group?*
2) *Can each member of your group play a role in advancing this concept or, is this just an excuse for getting together with friends?*
3) *Can your team set a realistic goal and sequence of steps to achieve that goal?*
4) *What will you or your team do when the goal seems further out of reach than anticipated?*
    4b) *What will you do when facing unexpected barriers, are you willing to do what it takes to overcome those barriers.*
    4c) *Are you willing to modify the goals as necessary and, as you learn a more feasible course for success?*
5) *Do you have a written agreement in place that spells out the role of each team member?*
    5a) *If a member fails to contribute, do you have a clear cut exit strategy for that team member?*

"When you get to the top of the mountain, keep climbing."
Zen Proverb

FREE ENTERPRISE

POWERPOINTER TWO
How To Build a Successful Team

One of the greatest problems my clients encounter has nothing to do with their promising idea or business but on occasion, the people they have chosen to be a part of their team. All of a sudden, the most well-intentioned beginnings deteriorate into personal disputes, with far too much time diverted from the original team goals. If you're stalled by team or personality issues or, if you need some guidance in forming the best possible team in the first place, here are some helpful guideposts:

For Team Building

1) Everyone gets excited about being part of a new venture but how well will that excitement translate into effective productivity and action? You don't just need enthusiasm and desire from teammates, they also each need to be capable of carrying out specific assignments. So as you build your team, be sure that everyone has a specific function and the ability to deliver.

2) Formulate a specific goal and purpose for the team and be sure that everyone signs on to that goal. As noted earlier, goals often have to change to achieve the original invention's intention.

3) Assign specific tasks to each teammate along with time-lines; Tasks achieved by certain dates.

4) Agree to detailed and confidential email communication from each participant to ensure diligence. If you are the leader, it is up to you to ensure that all of the assigned components are in fact, coming together.

If Somebody Falters..

If somebody fails to do their job or, falters for any reason, often a simple wake-up call will make all the difference. But if that earnest effort doesn't produce a positive change, and any individual starts to become a detraction or drain on the venture, everyone has to have agreed in advance to remove themselves from the team by unanimous decree and pre-agreed-to severance terms.

The exception of course, is the originator or originators of the concept who cannot be voted out and should agree to mediation or arbitration. If you built your team long before you got a hold of this book, and your venture is in a state of paralysis, you may have at least these four following options:

It's amazing, exciting and sheer fun to hear people talk about ideas but it's even more amazing what people don't do with their great ideas.

1) Walk away from the current venture.
2) Request that your former partners walk away.
3) Agree to buy out partners from future earnings.
4) Begin a whole new modified venture without existing partners or, with new partners.

How to Find People to Entrust

This is of course, the most vital element and in reality, you can't know whom to trust until you see what people actually do. That's why people often turn to friends but then if the friends don't have the necessary skills to contribute, that can place the friendship in jeopardy. Of course the most important advice here is to not rush into any choice until you are sure you need someone ongoing.

Consider bringing participants in for a limited period of time or, a trial period or thee to six months. The better your choices and understandings are in the beginning, the fewer surprises down the road.

"No, I Won't Help You"

You're trying to build a team and you need a break. It could be that distributor or manufacturer or that business that's willing to take a chance on your service; anyone who provides you with that catalyst to get things in motion.

Any of us who have been in business have on occasion, found ourselves hanging by a thread, waiting for that one possibility to help us make it through. But what do you do if that coveted team-player or, key decision-maker just isn't budging? If you call or email them constantly, you run the risk of putting them off. If you do nothing and just wait for fate, they may never turn in your direction.

1) No such thing as the one and only – We sometimes work very hard to win an account or sale that could be life-changing and we place so much energy into the prospect, that if we don't get the deal, we feel so defeated, that we don't have the energy or drive to press on. The lesson is clear: You have to have at least three options for any major deal you are assembling. If you're solely dependent on hearing a yes from one individual, you're always going to hanging by that proverbial thread.

2) Create Options and Alternatives. Depending on just one possibility or customer is a very risky prospect. Not only can this waste a great deal of time, it can set you up for tremendous losses even before you get started. You will always feel better if you seek out some good alternatives. That way, the prospect may start pursuing you instead of leaving you hanging in the balance.

An idea by itself has no power whatsoever unless implemented and delivered effectively.

FREE ENTERPRISE

3) Communicate, Communicate, Communicate. Now, this doesn't mean stalk and pester. It means, have a polite 'listening' conversation so you know the full reality of the situation. You especially need to learn if there are any barriers or problems with the prospect so you can address them. Sometimes deals go stale or dormant simply because no one was made aware of a small problem that could be addressed.

4) Create Options with Each Option. Knowing that there are always alternatives, you also need to know that there are options within each option. If the prospect is moving too slowly for you or, not at all, you need to find out why. Don't simply wait and hope that it's all going to happen. That's what a procrastinator would do. You to know if they are still even a prospect at all.

5) Bend but do not Break. Bend your offer as far as you can but do not break your own piggy-bank. If the objecting issue is money and fee-structure, find out where the middle-ground is. Sixty-percent of something is always better than 100% of nothing.

6) If you have no money and are seeking an affiliation with a company or individual, ask them if they will serve on your board act as an adviser or, offer a small equity position. The key is being able to assess what might attract a prospect to be affiliated with you. Is this relevant to their interests in some way, what will they gain by affiliating with you?

7) If there's just no way. If they say no six ways in seven different languages, at least try to find out why and learn from that input. The key is to create alternatives and options so the choices and your general fate is in your hands.

8) Remain Friends No Matter What. Good will and manners even after being turned down, will go a long way towards building trust in your character and integrity in the eyes of your declining prospect. These simple manners could be just that little extra edge that will prompt this prospect to come back to you at another time.

There is another compelling way to use this book which has been brought to my attention several times: You can also use it to try to make your 'day job' more secure. As we've emphasized, while doing what we love is key to a healthy life, many readers opt to keep their present job while using this book to make some money on the side. But these days, there is no such thing as job security.

You just can't walk into work and expect that someone else will take care of your company's financial soundness because if they do, chances are, they could take over your job as well.

Invention actually has two mothers: Necessity and Frustration.

FINDING YOUR MOST POWERFUL IDEA

Important Tips for Job Security

There is a solid solution that could not only help (but certainly not guarantee) you to keep your job but could possibly increase your job security. To accomplish this, you have to do two things:

1) Increase your worth and value as an employee. What other talents and services could you offer to make you just too valuable to let go?

Let's assume you take those measures which increase your value as an employee. Resultantly, your boss notices and does indeed appreciate how vital you are to the organization. But...what if the company runs low on cash not just due to lack of sales revenue which can often be shored up, but due to lack of available cash to maintain? No matter how talented you are at your specific skill base, if there's no money coming in, there's no way you'll remain employed. So you need to address point 2:

2) Become central to increasing revenue to your company. As you spend your valuable time perusing this book, you'll notice Hundreds of tactics for generating or increasing revenue for any venture, plus the 76 Core Strategies and Tactics interspersed at the end of each successive chapter. While keeping in mind the central goal of revenue generation, review these tactics to determine which ones might most effectively benefit the organization you're working for.

3) State Your Case. Learning to present ourselves effectively to the right decision-makers can be critical for job-survival. Let's suppose you identify 21 tactics in this book that you think might benefit the company. Consider presenting three or four each week. Start with some simple ones, like a 'call to-action' on business cards. Then present a few each week so that you are looked to as the idea man for revenue generation.

4) Help Make Ideas Happen. Now your best secret weapon, this book also shows you how to make these tactics happen. Get involved in that process so once again your value to the organization goes up. Survival of a job or personal venture is not merely about working harder and letting the boss see your office lights burning through the night. If he doesn't see you increasing revenue, he'll worry more about paying for that light bill. You must learn to be effectively strategic.

SCAMGUARD
The Downside of Moving Up

When you start thinking outside the cubicle and take a chance at raising your status in an organization, you also increase your vulnerability. Unfortunately, just because you know more or, precisely what your company needs to do, you may also end up ruffling the feathers of those who were supposed to be coming up with these strategies in the first

A good team is one that hangs in there when times get tough and money gets thin. Those are the people you can entrust.

FREE ENTERPRISE

place. Welcome to your first lesson in politics, where you'll often encounter people far more concerned at protecting their job than doing their job.

So yes, it's true, in some circumstances, you could lose your job by posing a threat to others because you're doing a better job of what they're supposed to be doing. So what do you do? Let's suppose you do nothing and the company goes under; you've lost your job anyway. Here are some tips to help you to both do a good deed for your company and, not get punished for it:

1) Go right to the top. If you feel that you can trust your boss or someone even higher up, go directly to that person and offer three solid ideas for revenue generation. Tell him that you want nothing in return except to help do your share to support the organization.

2) Partner with your Immediate Superior. Propose that you and your immediate superior work together to create enhanced job security, and present the ideas as a team.

3) Strength in Numbers. Bring up your ideas only in group meetings so the sources of the ideas become known.

4) Create an Adjunct Contract. Create a written agreement with your company so you will be compensated if your ideas work but, will also be protected if you do indeed run into political resistance.

5) Anonymously email one or two ideas to your boss each week. If he starts to implement them, then let him know why you did it and what your fears are about being known. This approach can backfire because company email can easily be traced and you could be accused of not standing up for your ideas.

Many readers may fully realize that their day job is in trouble and may in fact, already be feeling the knives in their back. Doing nothing may preserve your job for a long time. On the other hand, being pro-active may be the only way to ensure job security.

The people surrounding your idea are more important to the success of your idea than the idea itself.

FINDING YOUR MOST POWERFUL IDEA

CORE STRATEGIES AND TACTICS NUMBER ONE
Pledge to love your customer. Love is an abused term when it comes to business ventures except when it comes to understanding who and what keeps you in business: The people you are trying to reach. Learn everything you can about those who will benefit from your concept. Use this 'intimate knowledge to help shape and evolve your idea so it maximally benefits your customer. In addition, the more your customer perceives that you care about their well-being through excellent customer service, the more trust you will earn and the greater chance of building customer loyalty. Note all of the reasons why you love your concept, and why your customers should as well. And especially note how and why you need to show your customers that you care about them.

HOW TO SUPERCHARGE THIS TACTIC: Do more than just learn about your prospect's life; get involved it. Don't just talk about golf or tennis, set up a game; or a social function, get special show tickets for a preferred client. Remember that often a small minority of your clientele can comprise a vast majority of your income. If you can ingratiate yourself in a genuine manner with a prospect, they will be more apt to do business with a friend who shares their likes and appreciates their family. Also, consider hosting a customer appreciation day or, even an awards dinner.

HOW CAN YOU ENGAGE THIS RIGHT NOW FOR YOUR VENTURE?

_____

_____

_____

CORE STRATEGIES AND TACTICS NUMBER TWO
Ask how-to- questions about your idea of the best experts you can find. How would they set the business up? How would they promote it, etc? What would they do to make your enterprise as successful as possible? How could they achieve it while spending as little as money as possible? Accomplished people are generally flattered by your interest and will provide a wealth of useful information. Since you don't have the time to read every great book on your subject, seek out summaries of each book online. Think and evaluate all advice carefully.

HOW TO SUPERCHARGE THIS TACTIC: Contact the most knowledgeable people and the field and, ask to interview them. Often, these people will be flattered that

The more central you are to the core survival of a business, the less likely they could survive without you.

FREE ENTERPRISE

you asked and you will pick up valuable tactics that could save you endless hours of frustration. Go online and ask the hardest questions you can think of about your concept. Keep refining your questions until you get answers you can really rely on.

HOW CAN YOU ENGAGE THIS RIGHT NOW FOR YOUR VENTURE?

___

___

___

CORE STRATEGIES AND TACTICS NUMBER THREE
Look for Success Models. Is someone doing something similar to what you're doing? What can you learn from them and how can you combine those tactics with all the techniques in this book to do it better? Would there be a point where it would be beneficial to merge your respective talents to increase mutual outcome.

HOW TO SUPERCHARGE THIS TACTIC: Is there a way you might pool certain resources with your competition and go after far more business for both of you? Your competition is not always your opposition. Also, as you study heroes in your field, j\don't just learn what they did right, look at the mistakes they made and, how you could do things better.

HOW CAN YOU ENGAGE THIS RIGHT NOW FOR YOUR VENTURE?

___

___

___

CORE STRATEGIES AND TACTICS NUMBER FOUR
Create a Primary Goal. In one sentence of less, what are you trying to achieve? It can become very tempting to get side-tracked so keep that goal in mind whenever you feel challenged. It will help you keep your focus and drive. At the same time, if you determine that you customer base compels you to modify your goal, you need to either figure out how to integrate your original aim with the new ones demanded by your customer or, you may find yourself evolving to a new direction.

HOW TO SUPERCHARGE THIS TACTIC: Share your stated mission statement with friends and ask them to 'edit it.' This can help you to refine your goals and some-

A good idea is only valuable if you figure out how to make it work.

times discover aspects of your goals that you haven't previously thought of. Pledge to yourself that no matter what happens to your business, your goal must survive.
HOW CAN YOU ENGAGE THIS RIGHT NOW FOR YOUR VENTURE?

CORE STRATEGIES AND TACTICS NUMBER FIVE
Build an Instant E-Network. How many friends to you send useless chatter to each day? Why not put them to work by first telling them about your new venture and then, asking them to pass it on to any of their friends who might find it useful. This is a healthy expansion of simply talking to friends and, making new friends and most importantly, giving everyone at least two of your business cards; one for them and another for their friend. Best of all, you can do this on a quality level for no money.

HOW TO SUPERCHARGE THIS TACTIC: Refine your 'gift of gab' skills so you can engage these people as quickly as possible. Everybody gets flooded with slick email proposals from strangers but the sooner these prospects are emailing a real person, the better your chances of truly engaging them. See every opportunity when you're among people, as an opportunity for possible new business, but always be polite about it. Advertise a 'think-tank' and invite the smartest people you know.
HOW CAN YOU ENGAGE THIS RIGHT NOW FOR YOUR VENTURE?

CORE STRATEGIES AND TACTICS NUMBER SIX
Chat It Up In Chatrooms and Communities. With just some simple searches on line, you can find any number of websites, on line communities and chatrooms relevant to your venture. Note: do not use your real name and do not give out contact information until you're fairly confident about the people you've engaged.

HOW TO SUPERCHARGE THIS TACTIC: Seek these live chats out and contribute your wisdom, earn the credibility and trust of the other participants. That way, when

---

A Strategy is what you are planning; a Tactic is what you are actually doing to make that plan work.

FREE ENTERPRISE

you exchange contact information, there is more of a likelihood they will contact you, as opposed to simply placing your website out there right off the bat.

HOW CAN YOU ENGAGE THIS RIGHT NOW FOR YOUR VENTURE?

___

___

___

___

___

CORE STRATEGIES AND TACTICS NUMBER SEVEN
Answer a Question On Line. Go to *Yahoo Answers*, *Ask.com* or, any number of Question websites and answer a question relevant to your venture. This establishes instant credibility and your answer can be seen by a large audience seeking out your information and then, you. Make certain you have answered the question truthfully and credibly so that you have helped to solve the problem. Don't simply post a website or your email address, earn the credibility instead.

HOW TO SUPERCHARGE THIS TACTIC: Under another name, or a cloak, ask a few insightful questions about your topic so you can show off your know-how. Also make sure your register every relevant keyword, phrase and Meta tag you can think of.

HOW CAN YOU ENGAGE THIS RIGHT NOW FOR YOUR VENTURE?

___

___

___

___

___

CORE STRATEGIES AND TACTICS NUMBER EIGHT
Build a Wikipedia Page. Wikipedia is the ever-growing, ever morphing Encyclopedia online of just about everything. Your free posting or contribution to the knowledge of one or many Wikipedia topics can turn you into a ready reference, espe-

When a venture is in trouble, it is not generally due to lack of money but lack of the right strategies and tactics.

cially when the pages lead back to you. Most important rule: Be truthful and credible. If you are simply trying to sell, readers will be hard-pressed to believe you.

HOW TO SUPERCHARGE THIS TACTIC: In presenting your information, try to use your own company or name as a reference or informational source. This helps to build respondents and it helps you build your image and brand.

HOW CAN YOU ENGAGE THIS RIGHT NOW FOR YOUR VENTURE?

_____

_____

_____

_____

The right venture gets you out there meeting the right people you really want in your life. Go meet them now.

FREE ENTERPRISE

Progress Journal: (please feel free to copy or scan this page only)

_____

_____

_____

_____

_____

_____

_____

_____

_____

_____

_____

_____

_____

_____

_____

_____

_____

Your Signature_____Date_____

Email and online communications in general can be both powerful and effective forms of communication but don't hide behind them as a substitute for phone calls or face-to-face meetings.

CHAPTER TWO

ADVANCING YOUR CONCEPT

The Process of Self-Assessment
"If a man will begin with all certainties, he shall end in doubt; but if he will be content to begin with doubt, he shall end in certainties."
Francis Bacon

Overview

Having become more aware of what it really means to select the most appropriate idea, this chapter and its exercises will stimulate your thinking to help you to bring real momentum to your idea.

Activator Steps for This Chapter
1) Refine your self-understanding.
2) Determine your best idea.
3) Be open to new ideas to make the best choices for your venture

It makes no difference how simple or complicated your idea is. Everyone has the ability to act upon an idea that's personally important or just plain fun. Everyone we have ever met has some idea they want to develop and market. There has never been a more favorable climate than there is today for personal success. Coupled with our low-cost development and marketing systems, your personal possibilities are greater than ever.

This is not mere psychological cheer leading. Look at all the magazines and news items that now feature new products or services. There is clearly an increasingly receptive market for ideas from the individual dreamer, and we will show you the path of least resistance to get your share. If you really want your idea to succeed, you must have a love affair with your idea, and falling in love takes some time. So take the time. No success in sixty seconds here.

When you finish with this book, we want you to have more than just a gimmick. We want you to have something of value that celebrates your personal initiative. That's where we want you to be. That's our *STAGE 3*.

Do you have your idea locked down? The right idea? If you think so, let's see if it will hold up through this chapter. But so far, you're doing great. If you're following this system, aside from the cost of this book, your only expenses so far have been for pencils, notepads, or your PDAs, and you probably already had those.

Now it's time to move from dreaming to doing.

FREE ENTERPRISE

"Is this all there is? Can I find my market niche? What is my potential anyway?"

Scary stuff. Do we matter? Do we have what it takes to make a difference and make a little extra or a lot of extra money in the process?

Of the thousands of people we have lectured to or consulted for, the above are the major concerns we hear over and over again with one important difference — they have taken the initial steps to try to make a difference. It is that intent followed by action that will make a difference in their respective ventures.

Even if you believe you have your idea all ready to go - just one step away from the market, do not skip this exercise because the supporting theme of this chapter is to make certain that you have chosen your direction wisely and accurately.

Very often, you will discover that your idea is right for you, that it is the best utilization of your personal resources. You may also just be playing with something that will ultimately bore you, even though you already picture yourself as that lucky fraction of a percent of those in this world who are millionaires.

The goal is a fulfilling venture that augments your income either a little or a lot. It all depends upon you and your idea. Think marriage. That's right, marriage. A good marriage is what you're after here whereby in theory, you will stay with your concept for better or for worse. Some ideas are indeed big money ideas and some are not, it depends largely upon your dedication, imagination and your willingness to listen and learn at the early stages.

Still you can't just aim for the biggest money-maker. Instead, you find the idea that's right for you and then learn and grow with it and then maybe your next idea will be the real bonanza. What's most essential is to get comfortable with the process.

My Stumble Theory'

In general, the best successes and greatest adventures do not belong to the rigid but to those open to the new possibilities as they assume their direction. Be aware and prepared that opportunities may and will creep up that you may stumble into as you assume one direction or another. Be ready to recognize and capitalize on these unexpected opportunities.

Your first self-initiated venture is so important because you learn so much about patience and perseverance. And hopefully you will not have spent yourself into a financial dream-killer situation. What follows are a series of exercises to help you explore and expand upon the 3-stage idea development process.

Test the validity of your idea without expense.

ADVANCING YOUR CONCEPT

What the Global Financial Downturn Teaches Us about Developing Our Own Ideas

Should the current global depression, masked as a recession, come as a shock to anyone? Perhaps only to the naïve or those who simply chose not to see it coming. But right around Y2K, many did see that date as the epochal moment when financial Armageddon would be upon us and were confounded and challenged when it didn't happen. Back then, pundits proclaimed that banks were dangerously undercapitalized, , credit options were ridiculously liberal to the unqualified and that by 2001, there existed this giant 'bubble' that just was ripe to explode and would leave in its wake , the debris of double-digit unemployment and a real global depression.

Those pundits were correct. It just that there timing and catalysts were off. So Freddie Mac and Fannie Mae kept drinking in a steady stream of toxic mortgages. Other reputable and trusted financial firms, though well-aware of the dangers of this toxicity, chopped these loans up into separate burger bits and, mixed them with loads of very healthy loans in the hopes that they would be diluted and purified in these new packages. Then these companies sold these burger bundles to the globe, knowing how dangerous they were. When all the damage is done, the amount could easily exceed 100 Trillion Dollars.

Every bacteriologist knows that just one microscopic bacterium in a pack of meat with propagate, slowly and undetectable at first until it reaches the hapless consumer who only sees what looks like a healthy loaf of beef. (Sorry, my Vegan friends, it's just an analogy).

So from 2001 to 2007, all most investors saw was the fresh-looking red meat. But those financial organizations knew what was going on inside. Still they sold it to the world, as much as they could for as long as they could. Then they stopped selling them, not because their respective consciences compelled them to do so but because they drained the market (you and me) dry.

Suddenly, as they collected their absolutely criminal bonuses, they were making public proclamations of their shock and horror and, begging the government to pay them more money, not a penny to you and me. In the meantime, these financial vampires have drained the financial bloodstream of the world. And the Wall Street Bailouts will do very little, if anything for the consumer. So we are on our own and that's especially why you need this book.

In the end, after all of the mid-stream brokers and execs and you and me lose most of what we have. Then you are left with some eight to twelve thousand individuals who have actually benefited from the suffering caused to virtually every modern day investor in the entire modern world.

The approximately $100 Trillion lost to the globe is actually a fine for humanity taking itself in the wrong direction.

FREE ENTERPRISE

What the Bailout Foolishness Really Means To You

The worst part of the global financial collapse is that it could have easily have been avoided. It all happened because the world could not coordinate its true priorities. Our oceans are dying, literally suffocating, our polar icecaps are melting, forests are disappearing, our ability to safely grow crops or raise livestock is in jeopardy. We are fighting foolish wars that are only creating more enemies instead of encouraging global education and self-sufficiency. There are at least 5,000 true environmental and social causes that would have returned true and real value and benefit. But instead of working from our conscience and intellect, we gave into our more basal instincts or greed and we allowed ourselves to be marketed to in this manner. Another example is the steady decline of the U.S. auto industry who for years, have been marketing cars to our childlike needs instead of our need for common sense and the environment.

When you let the parking meter expire, you pay a fine. When you ignore the true needs of the global village and mother earth, the natural order of global and economic finances compels each of us to pay a fine.

That what this $100 Trillion-plus drain is to the globe – it's a fine against each of for allowing all the key priorities of the world, not just those who marketed this junk to us, but to those of us (myself included) who allowed ourselves to be marketed to.

Think about this as you build a business around your idea. If you do, you will greatly increase the chances of your global success.

ACTIVATOR FIVE

Who Are You? What Are You?

Scientist, blue-collar, white-collar, no collar, the exercise is still the same. Following is a connection exercise progression designed to help point you in the right direction. Don't Rush. This could take an evening or several weeks but do apportion your time so you will eventually finish. You are not allowed to give up half-way through.

The Current Me

1. When people ask what you do, you say, (list one primary occupation or whatever primarily occupies your weekday):

I am:

_____

_____

ADVANCING YOUR CONCEPT

2. Please list at least five things you love about what you do:

_____

_____

_____

_____

3. List up to five things that you dislike about what you do:

_____

_____

_____

_____

4. I feel that what people like most about me is:

_____

_____

_____

_____

_____

In the beginning, few great entrepreneurs or entrepreneurial teams are paid with anything but invaluable learning experiences. Hang in there for the greater rewards.

FREE ENTERPRISE

5. I am most bothered by the fact that I:

_____

_____

_____

_____

_____

6. Aside from your primary occupation, list any other skills you have, whether proficient in them or not:

_____

_____

_____

_____

_____

My Desires and Vision

7. Aside from becoming more financially independent (we'll get to that), I would also like to be more:

_____

_____

_____

_____

ADVANCING YOUR CONCEPT

8. List at least three things that you'd like to see changed or improved in your community:

_____

_____

_____

_____

_____

9. List at least three things you'd like to see changed in the world:

_____

_____

_____

_____

_____

Determine Your Best Idea

The next exercise will help you to build on your self understanding to determine your best idea.

Have you suffered enough to finally take real action to improve your personal economy?

FREE ENTERPRISE

ACTIVATOR SIX
How to Transform Your Vision into Action (Finding your best idea)

1. List any ideas you've had in the past, any ideas for products or services, whether you acted upon them or not:

_____
_____
_____
_____
_____
_____

     Remember to take all the time you need for the above. It is not a quiz and it's most definitely not a judgment on you. It's merely the most effective means we've discovered to help you find your best starting point; a sort of insurance policy to create maximum possibilities for your success. So relax. Have fun with it because that will be the foundation from which you will build.

2. Delete, combine and add to your ideas from the list you generated in step 1. Let your new self-understanding and you inner guidance lead you to the idea that is best for you at this point in your life. Write it down here for emphasis and focus.

_____
_____
_____
_____
_____

Often, the answers to your biggest business challenges can be found within the process of the struggle forward.

ADVANCING YOUR CONCEPT

3. Be open to new ways of thinking. Exploring new ideas and new paths always involve a little self-exploration and that can seem a little scary or just plain bothersome.

Many of our clients find it easy, having been in some form of professional life for quite a while. Others aren't sure who they are or what they have, but interestingly enough, the second category is often the most creative because they haven't been excessively preconditioned nor hardened by certain established or learned barriers.

It's helpful to remember that any life, and any situation, can be observed in either of two ways: as overwhelming, hopeless, and depressing, or as chock full of possibilities, promise and adventure. Find the fun, find the adventure or better said, make the fun, build the adventure. Any point can be a starting point upward.

Having said that and hopefully having cleansed your idea-producing palate, you should now be ready for the most exciting aspect of your personal idea- profile and this part is quite a bit of fun because you'll not only create a lot of new possibilities, you'll learn new things about yourself.

ACTIVATOR SEVEN
The Dream Ride

The concept of the 'Dream Ride' actually came from my personal and admittedly dangerous habit of coming up with my best ideas early in the morning, as if through dreams, while driving or while riding my mountain-bike. There they'd hit me and I'd frantically scribble them down before he really hit someone else. So obviously, we would never endorse writing while driving unless you're lucky enough to have a Dictaphone or digital recorder or a gracious passenger who will write for you.

It was all that daydreaming and driving, hiking, wherever it hits you, that really gets your creative juices flowing: new places = new ideas. The essence of the Dream Ride exercise for most of you involves simply carrying around a little pen and pocket notebook with you wherever you go. Whenever you have a thought, even a scant notion or question about something, enter it in your notebook.

As you occasionally refer back to your responses in the initial part of this exercise (some of which you may add to as time goes by), make notes about any ideas that might suit you; what do you like?

What could you make or what service could you create? Remember that money is not an issue yet. First, let's make sure you're matched up with the best idea and then we'll deal with the other issues in later chapters.

Aside from money which most of us would like to have more of, what else makes you happy and would you do more of it if you could make money at it? Write it all down.

A simple idea is born from seemingly complicated clues.

FREE ENTERPRISE

What do you do that makes you happy and that you wish you had more time to do? What talents do you have or could you develop to enable you to live that dream? Do you want your hobby to grow until it eventually becomes a vocation?

Daydreaming can awaken your best ideas

Naturally, we've seen quite a few of these notebooks from people who previously thought they couldn't fill one page. And of course, we have piles of our own. Loads of our own ideas and especially loads of fragments. It's those fragments, those puzzle-pieces that are most valuable.

Take several days, weeks or even a couple of months of note-writing (these could be some of the most important decisions of your life, so take whatever time you need). Anxious people rush to failure but enthusiastic people step to success.

And test, test, test! Tests make or break. Tests preserve or insure the potential of your dreams. Find ways to test your idea(s) even from the most scant beginnings - like when we're dream riding - exploring new ideas as we explore our own identities. There are many means to do so and are described in detail in this book.

As suggested earlier, it's scary stuff, looking at what we are and what we're not; until we remember that the very purpose of this entire chapter is simply to create a platform, a jumping-off point from neither what we are nor are not, but where we want to be.

Along with a new idea, this is about creating a new you, a new success or even a first success. As you undertake this process, you'll discover that no matter who you are or how successful or unsuccessful you have been, you have learned something every day.

Want a better life? No TV commercial or pop-up Internet ad has the answer, no matchbook cover has the answer, and no parent or relative has the answer. Most are distractions but some are puzzle pieces — opinions, especially the off-beat ones that you occasionally find yourself drawn to. What are they trying to tell you, what do they mean?

It's you who must make the final decision as to what might be the most fulfilling and challenging for you. All throughout the process of developing and nurturing your ideas, you may occasionally find yourself temporarily short of certain resources, but you'll always have an abundance of opinions which you must either validate or discard.

ACTIVATOR EIGHT
How To Test Your Dreams Without Consequence or Cost

These next three paragraphs are a little heavier than the rest of this book but they are very important for you and the ideas that you will be shaping and, that will be shaping you. So please bear with me and allow them to make sense for you. You'll soon see where they are going.

ADVANCING YOUR CONCEPT

In the eighties, noted journalist Studds Terkel came out with the book entitled 'Working.' Still popular today, this book contained over 600 pages of a celebration of the American worker, in particular, how people made their jobs more palatable. The overarching conclusion was that people loved to work but were happiest when the work was an undeniable part of their essence. And if it wasn't exactly what they wanted, fantasy and dreams of the future came into play. And if all of that didn't work and dreams were never truly realized, people were relegated to focus primarily on money, either for the future or, to be able to survive through the next month, or even this month.

How many readers of this book are primarily focused on money today and must do so as a means to justify their current job? Creating financial security or even survival does make logical sense. Most of us have to work and while we can fantasize or dream, we have to do what we have to do. We may be a great undiscovered writer or musician or public speaker or restaurateur but only in our dreams. We can't just stop what we were doing for a week or month or a year and just try something else. We have bills to pay and all the other responsibilities inherent to living in the real world. So then, let's take another visit to that fantasy world we all wish we could live in or at least explore.

No, you absolutely can not just trash your current life and just cast your fate to the winds simply because there isn't a whole lot of cash blowing around in those winds. But eventually, you may have to make a change if you ever really want to give the possibilities of your life, a real chance.

Nearly a century ago, famed psychoanalyst Carl Gustav Jung spoke of the importance of resisting mass movements and not losing ourselves by not knowing who we are.

It brought the thinking of Henry David Thoreau 'out of the woods' by not only inspiring us to make more of an effort to understand ourselves, but by warning us that to avoid doing so would find us lost in the forest of our own lives.

Mid-life crisis is nothing new and exploding your life in the midst of one is virtually accepted. But what if you didn't have to explode your life to make a 'course correction? And what if you could test the viability of your greatest career and life-dreams and fantasies without disrupting your life?

This book urges and guides readers though an identity crisis but without the attendant social consequences. Exploding your life, changing, career mid-stream or abandoning your marriage as I did with my first marriage is not always going to guarantee that the other side of the rainbow doesn't find you struggling with the same or worse challenges. The reason is simple: You always have to take you along with you wherever you go. That means good traits stay with you as well as unresolved issues. The net results can be the same, thereby explaining the high failure rate of second marriages or even second careers that can leave us just as lost as before.

When you go to the supermarket, they don't have one type of lettuce or one spice or one brand of diapers. When my wife shops, she loves to take her time and read every

Self-Assessment = Self-Invention = Self-Assurance = Self-Reliance.

FREE ENTERPRISE

label. I never go along with her because it can go on for hours; she loves to take her own time to study every option so whatever she brings home is what she really wants to bring home.

What if you could safely shop around regarding your life so that you bring the best results home. That's the magic and appropriate use of virtual exploration. When the Internet first came alive, we really weren't certain of where this space ship could take us but we all jumped on board and went there just the same. Many went overboard and just as a cheap replacement for oil will revolutionize the world (and it is coming), the Internet changed the way we all interact.

Today, we know things about the Internet that we could not have imagined even a few years ago. It comes from an agglomeration of both the opportunity for accelerated education and, extreme fraud. The accelerated education is a great advance and allows us to have needed data right at our fingertips. The fraud are the letters from impoverished countries promising millions to the recipient produced by promising writers, sitting in coffee houses throughout the world just throwing their hooks in the water.

Their letters get more and more clever. They create titles for themselves, phony passports and even phony companies with websites all designed to rob you blind.

The savvier we become the more clever and deceptive they become. But what if you could create your own Internet (Virtual) world not designed nor intended to harm, scam or bilk anyone? What if your efforts only had the intention of determining if there was an audience or any receptivity for your idea? For example, you work for a newspaper but you always wanted to be a musician. So you set up a Myspace describing your precise situation and dreams. Or, you place a series of free classified ads in any of the free classified ad sites.

What if you were always helping your friends write thoughtful things for weddings or other special occasions? Why not advertise that service to the world? If five or six people in your circle need the service, then it's fair to assume that Thousands need the service throughout your state or the U.S.

What's your dream? Many of us wonder or we really know for certain that we have other talents that could really make a difference to others if we could just find a way and means to reach them. Remember that the Internet age creates more of an opportunity to find the exact people you're looking for to make your dream happen but without compelling you to give up on your current life. In fact, you can test your ideas as a means to enhance your life and perhaps make subtle improvements that will help your to move in a more genuine direction.

Will the Internet stop the planet from mid-life wandering? No way but by engaging in the following exercise, your own identity crisis could not only prove far less harmful but, far more rewarding. All by simply making it virtual.

You'll never know if it's the dream you want until you wake it up a little with some free testing.

ADVANCING YOUR CONCEPT

What follows is a simple self-assessment test. As with all of the exercises in this book, this could prove to be yet another vital puzzle piece to help your entrepreneurial experience become a positive one: I am so lucky right now because I have the following in my life:

1) Home Life

_____

_____

_____

2) How happy are you 1 (not very 2 3 4 5 6 7 8 9 10 (Very)

    b) Career/Job_____

_____

_____

_____

_____

    How happy are you 1 (not very 2 3 4 5 6 7 8 9 10 (Very)

3) Here's what I would like to change and, why:

a) Home Life

_____

_____

_____

_____

In the virtual world of assessment, 'almost' is often good enough.

FREE ENTERPRISE

b) Career/Job_____

_____
_____
_____
_____

4) Here is what I would like to try if I could without upsetting my home life or career:

_____
_____
_____
_____

    The rest is easy. Just create a virtual identity for each of your dreams or fantasies and follow the systems in this book to test those dreams out without cost and without consequence. Then evaluate what you've learned about your intentions and direction:

> *1) Does the new idea make sense for you?*
> *2) Will you work on it to make it successful?*
> *3) Can this make supplemental money for you?*

But it's a secret!

    Does fear kill or preserve an idea? What do you need to protect an idea to ensure its success? If you talk about it with your friends, are they going to steal it?
    This is a great concern to a vast majority of our readers and clientele, and is addressed at various points in our progress.
    Just bear this in mind right now: To make any idea successful requires relentless initiative and very often, your best protection is both aggressive strategies and tactics and aggressive marketing. And yes, you may have to trust a small circle of collaborators. Remember that ideas, no matter how spectacular, are only the beginning. In fact free, com-

ADVANCING YOUR CONCEPT

petitive markets always consist of similar competitive products. Even if two ideas appear to be almost identical, they could still legitimately earn a share of the market. Further, no two concepts, even if identical, ever hit the market in the same way.

To be sure you don't restrict your creativity and potential with fear, think in terms of degrees. If you are a certified welder or have a PhD. in psychology, or perhaps you're an experienced home builder, the attendant certifications that accompany these competencies are ones you and you alone have earned. If someone stole the degree that belonged to you, all they'd have is the paper certification without the vital substance.

To really get your concept, they'd have to steal your brain and heart! So for most readers, part of your best protection is that your concept is too much a part of you for someone to come along and take it.

Then there's the issue of momentum. Hopefully, you'll use this book to be the most intelligent and aggressive in your marketplace which is in our own opinion, your best protection, i.e. earning a comfortable market share that's yours and yours alone.

Then there are the various patent, copyright, and trademark issues which we will go over in chapter 4. These issues will show you that the law is on the side of the dedicated originator. So protect, register, copyright trademark, patent pend by all means. Just be frugal, and don't let paranoia kill the potential development of a good idea. You have to trust some people and ultimately, you will find those people. And be aggressive in your marketplace.

The world is full of great beginning ideas that are totally worthless only because nobody knew nor connected with those who might have known how to act upon them. So explore on, dream on, and dream without fear.

At this point, you will have reached one of two stages: you either have a lot of puzzle pieces in the form of notes, or have added more dimension to an idea you already had, i.e. you are more certain about how to better direct that idea, in either case, it is now time to throw those notes on a table and see what puzzle pieces fit.

What fragments have you come up with that will constitute the best idea for you to pursue? Do not focus at this point on the money or labor you think it's going to take to develop your idea, what's crucial now is the proper starting point.

When you have indeed compiled your notes, or when you are fairly certain you know the direction in which you want to head, lay all your stuff (notes, etc.) on a table somewhere and begin putting the pieces together. Take heart - the answers shouldn't hit you right away. This is an intake time. You're a detective. We are working up to the point where you will learn how to relate your ideas with the appropriate potential contacts.

Saying this a million times wouldn't be enough: Your best protection are effective sales and marketing.

FREE ENTERPRISE

Summary

This is the point where dream becomes child, takes on a heartbeat and some tangibility. This chapter is crucial for helping to map out a clearer definition of your idea. To do this, you must be open to possibilities you had not previously considered.

-Refine your self-understanding.
-Determine your best idea.

-Be sure you've settled upon the best idea. Be certain that it's really a part of your personality.

- Do you really like your idea?

Is this something that's so much a part of you that you'll stay married to it for better or for worse?

- Will you be flexible as market reaction dictates turns and changes, not previously planned for or expected?

- Does your concept possess 'evergreen potential', i.e. perpetuity in the marketplace?

- Can it be utilized, improved, redeveloped and made available year, after year, like a hammer in a hardware store? Unless you're developing a fad-production business, stay away from fads unless you have a program for delivering follow-up products. The money-making pet rock and wall-walker were exceptions, not rules.

Are your expectations realistic?

Study the feedback until you really understand the best means for your concept.

Be open to new ways of thinking to make the best choices for your venture.

- Take a Dream Ride

- Show flexibility.

- Listen intently to the feedback and new understandings you have gained about both yourself and your idea.

- Be open to 'sideswipes' - directions not previously anticipated.

- Continue to make notes about your random and fragmented thoughts.

- Carry a little notebook.

- Write it down!

- Once again, dump your ideas on the kitchen table and look for patterns in your thinking.

- Keep at it!

ADVANCING YOUR CONCEPT

Potential Challenges and Solutions
Challenge: Can't Find an Idea

Solution: Fear of failure for those who have formerly tried and failed before is understandable but then again, you never had this book to help you before either. Fear of failure from those who have never tried a venture before is less understandable. First of all, you know some failures are unavoidable components of eventual success. Secondly, how are you going to know what you've got unless you give it a try?

Since we've attempted to take most of the financial risk out of it, the worst that can happen is you enhance your education about something and thus increase your value as a human being.

Assert your right to become a full and fulfilled soul. Don't be shy. Hitting upon the wrong idea generally results from bad listening or unrealistic planning. If you're building a boat, you don't begin by building a QE2. Work and grow within your gifts and abilities. Even something new must have a characteristic that somehow reflects that which has always been a part of you.

Challenge: Impatience/Anxiousness

Solution: Enthusiasm will give your idea energy, anxiousness will rush you to the wrong decision. Take your time and be open to the possibility that you may have not yet settled upon the best idea for you.

Challenge: Excessive Focus on Financial Gain

Solution: This book is designed to help you make more money. but orient first on your personal interests, then the appropriate financial formulas will follow.

Before You Continue . . .

- Can you describe your idea clearly and concisely?
- Is there a market for your idea?
- If so, where is it and what percentage of the overall population is it?
- What might your retail price be?
- What do other people think? Use reaction forms in upcoming chapters.
- Do you have or can you develop any talent relative to any phase of the development of this idea?
- Are you a resource or a liability to your own idea?

Is your idea useful, entertaining, etc? In other words, which of the following human needs and emotions does it appeal to, as pertaining to both your own needs and those of your potential customers?

- Love, greater feeling of self-worth
- Recognition/acknowledgment/popularity/pride
- Success/personal achievement

You'll gain more protection from focused direction.

FREE ENTERPRISE

- Self-congratulation/ego-gratification
- Physical comfort and/or improvement, pleasure
- Reduced fear (security) -emotional / financial
- Creativity enhancement/skill development
- Physical attractiveness

Heightened convenience/independence

POWERPOINTER THREE
How To Transform Unproductive Emotion Into Productive Energy

Are You Being Guided By Your Dreams or Your Moods?

The difference between your success or failure will be determined by the ongoing vision and spirit for success. When we create something new, it may not only change the world, but our personality as well.

Inventors and general business venturers, for that matter, become inspired and enthused. And the more they evolve their concept, the more alive they become.

So, at the onset, you need to begin shaping your mind for success. Attempting to figure out the answer to a problem when in a low mood is much more difficult than it is to find the same answer in a good mood. How aware are you of your moods, feelings and state of mind on an ongoing basis? That's why we say that good ideas not only generate financial profit but spiritual enrichment. And as time progresses, you'll earn an enthusiasm that will guide you forward to greater heights.

It won't come easily and we'll be there to support you with the best balance of instruction and solid motivational support. Anything that is worth doing takes effort. In that effort our thoughts will determine whether we are to be successful or not, not the physical barriers.

Cynics may disagree. That's what makes them self-limiting cynics. But what really separates the success from the failures is that the successful dreamers choose what they wish to think. Nobody does it for us.

Everyone has bad days which can stem from either external or internal reasons. But business opportunities pass us by if we wait to be in the right mood to work a deal or, make that vital phone-call. Still, most of us simply expect some days to be more lethargic than others. "Had a Bad Day" from Daniel Powter was a big hit song back in 2006.

While everyone could relate to it, accomplished execs and entrepreneurs alike know that in fact, opportunity doesn't wait for us to be feeling good about life and worse, if we try to approach tasks in a low mood, business could suffer.

So the pros learn to "check their emotions at the gate." and essentially, make everyday into a good and positive day, even if it's not. It's like a guy puffing out his chest

You can't be determined and depressed at the same time.

on muscle beach and then, deflating. They compartmentalize their feelings and, deal with them after the work is done. How do they do that?

Basically there are two approaches. The first is to learn some ways to take yourself out of a bad mood. For example, change or juxtapose your setting. I find that if I can make myself laugh about something, it generally sets be back on course. When working at Practice Builders, if I felt a little low, I would have a meeting with my author friend Steve Smith who probably also does not want his name mentioned in this book so I won't. There are some people that just make you laugh without even trying and Steve and I enjoyed that chemistry.

Other things can help such as taking a short walk, yoga, quick meditation or breathing exercises, a cup of coffee, a cute joke or story on the website, a uplifting not from a to a friend, or simple self-talk; all of these can serve to shift low thinking.

The second approach is the one I prefer which is to not let the bad or low moods creep up on you in the first place. If you get to bed too late or have too much sugar or alcohol at night, and you know these things diminish your capacity, pay attention to them.

If you know there are certain people who annoy you, either avoid them or, ask them to give you some space. If you know you have to deal with a difficult client or associate, prepare yourself mentally the night before.

Sometimes, our moods just start to drop, like when the coffee wears off or when we wake up feeling especially negative about life in general. The resultant feeling is the same. It is a sinking feeling like slowly dropping down into the fictional movie quick-sand. If we can see those signs just as they're starting, we can prevent ourselves from sinking more deeply.

Just as we monitor our marketing and business efforts and results, we often need to monitor ourselves before start really sinking in to something far less capable than we really are. If we don't and we get stuck in a low place, the longer we remain down there, the harder it is to bring ourselves back up.

With five children and a very busy schedule, I don't have the luxury of being able to have a bad day so before I start work, I do a 'brain-check' to make sure I'm in an attentive mental state so I can start every task with a strong, focused and clear mind. The luxury I do in fact have, is that often I can choose which project I want to work on so if I ever do find myself dropping a bit, I can switch to another more stimulating task.

State of mind becomes state of being so pay attention to the awesome power of your thoughts.

The different modes of thinking: Growing the enthusiast within.

The following will help you to identify and govern your thought-state into that positive self-inspiring realm that is characteristic of successful venturers.

EMOTIONAL THOUGHT - conditioned thinking draws upon memory, resistance, self sabotage, ego-mistrust, self doubt, and keeps you stuck — fearful and distracted

INTUITION - an inner voice — fresh, daring, insightful, playful, newborn — free. Helps to re-instill and grow new levels of confidence and competence.

AWARENESS - a willingness to look at one's own barriers while having the maturity to address them and move forward.

REACTIVE EMOTION - The situational reaction, based on our personal programming, and inherent coping skills. This negative or positive force either drains or energizes us.

As the valued cliché goes, remember not to get in your own way. If you are facing those "doubt demons," focus on the following:

- Quiet down inside.
- Notice your mood not by thought but by the feeling.
- Watch your mood without judging.
- Determine what tasks would be effective to complete in the mood you are in.
- Stay connected and aware of your mood throughout the day.

As the Buddha said, we are what we think. It's time to condition yourself to think and plan for your success.

ACTIVATOR NINE
How Not to Worry Yourself into Paralysis

"Why worry?" You hear that all the time about how unhealthy and unproductive it is but you do it anyway. Why worry? You can think of 20 good reasons no matter what others tell you about not doing so because to some extent, it is beyond your control.

There is a primitive instinctual mechanism in our brains that makes us worry, especially when we're striking out on our own into the unknown, to fulfill our dreams.

As we sail into that great unknown, we can't avoid thinking of some of those great fear-triggers, especially when we think about the great paralyzer: Running out of money. What if we really do run short and dry up our resources, what remaining security will we have? Didn't we get into this venture to increase our security and joy in life? What if things get worse?

Dealing with chronic worry is like dealing with an injury. Only the daily therapy of attempted efforts at solutions to your challenges can help to lessen it.

ADVANCING YOUR CONCEPT

First off, it's important to note that most people learn so much that things always improve. One key reason is the discovery that they key element they cannot afford to lose is their enthusiasm and worry is at constant war with enthusiasm and self-inspiration. It stops us from thinking and tries to overwhelm us like a great tidal wave. If worry had a mind of its own, and it definitely doesn't, worry seems to not just want to keep us safe and bored, but it wants us to fail or at least give up.

I've seen thousands of very successful entrepreneurs and dedicated small businesspeople lose some money at times but eventually succeed beyond their wildest dreams simply because they never lost their enthusiasm and hence, never lost their ability to try to be productive and through this book, you will see that there is always a ways to succeed.

You know all of this, you've heard it said it many different ways by many well-intentioned inspirational people but you keep worrying. How do we know? Because, you keep buying the same books designed to quell your worries or, perhaps capitalize on them.

You could argue that your worry has in fact kept you safe, stable and secure but in today's world, that safety is the most dangerous illusion you can harbor. You have to assume some risk just to maintain your current standard of living.

The most important thing you can hear from people is any pontification about not worrying. "Relax, don't worry," everyone tells you. "Everything will turn out as it should." In other words, give up.

We can't order ourselves to stop worrying but there are some specific guidelines that can transform worry into success. Here are some god guidelines to follow:

1) Are you worried right now or hopeful? Do you clearly understand the vast difference between these two states? One directs you forward one way or another, the other guarantees paralysis.

_____

_____

_____

2) Is your worry preventing you from moving forward right now?

_____

_____

FREE ENTERPRISE

3) Describe your greatest fear at present:

_____

_____

_____

4) Using the techniques found throughout this book, list five to ten specific action steps you can start today to solve this specific problem. Remember, they are action steps designed to lead to a direct result.

_____

_____

5) Observe how your action steps begin to reduce your worry.

_____

_____

_____

    Is attacking worry and tipping the balance to hope really that easy? Yes, it really is if you take some action. The problem has always been that the illusion of fear creates the illusion of personal ineffectiveness.

    Worry, fear and its close relative, a negative attitude operate like a virus that insidiously and slowly closes down the psyche and spirit until you find yourself nearly paralyzed with nothing but fear. The trick is in fact not to brave it all but to acknowledge when the virus of worry is creeping in and to listen to the message it is trying to tell you. What do you need to do right now to stop it?

    There is always a new proposal you can write, a new prospect you can call on, a new idea or dream you can test and pursue. There's always a new sale you can try to make or a new client you can try to win over.

    All of these actions will begin to shift your spirit from fear to hope and with growing hope comes stronger results. Use this book to solve these worries in ways you never

Play the Beach Boys Song, 'Don't Worry Baby' until you believe it.

ADVANCING YOUR CONCEPT

before knew were possible. There are so many new possibilities, enough to write a book. Believe me, I know. That is how I wrote this book and made my dream possible.

ACTIVATOR TEN
How to Brighten Your Outlook during Challenging Times

The greatest part of the brain is actually not any particular part. And it's not about size or intellect (Most brains weigh about 3 1/2 pounds). It's actually and aspect about being human.

It's free-will.

What is free-will anyway and, why is it such a big deal? Essentially, it means or allows that the very best time can follow the very worst time of your life. It means that any day, you can wake up and no matter how severe your problems, how dire your situation, you can choose a brighter perspective.

Why should this matter to you? Because if you're like most people, you've never really tested the power of your own free-will and like most people, you probably believe that defeat is a message telling you to give up. But to do so is anti-human.

No worthwhile venture happens without a real struggle. I get so depressed when I see and schemes promising 'easy' money or easy success. Sorry folks, but ads by their nature represent over-promise so you have to 'under-believe' them. If life is too easy, you learn nothing, and then when real challenge confronts you, you find it very difficult to cope. And challenge confronts all of us all the time. Accepting and embracing challenge is healthy because it forces (or invites) you to learn something new and hence, get stronger at your weakest places.

To create something new in your life or, to overcome a new barrier, you need to learn something new and that requires free-will. Free-*willingness*.

On the worst day of your venture where the biggest disappointment and discouragement occurs, fold your cards, close it down and go to sleep. The next morning, wake up with a new approach, new alternatives, a new way to do it. New approaches to your old list.

FREE ENTERPRISE

CORE STRATEGIES AND TACTICS NUMBER NINE
Communicate Effectively to Your Customers
- Think about the needs of the customers you are trying to serve. Who are they, what are their likes and dislikes? If you understand how they think, you will be able to reach them in a language they will
respond to.

HOW TO SUPERCHARGE THIS TACTIC: Observe how your clients are listening to you. Watch how they react. Don't just ramble on without knowing whether or not they are listening. This will help you to refine your communications style to the point of sale.

HOW CAN YOU ENGAGE THIS RIGHT NOW FOR YOUR VENTURE?

_____

_____

_____

_____

CORE STRATEGIES AND TACTICS NUMBER TEN
Create a free sample marketing plan for your Prospects.
In simplest terms, what are you going to do for your prospect and how can you do it better that anyone else? Sometimes, a one-page summary of tactics you would enact for a prospect is more valuable to them than a long drawn-out business plan that they may never read or understand. Your customer's chief concern is that they can rely on you to get the job done and a concise 'how-to' can often be enough to suggest to them: *"Hey, I know how to do this."*

HOW TO SUPERCHARGE THIS TACTIC: Consider either setting up a brief marketing plan within your company calendar. Include general action steps but leave out specific tactical details so they'll respond.

HOW CAN YOU ENGAGE THIS RIGHT NOW FOR YOUR VENTURE?

_____

_____

_____

_____

ADVANCING YOUR CONCEPT

CORE STRATEGIES AND TACTICS NUMBER ELEVEN
Create a One-Page Proposal/Contract To Help Get The Deal In Motion. Also, sometimes referred to as an 'M.O.U. (Memo of Understanding), this can show a prospect how serious and committed you are and can inspire a prospect to get off the fence and do business with you.

HOW TO SUPERCHARGE THIS TACTIC: Call your prospect and let them know you've come up with some ideas that you think would be very useful for them at this present time. Then send your brief summary with a note suggesting that you'd like to start working on these items, followed by your Proposal Summary. Be sure to follow through after a day or two. That shows diligence and a drive to get any job done.

HOW CAN YOU ENGAGE THIS RIGHT NOW FOR YOUR VENTURE?

_____

_____

_____

_____

_____

_____

_____

Too many people lament that there are no business prospects out there when in truth, they are everywhere but no one is communicating to them on their wavelength.

FREE ENTERPRISE

Progress Journal: (please feel free to copy or scan this page only)

_____
_____
_____
_____
_____
_____
_____
_____
_____
_____
_____
_____
_____
_____
_____
_____
_____
_____
_____
_____

Your Signature_____Date_____

Sometimes a good way to make a deal happen is to approach it with the same level of confidence as if you already have the deal done.

ADVANCING YOUR CONCEPT

Just because you're ready to make money doesn't mean your idea is ready.

CHAPTER THREE

ASSESSMENT

How to Test Your Ideas and Business Concepts for Free
"Life is either a daring adventure or it is nothing."
Helen Keller

Overview

It's not enough to have an idea, even a great idea. It's having the persistence and vision to find out how you need to mix with the world in order to turn that concept into something profitable. This chapter will help you to begin those vital evaluations steps.

> **Activator Steps for This Chapter**
> 1) Develop a familiarity and comfort with your idea.
> 2) Systematically seek out a broad range of opinions.
> 3) Analyze initial responses.
>
> *Develop a Familiarity and Comfort with Your Idea*

So here you are. You think you're all ready to forge ahead and see if your idea will hold water. Do you really have a good idea? We're going to be a little harsh on you for a bit to help reduce your chances of expending your energies in the wrong direction and should the idea hold water, help you every way we can to move in the right direction.

If you need to go back to the first chapter, it's only to increase your chances of success. If you don't agree, that's your right. Answer the following questions honestly:

- Is your idea something you just thought of the other day? You may have said to yourself, "Yeah, that's as good an idea as any." Does this describe you at all? That's fine. Go back to CHAPTER 1 and start over.

- Are you ready to risk a chunk of your hard-earned money on your idea? You are? Okay, you're demoted. You may be too anxious to see your idea clearly. Go back and make sure you've thought it through. Take the time to give your inspirations a healthy birth.

-Are you afraid of failure? Are you worried that your idea may not work out and that you'll be wasting your time? We are because we want everything we do to lead to success. Note that we use the word 'lead.'

Failures and stumbles are nothing more than temporary detours on your path to success. They are just one crucial component of the success formula. Wear your faults like a badge. If you understand what went wrong and how to make it right, you'll continually be able to promote your cause.

All businesses are in business to solve a particular problem. They attempt to turn that problem into an opportunity and hence, profit. See how important your failures can be?

So, you're confident enough about your idea to have continued on. What would a major manufacturer, advertising agency, or marketing company do at this point? If they liked the idea, they might spend hundreds of thousands of dollars, at the very least, to test the concept, then design, develop, promote and get it out to market.

Bad planning, bad feedback, and most importantly, bad listening wastes money. Bad listening destroys spaceships and melts nuclear reactors.

We must do our share to avoid that whether developing a product for a company or for ourselves. First of all, aside from yourself, determine who your idea will benefit. If you think it's only the user, think again. What about the distributors, manufacturers, all of the people involved in the production of the item before it reaches its final destination?

HOW TO CREATE BASIC PROTECTION

Before getting into the preliminary testing phase, there are many readers who are afraid that someone out there may just steal their idea. Most of the time, you'll find that people are trustworthy but, to put your mind at ease, you could do the following: Write down a brief description of your concept, including any supporting documentation. Make two copies and mail one to your lawyer and one to yourself. They are to be kept sealed until needed. Be advised, this mailing does not ensure that your idea will be protected, but it can serve as a small part of a general claim of origination.

If your idea is sufficiently unique, apply on line for a provisional patent. They are cheap and, will establish under the law that you were first with your idea. Additionally, if you are exploring your idea with a potential partner, or manufacturer, or anyone else involved in any capacity, you can ask your counsel to sign a statement that he or she will not replicate the idea you are about to discuss. This is generally known as an NDA (non-disclosure agreement). It's also prudent to maintain a log, dating and documenting your progress. What follows is a sample NDA, but remember that it's always best to have the advice of legal counsel in the execution of these documents:

A paranoid partnership is a paira non- achievers.

FREE ENTERPRISE

SAMPLE NON-DISCLOSURE AGREEMENT

Please check with your lawyer before enacting any legal document

     This agreement is entered into as of the ___ day of ___, 20___, by and between (your name goes here) (hereinafter "Y") and the (name of the other party goes here) (hereinafter "Recipient"). This Agreement shall govern the disclosure and furnishing by Y to Recipient of certain written confidential and proprietary information of Y which is marked as proprietary or confidential (hereinafter "Proprietary Information") and the use and return of such information by Recipient. Proprietary Information is either owned by Y, or is owned by a third party and is in Y's possession pursuant to an agreement of confidentiality.

     The Proprietary Information will be used by the Recipient only for the purpose agreed upon by the Recipient. Recipient agrees that Recipient shall receive the Proprietary Information subject to the following conditions:

1. Recipient shall not disclose the Proprietary Information to anyone except persons who have signed a non-disclosure agreement incorporating these terms.
2. Recipient shall not copy the Proprietary Information without permission and shall return to Y any portion of the Proprietary Information at any time upon request by Y.
3. The obligations stated herein shall be binding upon Recipient until the second anniversary date of this Agreement, or until:
    (a) The Proprietary Information appears in a printed publication; or
    (b) The Proprietary Information ceases to be confidential other than as a breach of this Agreement by Recipient.
4. Recipient shall have no obligations hereunder for Proprietary Information which:
    (a) at the time of disclosure is in the public domain; (b) at the time of disclosure is known to Recipient without an agreement to treat confidential; (c) is independently developed by Recipient without reference to the Proprietary Information received from Y; or
    (d) is required to be released by Recipient as a result of subpoena or order of a judicial body.
5. Recipient shall not export or re-export Proprietary Information.
6. Recipient acquires no intellectual property rights under this Agreement, except the limited right to use set out explicitly above.

Pick brains FIRST. Talk to authorities. Don't assume you know it all just because you were successful in another career.

ASSESSMENT

This Agreement shall be governed by and construed in accordance with laws of the State of (common venue).

ACCEPTED:

By:

Title: Date:

Company name:

By:

Title: Date:

Your name:

Whatever you do, if you insist on being paranoid, don't use it as an excuse to interfere with your progress. After all, you're going to become so knowledgeable about your concept, you'll be the authority.

When I come up with a new marketing system or product, I'm generally flattered and amused by our imitators; flattered because they copied my idea, and amused because they can rarely do it as well or as cost-effectively as you are I can.

In short, people are desperate for good ideas because they haven't learned to develop their own creative process by following our guidelines. They are afraid of the idea of the creative process. These types of people don't generally have what it takes to make an idea happen because they are not really a part of its birth. Thieves always get caught, either by others or by themselves.

But all philosophy aside, remember in business ventures, there is only one definition of a gift. A gift is any work, money, anything you contribute without a written agreement in advance. Always find a way to move ahead, but don't ever downplay the need to protect yourself.

So, if you're putting together a product, make sure that exact product is not already on the market. As long as you make an improvement or some significant modification, then you should be able to get your patent, if necessary, and move forward.

Millions of you have service or product ideas that may not require a patent. For the particular state you're living in, an attorney would best advise you in all areas of product protection.

It will take a lot more homework before your idea is actually ready for the development stages. You don't know exactly what you've got yet. Over and over again, keep thinking results, don't get stuck.

Listen effectively so you can learn more about your idea.

FREE ENTERPRISE

Systematically Seek Out Broad Range of Opinions

Time to pick some brains. There are scores of people out there who will be only too glad to give you free time and advice - FREE ADVICE. Some of it will be questionable but some of it will prove highly valuable. As you become more intimate with your product, and if you use this book as a guide, you'll soon learn to decipher the usable from the stuff you throw away.

We said free advice. Why will so many experts generally be glad to give you some free time? If your product takes off, some of these people know they may become involved in the production process. A little investment of their time could really pay off.

Tell these valued advisors what you are thinking of and make notes. You're not always going to like what you hear but a little criticism can save you a fortune. Remember that underwater safety switch described in the last chapter? Here's a good lesson: AFTER we gave the distributors thousands of these single switches, we met with them to find out how it was doing.

Unanimously, they told us there was no market for a single switch, only a DOUBLE switch. Had we picked their brains before we hit the drawing board, the client would have saved a lot of time and money.

Senior Helpers

A number of our clients are in their sixties and seventies and are a wealth of knowledge and success in one area. Invariably, the first thing we work to convey to them is, just because they turned sixty and were successful at one thing, doesn't automatically make them an authority on everything.

However, in no way will we ever deny that one of your greatest potential assets for procedural guidance could be the great and untapped wealth of retired persons and senior citizens. Seek them out via your local senior citizens organizations. Generally, you'll make some great friends and your product will enjoy a much better end result to success. Seek out the:

Service Core of Retired Executives (SCORE)

Keep the following in mind: As long as your idea has some merit to someone, there's always a way to put it together. Listen, think and accept no one as final authority except yourself.

You can spend $150,000 to make a mold for an injection-molded plastic product. But if you could source out the same high quality task for a fraction of that cost, which would you choose?

In general, the only theft that kills most ideas is when we choose to rob ourselves of our own confidence.

ASSESSMENT

We've discussed basic products so the points would be clearly understood, but many readers have very complex ideas or services. Essentially, the same query-approaches apply. In fact, if your idea is service-oriented, you can often see the possibilities blossoming at a very rapid rate.

Let's suppose you want to create an information source for a senior citizens organization. You might begin by discussing it with a local senior center, or even city hall. Such was the case in New Bedford, Massachusetts. After a homemaker's children had grown and left the nest, she sought out a means to best utilize her existing skills. She successfully obtained start-up funds and now runs a newspaper exclusively for seniors. She had done some writing in the past and she wanted to make a useful contribution to her community.

Her paper is now a model for similar efforts around the country. All she began with was an intelligent idea that complimented her potential, and a little homework. What a perfect inspiration and example of finding one's star.

Keep your eyes open and allow your mind to wander a bit here and there. You never know who you're going to meet today that could help to change your life for the better.

Talk to potential customers. What do they want from a better widget? And what about the existing product that may be similar to yours? What's wrong with it and why is yours an improvement over it? What are the problems that you can eliminate? Ask, Explore, LISTEN and Digest. Keep thinking Concept, Research, Refine the Concept. Focus the Research.

Keep asking yourself "Who can bring my idea to life and, to its intended market?

As you progress in this area, something exciting begins to happen. Your ideas begin to come into focus. As the dust settles you have begun to get a much better idea of where you're going and how to get there. Best of all, you haven't spent thousands of dollars to test your market or shape your gem. For this chapter, you have spent some money on gas, phone calls, emails, Internet surfing, and some more pads and pencils. That's a reasonable investment to explore your dream.

How's your concept building? Are you ready to make it come to life? Let's find out.

How To Build Free Focus Groups

Qualified field experts and/or most companies with start-up products very often spend more on evaluating the feasibility of a product/service than most of us might see in our lifetime. But then why are so many millions of everyday people like you successfully

What others think can help you sharpen what you think.

FREE ENTERPRISE

launching concepts with hardly any resources? The reason is simple; because you can get vital and often valuable feedback on your prototypes or plans, etc. without all the expense and often with hardly any of the expense.

The people you will seek feedback from are broken down into three categories: personal friends, professional people that you know, and finally, relevant people whom you don't know who have some relevance to your venture with respect to production, prototype planning and overall marketing. Be sure to seek out those who may already understand your market. Remember you are not to hire anyone at this point. If you do, you might financially discourage yourself in a hurry. What we're really doing is making sure that your next step will be your most sensible one.

Here Comes That Old Paranoia

You're still concerned about the protection of your idea and we will delve into most of the protection issues far more aggressively. You may want to go through Chapter 4 right now and then come back and finish the rest of this chapter. As we've suggested earlier, our own view is that while theft can occur, and while some ventures require patents; for the most part in today's marketplace, your best protection is your personal commitment to aggressively marketing your concept. Don't be afraid to learn and then to energetically apply what you have learned to your sales efforts.

As we write and research, we have gone back to several patent attorneys and scores of associates and the stories are all the same: Most people you deal with who are in the various facets of legitimate business are trustworthy. They would have to be or nobody would deal with them.

While always respecting the privacy of our clientele, we have (with permission) talked about or pitched countless ideas with potential contacts and no one has ever stolen an idea from us. Most of our associates share this feeling.

Then one of us will be giving an interview or seminar and someone will tell us that they had an idea for a better rake or book or you-name-it. "Next thing I know," they'd tell us, "someone else is coming out with my idea." In almost all cases, this happens because someone did indeed come up with a similar idea all on their own, and this happens.

Sometimes people observe similar trends and resultant needs based upon those trends and hence come up with similar ideas, like the computer, the cell phone, plasma TV, or the chocolate-chip cookie, again, you name it! Well, that's just free enterprise.

Don't ever aim for nor expect 100 percent of any market. That's unrealistic. What is realistic is that you create, listen, learn, bend, adjust, thrive and survive by earning your market share; your piece of the pie.

Going back to the patent attorneys we've interviewed, most expressed concern that so many clients would spend so much money on protection and then fail because they spent no energy on marketing. When my book, *Good Idea! Now What?* was first written,

This is a time when friends and colleagues can prove their true worth.

one attorney jokingly suggested it be called, "Good Idea! So What?" But looking back, his idea wasn't all that unrealistic because that book made it clear; anyone can have a good idea. It's the ability to act upon that idea and respond effectively to the needs of the correct market that will make it successful.

If you still have concerns when speaking to certain parties, describe your idea in general terms. Often an idea can be conveyed without giving away details, allowing the potential consultant to understand the prospective market, and to give opinions.

Ultimately, whatever protection you may or may not have, in order to connect and move ahead you have to trust some people. So yes, be careful; don't give away the farm, don't spend a lot of money to start the idea, but on the other side, don't allow paranoia to become an excuse for not progressing.

To a great extent, your commitment to finding the right marketplace is your best protection and your best chance at success.

So assuming now that you may have already read Chapter 4 if you are so inclined, let's now proceed with this vital evaluation phase.

POWERPOINTER FOUR
How to Keep Adding Value to Your Idea

As you develop your idea, your first step is to visualize the service or function you are striving for. How will your concept or service function; what do you see yourself achieving? These are healthy business fantasies and should become a habit. The reality is that when you finally bring your idea to life, you'll want it to be an improvement on what already exists.

Here are three steps to help achieve that:

1)Picture Your Basic Concept. Can you describe it in a simple paragraph, do you have a clear understanding of what your concept is. This is known as the foundation of your concept and from this, you'll build up or out in all directions.

2) Learn From Others in the Field. Who is successfully doing what you want to do or if your concept is completely original, who has a business model that you can learn from?

I've sold books mostly successfully all of my life but when I started watching how Kevin Trudeau sell his Natural Cures and Weight Loss books by a no-nonsense infomercial, I sensed that would be an ideal format for me as well. When I later learned that his efforts had generated a mega bestseller, I knew that this was a format that would allow me to reach and be of service to the maximum number of people.

I learned everything I could about what he did and how he did it. I watched his infomercials over and over again. I read all three of his books. Next, I studied how

There's something interesting, relevant and insightful in each of us.

successful books are being written today. I've written many books but it is especially vital today to keep up with how the most well-received books are structured. Since books are just the foundation of a delivery system, promoting that system is a critical element of the process. In addition, people are ever more jealous of their time. They want information fast and now so a book has to work somewhat like a website or a laptop computer sans the electronics.

I realized that some of the most successfully structured books were written in the Dummies series and good old Dr. Phil McGraw. Every page has something you can use and benefit from.

Finally, I watched the presidential debates which were happening at the time of this writing. Presidential candidates spend millions just on their personal image so I carefully observed the results of those millions. What was believable and what seemed contrived? I determined that there of course was no substitute for truth but that truth had to be presented with appealing energy.

While my book is in a vastly different field, I believed these elements would work in concert for me and hence, my prospects who could benefit from this information. And I was right.

It's important to identify relevant mentors and examples for as many aspects of your project as you are able for your venture and then, learn all you can from them. But the next step is the most important.

3) ***How Can You Improve on What's Already Out There?*** There is always a way to do something better. That's how society and technology evolve. Once you've envisioned your concept, step back and just imagine how you can do it a little better. If your concept involves direct retail storefront sales, what little things can you do to make your customer feel just a bit more cared for, why would you buy your product or service instead of the competition, what are the several ways that your value is better?

ACTIVATOR ELEVEN
The Reaction Formulation

"Measure Twice, Cut Once", the old adage goes but you can see that we measure far more than that for some very important reasons. Far too many people are guided by anxiousness and figure they'll just change course along the way. But there is a critical point where an entrepreneur can just run out of steam if they've traveled too far in the wrong direction. The purpose of this connection exercise is to determine what kind of long-term relationship possibilities you might have with your idea because the long-term is what truly matters. We are not simply talking about need or marketability; we are talking about something you will want to grow with until it takes you to a better place in your life.

There are two kinds of sales personalities: Those that wait for customers to come to them and those who go out and find those customers before they walk into a competitor's door.

ASSESSMENT

What we are most interested in here is finding out how well your idea will fit you. Assuming your concept has survived our previous interrogatories, let us now try to get an indication of what the rest of the world thinks. Now, of course, the ultimate test is whether the end user (customer) buys (accepts) it but this next evaluation is a strong one.

Following is the initial primary reaction category. Under each heading, get opinions from that group and evaluate and summarize and evaluate their reactions as briefly as possible.
- Do they like it? Why or why not?
- What changes would they make?
- What retail price would they pay for it?
- What manufacturing procedure might they follow?
- Where do they think the customers are?
- How would they propose reaching those customers?
- Why do you think they reacted the way they did?
- Who do they know who might be able to assist you?

Category 1 - Personal (friends, relatives, co-workers)
Name, Opinion

_____

_____

Your Reaction

_____

_____

_____

Name, Opinion

_____

_____

_____

Some people don't make money from their idea simply because they think they don't deserve to.

FREE ENTERPRISE

Your Reaction

Name, Opinion

Your Reaction

Category 2 - Professional Acquaintances

Name, Opinion

You and you alone must be the primary catalyst for bringing your idea into reality and viability.

ASSESSMENT

Your Reaction

Name, Opinion

Your Reaction

Name, Opinion

Think of the easiest and least costly ways to test your concept.

FREE ENTERPRISE

Your Reaction

Category 3 - Other Relevant People

Name, Opinion

Your Reaction

Name, Opinion

Implement Free or Low-Cost Ways to Utilize Effective Resources.

ASSESSMENT

Your Reaction

Name, Opinion

Your Reaction

If you're willing to promise yourself to do the work to make your idea work, promotion becomes far simpler because it's sincere.

FREE ENTERPRISE

Note: In filling out these forms, be sure to list subject's possible relevancy to your concept! You may make additional copies of any of the forms in this book for your own personal use. It 's also helpful to collect a business card, email address, website URL, and make notes about each individual on the back of each card.

Briefly summarize all of the opinions:

_____

_____

_____

_____

_____

_____

_____

_____

_____

_____

_____

_____

_____

_____

_____

_____

_____

_____

_____

ASSESSMENT

Use These Opinions To Improve Your Idea

You've spent a long time getting to this point and you've sought out many preliminary evaluations. Hopefully, you've done a $100,000 job for either very little or no money at all.

Before completing this page, study your progress. How has your idea evolved? How much money and time have you saved by utilizing this chapter? How good of a listener have you been? Do you now have a better focus on your market (who will really buy what you're selling, who won't?)

Having studied the new puzzle pieces in this chapter, now describe your concept and the changes:

My New and Better Idea Is:

_____

_____

_____

_____

_____

_____

_____

_____

Parties and Barflies

Earlier on we admonished you not to bore people at parties. Well now you have something more interesting. If you feel sufficiently comfortable about your concept, test it, at least verbally and maybe just in general terms, at parties or see how it flies at the local bar, etc. - any gathering where people feel relaxed and where you'll hear what you need to hear instead of what you want to hear.

If you're not constantly thinking about alternatives to all the roadblocks you encounter, you're not giving your business survival a legitimate chance.

FREE ENTERPRISE

Summary

This is the point where the dream assumes sufficient shape to relate it to other people. A dreamer, who really wants dreams to happen, will listen carefully and patiently. Don't fight with your critics; seek them out and draw them out. The better you've done with these three previous chapters, the fewer regrets you'll encounter in the future. Your idea should be much improved but still it is only as good as your ability to earn your market share.

Make sure that you:

Develop a familiarity and comfort with your idea.
- Secure appropriate protection for your idea. Protect but don't let fear of theft impede your progress. For additional information on protection issues, see Chapter 4.

Systematically seek out a broad range of opinions.
- Seek out consultations from authorities at every level
- Personal - friends, relatives, and co-workers
- Professional acquaintances
- Other Relevant People
- Listen carefully, without ego
- **Ask the valuable authorities every question you can think up concerning your project**
Analyze initial responses.
- Complete Connection #4
- Incorporate the feedback to make a better product.

Potential Challenges and Solutions
Challenge: Insecure about releasing the idea without sufficient patent protection.

Solution: People generally have the following choices once they have received their patents: They can sell the idea, lease it, they can put the patent certificate on a shelf to show their grandchildren, or they can make the venture happen themselves.

Though many of you do require exacting protection, review all the alternatives with your attorney. Get your protection and then move ahead. Generally, an inexpensive Provisional Patent is all you'll need. In our experience, we have seen paranoia kill more ideas than even greed kills. Don't use fear as an excuse not to proceed.

Your other innate protection is that, for most cases, no one has your specific technical skills, motivation or tenacity to make your venture successful. This book has shown

'Patent Pending' does not mean 'Hard Work Ending'

ASSESSMENT

you that you have things of far greater value to offer your prospects i.e. your know-how from concept all the way to customer.

Challenge: Can't find authorities to talk to

Solution: For simple products or ideas, it's just a matter of time before you track down the right people. The only problem may be distance.

If you live too far away from the right people, don't just send your product with a letter. Before you run up huge phone bills, see if your target company has a toll-free phone number. Or, consider one of the outstanding computer-fed phone services like Scype, Vonage , Magic Jack or Oovoo. The Internet has every form of phone directory you can imagine. And in this day and age, most every venture requires a website (which you

can also create for free). This, of course, accelerates the prospect's education and response-time. It is not uncommon to transmit photos and actual (streaming) video.

If your venture is fairly sophisticated, break it down into components and seek out the makers of those individual components. You can also locate products with some similarities to yours which might be marketed in a fashion similar to yours. Those experts could also benefit from your marketing prowess.

Challenge: Afraid or unable to approach these experts

Solution: People are people first, just like you. Many of this country's biggest success stories were once nothing but an idea, perhaps like yours, with the same doubts you may now be experiencing. Those types often welcome someone with a similar ambition.

If someone refuses to meet with you, after much effort on your part, move on. After you've succeeded, let them come crawling to you. For the most part, we find that most people are more than happy to teach you what you need to know. Just ask. If someone acts in a very intimidating manner towards you, don't be affected by it. You are there for knowledge. If you have to cut the meeting short, leave politely and seek your information elsewhere. There are plenty of successful human beings out there who can help you and who will treat you with respect.

Before You Continue . . .

- Have you not found an adequate means to relate, test, or demonstrate your idea? There's always some way to relate it, even in the most general terms.

- Remember that enterprises are all ultimately dependent upon the support of the appropriate people. Are you seeking them out? Focus your search, and continually refine both your presentation as well as your people-skills.

Marketing is a two-way path: You need to find both a pathway to them, and you need to inspire them to find a pathway to you.

FREE ENTERPRISE

POWERPOINTER FIVE
Insights

How to Familiarize Yourself With Your Inner 'Inventor'

Insights are thoughts that appear from an intelligence within that we do not understand fully yet. They are flashes of knowledge that speak to us when our busy mind has taken a break from the mundane conditioned thinking of our past. True genius is born each moment from this place because it is fresh thought that has yet to be contaminated by the destructive effects of the ego. We all have insights, but most of us are unaware that they exist and that they are trying to communicate to us all the time.

Allow your mind to be free of distractive thought.
- Ask yourself a question which needs an answer you may not yet have.
- Stay very quiet. You will see that the answer may already be within you.
- Don't allow your thinking to take over or the insight won't reveal itself.
- Make a note each time this flash of intelligence comes to you.
- Notice where you are and what you are doing at the time.
- Don't act upon each insight, just watch and listen.
- Keep a journal of insights. You will need them at a later time.

ACTIVATOR TWELVE
Are You Now Ready To Commit To Your Idea?

It is well worth the time to examine whether the idea you have settled on is not simply a concept you have settled for. We have to make sure that you have infused a fair measure of creativity. You cannot claim that you are not creative or enterprising in some way.

Creativity and inventiveness are natural gifts that everyone has in one way or another. What you can claim is that you haven't found your best idea yet. If that is the case, now is the time to engage that process because it is only by process that we discover our truest and best capabilities.

Everyday that I am writing, teaching, or speaking, I am happy. For everyone, there are certainly daily work activities that both challenge them and afford them a sense of fulfillment. It is human nature to not just work on something that's going to make a lot of money, but to work on those meaningful things that you enjoy, and then strive to evolve that into your eventual primary income source. So, if you find yourself saying that enterprise is for the other person, then you are denying your birthright. So no excuses; everyone something to share or sell. Let's find out what you have:

If everyone worried about theft of their concept more than production of their concept, we'd all be walking in the dark.

ASSESSMENT

The Commitment Evaluator

Please reply to these questions with the first positive notion that pops into your head:

List Your Highest Educational Level:_____

What Specific Skills Do You Know, have simply figured out and/or have been trained for?_____

_____

_____

_____

_____

_____

_____

_____

If currently employed, what is your current occupation?_____

_____

_____

_____

_____

_____

_____

_____

The right people will always tell you the right thing about your venture. But you only know if they're the right people after you hear their opinions.

FREE ENTERPRISE

How happy are you with your current avocation? 1 2 3 4 (very content)

What do you wish you could be doing specifically (do not answer with "winning the lottery", etc)?

___

What were you born to do? Even if you've never done it before, what have your often noticed is in your nature that you've just never been able to do? What daily work activity makes you happiest and how can you incorporate that into your project?

___

Test, observe, evaluate, adjust.

ASSESSMENT

What are some of the most helpful things you do for others?

What kind of work or hobbies do you think would most motivate you to get up in the morning?

FREE ENTERPRISE

What do you observe that is preventing you from realizing that dream in some fashion, besides money? What excuses have you invented to prevent your invention from happening?

___

Assuming for a moment that there are no restraints for reaching your goals, what do you really want to be doing? How do you picture yourself as more content in your work or general occupation? "I don't know" is not an acceptable answer. Hope is always an element of human nature. So, allowing for that, what is it that you most hope for? What do you love to do? (Lying on the couch is not an answer) Don't fret about the details for getting there. We'll take care of those in all the upcoming steps.

Please describe how you see your venture changing your life:

___

Rejection is really just an invitation to try it another way.

ASSESSMENT

How are these questions affecting your innovative thinking so far?

Believe the result, not the promise.

FREE ENTERPRISE

CORE STRATEGIES AND TACTICS NUMBER TWELVE
Offer a Free Mini-Consultation. If you have the time to show what you know, this can be a highly effective tactic for earning a new prospect. This is another form of a bit-sized sample that can show prospects that you have a specialized product, knowledge or capability that is of real value to them.

If you prove it, they will buy.

HOW TO SUPERCHARGE THIS TACTIC: Emphasize strategies but go light on tactics. Inform prospects that you have a whole lot more for them if they are willing to give your product or service a try. Create a response deadline to help motivate them.

HOW CAN YOU ENGAGE THIS RIGHT NOW FOR YOUR VENTURE?

_____

_____

_____

_____

CORE STRATEGIES AND TACTICS NUMBER THIRTEEN
Host a Free seminar at Whatever Level you can afford.
Often, you can find available free space at your local library, or you could host a breakfast. But if you have something exciting and interesting to talk about, this can be a highly effective and free or nearly free way of gaining valuable prospects.

HOW TO SUPERCHARGE THIS TACTIC: Is here an existing gathering or club you already belong to? This can be an ideal place to begin trying out your presentation skills; even if you simply ask them for any clubs or organizations who you could talk to.

HOW CAN YOU ENGAGE THIS RIGHT NOW FOR YOUR VENTURE?

_____

_____

_____

_____

There is always a way through if you're willing.

ASSESSMENT

CORE STRATEGIES AND TACTICS NUMBER FOURTEEN
Be in the Right Place. Don't just rent a store because it seems like a good bargain. Make sure you are locating yourself and your service or product in a place where customers are. You've heard the old cliché, "Location, location, location." Also, make sure you employ all the tactics that will let prospects know exactly where you are.

HOW TO SUPERCHARGE THIS TACTIC: Look beneath the surface. Don't simply accept that this may be a good location. Take the time to physically observe rates of traffic, ease of entry and egress for customers, image of general area. What are the real reasons that this place is vacant? And always, if you can start off by simply paying a percentage of sales instead of rent, which could reduce your start-up risks.

HOW CAN YOU ENGAGE THIS RIGHT NOW FOR YOUR VENTURE?

_____

_____

_____

_____

_____

_____

CORE STRATEGIES AND TACTICS NUMBER FIFTEEN
Go for the Show. Are there seminars, tradeshows, associations or meetings that you should be attending or displaying at? Often, these meetings, relevant to your area of expertise, can help to establish you as an authority in your field. If you can't afford to have a display, just being in the audience and asking compelling questions can make a big difference. Also, offer to give a speech or presentation at the gathering and promote your appearance with brochures, a free announcement in the show directory and maybe a couple of free radio interviews.

HOW TO SUPERCHARGE THIS TACTIC:
Be Unconventional at Conventions. Can't afford both space at a convention, seminar and show where customer and colleagues may be lurking? Go anyway and just be a browser/schmoozer. Shake hands with as many people as you can,

Even if you find yourself stumbling forward, it's still forward.

FREE ENTERPRISE

hand out a business card, brochure and your website URL to everyone you might be able to work with or sell to.

Event Marketing: Conventions & Shows. Event marketing is effective if it addresses your target audience's needs and/or wants. Seek out those happenings where your product is relevant and make your presence known.

HOW CAN YOU ENGAGE THIS RIGHT NOW FOR YOUR VENTURE?

_____

_____

_____

_____

CORE STRATEGIES AND TACTICS NUMBER SIXTEEN

Cash- Flow. Be careful with every penny you commit to. Don't start signing all kinds of distribution or advertising contracts that will require small payments. It all adds up. Don't rent or commit to shows, conventions or space unless you absolutely need them. Store your product in your house and work from your home if possible. When it's time to negotiate for leases, rental space, etc, be sure you shop around for the very best deal and location. For collections, be sure you set up clear payment terms. Can you create automatic billing?

How to supercharge this tactic: Often people carry their impulsive shopping habits into their business buying and commitments. Evaluate every prospect carefully. Ask *them* for a free sample to prove their worth.

How can you engage this right now for your venture?

_____

_____

_____

_____

ASSESSMENT

Progress Journal: (please feel free to copy or scan this page only)

_____

_____

_____

_____

_____

_____

_____

_____

_____

_____

_____

_____

_____

_____

_____

_____

_____

Your Signature_____Date_____

A little time with hunches can improve your prospect bunches.

FREE ENTERPRISE

POWERPOINTER SIX
How to Step Over That Critical Boundary between Dreaming and Doing

There is a place we all get to or, don't get to where the spark of our dream seems to fizzle out. For most people, that point of paralysis arrives far too early in fact, often right after the inception of a really good idea.

The problem is we too often feel that we are not equal to the great promise of our idea and there are in fact, many ideas that are way out of our realm of capability. But for most of us, coming up with an idea is often an evolved and unconscious mesh of a dream that's somehow relevant to our lives and we are often more capable of attaining that dream than we think. So it's not patent fears or money that kills our best ideas, it is something within ourselves, that same mechanism that our mothers instilled in us when we were little to keep us safe, keeps us from taking some very simple steps to try a dream.

A year ago, one of my top twenty dreams was to write, produce, sing and successfully distribute a CD of my very eclectic music. All my friends told me I was crazy and those who felt I wasn't crazy, felt I was incapable in every regard. But I wanted to make this work. I have been a writer all of my adult life and music was one form of writing where I felt I had ultimate freedom of expression.

With no formal musical background, I kept writing songs and then, with great embarrassment, finally got up the nerve to sing some of them to my some of my musician friends and to my shock, they actually liked some of the songs (I did not say 'love'). Since that time, my CD is well into production and will be released shortly. The point of this story is that every time was willing to take a leap in the unknown, I discovered new capabilities within myself.

There is a scene in the second Indiana Jones movie where he steps onto what appears to be a deep chasm that actually turns out to be a camouflaged bridge. It is that small leap of faith that can open up our worlds and motivate us to drive our ideas forward.

You bought this book as a promise to yourself to take the leap and give your idea a chance to really grown into something. Take that leap now.

How to Steer that Hobby-Horse into Business

I have a hobby that I really love to do. When engaged in this hobby, time stops, I feel relaxed, fulfilled and uplifted all at the same time. That hobby is writing. Writing is also my avocation so it's fair to say that even when I'm working, as long as I'm writing, I'm reasonably content; perhaps more content than most people at work. Even when I want to relax and escape, I play online Scrabble so I'm always surrounded by new words. Words are the architecture for my dreams so essentially, I am paid to enjoy myself.

There is always a way to find the time, resources and money, if we simply use a little imagination and flexibility.

ASSESSMENT

You too can certainly consider transforming a hobby into a business but it depends upon what that hobby is and if you really want to make it into something more than a hobby. For some people, if a hobby like repairing lawnmowers or milking rattlesnakes became a full-time job, it may no longer prove interesting or fulfilling. For most who turn a hobby into a living, they also lose that part of their life as a hobby. All that said, there are most likely elements in your hobby that you want to experience in your work. Ask yourself:

1) Do you really like doing this or is it just a way you think you can make some quick money?
2) When working on your new business, do you ever feel tired or fatigued?
3) Does your business make you happy or give you hopeful thoughts?
4) Does your business concept encourage you to imagine even bolder ideas?
5) Do you like to talk about your work?
6) Are you so wrapped up in your work that you don't want to be anywhere else?

If you answered at least five of these questions in the affirmative, you're on the right track. In terms of replacing your hobby, it may be best to seek alternative means of relaxation, especially if a hobby takes up too much time. More promising things seem to happen around your idea when a hobby can be intermixed with a vocation.

Ideas and services evolve as if a living breathing entity.

CHAPTER FOUR

DO-IT-YOURSELF R&D

Creating a Model

"A great substitution for cash is the burning desire to succeed."

Howard Bronson

Overview

It doesn't necessarily take money to make money. What it does require are the right resources, the right team, keeping the right attitude, and perhaps a corner of the living room, kitchen, garage or basement.

> **Activator Steps for this Chapter**
> **1) Bring the idea into a tangible form.**
> **2) Implement low-cost ways to utilize effective resources.**
> **3) Pursue protection if necessary.**
> **Bring the Idea or Business into a Tangible Form**

Science fiction films have become so creative and convincing, we essentially accept their portrayals of the future as gospel. Deep space adventures are presented with a clever intermesh of intelligence, compassion and photon torpedoes. We often find ourselves focusing on the melodrama, accepting all the glitzy special effects as standard background.

No space vehicle or home will be complete without a transporter which will demolecularize any human or object and make it come to life at any other given point in the universe.

If you think transporters are either totally fictitious or light years away with no bearing on today's world, think again. Star Trek has landed at places like the GE Plastics Technology Division in Pittsfield, Massachusetts.

Things of all types, born of ideas are transformed from the center of the mind onto a computer screen, where it may be plainly seen from all perspectives. It does not stop there.

Right there, within the heart of the computer, the image can be engineered, even to the point of stress analysis and performance testing. Turn on the transporter. Here comes the real magic. Before thousands of dollars have been spent drafting, testing, etc., the

We only run out of time when we run away from what we were meant to do.

FREE ENTERPRISE

computer actually transforms the design into a physical product mold, from which the product can be made.

Computer aided design and engineering is carried out at many levels in many companies throughout the world. These are the ultimate dream into- reality machines riding on the leading edge of the future. Virtually concept to customer at the push of a button, but they cannot tell us if the people will actually accept a product no matter how perfect it may be.

We operate from the standpoint that most readers do not yet have access to such million-dollar technology, but we shall still achieve viable test results well within or below your budget. You're about to discover the vast difference between image and substance. The development process is also the second phase of the evaluation process. Here is where we beam our ideas into something real. You've kicked your idea around with everyone.

Some of your friends will think you're really into something interesting. Some think you're all talk. Attitudes will really change as your image transforms into substance; as your dedication gives steam and energy to what began simply in your head and heart. How do you build a model if you've never built one before? Do you begin at the beginning? Not necessarily. But you must begin.

Creating Your Initial Business, Virtual or Physical Model

Don't get so confused or rigid that you're afraid to begin. Now that your ideas are starting to come into focus, throw it on the canvas or paper or whatever. You probably won't love what you see at first. Doing is more important than asking why at this stage. Even if the physical birth of your idea is a little ugly, don't worry about it. At least it's a birth. The first three chapters have already helped you build a wealth of knowledge. Don't be too disappointed at this stage.

This is a time to be flexible. Too many times in our careers, we have seen great ideas get trashed just as soon as its creator decides an obstacle is too great to overcome. This sense of being overwhelmed is common.

The advantage you have now with this book is that you can press on, bit by bit at times, if necessary, without draining your bank account.

If you don't try to make your idea happen, it will most likely never become real. Your aim here is to create something that will help start the wheels of production turning. Don't cut corners. You could imagine that you could go to a particular manufacturer and tell him about and maybe sell him your concept. Most major manufacturers get these kinds of proposals every day from starry-eyed conceptualists.

Our experience has taught us that this is not the best way to make your product come to life. As mentioned earlier, consult with the heavies but assemble the overall technology yourself. The working or nearly working model is of much greater financial benefit to you than just an idea.

You worked hard to get that idea! Are you just going to give it away for a few dollars, when you can make it yourself? But what if you could turn many of these sizable corporate heavies into valuable consultants for your enterprise and still own your project? Read on.

There is a barrier here, and it's generally you. If asked to come-up with the key point that separates the successes from the failures at this stage, we arrive at one simple stumbling point: Shyness. Too many people are afraid of looking foolish and will therefore not take the appropriate chances of making low-level presentations which in turn, can lead to greater-level presentations. It's important to bear in mind that this is the time to make mistakes. This is the time to learn, and you are making these initial presentations to learn.

We get emails daily almost always containing these phrases; "I'm no mechanic. I'm no artist, I'm no sculptor. I'm afraid to approach person 'X'. I'm no writer." In order to save you some anxiety-time, allow us to respond collectively. We're not interested in what you can't do. We're only interested in working with what you've got. Just talk to these people as people and discover what you have in common and learn, learn, learn!

If your idea is a physical product, make it out of clay, Popsicle sticks, wires, or whatever. Have fun. Relive your childhood. Creativity is fun because you're giving birth to something new that has never been done quite like you're doing it.

Once you feel you have a rough idea of what you wish your blob of clay would have looked like, take your blob to your local starving artist or sculptor or drafting student. Tell them what you were trying to do, get a solid price (anywhere from free to $100, or find someone else) and a firm deadline (one-to-four weeks depending on the sophistication of your blob).

Warn your model-refiner that you may call once or twice with a few slight modifications. It's important to be clear about your thoughts, and it's equally important for the artist to be sufficiently flexible in order to make your idea happen. Establish a clear understanding from the beginning. If your project requires drawings, diagrams, or a proposal, do what you can first, and then follow the above procedures. Written descriptions can be a bit more traumatic for many, but they shouldn't be.

As you write, pretend you're writing a letter to your best friend or anyone else who you feel can understand what your thoughts mean. If you still have a problem, get a little digital recorder (most cell-hones have one built-in) and talk away, or work it out on your personal computer, if you have one.

If your written proposal doesn't convey what it should to your particular target, bring it to your local high school English teacher who may be willing to refine your draft for free or for a modest fee (same formula as with models described earlier). Just re-

If you take a little time to get just a little more organized, you will end up giving yourself a lot more time to become successful.

member there's always a way to do it and do it well. Don't look for excuses for yourself. That's the easy way to quit.

A few weeks later, you'll see the first signs of genuine encouragement for your project. That spark we've been looking for and struggling with from page one suddenly is showing some promise of life - from brain and heart to something real and potentially commercially viable.

When you get the preliminary phase product in your hands, hold it, stare at it, sleep with it, make notes about it. Get it into your psychological bloodstream. You can see for yourself how you're increasing your idea's value. Aren't you glad you didn't run to the first major manufacturer you could find?

The Promise vs. the Overpromise

From the time when the first jar of snake oil was sold as a promise to cure all ills, to the present when more sophisticated deceptions confront us almost every few minutes, advertising and honesty have always have not always gotten along all that well.

The basic premise with any ad is that it wants you to buy something, so it promises you something but since it knows you won't believe that promise, it adds more finesse until studies show you will believe it. Testimonials, scientific backing, iron-clad guarantees; whatever it takes to motivate you to spend your money, you will see.

The media world is your great research Mecca; every ad you see, every promise that serves to awe you, even slightly, and makes you wonder "Can I really get 200 shaves with one blade, can I grow hair, will this book heal my broken heart." The list is as endless as the promises each ad makes and of course, as you'd expect, the biggest culprits are found in *electronic integration media*. The internet and all of the specific technologies borne from it now lead the way in the 'world of endless and amazing promises.'

When you poll the top ad execs about the promise, the answers are as many and varied as the ads but there seem to be two distinct camps: One asserts that advertising simply should be a process of communicating the truth so effectively, that people are motivated to buy. The other argues that simply to gain attention and compete, you must make the same level of overpromise that everyone else makes.

In my view, camp One wins the debate handily. The use of media and events to promote a cause, brand or any concept is known as a *campaign*. A campaign is generally known as a *process*. If you aim to tell the truth about your concept, over time, you can mount the argument or campaign to persuade a prospect. If your promise is too extreme and your concept doesn't live up to the promise, you may enjoy some success in the short run but you will destroy your future.

A team always has two choices: Either pull together and take action or, pull apart and collapse the venture.

DO-IT-YOURSELF R&D

Part of the Blur

Internet advertising can borrow from so many genres of advertising and, from other professions, like the legal profession. For very little money, an internet ad can utilize many pages and angles to support its argument. These extravagant presentations are popping up everywhere to sell novel products, life-changing seminars or, sure-fire ways to make more money than you've every imagined. No education, no experience, no work; Thousands will start flowing into your bank account if you just buy their promise.

The problem with any media genre is the more they appear in front of you, spectacle and all, the more they all look the same and once so diluted, what they eventually get from you is doubt and mistrust. So what they give back is an ever more extreme over-promise and ever-more powerful guarantees.

The biggest problem most of these campaigns is that most of us don't really need this stuff in the first place. They are discretionary commodities. But if you consider a more necessary commodity like travel, key sites fall all over each other to lure, win and keep your business and the most important way they do that is to *prove* their worth.

If I go to Hotwire or Travelocity or Kayak and consistently receive the best service and, save the most money, I place them on the top of my travel search list. Their offers and technologies get better and consumers benefit.

The best truth is what your service actually does for a prospect so if you can communicate the truth effectively and win over prospects.

Getting Your Promotions in Motion

When preparing your campaign, you need to consider these elements:

1) What is your true deliverable; what is it that you can genuinely promise? If you're in the flower or greeting card business, perhaps your business is love and caring. If you're a plumber or architect, you'll generally have a lot of competition so you're selling superiority of skill and service.

2) How can you consistently make that promise in your campaign and, deliver on that promise? We're still in two phases simultaneously — development and assessment. As things develop, you evaluate, assess and make the appropriate modifications that permit you to move forward. Let's really get a jump on those manufacturers.

Let's make a working model. It doesn't matter at this point how well it works as long as it's clearly understood. It merely has to make a point that it can do what you promise.

Look what you've done. You don't need an expert to tell you that it's not perfect, but is it something real that begins to validate your dreams? At this point, many of you are so excited that you're ready to go running to the nearest manufacturer or distributor **We always have something of value to offer someone.**

FREE ENTERPRISE

or franchise attorney for instant wealth, fame or whatever. You've made it this far now all you want to do is get it out to your end-user.

Most of you, however, are not ready yet to go to market. So if you begin to work with a manufacturer at this level of unpreparedness, what happens to your own credibility, value and momentum? If your idea is more in the service realm, all down on paper and ready to wow your prospects, stop!

Pursue Protection if Necessary

Soon you will be scheduling a meeting with a group of potential producers of your idea. Before you meet with them, you will want to have some working knowledge of product protection. So, we've interrupted Chapter 4 to address many of your questions and concerns about concept protection.

We each keep a written track record and dated journal of all our concepts. Yet in hundreds of radio interviews, almost a third of the callers are totally focused and concerned about theft and protection. How can they be sure their concept won't be stolen?

The following is a reflection of almost three decades of concept development and why we believe that while patents may be crucial for some concepts, momentum may be as critical for the success.

POWERPOINTER SEVEN
Patents, Protection, Paranoia, Copyrights & Trademarks

"Yeah, I've got a good idea, alright. In fact, I bet it's so good, that's someone's going to steal it if I talk to anyone about it. I've heard stories. But I have to relate this to some people or companies. What should I do? Must I have a patent at this stage? What if my idea doesn't make millions? Are there less expensive alternatives?"

This is the vital section, the one that even many experts just won't touch. Many recent articles about idea protection have actually questioned the importance of patents in some cases; others merely question the timing as to when people should search and/or apply.

The intent of this section is to address and evaluate the varying needs for certain forms of protection. Ultimately, you may elect to obtain a patent or you may determine this process to be wholly unnecessary with the exception of simply attaining a provisional patent.

There are many competent and reputable patent attorneys who may differ with our findings. Not being attorneys, we must defer to the professional legal advice of such attorneys.

Your idea has value because you have value.

DO-IT-YOURSELF R&D

However, we are in the front lines, dealing with thousands of everyday people with ideas that are thriving. Some are patented, but more than half are not.

It just either wasn't necessary at their own particular point of development or it wasn't necessary at all. Do not spend twenty thousand dollars on legal fees to protect a worthless idea.

If you are familiar with the history of United States, you know that it was founded, built, based upon and designed to support and protect two primary forces — the family and the courageous dreamer. Just as the life-blood of any business is new business, the survival and growth of any country is based upon new ideas somehow evolved out of the old. Many countries want to protect and insure your concepts because they know their survival depends on you.

Yes, you might need protection, especially for a highly technical enterprise and it might cost you quite a bit. But for a great majority, your cost for initial U.S. government protection is under $100, which is about the cost of a disclosure document registration fee and which generally establishes your origination date and basic protection for the first two years of your venture..

The Law of Protection and the Law of Human Nature

What is protection law and what rights does it entitle you to? The word "first" is the primary issue here. The idea of protection law is to establish and prove that you were the first to come up with the idea. But just because you have established such a precedent, doesn't guarantee you protection even if someone does allegedly steal or extrapolate from your genius. First you might have to sue, and you might not win.

Unfortunately, that's the reality of the protection law today; otherwise there would be only one computer manufacturer, one fast-food chain, and one brand of car.

The entire system contradicts itself unless you consider the foundations of free enterprise: competition and marketing, marketing, marketing!

Corporate giants and a host of wealthy venturers can sometimes spend the money to protect some of their most valued concepts which often causes a technological détentes in those circles. But you should be encouraged and not discouraged because if you have proven yourself to be first and a giant steals your idea, there are many attorneys who might love to represent you on a contingency fee.

So corporations try to be careful not to knowingly lift ideas that belong to others. As you will learn, many corporations have specific submission procedures that require certain releases to protect themselves. And you should be encouraged by the millions of ideas that are evolving daily at various stages, as well as the thousands of new ideas that crop up each week in so many forms. You see them on television and on the Internet all the time.

Make sure others appreciate the value of your idea.

FREE ENTERPRISE

Again, a great majority of these endeavors are not patented but are protected by one crucial and underlying factor: momentum. These dreamers, builders, inventors, manufacturers and retailers are working on their ideas, making them grow and earning by their efforts, a solid piece of the pie.

As we together work to maximize your results on minimal budgets, you'll not only save a great deal of money, but you'll also give your idea a much greater chance of succeeding. In our collective years of consulting, we have never found magic nor instant easy money. Everything takes work and must be earned, and what we have often learned are better ways to work and deliver more effective results. Momentum- your best defense is the correct marketing offense. Keep that in mind as we systematically examine the various forms of protection you need first.

What up, 'Docs'

Each and every week, thousands of people simply assume that they will immediately require a patent and do one of four things:

1) They discover it might cost over $1,000 and proceed.
2) They discover it might cost over $1,000 and give up their entire idea.
3) They merely proceed without any protection.
4) They file a disclosure document or a one-year provisional patent.

This simple disclosure process which, providing you are indeed first, will protect you for the first year to two years of your venture - giving you time to generate revenue for a patent pending application and formal process, a patent search and, finally, a patent or whatever else you may need at that time.

How do I file a Disclosure document?

To file a disclosure document, send duplicate photos, illustrations, diagrams, written information, etc., with a self-addressed stamped envelope to:
The Commissioner of Patents and Trademarks
Washington, D.C. 20231
The 24-hour information telephone number is (703) 557-4636. But before you write or call, the best way to learn about all the latest details about the patent process as it relates to your concept, is to visit their website: www.uspto.gov

This is an excellent site which will guide you every step of the way in your patent process. Since the advent of the Internet, there has been a concurrent explosion of ideas from the general public.

Let them see your idea's value but never let them see your anxiousness.

Be sure to include the appropriate fee for each concept or process you wish to register. Remember, the provisional patent document is not a patent and does not offer you the comprehensive protection you may need in the long run, but it's sometimes the best first step and will give you a year to decide if you're certain that you need a patent.

Straight Talk about Patents

There are basically three types of patents:

1) Plant - for the protection of any new plant, tree, vegetable, etc.
2) Design - for the protection of decorative and/or visual outer "aesthetic" properties of any item, but not the internal core frame or structure.
3) Function or Utility - to protect mechanical designs and functions, most specifically in regard to inventions.

There are well over 350,000 patents awarded each year and well-over two million patent applications made each year. Unfortunately, a patent is often all that people ever get for their idea.

There is another interesting statistic of which you might not be aware. Each week, thousands of new at-home businesses and general businesses are started. What this means is that to merely look at the number of patent-applicants is deceiving. There are literally millions of people trying to get their piece of the pie working or they may be stuck at various levels of progress. Also, do not confuse this with job creation statistics. New ventures are not yet categorized as jobs.

Getting a full-blown patent is a detailed and expensive process. If you do indeed really require a patent, there are many competent attorneys who know all the right steps to take. So, if you are convinced or even if you're not certain, following is a valuable resource to help you best address the issue. If you are looking for a patent attorney to guide you, the least expensive procedure is a free consultation with a patent attorney for a half-hour. This is available through the American Intellectual Property Law Association's Inventor Consultation Service. F

What does having a patent mean?

Let's assume you have visited a patent attorney who quotes the various options that protection laws may provide for you - maybe in a similar fashion as we have done so far in this chapter. Suppose she then says, "Okay, it's up to you, what do you want?" What are you then supposed to do? To be extra-cautious, your attorney might insist that you begin with the maximum patent-protection available under the law. After all, the purpose for creating patent, trademark and copyright laws are to protect, support and encourage your creativity.

To grow our idea successfully, we need to evaluate receptivity.

FREE ENTERPRISE

While I often find myself in similar positions regarding patent questions and often make referrals to patent attorneys, I hope this chapter leaves you with more of an understanding of what your actual options are. I hope that you will keep the basic intent of the protection laws in mind - to not let your good ideas die and to find the best way to bring your ideas to life.

We have worked with many un-patented products as well as many patented ones. Ultimately, you'll have to decide where your resources and hard-earned money will be best utilized. Whatever you do, remember that no patent in the world is a guarantee of financial success. What matters most is the work you do and the choices you make to put that patent to work for you. The following connection exercise may assist you.

POWERPOINTER EIGHT
Protection Screening

Answer 'Yes' or 'No:'

- Is your product or idea totally original but highly simple? Y N
- Does your product represent a breakthrough (either high-tech or low-tech) that in a competitor's hands could lose you or cause you to lose money? Y N
- Have you fully explored other less expensive protective measures that may give you all the protection you need at this point? Y N
- Has your attorney discussed your options and recommended that you still pursue a patent? Y N
- Do you have investors or are you able to risk up to $20,000 on a patent search, application and possible challenges, including legal challenges? Y N

If you have answered yes to more than one of these questions, you probably should seriously consider pursuing a patent. However, if a disclosure-document, which essentially protects your venture for its first two years and only costs around $30, will suffice until you have proven to yourself and perhaps your associates that your concept will make money, then you should seriously consider that as your first option.

How Do I Submit an Idea to a Corporation?

Some companies charge sizable fees just to supposedly shape your concept and then present it to the appropriate industry. You come up with the idea, pay one of these brokers some money, and bingo, you're rich! Don't you wish that were true! It is of course, not true for most cases. What is true is that most companies, large and small, have their own parameters for agreeing to review your idea.

Most companies are built on ideas and need new ones or improvements upon old ones in order to thrive and survive. So, most companies do have their own internal research and development organization dedicated to monitoring and meeting the needs of

'Forward' is not always the direction you assumed it was.

their product or service-line. But every once in a while, someone like you comes along with an idea, and while a high percentage of these ideas won't be accepted by these companies, some do spark interest.

Your best bet for submitting an idea to a company, via its proper guidelines, is to contact that company and ask to be sent the company's conditions for agreeing to review your idea. That's where you start. You may find that some companies won't even glance at your idea unless you have a patent - others are not as stringent. A good tip is to begin by seeking out smaller-sized manufacturers/distributors that have a relevant product or service-line. Please note that the more preliminary and low-cost research and development you undertake, the better prepared your concept will be for a presentation to the company.

Also, don't discount friends in the business. Friends contacted or made at the right time in the right setting can sometimes help you with a vital short-cut just when you really need it.

Non-Disclosures

Smaller, local companies are generally more receptive and often easier to work with, but again it depends upon their abilities to work effectively with your idea. Most of you will want to make sure that after submitting your idea, no one will use it without your authorization. Sometimes you will produce non-disclosure forms or contracts that resemble something like the form in this book.

However, what you might not be prepared for is that some companies will sign your non-disclosure form and some won't. Almost all will have their own protection form for you to sign, which essentially states that, while they may agree to look at or discuss your idea, their research department may have already thought of the idea long before you did.

And if that's true, they won't want you to come after them for an idea they actually thought up first. One gets the impression that it's just a matter of the old principle, "you just have to trust someone," and since most long-term business is built on trust, you may have to take a chance like that.

Again, if you're still not sure, let your attorney have the last word. Get a second or even a third legal opinion (all free, if possible) before you commit to any legal expenditure.

While we have learned a great deal about protection laws in this country, we do not have the legal training or certification of a qualified and reputable attorney. Our expertise is in protecting you by helping you to find the most viable ways to produce and market your concept - protection through the strength, power and earnings of sales.

Never underestimate your good intentions or your great potential.

FREE ENTERPRISE

Trademarks and Copyrights

First, we'll explore the trademark or service mark because, as with patent issues, trademarks are still under the auspices of the commissioner of Patents and Trademarks in the U.S. Department of Commerce (Note: If you're utilizing this manual outside of the U.S., please refer to your country's own protection system, and/or U.S. International patent law).

The simplest way to explain what a trademark is would be to say "Coca- Cola," "IBM," etc. A trademark is a word, logo, symbol or any generally visual device, imprinted on each and every product or packaging of any service to indicate ownership, origination, quality and identity as it relates to publicity and advertising.

Trademarks, built-up over time, can be worth a great deal of money and cannot be copied or used without permission. A trademark or service mark symbol protects the right and ownership but does not, in itself, prevent others from making or selling the concept, as does a patent and patent-pending.

Just as a lawyer will conduct a patent search to assure potential originality of your idea, there is a Trademark register of the United States available in most libraries. Similar to a patent search via satellite patent offices, you can save money and make sure your trademark is indeed original by conducting your own trademark search. You can register any of your own original trademarks providing:

- They do not depict anything suggesting deception, immorality, or disrespect for persons living or dead regarding any individual beliefs.

- They do not depict signature or portrait of a deceased United States president, as long as the widow is still alive, unless she grants permission for such use.

- No flag or coat of arms may be used or incorporated.

- No common mainstream language term is used.

Copyrights

The key issue of a copyright is that it prevents someone from copying those written works which you originated. Believe it or not, a copyright is your protective right against being copied. Copyrights are inexpensive and are geared to protecting original works of authorship.

If someone should attempt to use anything you have originally written without your permission, and you do wind up in court, the law recognizes your copyright as legal proof of your origination.

Examples of copyrightable material are:

- Manuals
- Photographs

When you sell, sell well.

134

DO-IT-YOURSELF R&D

- Seminar guides and other guides and the actual presentations
- Original descriptions of original products.
- Books
- Sound recordings, CD's, DVD's
- Software
- Graphic design
- Most advertising and or promotional presentations via most
(print, radio and TV, Internet).
- Certain website concepts or names.
- Any established or electronic media. (This is an ever-evolving frontier).

Everyday symbols, such as stop signs, etc., slogans, phrases and other related issues, cannot be copyrighted. A copyright gives the processed applicant full ownership and exclusive rights to handle or sell that material.

For complete details, including copyright applications, contact:
www.copyright.gov where you will find full instructions and all forms. NOTE. The forms cost nothing but there are filing fees for most of the forms.

- For further information on copyrights, request publication 'R-2'
- To copyright a book, booklet, or most written items, request form 'TX'

To keep a free society truly free, the law must protect the creator, originator, inventor or pioneer, and indeed there are laws to protect virtually anything you can dream of creating. Just remember that you are always better off if you're part of the sales-chain. Because even if you do have your protection in place and launch a lawsuit — which can cost a lot of money — the suit might not be heard for several years, and then you could lose.

Dear Me?

Many people ask about postmarking a written form of an idea. In other words, paying your local post office first-class stamp cost so they will affix that day's postal imprint, complete with date. Again, with a good lawyer and a sympathetic jury, this might be considered as a small element of evidence, but this fundamentally does not stand on its own. It could, however, be useful if your competitor is smalltime and you show them your postmark. This information also regards the doing business as ("DBA") certificates available in most city halls.

On the other hand, email communications can be more readily documented and, can be used as evidence. Same with phone records.

So copyright, patent-pend and trademark when you can but, be fairly certain about a patent before you proceed. Then, channel your energies and frustrations into getting your idea developed and marketed. If you focus on listening to the needs of your mar-

FREE ENTERPRISE

ket, produce a reliable and good quality product or service, and remain determined and focused about where and how you work, you should be able to earn, keep, and even grow a market share.

It is deceptive for anyone to say that any particular protection or sales methodology is a guarantee for money. A patent is no guarantee for cash, nor is an ad, etc. But if you'll work hard and follow these steps, I believe you'll succeed and you'll discover that your best guarantee is directly contingent upon your own sales initiative. Be protected but most importantly be very pro-active about marketing.

Always describe your venture in a manner that is far more favorable to your client than to yourself.

DO-IT-YOURSELF R&D

Summary
Now that we have our blueprint or general performance plans, it's time to create some form of prototype or functional guide. If you've followed the steps to this point, your concept should have sufficient clarity to relate well to your initial subjects.

Bring the Idea into a Tangible Form.
- Create an initial model.

Implement Low-Cost Ways to Utilize Effective Resources.
- Locate and organize resources to assemble detailed model and/or written proposal.
- If any fees are involved, get a full understanding of what they are in advance.
- Be extremely clear when telling artists or other vendors what you want.
- Continually check on progress.

Pursue Protection if Necessary
- Send your Idea to yourself and your lawyer to obtain postmark as proof of your idea origination date.
- File disclosure with The Commissioner of Patents and Trademarks.
- Investigate if you need a patent at this time.
- Complete Connection #4 - Protection Screening
- Get free consultation from patent attorney.
- Obtain a trademark or copyright for your idea.
- Prepare to submit your idea to a corporation.
- Create a non-disclosure agreement.

Potential Challenges and Solutions

Challenge: Can't make a model
Solution: If you feel you just can't put together some kind of model or written description, you may need to do more homework. With sufficient knowledge, you should be able to put something together if you're really serious about your idea.

Solution: Re-examine your sources. Someone may be giving you misleading or unqualified advice which is creating an obstacle for you.

Challenge: Can't get anything on paper
Solution: Even if you're barely literate, if you can relate any thoughts to other people, you can find help to get those words clearly on paper.

Solution: Break through this fear and give your venture a chance to succeed.

"Look mom, someone said something nice about me online."

FREE ENTERPRISE

Before You Continue . . .
- Have you found a means to create a working demonstration of your idea?
- Are you continuing to find ways to advance instead of excuses to stop?
- Are you seeking out qualified critics/consultants?
- Are you listening constructively?

POWERPOINTER NINE
Understanding and Overcoming Success Barriers

You might remember thinking, "Wouldn't it be a great idea if..." "Why hasn't someone invented a way to... "Or you may have a reaction to someone else's insight that became real: "What a great idea! Why didn't I think of that?"

Simple self-doubt is the destructive voice inside you that will keep you from believing in your insights (your true self). Scrutinizing is healthy, self-examination is healthy as well, but an overall negative tone will nearly always sabotage your good intentions and fresh ideas by telling you that you are not good enough, smart enough or brave enough to step into the unknown and risk your safety for your higher good.

Think you've heard all this before? You haven't because you haven't listened to what seems so simple and you haven't yet produced your desired effective action which proved you are being guided by a faith in your vision, instead of enslavement by your doubts.

When you're ready to succeed, you will refuse to believe the negative messages that are kept alive through by playing emotional 'tapes' or memories of fear, intimidation, greed, power, selfishness and self doubt. And these dark feelings will find you when you are most vulnerable; when you are tired, in a low mood, in light sleep or frustrated. The effects? Well, many of you are living them not just right now, but for many years prior.

It's time to stop. Here are some insights for overcoming these success barriers:

1) Understand that all the negative messages preventing your success are coming from your thoughts.
2) Feel how your doubts feed your, fear and general lack of progress.
Notice when it attacks. During times of vulnerability.
3) Realize that it is not the real you, and that through the development of your new venture, you can evolve to a higher place.

For a worthy venture, all media has a place where you can communicate to your audience for no cost.

DO-IT-YOURSELF R&D

ACTIVATOR THIRTEEN
How to Protect the Spirit of Your Idea

Here is the Number Two reason that people stop before they even get started. They assume that they have to spend thousand of dollars on protecting their idea, or someone is going to come along and steal it right from under their noses. They've heard stories.

Well, we're not going to sit here and say that most ideas do not get stolen. The reality is that there are unscrupulous people in this world who will steal. But your bigger worry is getting robbed by consultants who flatter you and make inflated promises about your concept. The next thing you know, they are asking for hundreds or even thousands of dollars to help protect your idea or to do a patent search. Just a minute here! You already know that you can file a **Disclosure Document** with the U.S. Patent Office for under $100.00 This is not a patent but if you have a product in development and you're not sure if it's going to be the one, this simple document at least establishes a record and time line. You can also file a Provisional Application for a Patent for very little money, directly with the U.S. Patent office.

What if you have a book, or songs or anything related to expressive creativity. You can use **Form TX** from the U.S. copyright office.

The patent and general protection forms are *free of charge* from the U.S. Patent and Trademark Office or website and anyone charging you for these blank forms may be most likely be taking advantage of you or better stated, ripping you off.

We are never going to tell you that protecting your concept or intellectual property isn't important but we must expand that definition of what protection really looks like in terms of your potential success.

Patents, copyrights and trademarks are some of the greatest vehicles afforded to us, second only to our basic constitution. They endeavor to protect who we are as creative individuals. Patents are also very beautiful documents that look wonderful hanging on the wall. *But a patent or other document of ownership hanging on the wall is not guarantee of success.* Our government, like a patent does not guarantee our success, but only an environment of free competition, and you will have competition.

So what does guarantee success? Marketing. You can't just create something and seek massive protection. *You have to find the way to market it.* In other words, *you have to create a way that it relates to the public in a commercial or other intended form.* This is where people fall short and that's why marketing is your best protection. We will spend a great deal of time on how to get your concept in the hands of your target customers in subsequent steps because that will be some of your best weaponry for success.

And nothing feels more protected than a venture that you created that is making money. You'll have a deeply motivating sense of ownership from something that you cre-

If you don't keep in step with simple free technologies that will really help you, you run the risk of getting stepped on.

FREE ENTERPRISE

ated. So if you thought that protection only meant getting a patent, you're only getting a tiny part of the story. That's why some of the most successful concepts always find a way to keep moving forward.

If you believe that your idea requires special additional patent protection, we urge you to pursue a qualified attorney. It is neither our intention nor qualification to advise you on patents for your particular venture, but to make you aware of the importance of getting your ideas successfully to the end user.

How is your concept changing or evolving as you process these guide-points?

_____

_____

_____

_____

_____

_____

_____

_____

Every person you meet may somehow teach you something and therefore, present a new possibility for your idea.

DO-IT-YOURSELF R&D

CORE STRATEGIES AND TACTICS NUMBER SEVENTEEN

Commit to Excellence. No matter what your budget, or even if you have no budget, never sacrifice quality for any reason. Make certain your staff is properly trained, enthusiastic, and dedicated to helping you achieve your goals. Invest in the best equipment and choose the best office facilities and location you can afford. Neatness counts because it infuses trust. The formula for success is: A well thought-through concept coupled with strong strategic planning + strong execution = marketing success!

HOW TO SUPERCHARGE THIS TACTIC: Every chance you get, show your client that you are willing to go the extra mile for them.

HOW CAN YOU ENGAGE THIS RIGHT NOW FOR YOUR VENTURE?

_____

_____

_____

_____

The Plane Truth about Excellence

On a cold afternoon back in January 15th, 2009, anyone looking towards the Hudson River at just the right moment had to wonder if their eyes were playing tricks on them: An L-1011 traveling at over 100 miles-per hour glided onto the surface of the Hudson River. Within minutes, all boats nearby came to the aid of the plane and shortly thereafter, all of its passengers found their way safely to shore. Virtually no injuries.

The moment the plane hit the Hudson River, all that CNN initially reported was that a plane had gone down in the Hudson. My colleagues and I assumed the worst. Who wouldn't? The history of water landings is not good. So to later learn that everyone walked off that plane with virtually no injuries, struck our hearts with sheer amazement. We were not alone. This was one of those moments where the most subtle mistake would have killed all 155 passengers aboard that craft.

"You can't always control what happens to you, but you can control how you deal with it."

FREE ENTERPRISE

So what saved them? In a word: Excellence. The pilot Chesley B. "Sully" Sullenberger III was "the right guy at the right time at the right moment," to quote his neighbor John Walberg. A former air force pilot as well as a safety and glider instructor, Sullenberger was perhaps one of the few pilots who could have brought that plane down safely.

'Sully's genuine accolade of excellence could only be defined by one fact: Everyone survived because he did absolutely everything right; the pitch (angle of approach), speed, position of flaps upon impact, assessment of water current, wind, weight distribution of the plane, specific safety instructions to passengers. All of these parts equal the sum total of excellence. If anyone of them were off, the result would have been far less than excellent. "Sully' had to be excellent.

Volumes have been and, will be written, about the definition of excellence. It is taught everywhere everyday but there is no better way to truly understand what it means than by a true story like this 'Miracle on the Hudson'. Excellence in action. The challenge to each of us then becomes: How can we dedicate ourselves to excellence in whatever we are endeavoring to do, as if our lives depended on it, as well as all of those we serve. Study this story and other like them and you will know excellence.

CORE STRATEGIES AND TACTICS NUMBER EIGHTEEN
Create a Cool Logo and Tagline. Every company needs the right image. Your image should not be something that just looks cute, clever, or amusing to your friends, but also something that will sell your service to new prospects.

HOW TO SUPERCHARGE THIS TACTIC:
Your logo is often your first impression and your tagline your second, but both work together to communicate your service so make the right first impression.

HOW CAN YOU ENGAGE THIS RIGHT NOW FOR YOUR VENTURE?

_____

_____

_____

_____

The greatest success is being able to identify and then, overcome your greatest barriers to success.

DO-IT-YOURSELF R&D

CORE STRATEGIES AND TACTICS NUMBER NINETEEN
Get High Quality Professional Photos. Professional photos are not that expensive and are well worth the impression they make. People want to see who you are. Or, visual proof of the quality of work you do. That is part of the trust-building process.

HOW TO SUPERCHARGE THIS TACTIC:
Unless inappropriate, smile as that can help instill trust. Whenever you can tell part of your story visually, do so as prospects will grasp it more quickly.

HOW CAN YOU ENGAGE THIS RIGHT NOW FOR YOUR VENTURE?

_____

_____

CORE STRATEGIES AND TACTICS NUMBER TWENTY
Answer phone calls professionally. Answer the phone clearly and distinctly with the company name followed by your own name to help the caller remember it, such as "Jones Public Relations. This is Sally Jones." Also, try to smile when you're talking on the phone and, stand up, if you are able. Body language, facial expressions and attitude can be readily be transmitted through the phone lines. Make use of the customer 'hold' time with a timely message further educating your customer on your services.

HOW TO SUPERCHARGE THIS TACTIC:
Record a Professional-Sounding Voicemail Message. A professional voicemail makes a great impression on new and current prospects. It may sound like a small measure, but they all add up to build your positive image. Also, when people are on hold, this is a great opportunity to explain services and create a greater sales opportunity.

HOW CAN YOU ENGAGE THIS RIGHT NOW FOR YOUR VENTURE?

_____

_____

_____

The secret to your success will be your willingness to get up one more time than you fall down.

CORE STRATEGIES AND TACTICS NUMBER TWENTY-ONE
Be Ready to Describe What You Are Doing Clearly and Concisely. As with the earlier exercises, know how to describe what you're doing in one or two sentences. You never know where you're going to meet a prospect or, how much time you'll have so have those sound-bites ready and hand out that business card.

HOW TO SUPERCHARGE THIS TACTIC: Write down a few Soundbites that clearly and positively describe your venture. Keep them by your phone and in your pocket, ready to use at a moments notice.

HOW CAN YOU ENGAGE THIS RIGHT NOW FOR YOUR VENTURE?

_____

_____

_____

_____

_____

One of the most meaningful forms of success is overcoming seemingly impossible odds.

DO-IT-YOURSELF R&D

Progress Journal: (please feel free to copy or scan this page only)

_____

_____

_____

_____

_____

_____

_____

_____

_____

_____

_____

_____

_____

_____

_____

_____

_____

Your Signature_____Date_____

When you're succeeding in one direction, put even more marketing in that successful direction but protect your growth by continuing to seek out new markets.

CHAPTER FIVE

FIRST STEPS TO MARKET

Materializing Your Concept
"Successful concepts are understood in ten seconds or less."

Howard Bronson

Overview

Even more important than testing is evaluating the data and then, genuinely applying this new knowledge to the improvement of your idea. This requires careful listening, especially to potential buyers. Actively seek out critics and be grateful for their valuable time and input.

> **Activator Steps for this Chapter**
> **1) Incorporate feedback.**
> **2) Earn and learn each step of the way.**
> **3) Present your concept.**

Incorporate Feedback

Chapter 4 addressed the battery of protection issues for most of you, hence, giving you the impetus to carry on with your research and development. At this point, you're actively seeking out the experts in relevant fields who will spend some free time giving you their opinions. At these meetings, expect to be insulted occasionally. After all, your concept is a part of you, but you're looking for hard core critiques now before any big expense is involved. Write down a list of hard questions. Let them rip your idea to shreds. They may finally kick you out. They may make you an offer.

In any case, if you do as much ego-free listening as possible, you will invariably leave these encounters with more than you came. Some of the best ideas we ever came up with were more than put down. With one, we were actually warned by the head of a highly reputable firm not to pursue a particular venture that it would definitely fail and would be of no benefit to the public.

That venture was the highly successful predecessor to this book. The gentleman warning us was actually the head of an advertising agency who felt that the book would

FREE ENTERPRISE

threaten the ad industry. So obviously we saw that as an opportunity, and the rest is history.

You need to make sure that you understand the reasons for criticism. When I wrote *How to Heal a Broken Heart in 30 Days*, my co-writer and famed marketing guru, Michael Riley heard from various therapists who blasted the book, which turned out to be highly successful. So consider both the value of the criticism and the source.

Whatever you hear, you'll make no decision at this point. You may now want to forget your entire idea, or you may want to jump at the first offer you've heard. Instead, go home, or go back to work and don't think about your venture for a few days. Then, slowly digest all these new ideas. Your goal is to find a way to make your idea more viable and to advance it. Some of you will destroy your original models and proposals.

Some of you will make slight modifications. In either case, you will be finding ways to enhance the value of your product.

Keep it fun. Keep your sense of humor. Revel in the fact that throughout our careers, we have already made the big mistakes for you. Many times over. Are we proud of our mistakes? No. You can't simply say that all mistakes are okay. You have to learn something. We are never proud if our efforts fail to achieve what we know we can achieve for others. But we try to learn to do better with each new time. We fall forward. So there is a lot of learning to do, but there is some pain inherent in that learning. That's just part of the process that will mold both your venture and your character.

You have reached this crucial development stage without spending any significant money. Discouragement can and will be corrected, but a squandered life-savings over a half-tested idea? You can avoid that. We've seen it happen to people of all levels of intelligence. We wish they had the sense to invest a few dollars in this book. Think of the money they could have saved, and that's not the only loss. Their wonderful idea becomes only a bitter memory. So, no matter what stage you're at (and many of you will have suffered severe setbacks at this stage of the game), it doesn't matter. What does matter is the heightened awareness and education you now have about your idea. Your small failures are crucial for paving the way to a more genuine success. Young or old, you don't have time to mourn your mistakes. Just learn from them and move forward. Remember, regret is the greatest waste of human resources!

What is your idea trying to tell you?

As writers, we love the computer and Internet because it allows us to research and play with ideas and rewrite the same page as many times as necessary. We can give the impression of being able to take criticism well on any of our writings because the computer allows us to test and perfect the product on a virtual basis without the traditional labor and frustration. Ego-free listening and the pursuit of excellence become easier all the time.

The point is to patiently rework your model until it works. That way you get the experts' stamps of approval, but you still own the idea! By sticking with our planning and development advice, you've created some exciting options for yourself. You didn't sell out, so as a reward, you can now offer potential players the option of "buying in." Now you've got something, and Chapter 6 will help you begin to make the best of it in some very exciting and profitable ways.

The Perfect 10 Test

"Don't tell me I need tests. I know this is a great idea. This is me; this is my child, my baby. I haven't felt this strongly about an idea in years. We'll make thousands of them right away. Wait a minute...babies learn to walk by falling.

Maybe I'd better go a little more slowly here."

Smart person, whoever spoke these words. Does it describe you also? Are you anxious or enthusiastic? Are you listening well, and are you evaluating what you've learned and incorporating it properly into your mental model?

That's good but even if you feel comfortable and have done batteries of sophisticated tests, nothing will save you more money and heartache like the real perfect 10 test.

Most of you are proceeding cautiously out of necessity, but some of you are reading this while nervously wondering what can be done to unload a warehouse full of unsold items you made or stocked up on. Well, sometimes we can indeed develop ways to move those items, but hopefully you've learned an important lesson that you'll remember forever; in most cases, do not manufacture too far ahead of your demand and keep watching your market for changes and incorporate those changes into your product. Moreover, always remember the perfect 10 test.

We all know that, aside from the one we love, there's no such thing as the perfect 10. But now we'll tell you about another perfect 10; one that can save you loads of money and even save your business from complete disaster. Most importantly, the '10' test can preserve the vitality of your dream. You are at this point in the book because you have researched, conceptualized, re-worked, re-conceptualized and possibly protected your concept to the point where you think you are ready to go into production. There is one more crucial step which you shall be using throughout the life of your idea - the model and/or the test.

If your idea involves a service, start small - don't over commit. If it's a product and you've made a model that seems to work well, still for your first production run - make ten. That's it - just 10. We will be discussing models, prototypes and pre-production planning but progress is determined much less by luck and far more by gradual testing and evaluation that begins on the smallest scale possible. Especially those first 10 units.

The choice to have courage is just the beginning. Next, we have to nurture, test and grow that courage until it sustains us.

FREE ENTERPRISE

Whenever we are personally involved in the development of a product, after we are satisfied with our model, we then attempt to make ten perfect prototypes. The prototypes are exact replicas of what we believe will finally be in distribution, with possibly the exception of packaging (since certain retail or other sales may require varying forms of packaging).

We then present these prototypes to prospective distributors, as if we are presenting any product for a sale. The distributors we approach are usually the biggies, i.e. the ones who would buy in the largest quantities.

Hopefully, if we are polite and professional in our approach, this prospective buyer will respond honestly with one of the most vital components you'll ever get for your idea - professional criticism. If the buyer says no, find out why. What changes could you make to make him say 'yes'?

Of course, as we've indicated earlier, don't exclude your local retail market. Those down-home responses can teach you as much as any others. Are you beginning to see the value of the perfect 10 test? Before you over- manufacture or over-commit, these buyers could give you the most valuable advice you could ever hope for.

Testing addresses and, hopefully, solves simple issues before those issues become major problems. It's better and, in fact, it's okay to make a thousand mistakes in your testing phase as opposed to even one mistake in thousands of an untested item.

Why We Test and What We Test For

SAFETY
- Has it met, or preferably exceeded, all safety standards as required by all pertinent laws and codes in all designated sales areas?
- Apart from legal requirements, can you anticipate potential safety issues, exclusive to your concept that must be addressed?
- Have you addressed as many safety problems as you can possibly think of before you allow anyone to actually try your concept?

MANUFACTURING
- Are you using the most appropriate materials?
- Is your assembly/manufacturing process the most efficient, economical and hazard-free?
- If possible, are you utilizing biodegradable materials?

FUNCTION
- Does your product work consistently and repeatedly?
- Can your service deliver what you promise it will?

It's not real until you make it real.

FIRST STEPS TO MARKET

- Is your product designed to last for an amount of time comparable to or in excess of the competition?
RESPONSE
- Has your target market indicated interest?
- Have you incorporated legitimate suggestions into your concept?
- Can you produce concept at promised price and still make a profit?
PRICE
- Is your price competitive?
- Can you test at different pricing levels?

Service and Needs

Everyone used to joke about selling refrigerators to Eskimos, but today, many modern Eskimos have refrigerators, just like anyone else. So, to apply the *Ten test* to a service idea, you must take much of what you have learned about the need for your service from the previous chapters.

What percentage of the population would utilize this service? Will there be competition? Could you try out your idea first through just an ad in the local paper or yellow pages? Again, determine response and demand and then respond and progress accordingly, but do not go right into an office space without first taking a step-by-step process of determining if the population will support your idea, or if you can sufficiently market your service in order to make your venture profitable.

How To Use Rejection To Help You Succeed

"*No* is just a yes waiting for another question." From Jason Alexander's 'Bob Patterson Show' (unfortunately, the show got a big 'NO' very quickly).

But he was right about that: *A negative response is only a temporary learning phase to a genuine small businessperson.*

Of course, as noted earlier, the responses are a bit more detailed. If you're fortunate enough to get a positive response, what does that mean? And does a 'no' really mean 'no way'? The key will be finding what's wrong and how to correct it. Did you speak to the right person?

Were they busy? Always get to the core of your mistakes so you can progress. You will be referring to the upcoming "Connection" throughout many phases of the development of your concept. It is designed to aid you in making clear-cut analysis to enable you to get closer to a sale.

Pay attention to all the components that will make your venture profitable.

Moreover, to conserve our financial and other resources, we are always looking for the shortest distance to a sale or the promise (letter of intent) of same. Hopefully, before you even talk to a prospect, you will study this so as to get an idea of what you are aiming for. Right after that , we will explore the current state of your concept and what we will have to do before we give your idea a test-run.

Finding the Decision-maker

You will notice in the Connection #6 that the terms 'buyer' and 'prospect' are frequently used, but in fact, there are many labels your prospect may assume. Be sure you are speaking to, or eventually will speak to, a genuine decision-maker who has money and authority to commit. If it will be a committee decision, can you meet with the entire committee?

Everyday, hundreds of new prospects are created, new items, new stores or services that may be ideal match-ups for your service. So how do you find the right buyers? There are several ways:

A Key Sales Motivator

The first place I ever sold my book, *Good Idea! Now What?* was in a local, independently-owned hardware store, since I theorized that a lot of do-it-yourself types would appreciate the intent of the book. The local owner/buyer agreed to try ten on consignment - and they sold within a matter of days. From then on, I sold on a cash basis.

A key motivator for successful sales is to disdain inventory that sits around, as you would any employee that sleeps all day. Get it moving! Are there local shops that can prominently display your product? It's a good, inexpensive way to test your idea and build your sales-confidence. Then, if your item will do well in a few local stores, how do you reach hundreds or even thousands of similar stores?

There are so many ways to link up and interconnect with the various sales avenues, and not just on the retail level, as we will learn. However, if you have created a successful local retail test and want to expand, there are two viable ways to approach this:

Back-tracing

Who sold the local store the major products they sell? What distributors did they deal with? Pick a product or products that, while not identical or specifically competitive, could be sold to the same retailers which yours could be - a similar family of items, so to speak. Now back-trace. Who sold those items to the retailer? Ask the retailer for the name of the distributors who may be relevant to your concept.

Find your market and then market to your market.

FIRST STEPS TO MARKET

Directories and E-Directories

While back-tracing is a very powerful vehicle to help get you started, the ever-expanding and ever-changing world of reps, distributors and buyers is a vast and often complicated one; so, don't over-commit to any rep or distributor unless you have some evidence of their capabilities (and the freedom to fire them if they don't do their intended job!).

If you are seeking a more systematic approach in your retail distribution hunt, the internet has hundreds of thousands of free resources and directories for just about every concept. Listing those sites just for your concept alone would fill another book.

Here's merely a simple example of where to get started. Also remember that the key to getting the best internet support is realized by asking the right questions.
For Sales Representatives, check out the United Association of Manufacturer's Representatives. www.uamr.com
For Retail & Distributor Information, contact: www.nrma.com
To present to manufacturers, go to www.thomaspublishing.com

Hopefully at this point, you've googled your markets, your competition and, everything related to it. How are they getting their concepts to market and how can you do it more effectively? What can you learn from them?

You may or may not be ready to make use of the above associations and directories, but if you are ready to use the upcoming *Yes Chart*, you should then have a broad base of target (prospective) markets to hone in on.

Our experience has been that no does not always mean 'no,' but more usually, it means not yet or not under either the terms or the conditions which you have presented your item. What's exciting about the internet is that if you learn to use it with some savvy, you can always find an alternative possibility to make your concept fly.

POWERPOINTER TEN

How to Rise above the Competition

Remember, all you need is a market share. You may not need to dominate the market but how do you earn your place in a competitive market.

Let's suppose you have a new concept that you're selling or ready to sell. Or at least, it's new to you. You know you have an idea that will work and sometimes, you r concept will be so unique that it will create a market niche that's unique and untapped simply because your concept is so unique. But even if you did indeed create that better mousetrap, how do you convince the world that it's better, how do you steer them your way?

Dealing with competition can seem overwhelming because competitors can be, well, competitive. Even if you know you have a better product or service, an aggressive

Let the world know you exist and show them how they can benefit from your venture.

FREE ENTERPRISE

competitor can overwhelm and steer customers away, even if those customers would be happier with your offering.

For outsmarting the competition and, for bringing the customers home to you, keep these three elements in mind:

1) Listen to what the prospective customer is asking for. If you watch many of the recent car advertisers, most are emphasizing MPG economy and Honda especially talks about a multitude of gas economy features with a little more technological description. What the spate of general auto ads show is that the automakers are listening but Honda's ads suggest that they are listening better and are doing more to address the needs of the consumer.

Even when car sales are slumping or, especially when care sales are slumping, car makers have to steal customers away from each other like never before. Honda knows that even in a tough economy, people will still pay a little more for a more economical and reliable vehicle. Even if the vehicle may take a few more years to cost-justify, Honda knows that many people will spend more to feel better about using less gas because Honda knows that there are millions of prospective customers who have a guilty conscience about wasting resources.

The more you listen, the easier it will be to sell. We've all been in those uncomfortable situations where we felt like we couldn't say no to a slick salesperson. Often, that form of sales aggression happens because the product or service isn't selling itself sufficiently. But for those whose concept reflects good listening to the needs and wants of a customer, selling is a matter of clear and calm communication, again, like the spokesman for the national Honda ads.

2) Respond. We've all run into people who seem to listen well but that's all they do. They seem to show real care, compassion and concern but they don't do anything. A real measure of good listening is response by specific action. If a prospect is screaming for a better way to test toys for lead at home, what are they looking for and how can you deliver that?

3) Communicate. You don't have hundreds of millions of dollars to call attention to your venture but through this book, you've learned how to get lots of quality attention for free. You've learned how to identify the right prospective audiences and how to reach them.

Don't fret when the economy's bad. People still buy but their spending habits change. Listen, adjust and deliver and even in tough financial times, prospects will orientate towards you.

There's a sense of satisfaction when a prospective buyer feels that a seller is listening and responding. Driving a high quality, more fuel-efficient car like a Honda that

The key to finding what you need is asking the right question to the right source on the internet

will deliver even better gas mileage makes the customer think, "They are listening to my needs, wants and concerns and they are doing something about it." Their purchase is their vote of confidence.

The sooner in the sales process that you can show your prospect that you're really listening, the better chance your well-perceived service will lead to a sale.

The True Secret for Sales Success

What is the real and true secret for maximum success in your marketing campaign? If you google or Amazon-search all the books about Marketing and Sales Secrets, you'll discover two things; first, obviously most sales and marketing authors can't keep a secret but even more importantly, there are just too many secrets to afford any of them real credence. Their secrets imply that once you learn them, you'll become a master sales and marketing guru. The great Panacea.

In the early seventies during the first post WWII gas crunch, those who survived through that one will recall the even-odd gas days and the long lines waiting to pay a bone-numbing 67 cents a gallon. Any crisis precipitates two things: Inventiveness and exploitative fraud. At that time, there were literally hundreds of gadgets, elixirs and general tips for maximizing gas mileage. Some even promised to double gas mileage.

So a savvy news reported in Denver decided to test the top ten. He ordered each one, from a water-injector to a major electronic box, to all the additives. He tried each separately and then, combined them all. Separately, he claimed that only the water-injector may have increased mileage slightly. Then, he combined them all and his mileage actually decreased.

That's kind of what you deal with when you follow every 'miracle' marketing tip as opposed to the ones that truly work. Because no matter what anyone claims, there is only one real and true marketing secret: *Effective Communication*. That's it. If you are successful in communicating the importance of your offering to your prospect, you will earn a customer.

See the Internet as Accelerated Networking in the Real World

FREE ENTERPRISE

Tips for Communicating Clearly about Your Idea

Effective communication is not all that difficult. Simply pay attention to the following:

1) RETURN CALLS AND EMAILS. Not only does this help to develop a rapport with prospects, it displays common courtesy. When people do not return calls or emails, it says one thing: "I DON'T CARE." No prospect should feel that way and anyone could become a prospect.

2) LISTEN INTENTLY TO THE NEEDS OF YOUR PROSPECT. If you try to force anyone into a sale, they will try to avoid you. However, if you listen to a client's needs FIRST, you can then work to meet those needs and selling becomes easy and ongoing.

3) MAKE EVERY CLIENT YOUR FAVORITE CLIENT. Excellent service is a powerful way to communicate to your client that you really care about the quality of your and, your client.

4) BECOME A RELIABLE SOLUTION. If you become the one resource that clients can turn to as a resource of solution, your phone and email will constantly buzz.

5) NEVER FIGHT WITH A CLIENT. Choosing to fight with a client is always the beginning of the end. Even if you vigorously disagree, don't assume that you are display mastery. Instead, re-frame your dialogue to the effect of: "I can appreciate and understand why you feel that way. May I make a suggestion that might get us close to our goals?"

6) BE AN 'US', NOT AN "I". If you stand shoulder to shoulder with a client, working together to solve a problem, you become one effective force joining together.

7) FOLLOW THROUGH. No project is complete until the intended results are achieved. Show your client that you are dedicated to a successful completion of any task, no matter what it takes.

Learn how to make the internet work for you while you sleep and when you're wide awake.

The Yes Generator

This is intended to help you overcome obstacles when presenting your concept to your designated market. Review it a few times until you can change all of your 'No's to *Yes's*

The No Part: "I'm not far enough along to present my concept"

How far along should you develop your idea before making a presentation? That obviously depends upon a lot of circumstances, including your own personal capabilities and relevancy to the idea. But sometimes, you can sell a service or product before it exists.

Another key element of early presentation is you may be able to secure additional funding or other resources to advance your success but only accept alliances if you really need them and, if those partners are suitable qualified.

We've talked about protecting your idea so be sure to secure your non-disclosure from prospects and maintain a good paper trail to establish who was first with the concept.

The No Part: "I can't get myself out there! I'm not a salesperson."

Yes you are. In one way or another, everyone has to represent themselves at some level just to survive. All selling requires is honesty and a willingness to listen and learn. Don't force; let your product do the selling. As far as confidence is concerned, you'll earn it as you gain sales. Also, don't let any fear of rejection slow you down. That's just part of the process.

Success belongs to those who get knocked down (as we all do) but are willing to get up again because they have enough faith in the promise of their idea.

What's the response to your initial presentation?

Will the prospect issue an order or, what is the possible nature of the agreement?

_____

_____

_____

_____

FREE ENTERPRISE

IF **NO**, find out why and accommodate prospect with new presentation.

IF Yes, Go to next step

___

Still Stuck in **NO**where land?

Are you pursuing the correct market, prospect, or buyer? If **NO**, research your market, develop better sales targets and start again.

___

Ask the prospect what improvements you need to make. Have you left too much up to the buyer's imagination? Start over.

___

Do competitors offer better products? Better terms?

___

How effective is your team or advisers? How positive is their support?

___

Selling is showing and 'telling' others how and why they will benefit from your concept. Be clear, friendly and confident.

Rethink all of the elements that will improve your concept

_____

_____

_____

_____

Did the concept sell itself, or did you sell it too forcefully?

Slow down! Believe in yourself and your idea. It costs you nothing to look at a concept from many angles. Remember that many solutions exist even if we can't see them at the moment.

POWERPOINTER ELEVEN
How Humor Can Help To Keep Your Idea on a Serious Path

Laughter isn't merely the best medicine, as the expression goes. Laughter really is good medicine. Studies have shown that for people who have had at least one good laugh each day, enjoy not just a healthier emotional outlook but a biological one as well.

The other side of laughter, at least as far as your body's health is concerned is fear and dread but not necessarily sadness. Often times crying can be as healthy a release as laughter because tears of sadness release toxicity. But not depression of course.

Imagine something funny, a joke or, funny happenstance. You laugh. Think of how good your body feels; relaxed, content, pain-free. Your belly feels good and relaxed. You feel safe.

Now, think about how you feel when you think about debt, or a lawsuit, or, someone yelling at or, insulting you. Your belly feels different now, your body doesn't quite feel right and over time, this feeling will cause physical harm.

How do you prevent yourself from feeling the very real effects of real fear? Some people simply deny feeling afraid but the body knows better. That's what they call it a brave front. But some people learn to laugh at fear or, learn not to be affected internally and, can really laugh it all away.

This book is designed to help and support people in the quest to make money with their ideas. For the vast majority of people, more money means less anxiety and dread. Sorry, platitude devotees, money can buy some happiness. But as you make money, if

FREE ENTERPRISE

you do not learn to cope effectively with fear as you're struggling to succeed, you'll simply find new things to be afraid of after you succeed.

I believe the human body, soul and spirit are designed for joy and that we function best when we can appreciate and see some fun in our lives. Otherwise, why succeed if there's no joy? That's why I've included these activator tips to help you more effectively cope with the business and general stressors of life so you can enjoy it all just a little more:

The 'Lighten Up' List

1) Remember, your whole view of life comes from that few pounds of brain we each have. All your fears come from your brain so why not train it to be less afraid and more joyful. It's your brain and your choice.

2) If you're afraid of simple non-life or health-threatening things, ask yourself why and imagine the worst thing that could happen. And what is the likelihood of that happenstance. For example, if you get sued over some business dispute and the sheriff comes to your door to serve you, the whole scenario makes you worry and afraid. That's largely the idea of lawsuits: To scare you into doing something you ether cannot do or, so not want to do. And really, what's the worst that can happen? if it's a money dispute, you'll resolve it somehow but your 3 1/2 pound brain is worried that you'll lose everything and a few months down the road, it will be resolved one way or the other so why worry in the first place? And what will worry do other than make you sick and why make yourself sick when being healthy is more fun?

3) Remember that as serious as life can be, business ventures are like a game. Sometimes you win, sometimes you lose. If it doesn't work this time, perhaps you can learn something to help it work out the next time. But if you worry yourself into paralysis, you won't have the ability to take what you've learned and create a next time.

4) Find the humor in your situation. Find the irony or the contradiction; something you can laugh about. See the humor in your problems and you will cope better.

5) There's always another side and a different perspective. As I've said many times before in many ways, where there's a problem, there's also a new opportunity and where you can invent a new opportunity, you can find hope. Hope like laughter is a great guiding force that feels good.

"Wherever you can test, will plan your future best."

6) Hide in a nap. We all know rest is important for clear and sober thinking and general health. Sometimes when feeling overwhelmed by a problem, try taking a short nap. Not only does this strengthen our ability to cope, this form of mini-escape allows the brain to process the problem so you often times awaken with a solution.

7) Have a great laugh. Call a funny friend, sing out loud, watch comedy; dance. List all the things that make you laugh and pursue them. Lift your spirits because they higher your spirits are, the harder it is for negativity to reach you.

Humor means more than being goofy or funny. It allows us to make the unbearable more tolerable, it helps us to cope and it makes the struggle to success fun because struggle is fun if it leads to a higher place.

There's always a ways to move forward. Your brain, coupled with a clear-thinking, fear-free positive attitude is a hard combination to beat. At the same time, you must temper your anxieties. The brain is just 3 1/2 pounds. Don't let something that weighs just 3 1/2 pounds bully you.

'Entrepreneur, Heal Thyself'

Along my struggle to entrepreneurial enlightenment, I've had the privilege of learning from many great minds. One was an elderly gentleman named John Shaw who when he saw me struggling to raise the necessary resources to make this book happen, he turned to me and said:

"Entrepreneur, heal thyself."

That was a turning point in the development of this project. I have been through so much frustrating struggle with this project, just like my readers; so much so that I forgot about my own capability and power I had to make my dream happen.

What I was impelled to remember was that if we have a task to accomplish and require a bridge or catalyst to make it happen, we often assume that we have to look to someone else to provide that magic break to make it happen. But there are problems with that thinking because unlike, the necessary process of building a team, this suggests:

1) That you are dependent on one company or individual to produce your success.
2) You are not looking at a diversity of prospects or creative options.
3) You may not be looking at your own specific ability to help you solve the problem.
4) You may not be exercising sufficient will and initiative on your own.

Wake up to the fact that you are what you choose to be.

FREE ENTERPRISE

This is a critical issue because it represents one of the key 'stuck points' that entrepreneurs encounter. They reach a point where they are certain that someone else money or counsel will get them to the next step. Failing that, they simply stop, close down temporarily or just give up.

What's Stopping You?

We've talked a lot in this book about seeking answers both within and without and how to know the difference. When you find yourself at one of these stuck points where you're holding your own dream hostage, you need to take a careful look at what you're doing:

1) Look at your problem clearly. Write it down. Examine it from many angles.
2) Ask you team to each write down at least three potential solutions.
3) Review those solutions and determine which will get things moving again.
4) Place both a log of the problem and solutions in a solutions file.
5) The next time a similar problem arises, you now have a written roadmap of solutions that you can refer to.

Your personal economy is up to you.

Summary

In this chapter, your new feedback will often come from many of your potential buyers, who often become your unwitting production associates, as they will often tell you exactly what you'll need to do to get them to buy, invest or distribute your concept. Many giant leaps are often made in this chapter.

Incorporate Feedback
- Use the 'Perfect 10' concept.
- Progress effectively but with minimal risk.

Earn and Learn Each Step of the Way
- Shape your concept to potential buyers, distributors, etc.
- Make them your most valuable ally.
- Take note of Power Up Tip #3.
- Investigate prospect sources:
- Local outlets
- Back-tracing
- Directories
- Find the Decision-makers.

Present Your Concept
- Actively seek out and listen to their best criticism.
- Research-Refine-Research-Refine.
- Get to 'Yes' with the assistance of Connection #6.
- Keep increasing the value of your product and service.

Potential Challenges and Solutions

Challenge: Can't seem to muster resources to generate any kind of interest.

Solution: If your heart's in the right idea, you won't stop until you've actively sought out those resources that can assist you. Are you seeking out seeking critics?

Challenge: Can't find the means to make my concept into something real and functional.

Solution: Coming up with something new requires a great deal of creative thinking, of which we all are capable. Look at the same old possibilities in new ways. Also, since large ventures generally begin with a single seed of a notion, how can you find the new doors that will carry your concept forward?

Before You Continue . . .
- Is your concept a by-product of disciplined motivation or careless over-anxiousness?

Relevance allows you to maintain control; inspiration allows you to maintain stamina.

FREE ENTERPRISE

- Are you listening well to your team players?
- Have you approached a potential review or sale with confidence?
- Do you now have new ways to increase your concept's value?

POWERPOINTER TWELVE
How to Build Your Own Inner Coach

It seems everyone's a coach these days, helping us to manage virtually every aspect of our lives. Sometimes, outside opinions and guidance are great and powerful things. Other times, they annoy and degrade us simply because we already know the right words of wisdom if we will just take a moment to listen to some-thing inside of each of us. That inner voice.

The inner voice is not, in literal terms, a voice, but a feeling inside that resonates with who you are. It is the feeling that strikes a cord when something makes sense to you. The inner voice is not always trusted by our logic because logic is based on what we have learned from social conditioning throughout millennia.

The inner voice is based on what our true inner self feels is right to us personally. Learn to identify with the Voice. Listen for feelings that do not necessarily make sense, but feel right. It will feel right because it is right.

Throughout the day, notice the difference between the inner voice and the media-bombarded mind.

1) Identify the two via a feeling.
2) Trust the easy, light feeling to be the inner voice.
3) Move toward the messages from the inner voice. Be trusting.

Example: My friends are all talking negatively about another person that is not present. My inner voice says this does not feel right to talk about someone behind their back. That feeling of knowing is your inner voice.

POWERPOINTER THIRTEEN
Should You Quit Your Day Job?

"Don't quit your day job." You hear that expression all the time especially if you're trying to venture out on your own. People will insist that you require two primary components to make your venture successful: Time and Money. Most people don't have much extra money, or time, especially these days. In fact, that's why they're trying to create a new venture in the first place, not to spend more money or waste time but to make more money over time.

When you experiment and combine, layer or integrate these strategies and tactics, you have literally Thousands of marketing possibilities.

Still, everyone insists that you need time and money to make a new venture successful. Everyone is wrong! What you need is *profit* to make your venture successful. And even if you find some extra time as you'll learn in just a few pages, what good is carving out a bunch of extra hours each month if you're not seeing a profit? In the meantime, there are people who are following the systems in this book right now, spending far less time than you, and they are seeing a real profit. So what you need most of all to even consider taking a leap from your day job to your new on a 100% basis, is a growing net profit.

So how do you balance an already busy life, laden with family obligations to make the new venture work? In addition, you may look to them for encouragement but all you get is criticism for being less available or, less of a provider.

Becoming an entrepreneur where you begin a pathway to do what you are truly born to do, can be one of the most rewarding experiences of your life but it can also be a lonely, frustrating road, especially when those you would expect to help, seem to be doing everything possible to prevent your success.

In truth, we always have more time and resources than we think we do. A recent small e-consult client was looking for just $1,100 more each month to set up a retail storefront for his outstanding line of homemade computers but lamented that he just didn't have the funds. But he did have $11.00 each day to eat breakfast out and, $5.00 for a special cafe latte; he also had an extra $78. each month for his favorite sports channels. So in reality, he had nearly half the money. For the other half, the landlord agreed to let him rent the store front for half-price for the first three months, plenty of time to realize enough of a profit to cover full lease, especially since he was using my systems to promote his business.

ACTIVATOR FOURTEEN
Reality Check for Your Idea

Okay, you've settled on an idea, so this is the time to explore the feasibility of your vision. Is it the right idea for you, or are you just so excited about the whole process that you haven't really thought it through? This is the time, before you expend your resources, to go through that very tough process of second-guessing yourself. This is time to do all the mental exercises when all it will cost you is a little time.

This process involves asking yourself the following questions:

a) Could you explain your idea clearly in less than ten-seconds? This is important not only for your own focus but for making time-sensitive presentations and for building effective ads or displays. Try to write a simple sentence that describes your idea in a way that anyone would understand it.

Learn from relevant businesses that are more successful at getting customers than you. How are they doing it?

FREE ENTERPRISE

b) Who are your customers? How big is your potential market (buyers)? Why are you so sure they would be your customers? Have you asked them?, Have you conducted any end-user research, formally or informally?

_____

_____

_____

c) Is your idea unique or will it at least be competitive with similar ideas? Why? What makes your idea better?

_____

_____

_____

d) Why is there a need for your product or service?

_____

_____

_____

_____

e) Are you confident that you can secure the talent to make this idea a reality? If not, what do you need to learn or, who can fill that knowledge gap?

_____

_____

_____

_____

Getting your attention and interest is half the battle. Getting you to act and buy is the victory.

f) Are you either a central or, a reasonably valuable resource for making your idea happen?

g) What have friends and experts alike said about your idea? Have you discussed it sufficiently with trusted colleagues? What helpful suggestions have they made?

h) What contribution will your idea make to the world?
Is it just for entertainment?
Does it make life easier in some way?
Does it help humanity?
Is it a needed service?
What is the purpose of your idea? How will it affect or benefit others?

If they believe, you will receive.

FREE ENTERPRISE

i) Why did you end up choosing this idea?

_____

_____

_____

_____

Let Me Give You Some Extra Spending Money

Some of you have all the money and resources in the world to use these systems to test your ideas at will. But for the vast majority of you who are barely getting by, the last thing you need or want to do is to incur any additional debt. Since your production and promotions costs will generally be negligible, you may only need a few hundred extra dollars to make your concept work. If you're an ongoing or high-end business, the technique in this book will save you untold amounts of cash. But if you're that little guy looking to find just enough to get your venture off the ground, you may already have that money hiding right under your nose.

Unconscious Graduated Deficit

The vast majority of Americans are spending beyond their means and they are often not at fault. We hear about a new computer, cell phone or consumable and we have to have it sometimes, without even knowing why. We subscribe to some newsletter or other service online and suddenly, a little chunk of money is just disappearing from our bank account each month. All of this happens because the advertising industry is masterful at confusing your wants with your true needs. We buy that new car or new outfit because we think we need it and suddenly, we find ourselves just leaking money everywhere. And we get so caught up in the frenzy, we can't stop ourselves. Well, what I'm suggesting is that if you do in fact, pause for a moment and look at what goods and services you are paying money for, you might start to feel like you're being robbed or worse, that you're robbing yourself.

Consider what you may be paying too much for and how you can start saving instantly.

Change all Your Credit Card and Bank Account Numbers – By some estimates, over 80% of all Americans believe they have either an unnecessary or unexplained charge on their credit card or bank statements. Perhaps it's that dating service you once subscribed to or, a repeating charge that you never authorized because you thought you were buying a one-time trial offer. The moment you change all of your credit card numbers, it all stops. Then, you can go back and only authorize legitimate debits. Also, if you process credit cards, see if you can find a service that will charge you a lower processing fee.

How much money will you waste today simply because you haven't thought about it?

When I personally did this, I discovered that I had an extra $300.+ each month all from little services I subscribed to including trial offers where I though I would only be charged one time. (Later on in the book, I recommend using gift or pre-loaded cards that cannot be connected to an ongoing line of credit or bank account). Do this now and as you do this, be sure that both your bank and/or credit card companies are charging you the lowest fees possible.

Estimated Savings_____

Your Cell Phone Contract – These days, there are hundreds of contract offers at any given time for your cell phone service. That means that the chances are excellent that you can save money on your service by asking your cell phone rep to shop those contracts.

Estimated Savings_____

Your phone service in General – Skype is a totally free phone service for you and other Skype users and their rates to non-users are dirt cheap.

Estimated Savings_____

Your Cable or Dish Television – Same thing. If you don't listen to satellite radio, or don't watch sports or all those movie channels, on your television, why are you paying for it? Or, do you even need cable. In many areas, you can download free radio, TV and even movies On Line.

Estimated Savings_____

Bottled Water – Americans spend $15 Billion (with a 'B') on bottled water, much of which has been proven to be no better than most tap water. At least consider switching to a water filter.

FREE ENTERPRISE

Estimated Savings_____

Your Driving – Can you use alternative transportation, take public transit, carpool (even for errands or shopping). Even if you simply slow down and glide down hills (where safe), you can save a few gallons.

Estimated Savings_____

Your Monthly Bills - Air Conditioning/Heating – Could you get by with ceiling fans? Do you have energy-efficient bulbs, is your refrigerator set properly? Are you paying too much for your car or home insurance, can you refinance your home or car loan, are you paying too much for your credit cards?

Estimated Savings_____

Food – Most people have been so conditioned to eat out or, stop for coffee and a baked good, that they often don't realize they're doing it. Review your grocery list. Can you save more by eating breakfast or, having that cup of coffee at home? Are you buying too many pre-made dinners when cooking can be much cheaper?

Home Upkeep – Do you have gardening or cleaning service when other household members could help a little more?

Estimated Savings_____

Paying Bills – The average home still pays their bills by putting a check in an envelope, buying a stamp and, making a few special trips to the post-office. Virtually any bill can be paid on line these days, either for free or, a minimal fee. Or, you can set up automatic bill-pay for many key bills.

Estimated Savings_____

Sell Your Junk – Have a garage sale or, sell stuff you will never use, on e-bay. You can realize hundreds of dollars of found money immediately.

Estimated Savings_____

Before you purchase anything, check the internet to see if there is a similar offer of the item or service for free or via a sponsored site. There are many movies available on line for free! Even if you don't have a home computer, most libraries will let you use their computers for free.

- Estimated Savings_____

    Family Fun – Do you haul you family, boat and ATV's in tow only to get to your location and run more motors? Why not consider a family walk or hike, or a less expensive day at the beach or local park or, free outdoor concert?

Estimated Savings_____

    www.missingmoney.com Visit this website and enter your name.
This is an absolutely free site that finds any missing money you may have forgotten about from old stock certificates to store credits to tax refunds. I tried this with my friends and many found anywhere from $100. up to several hundred dollars in their own unclaimed money, <u>all for no charge.</u>

Estimated Savings_____

Estimated Total Monthly Savings_____

Estimated Total Savings_____

Congratulations, you now have $_____ to help Advance your idea or to do whatever you want.

    See, I told you I'd give you some extra money (you just didn't know it would be coming from you). Now, , how about that extra time I promised you:

Ask and you shall 'Receipt'

FREE ENTERPRISE

Let Me Give You Some Extra Time

Most budding entrepreneurs will tell you that the recipe for success is:
Time
Know,-How
Confidence
Persistence and
Money.

But often because they believe too inflexibly in this formula, they remain budding instead of blooming. Why? Well just look back at what we've learned. Take any of these five elements and this book has shown you how to get them. Still, you can make the excuse that even with the others in place: Money (or it's substitute of all the free resources we've told you about), know-how, confidence and persistence; even if we understand that we can really do this, we still come up with that unbeatable excuse: "Sorry, I just don't have the time." If we look at our lives and our precious time, our schedules can appear pretty tight. Phone calls, emails, kids, significant others, extended family, alone-time; by the time the day is done, we barely have time to think. Most of us have to plan everyday just to make everything fit in, not realizing that we are probably wasting far more time than we realize.

Unconscious Addictions

When it comes to time, even the most time-efficient among us wastes more time that they realize often using the very technologies designed to make our lives more efficient and, to save us precious time. Computers, cell-phones, P.D.A's video games and even fast food have all found ways to waste our time, while selling us on their convenience. These are the primary unconscious addictions because we are unaware of how they are fighting for and carving up our time and priorities. And what's the worst thing about addictions? They rob us of time that can never be recovered.

It's not all our fault. All these new or evolved techno-wonders compete for our time. The more of our time they can usurp, in the name of convenience and efficiency, the more money they make. So cell phones, lap-tops, video-players etc, all compete aggressively for your time by offering more supposedly essential services. Before you know it, you are so electronically-connected that you feel you need each device even more. More precious time. Hello, unconscious addictions.

You can plug into some hope by doing a little unplugging. When my wife and I want to redecorate a room, the first thing we do is remove everything from that room. Then we carefully lay in what we really want or need. Same with your electronic world. Try the following:

The first step to selling is to relate to your prospect.

1) Declare a non-electronic weekend. Just shut everything off, even the cell-phone (unless needed for emergencies only). Computers, Video games, TV's. ATV's.

2) Do something non-electronic and non-mechanical. Walk, hike, bike-ride, visit friends, mow the lawn. At this point, you're probably already beginning to shudder at the thought of becoming unplugged. It's a very uncomfortable feeling in fact, it can be downright irritating and boring. That's because you are feeling the subtle effects of electro-detox. Withdrawal. So, as with any addiction, endure the transitional discomfort in the knowledge that this will take you to a better place.

3) At the end of this 'painful' weekend, reintroduce these devices into your life but in a manner where they now really save you time instead of causing you to unconsciously waste it. People are amazed to discover that they find three to six extra hours every week just from this exercise. And that could be all the time you'll need to make your idea successful.

Your Time Machine

Before	Time Used	After	Time Used

Cell Phone

Television

Video Games

**Online Services
or Games**
P.D.A's
IPOD

Other Time Bandits

_____

_____

_____

_____

The key to increased Internet response is maximizing the impact of your key words and phrases.

With this new data, the best way to begin is to start managing your most severe time-bandit because you know you'll find lots of extra time there. Then, work your way down your list.

What do you know; the one final excuse you thought would prevent you from bringing your idea to reality no longer exists. It's about time. It's about that great human penchant for wasting time where one lost hour can turn into hundreds. Time to re-set your clock.

Let Me Help You Get A Bit More Organized

For a hurricanic entrepreneur like me to suggest that I am any example of maximum organization would be an act of fraud. The fact that I do indeed make the effort to get more organized in spite of my genetic proclivities means that anyone can do it.

In business, time is a precious commodity and how and where you apply your time can make the difference between profit and loss. One of the key elements for saving both time and money is to get organized, even if you're a sworn member of the chronically disorganized. Being disorganized is not a fault; it is often a characteristic of the entrepreneur whose vision is transfixed on greater and more distant things. Still, being organized can make those things more accessible and that's good for business.

I am one of those people who spin a million plates all at the same time so what helps me is a simple list. Many people swear by their PDA's so the information is readily accessible. For me it's a combination which all begins with a prioritized task-list that I review every morning and evening. I need to know what the most important tasks are, deadlines and, how much time I have for each. I also need to be nagged when I have an appointment or other obligation.

There are many great websites, software and freeware to help you both get and remain organized. I like www.Iwantsandy.com but you have many options. The ten minutes I spend regrouping at the beginning and end of each day make my days far more efficient and, far less frustrating. A dreamer needs to dream and taking some simple steps to organize can permit that with far fewer distractions.

People are looking for your business all the time but you have to let them know they are looking for you. It's Up To You.

CORE STRATEGIES AND TACTICS NUMBER TWENTY-TWO
Put Your Customers to Work. There's no better advertising than a satisfied customer who relies on you. Who does that satisfied customer know who would appreciate the same service?

HOW TO SUPERCHARGE THIS TACTIC: For customers who can deliver prospects to you, offer them a surprise reward, bonus or commission whenever they bring a prospect to you. Some customers may actually become sales reps for you.

HOW CAN YOU ENGAGE THIS RIGHT NOW FOR YOUR VENTURE?

_____

_____

_____

_____

_____

_____

STRATEGIES AND TACTICS NUMBER TWENTY-THREE
Put Teeth in Your Soundbites. Why should someone do business with you instead of your competition? Create a list of those benefits where your customers and prospects can clearly see them. If you let customers know of your key advantages in the beginning, they will always remember that about you. Be familiar with your professional 'one-liners' and update it whenever you get a new idea.

HOW TO SUPERCHARGE THIS TACTIC: Write down the key befits or your service and memorize your list. The more people hear of your superior or advantageous offerings, the more they will be prone to try your product or services.

HOW CAN YOU ENGAGE THIS RIGHT NOW FOR YOUR VENTURE?

_____

_____

_____

_____

Build an image but be sure to match that image with real substance.

FREE ENTERPRISE

CORE STRATEGIES AND TACTICS NUMBER TWENTY-FOUR

All Employees are Also Salespeople. Everyone who works for you is also a representative for your business. They should each be handing out at least ten business cards a week (and they should be collecting twice as many cards, relevant ads, and email addresses).

HOW TO SUPERCHARGE THIS TACTIC: Create a contest amongst employees with a monthly celebration.

HOW CAN YOU ENGAGE THIS RIGHT NOW FOR YOUR VENTURE?

_____

_____

_____

_____

_____

_____

_____

Everything you do in business sends a message to your prospect.

FIRST STEPS TO MARKET

Progress Journal: (please feel free to copy or scan this page only)

_____

_____

_____

_____

_____

_____

_____

_____

_____

_____

_____

_____

_____

_____

_____

_____

_____

_____

Your Signature_____Date_____

Prospects need to understand function and benefit quickly.

With all of the ways to get your message to your potential customers, there is often no substitute for the simple places where many exclusively get their information.

CHAPTER SIX

TESTING THE MARKET

Listening With Logic vs. Emotion
"Ideas are like children. Raise them well and witness success."
Anonymous

Overview

This is an exciting stage where you will not only be seeking out potential distributors, manufacturers or various other buyers, you will also be soliciting their strongest critiques. In essence, the very people you are going to sell to are going to tell you exactly what you need to do to get them to commit.

Activator Steps for this Chapter
1) Maximize your concept's value.
2) Present your prototype to the market.
3) Create inexpensive resources

Maximize Your Concept's Value

You have made strides in developing your idea and now have to face the challenge of testing it while building your own personal value to any future prospect.

Can you imagine giving up rights and ownership of your idea only to discover that someone else ended up making a fortune on it - just a few pennies for you? You didn't think you were capable of making it happen, so you sold out. The multi-billion dollar Microsoft bought the original core DOS software for only $75,000 from someone who had an evolved idea. After you read this book, you should have an entirely new attitude about selling out.

You don't have to be a non-professional to unwittingly give away all of your hard work. People at all levels get short-changed on their ideas to the tune of billions of dollars daily. Why do you think so many lawyers get rich? They often rake it in from the simple and avoidable mistakes.

Believe it or not, lawyers and good advice can become your best allies if used before the crisis erupts. A lot of you are afraid to pursue your best concept past the thrill of the romance stage. Seeing your concept at the model phase is gratifying for your ego

For new product or service releases, don't be cute or even clever, just be clear and clearly support your claims.

FREE ENTERPRISE

but serves little other purpose toward your goal of marketing, control and profit, and self-actualization.

A lot of our new clients come to us as bitter people, convinced that market savvy and success can only happen to the other guy. So, they offer us hefty fees because they've either given up on their own talents, or they haven't read this book.

People become bitter when they try it the wrong way and then refuse to learn the right way. They become convinced that their way proves that the system doesn't work for them. If they had done it right, maybe we'd be out of a job, but they would be happier people. There's nothing like participating in a success, but you must have incentive.

Much of our work involves keeping people excited by showing them the fruits of their efforts at each step. One should never underestimate the power of instilling incentive and confidence.

Lee Iacocca's incentive plans for Chrysler were so good, they were actually greater than he was. Against his wishes, a strike in late 1985 was settled by paying his workers fees that gave them parity with competitive autoworkers. Iacocca was not terribly keen on the idea. He thought it would drain the company dry.

The strikers won and a month after settlement, the company posted some of their strongest earnings ever. His own philosophy of incentive; of employees standing up for the best within themselves, triumphed. That which is perceived as an "Ultra-incentive" will produce Ultra-results. (By the way, Iacocca's recent venture involves the development of mini-electric cars for local driving, with part of his profits going to diabetes research. A great mind is always creating.

You will always keep your incentive in your pursuits because you will always create for yourself the proper involvement at each step. Never sell out unless you're talking fortunes and retirement, even then, it's nice to keep a hand in just in case you need the production resources.

In fact, you are going to learn to have more than just an interest. Your prospects and associates will realize that you are uniquely qualified to merit a controlling and supervisory interest. After all, it's your baby.

Don't Use the Dime-Store Approach

Your first premise is to never use the dime-store approach when selling your product. The dime-store approach entails taking a flat fee for a product or idea then just walking away. You're paid a fee that may seem sizable to you at the time and then you go home and wash your hands of the whole thing. The idea has been so much a part of you and so important to you, and now you're just going to cash out? You've turned your dream into something that someone will buy from you. Sometimes the first-time thrill of that idea makes people lose their perspective.

It's up to you to make sure your idea gets the quality attention it deserves; attention that makes that phone ring!

The final decision is yours. If you want to just take the money and run, we can't stop you, but obviously, we don't advise it unless we're talking BIG bucks. Even then, as with the situation we just described, selling out may not be your best option.

What you have learned thus far has helped you to get started but it's only the beginning. You're still caught in the thrill of a brand-new romance. Now comes the marriage.

You've brought your idea closer to perfection, and now, you just can't wait to go back and show up your critics. You probably think that our next piece of advice is to make just such a presentation. You couldn't be more wrong.

You began with an idea and then you turned the abstract into something tangible, a product or service, at least twice critiqued and refined at this point. You started as a shaky dreamer. Then we transformed you into a researcher, an inventor, a designer and a developer. That's quite a company you're becoming.

We've worked hard to increase the value of you and your company. You may indeed go back to a manufacturer or distributor and work with them. You'll have to ultimately make the best determination for you and your venture. After this chapter, your options should clarify.

"Sell-Out" Caution

If you're thinking of becoming a "sell-out," be aware that many ideas are purchased and are then never released. Companies often buy out competitive ideas just to crush any potential competition. So if you do sell out, do one of two things:

1) Get a production commitment which will return the rights of your idea to you after an agreed period of time if the buyer does not produce and sell it, or
2) Negotiate a GENEROUS sum of money.

As you have already observed, many ideas die from a simple case of misdirection. The bottom line is - don't let your good ideas die for any price. The world always needs better ways to do things. Your idea could make a difference.

ACTIVATOR FIFTEEN
Describing Your Idea

Here's your assignment; write three paragraphs describing the features and benefits of your idea. Is it new? Say so, and explain how your idea may render existing competitors obsolete. Don't explain how. Don't be too technical and don't give away too many hints about your research conclusions. And, by all means, always include at least a mail-

---

Never assume that any older or traditional form of media can be completely substituted with a more modernized form. Every layer of communication has its place.

FREE ENTERPRISE

ing address and preferably a phone number. And of course, the idea means of communication, barring a personal meeting: the personal email address.

Convey that your product is available for distribution or participation (if appropriate). This is done to officiate and lend credibility to your product or service. DO NOT EVER lie about your product. You'll have enough to remember when making actual presentations so if you tell the truth, you won't need a good memory. Genuine advertising is a responsibility to the public to tell the truth in an attractive and appealing manner.

You have no doubt noticed that some of the most outrageous claims are made for some of the most inferior products. The harder someone tries to sell something, the more dubious you should become. Don't promise magic, just honest better features and benefits than the others (and you'd better have better features than the others!). Write something that you would believe yourself. Run it by some friends.

Ask for feedback by email; that's usually most convenient for mass response. We're not looking for cute copy. Cute is dangerous if not used skillfully - "just the facts, ma'am."

Is your writing understandable? Can people get an idea of what your product is about just from your paragraphs? Have you created curiosity?

Spend a week writing if you need to, but no more than that. Don't get stuck. We write these types of descriptions all of the time and our blurbs appear in hundreds of magazines and websites each year. Since we've been doing them for years, we can usually churn them out in less than an hour. Ultimately, you'll be able to do the same thing.

You should be able to write as fast as you can clearly relate your ideas in ordinary conversation. But do get help to ensure your writing is reasonably clear. A sloppy presentation will jeopardize your credibility.

Now that you have produced this description of your product or service, the trick is to get the message to the right people. This book is laced with the common theme of bringing each task to a successful conclusion. This is both exhilarating and terrifying for many of you who never dreamed you would ever see anything of yours in print.

You'll soon discover how easy it can be. Nothing is easy until you master it, but if you've made it this far, you can make it the rest of the way. Many of you don't believe it, and we used to lose a lot of promising students at this stage. It's easy to get stuck right before your big debut. Let's continue on . . .but first these important words from your sponsors . ..

If you have lived and worked in the United States, you know it can be a very exciting place because it attempts to encourage free thought and of course, Free Enterprise. This type of environment is most conducive to heightened productivity.

If you allow yourself to be left behind, you deprive all of us. In the next section, we begin dealing in earnest with the shenanigans of the concept development game.

It's tempting to believe that the Internet is the Panacea of all communication needs but there's still an entire universe of ways that people get their information without it.

We'll give you the best idea possible as to what to expect, but life is always full of surprises. And it is you who will move it forward.

If you are still having trouble making it through this critical time, you're not alone. Everyone reaches a point where they simply feel overwhelmed and overburdened. People talk about getting tired of all the barriers to success for their ideas. And sometimes in that tired state, we forget the worth and value of our idea. So if you need a break take it. Persistence doesn't mean to work yourself in the ground. It just means keeping your healthy focus so your idea stays healthy. And if you need help bouncing back sometimes, consider the following:

ACTIVATOR SIXTEEN
How to Bounce Back From the Edge of Business Defeat

Sometimes we all just run out of steam without really understanding why, and then our concept or dream begins to flounder. If you ever find yourself with those feelings, refer to these primer points:

1) Forgive yourself for any mistakes you made or commitments you couldn't keep. Learn and seek to move ahead to the best of your abilities.
2) Believe in your own talents and capabilities.
3) Recall that in the past, there were certain goals you thought you had to have but didn't really need. Maintain a strong vision but a realistic one as well.
4) When it comes to sales, don't finesse, impress. Customers will make their own choices, no matter what we want them to do.
5) In time, you'll always view the time you spent feeling discouraged, to have been a waste of time. Learn, heal and move ahead. Build from the old to create the new. That is nature's way.
6) Don't allow yourself to be paralyzed by envy or anger at some other high achiever. These emotions are really a wish that the challenge was easier than it really is at the present moment. Use logic to tame negative emotions so you may share your best with the world.
7) Act or be acted upon. Inaction is a choice to deal with issues through weakness instead of motivation.
8) Those that don't have the good sense to recognize your potential do not deserve to profit from your ideas. Learn from them and move on.
9) Work with the possible and remember that you can always create new possibilities.

The business world is on a web-connected computer screen that travels everywhere. You need to be there in front of that viewer that's looking for you right now.

FREE ENTERPRISE

Moving Ahead With Interest

Some of your respondents to your initial public exposure may be from some of the contacts you made in your initial research phase. That can prove to be a very encouraging development. Last time you encountered these experts, you were just a babe in the woods, and they were the authorities. If you did your homework properly, the tables have now turned. Your efforts have elevated your value to your potential associates.

Hear these prospects out, but make no promises. Ideally, you'll want to entertain many possibilities before creating any type of written agreement. We're going to present a host of your basic options, and then you can decide what best suits you. Whatever you do, sign nothing, agree to nothing until a competent attorney reviews any and all proposals.

Some of you honestly feel that you have gone as far as you can on development and production planning. The nature of your product requires a specific manufacturing technology to move ahead. It may indeed be the correct time to explore potential associates.

If this is the right time to approach the heavies, let's do it right. We want you to be well protected. Arrange a meeting with the company's decision-maker(s) so you won't have to duplicate efforts or waste time with a go-between who could distort the hard information.

Be very open. Find out exactly what they want to do with your concept and what they are willing to offer you. Remember, you are never to sell out completely. After all, as an expert on your product, your services could be of great value to them. If your prospects are smart, they will realize that they need you as much as your creation.

"Aren't I Supposed to Be Risking Something?"

You-Can-Do-It seminar coaches will all say about the same thing, "There's no opportunity for reward without risk." That phraseology is very deceptive for the vast majority of our readers and clientele. It's easy for someone else to encourage you to risk your money, but we think you can always afford to be careful. In fact, you must not jump ahead or risk heavy capital until your actual orders can support that risk and even then, study the alternatives, spread the risk and reduce the risk!

If you do your job and connect effectively, you will meet all kinds of people with all kinds of ideas for your idea. Sometimes there will be opportunities for strategic alliances and sometimes, simple affiliations. If you suddenly find yourself facing an offer, approach it carefully.

POWERPOINTER FOURTEEN
A Piece of the Pie - What, When & How to Give

What do you give an individual or company or investor who offers their services or finances in exchange for a potential piece of the profits of your company? While this depends upon a number of factors, there are some hard and fast rules to consider:

1) Don't give away long-term interest for short-term favors

If someone's doing a small money job for you, try to arrange liberal payment terms, if possible for the amount they are owed, plus agreed-upon interest. If you absolutely believe you have no other option, then get as much as possible from this supplier as you possibly can.

2) Don't make promises you can't keep

Liability and accountability are increasing legal buzz words and production and service suppliers lose more sense of social responsibility. So while you want to wax enthusiastic about your concept when presenting it to others, don't promise untold riches! Always let the prospects draw those conclusions themselves from your presentation, but never make large financial rewards the reason for inviting participation. Remember, relevancy should come first.

3) Insist upon 'maximum flexibility'

If you have been told to make a plan and then stick to it, you are hearing incorrect information. The 'Connection' exercises of this book will be your marketing plan, and it will change and adapt as often as needed to meet your production and sales needs. Plan to be flexible, and insist upon the same behavior from your participants. Be crystal clear that your venture is a risk and may not yield any money for several months, years, or possibly never at all. If you encounter or discover you are dealing with an inflexible, demanding type, either let them know what the rules are in writing or plan to phase them out. Impatience pushes good ideas into failure.

4) Non-lawsuit clause

If you require your participants to sign just one document, make it a mutual written promise that no one may sue anyone else involved in the venture for any reason. Moreover, should a dispute arise, a mutually agreed-upon arbiter shall be appointed to resolve any and all disputes and claims competitive ideas just to crush any potential competition. So if you do sell out, do one of two things:

5) Get a production commitment which will return the rights of your idea to you after an agreed period of time if the buyer does not produce and sell it, or

6) Negotiate a reasonable sum of money.

As you have already observed, many ideas die from a simple case of misdirection. The bottom line is - don't let your good ideas die for any price. The world always needs better ways to do things. Your idea could make a difference.

FREE ENTERPRISE

7) Stop at '51'

Unless you and your associates (shareholders, investors, co-venturers, etc. are offered a sizable cash advance for a majority of your company, always retain over 51 percent of your company, and always maintain personal veto power. There can be majority opinions against you, but you should always have the final say.

8) Net not gross

Your company could be taking in a great deal of money (Gross Profit) but after all expenses, including taxes, are deducted, there may be no actual remaining cash (Net Profit). Only offer pay-outs from net profit.

9) Start at '5'

Offer your long-term, permanent players a starting net pay-out of 5 percent once such net is realized. Also offer certain participants an opportunity to increase their profits providing they increase sales in some fashion.

10) Don't be too generous

While the success of your venture may hinge upon assembling the appropriate team, test your team first. Make sure you're working with the right players and be sure each is making best use of their respective gifts.

Inform your prospects that you feel it would be to their benefit if you stayed with the project through all stages. After you finish this book, you will find that you really can be of great value to them in many key areas.

You may consider suggesting to these serious prospects that your compensation be in the form of a modest monthly consulting fee plus a percentage of the gross profits that your product generates. This type of option can prove highly appealing to a company who originally had thought they were going to have to pay you a small fortune up front. The way we have suggested represents a better risk for all parties concerned.

A business deal is not a good one unless it benefits all participants involved. Some of you may indeed require the services of a major distributor but may not need the manufacturing end. Don't worry, you'll learn all about our special promotional techniques in the upcoming chapters. In the meantime, don't rush to give your product and profits to a big company who might end up using the same manufacturing company you would use.

On to the Market

So where do you go from here? How about to the marketplace? That's right; you read it right. All you have is a rough prototype. You're in the infancy of production stages yet we are going to expose you to the marketplace.

You are about to undergo what is commonly known as a market test. You've gotten samples in the mail of new products. That type of promotion or test can cost millions and what if the product has to be modified? The cheapest market surveys can cost thousands of dollars even before you know if your product is ready.

You don't want to spend that kind of money on your project, but would you be willing to invest less than $10 plus a little time to test your idea?

We have to find out how the public and related industries feel about what we're up to. We have our legal protection and research behind us.

Let's find out what the world is thinking. This is a more comprehensive form of focus group assessment. You may already have a distributor and/or manufacturer in mind. Wouldn't it be simple just to build that relationship and move ahead? Be advised, there may be several people out there who can help your product come to life. Don't limit yourself to one chance prospect.

POWERPOINTER FIFTEEN
How to Breathe Life into an Oxygen-Starved Idea

Ideas die when people don't know what to do next to move them forward. It happens all the time. Lack of the right and often very simple information combined with a lack of confidence are the leading cause of death among promising ventures. Even business professionals can be afraid to admit that certain delays are caused by procedural ignorance, so all you hear from them are excuses and stories. Pride or fear of job security shields ignorance and then, the idea falls victim.

Good business health is determined by any measurable signs of moving forward. Even when struggling, people who dedicate themselves to making their product move ahead are rarely depressed. Keep it going. If you don't know, ask, learn. If you have a problem, solve it. There's always an economical, ethical and effective way.

As we were putting this book together, some of our critics told us to cut any words of encouragement and just stick to the "How To Stuff." This was one time when we found our critics to be dead wrong. The world is full of "How to" Encyclopedias on how to do anything, but with little understanding of how you, the reader, is thinking about each step. So instead of learning "How To" with many of these books, you learn "How NOT To" once you run up against your first inhuman directive that you don't understand. You learn how not to permanently by creating fear and lack of confidence as your biggest enemies. The success of your venture is a highly personal issue, and we want no one to be left behind.

We can't get too heavy, and we can't play psychologist. All we can say is that, if you're stuck, there's always a way to get through it if you're willing. Find it. The key is to keep moving forward no matter what happens.

When you know where and how to go, you run the show

FREE ENTERPRISE

To those of you who are now ready to move forward, go get 'em! You're going to encounter a lot of characters who might try to raise your blood pressure and steal your sleep and worse. My intention is to not have you lose a single night's sleep.

You see, it doesn't make any difference what kind of characters approach you, we'll teach you how to deal with them. You'll have the control and the upper hand. If anyone loses sleep, it'll be the other guy, not you. Fear no one. This is your game and you make the final rules. Alas, there is still a segment of you who have never finished a "How To" book or any venture, for that matter. You began with the best of intentions and hopes, but then repeated the same old pattern of fear and failure, like a worm crawling around the inside of a cup, round and around until it dies. Maybe you have spent years training yourself not to succeed, and therefore, have never had a success past a certain level. You now will have the know-how to break that cycle. Know that you've got it, believe that you've got it and go for it.

If you have lived and worked in the United States, you know it can be a very exciting place because it attempts to encourage free thought. This type of environment is most conducive to heightened productivity. If you allow yourself to be left behind, you deprive all of us.

In the next section, we really begin dealing with the shenanigans of the concept development game. We'll give you the best idea possible as to what to expect, but life is always full of surprises. Just remember to keep moving forward.

Suppose you're planning to start up a small hometown paper or ezine. You could go to a local publisher who could essentially take it over. Or you could find a printer or web designer with periodical printing experience. No matter what you've got, if you attempt to line up your "jobbers," you can reduce your dependency on any type of parent operation.

Safety, Safety, Safety . . .

In pre-production, aside from protection, there is one other key element that cannot be ignored nor overlooked. A lot of inventors are very rebellious and then there are many of you who are strict conformists. The nature of your concepts could be as different as night and day, but in the area of state and/or federal regulations, safety standards or any other mandatory codes or laws regarding safety and approval of your goods or service, there are no shortcuts. If you think you know one, forget it.

Safety standards and the like are in place to protect all of us. Adhere to them like Krazy Glue®. Determine if you need certain safety, and/or other approvals and take proper steps to get them.

Have you ever bought a new screwdriver at a flea market only to find that it chipped away after its first use? What if a fragment caught in your eye? What kind of bargain is that? There are millions of such stories with far worse consequences. A bargain is a quality item at a lower price, not a substandard product that looks like a steal.

If you're out to make a quick buck and you have any intention of taking safety shortcuts, don't. You pose a real danger to the safety of all of us that you deceive into buying your product. Enough said.

Money Falling from the Sky?

It won't always happen and you may have to try several times but as a result of your P.R. campaign, sometimes money does seem to fall from the sky. Some of you may be approached by people who want to help fund your efforts. You never know who's out there reading and the more relevant your media targets, the great the possibilities of hearing from real prospects. These prospective customers or buyers fall into two basic categories:

1) The first is one who will give you a sizable amount of capital, essentially as a loan secured by your product. That kind of offer can tempt a lot of us but it may be plain foolish to take on a loan burden at this stage of the game.
2) You could also be approached by the venture capitalist. This person may advance you a certain amount of money for the development of your product. You will pay him back by pledging to this person a modest percentage of your net profits for a specific amount of time.

My rule of thumb for money offers is - don't take it unless you legitimately need it for your venture. Money, by itself, at the wrong time doesn't always spell opportunity. Even with the absolute best of intentions, you are going to run into situations that may shock your sensibilities to the core. Broken promises, broken contracts, snake oil - the lessons come hard and fast. As long as you keep your sense of humor, you can persist and prevail.

Each chapter has represented specific missions for you to focus upon and achieve. You've come this far so you know your idea is a feasible one. A wonderful elderly Mexican friend always used to say, "Poco a poco, Caminos lejos." Translation: "Step by step, we walk far."

So keep walking and protect yourself by protecting your interest in your creation. Economically successful nations are built on productivity, and productivity makes money, not the other way around.

FREE ENTERPRISE

How To Present Your Prototype to the Market

You have now gotten your product to the genuine pre-production stage. You have either married a company, or you have ventured out on your own. In either case, we have just barely begun to make things happen. Something you created or some concept you introduced is ready to happen on a level where it could prove profitable. You're excited, and you're already picking out the color of your Rolls Royce. Or your associated company, usually small, is hopeful that your product is going to work out. What do you do? Do you make thousands of 'em? Millions? "Why not!," you think. Everything's ready to go. You and/or your developers have worked all the bugs out, and everyone seems to be suggesting "Full Speed Ahead." Even if that's what your manufacturing associates or whoever are suggesting, present them with this premise and option.

Premise: All parties with a vested interest want your idea to bear fruit as soon as possible so that a healthy road to profit can be realized. Of course! Well, if your associates agree with this premise, then you should propose the following option.

Option: In that no one wants the road to profit interrupted once full-fledged sales begin, you need to do one final test. Your associates may be somewhat annoyed at your insolence and suggestion of any delay at this point. You've already run a P.R. reaction test. You and maybe some technicians have tried to anticipate each and every pitfall. You never know how your users are really going to react once they start using your product. Up to now, all of our tests and theories are only models that may anticipate what consumer reaction will be.

Even some consumers have told you they know the idea is going to be a hit. Will they say the same thing after they've actually used and worked with your product? No guarantees. One final test may save you a lot of problems down the road. If we are representing a new product, we attempt to give away 20 to 100 of the product before releasing it for actual sale. With high-tech products, your budget may limit you from doing this. Even if you can get a few out in a good public field test, the benefits could save you a small fortune down the road.

Some pre-market tests involve thousands of giveaways or test-sales in various geographical areas. The majority of you will not need to go to such extremes.

Find Out Before You're In Too Deep

The time to make your mistakes is backstage, i.e. our testing phases. Relatively private mistakes are nothing compared to that same mistake times a thousand or a million. Protect yourself. And take chances? Absolutely. You gain nothing if you take no chances, but concurrently, you'll make no progress if you don't protect each step.

You've heard the expression, "Worst Case Scenario." What if wayward finances turn your best friend into your worst enemy? What if you're sloppy about the test-

Sometimes, all your media efforts have to do is start the ball rolling and then, let the media take over.

ing phases? Who's liable? You? Your affiliates? Plan and aim for success, but don't let your anxieties stop you from protecting yourself. And keep up that friendly relationship with your attorney. You can haggle most of the details, but your attorney can often very quickly insure that you made the agreement you thought you made.

Building good solid business friends can make a real difference. If your concept doesn't quite work out as planned the first time, don't write off some of your original associates. If they like the way you have presented yourself and your ideas they may well be apt to try it again with you.

After all, who is going to know more about what steps not to take than you? So let's see how well you can observe, anticipate and correct mistakes. Give your product or service to some average users for no charge, if possible. Let them play with it and run it through the mill for a few weeks or longer if necessary. Major corporations do this all the time.

Encourage your subjects to be ruthless and excessive but not dangerous. Then go back to them and beg for their worst, meanest criticism of your concept. If they love it and have nothing rotten to say, persist until they come up with something good and negative.

Make certain you are in the proper frame of mind. Listen carefully to what your test market has to say. Write or record this feedback, and thank your subjects. Do not argue with them. Even though your concept may be very dear to you, just throw your pride out the window for now.

Then go home and decipher the valid from the far-fetched. If you evaluate your data correctly, your pride will prevail in the end. If necessary, retrieve all of your products and bring them back to the drawing board.

If you had, say 100 random test subjects and their responses were generally and genuinely favorable, that can be interpreted as a very healthy sign. If some of your subjects almost fight you and refuse to give it back, that's an even better sign, as you'll see in the next chapter. If you got a lot of tomatoes in your face, fine. Go back and patiently make those changes. Then take a moment to thank your lucky stars that you have saved all interested parties from a devastating recall or worse. If ever you could tastefully recite the phrase, "An ounce of prevention is worth a pound of cure," and sound convincing, this has to be that time.

Don't Neglect the Details

You may not be ready to present your idea which may be perfectly fine at this stage. But for those who are ready for their first phase of presentation to your prospects, the time is right.

In a tough economy, you need to reach far more prospects to achieve the same level of sales as in a healthy economy. Direct Response advertising can help to make up that difference.

FREE ENTERPRISE

Create Inexpensive Resources While Maintaining Quality

"Let's see. Do I want to spend thousands of dollars or hundreds of dollars (or even less) to achieve the same result?"

Of course you want to spend as little as possible to achieve a quality result. Your job is to convince your buyer of your professionalism. And if you can make a perfect-prototype that will impress and convince your prospect, isn't that the wisest way to go?

We've seen it all or maybe we should say, we've seen them both - the big money deals and the small money deals. We've seen plastic mixing cup sets designed, engineered (including molds made) for over $150,000 (yes that is a ridiculous amount of money). We have seen a similar competitive set made for almost no money. What's true here, as in most situations in our lives is that some people buy more wisely than others.

In the following Manufacturing *EconoGraph*, our first subject (A), could have developed that same concept for as little money as was spent by our second subject, the much more astute **(Subject B)**. Don't be alarmed by the extreme cost differences. We've been around a long time and that's why we've been able to come up with examples like this one.

The *Econograph* on the following page reflects the absolute best and least expensive and the absolute worst and most expensive ways to put a product or service together.

You may very well not be able to put together all the resources required to do as well as subject 'B', but hopefully you'll learn how to get as close as possible. But for those of you right now who are 'A's, study B's approach very carefully.

A true cause, draws.

Which Way Do You Want to Do It?

	Subject A	Subject B
Product: Water Bottle with Self-Contained Filtration System		
Prototype/model made?	Yes	Yes
Prototype Made From?	Clay	Scrap Plastic
Cost of Prototype?	$25,000	Under $200
Was prototype shown to prospects?	Yes	Yes
If yes, to whom?	Investors, Manufacturers	Investors, Manufacturers
Press via news releases, etc.	No	Yes, to test concept
Were critiques carefully evaluated before production?	No	Yes

FINAL MANUFACTURING

	Subject A	Subject B
Materials:	**Polypropylene**	**Plastic Polypropylene Plastic non-Toxic, Basphenol-free**
Design cost	$10,000	**Under $100 with balance paid by manufacturer**
Engineering costs	**$140,000 for mold, tool, die**	Paid by Manufacturer
Most work done by...	Outside vendors	Inventor/Owner
Inventor's experience relative to the idea?	**None**	**Apprentice draftsman for an injection molding firm**

PRODUCTION

	Subject A	Subject B
Quantity of initial run?	20,000 units	300 units (after '10' test)
Cost for initial run?	$8,000 - $1.60 per unit	$1,200 - $4 per unit
Feedback from initial distribution trials:	**Minor changes but must scrap first 20,000 units**	**Positive with minor modifications**
Results P.O. received.	**Yes**	**Yes**
Profitable by:	Two Years	Month 3.
Total Investment	$160,500	Under $1,900

FREE ENTERPRISE

You could swap out chocolate chip cookie, audio or video production, anything. Or anything. The key is to not overdo development until you are reasonably confident that you have a market.

Though these contrasts seem hard to fathom, these stories happen all the time. Why is it that some people work wisely into profit while others merely spend themselves into discouragement? Which are you...perhaps a little of both? Well, that's why you bought this book. Are you getting your hands dirty or are you paying to watch from behind the front lines. Are your labors or value or talents somehow contributing to the profit or loss of your venture, are you shopping around, comparing costs, looking for team players or co-venturers?

Aim to think and work like Subject B because that's how everyday people create opportunities for themselves; by truly becoming an integral part of their idea, while teaming up when necessary with appropriate players versus merely contracting with various vendors.

How to Be a 'B' From A to Z

We already know how Subject A thinks. He believes you need to spend your way to success. He either has a lot of money or, has raised a great deal and is simply buying whatever he thinks he needs. Subject A figures: why analyze a problem when you can purchase a solution.

Whoever thought having too little money could be an asset? Not people who starve, or who have to sleep in their offices and skip meals to make ends meet. But there's one thing a poor entrepreneur/creator/dreamer does have and that's the no-money option. Subject B had to approach every step as if he had no money for one simple reason — he had no money. Buying a solution was just not an option. But he did have determination, creativity, some applicable talent and a little space in his dirty little garage.

Now of course each situation is different. Maybe you do have a lot of money. It doesn't matter. The lessons are still the same. Every time B had a challenge or problem, he would find a solution using everything he had, with the exception of money. Having no money compelled him to think and make maximum use of his creativity and resources. He was determined to earn his market share.

While B wanted to make a model, he did not have the money to hire a draftsperson or designer or anyone. But he did have some scraps of plastic and some glue and some sandpaper and a can of spray-paint. And he also had the commitment to spend most evenings after work in his garage working on his model using whatever he could find. Until many months and many inexpensive failures later, he is concept began to work close to what he had envisioned. In lieu of money he gave his labor, his time and his own resources.

News to your relevant industry should embrace one consistent thread for your efforts: No Cost.

Alternatives and Connecting Those Dots

Still, Subject B's approach was not, and is not, the only way to proceed. Some ideas can be presented merely as a drawing or in the case of service ideas, a brief report. The key is structuring your concept so it captures the imagination of that right manufacturer, distributor, buyer or rep.

Sometimes that will require a long hard road, and sometimes the right conversation with the proper trusted prospect can get you well on your way. If your idea has some relevancy to your gifts or your developing gifts, don't kill it with bad financial decisions. Find a way. Know that your aim is a top-quality result, but think as if you have no money.

Here's where we learn the importance of 'starting small'. You don't rent an office right away when your living-room, garage or kitchen will suffice. And you don't expand without demand. All of this backdrop should be stimulating you to rethink any previous notions you held about building your model. We know from experience that a great many of you previously assumed that you simply had to hire someone to build a model or to consult on the beginning aspects of your concept. The following is designed to dispel those thoughts.

FREE ENTERPRISE

Creative, Money-Saving Alternatives for Starting Your Concept

Traditional Method		Creative, Money-Saving Alternative
1) Raise Money To Fund Venture Create basic Goals and steps to get there	OR	**TEST IT FOR FREE**
2) Pay substantial fees to consult with various with various experts in the field.	OR	**Get the same Advice for free by simply interviewing experts in the field**
3) Hire and pay a general staff.	OR	**Build a non-paid Team of relevant experts who will share in the profits**
4) Hire (and pay) a design/ engineering expert relevant to field.		**Nope**
5) Hire a designer or artist to create a non-working model.		**Nope**
7) Purchase fully functional components and then assemble concept or with hired experts.		**Definitely Not**
8) Hire various marketing and advertising experts to present concept to market and spend Thousands or Millions	OR OR	**develop a series of free press releases to advertise and test feasibility of concept. If a businesses or service concept, describe in detail as if your are already in business. If testing a product or If testing a product, include a virtual drawing.**

RESULTS

Concept infeasible. Losses significant. Company dissolved.	**Concept also infeasible but since virtually no money was spent to test and evaluate the same concept, team easily moves onto the next idea.**

Don't believe what you're told or sold, believe what's proving to bring in the gold.

What were <u>you</u> going to pay to start your venture?

Spending an uncontrolled amount of money on the model/test stage before gauging the reaction of various prospects can become a lesson so expensive as to cost you the hope of an idea. Even if you have spent too much on your product so far, now you know better and now you can better manage your budget.

Given the base from above, let's now consider some of the creative ways to put your venture together, understanding that we are only limited by our own temporary lack of knowledge. So let's explore some additional alternatives.

POWERPOINTER SIXTEEN
Thinking Success or Failure

Negative Thinking in the form of paralyzing fear or anxiety can overtake us at any time. Thought attacks are harmful, destructive thoughts that have destroyed some of the best laid plans.

Thought attacks are one of the subconscious mind's greatest tools to disarm the unsuspecting victim. The great thing about thought attacks is that it is only a signpost that our thinking has become contaminated by our over-active minds. Gently become aware that a thought attack is occurring, quiet down and let it pass.

1) Identify and admit that you are having a thought attack.
2) STOP whatever you're doing or whatever conversation you're having because it can only bring out the worst in you and others around you.
3) Take a couple of deep breaths and bring yourself to a rational and non-hostile place.
4) Recognize that the negative thoughts were simply created by your thinking and that, you can choose to change course and, think differently.
5) When you feel like you're back to a rational place, observe how much better things look and how many more possibilities you have.
6) If you're in a conversation, restart by saying something to the effect of: "Let me approach this another way…"

Often the best thing is when things don't go as we plan because that helps us to discover new possibilities. Don't panic, simply learn, adapt and use the lesson to improve your process.

FREE ENTERPRISE

CORE STRATEGIES AND TACTICS NUMBER TWENTY-FIVE
Create a Guarantee. Guarantees come in many forms but the key point is that they stand as a commitment to excellent service and a job well done. Prospects feel more reassured with a guarantee in place.

HOW TO SUPERCHARGE THIS TACTIC: Let the prospect see that you'll do whatever it takes to get the job done right and they will come to rely on you for a broader range of services.

HOW CAN YOU ENGAGE THIS RIGHT NOW FOR YOUR VENTURE?

_____

_____

_____

CORE STRATEGIES AND TACTICS NUMBER TWENTY-SIX
Sell While You Sleep. Your website, radio ads, infomercials, yellow pages, or any exposure you create should be working for you 24/7. If relevant to your venture, your website should have e-commerce capability so every time you wake up, you're richer. Also, offer a small discount for Internet, email, or orders by fax. This encourages customers to make use of your automated ordering systems and helps you to conserve valuable employee time.

HOW TO SUPERCHARGE THIS TACTIC: Create web specials and then refer to them in your print or radio ads and even your brochures. You can and should rest but your communications to prospects never should.

HOW CAN YOU ENGAGE THIS RIGHT NOW FOR YOUR VENTURE?

_____

_____

_____

CORE STRATEGIES AND TACTICS NUMBER TWENTY-SEVEN
Make Your Website and Yellow Pages Ads Work Very Hard Together. Having a website and Yellow Pages Ad are essential for building virtually any business. In your website you must create something that gives visitors a rea-

son to return and via your keywords and multitudes of free directory listing both on line and, in print, you need to be the easiest to find for those already actively seeking your services. If you're running a restaurant, why not offer a daily Internet work lunch special for groups. If you have a business for saving wildlife, have the latest news feeds about your work and how it relates to your visitor. Most importantly, give people a good reason to use your service instead of the competition, similar to your call-to-action in your brochure.

HOW TO SUPERCHARGE THIS TACTIC: Create ever-changing web specials. Also, advertise a special website discount code in your Yellow Pages ad.

HOW CAN YOU ENGAGE THIS RIGHT NOW FOR YOUR VENTURE?

CORE STRATEGIES AND TACTICS NUMBER TWENTY-EIGHT

Market Time. We've discussed earlier how to find more time for you. It's just as valuable to your customers so wherever you can help save them time or aggravation, do so.

HOW TO SUPERCHARGE THIS TACTIC: When selling, consider producing a chart that shows prospects all the advantages and degrees of savings in time, money, headaches or anything else you can document to them.

HOW CAN YOU ENGAGE THIS RIGHT NOW FOR YOUR VENTURE?

Products don't roll when prospects roll their eyes.

FREE ENTERPRISE

Progress Journal: (please feel free to copy or scan this page only)

_____

_____

_____

_____

_____

_____

_____

_____

_____

_____

_____

_____

_____

_____

_____

_____

Your Signature_____Date_____

CHAPTER SEVEN

INITIAL SALES

"Hello Out There. What Do You Think?"

"For entrepreneurs, the most beautiful words in the English language are: 'I think I'll buy it'."

Overview

Ideas that give us growth and enlightenment are well and good, but when we convert these ideas into potential sales, now we're really connected. We now move on to building from feedback to refine your concept.

> **Activator Steps for this Chapter**
> **1) Create initial target linkage.**
> **2) Turn respondents into sales.**

Create Initial Target Linkage

It was frustrating in the beginning when we told you not to bother your friends at parties. You wanted to brag about this spectacular romance you were having with an idea.

Think back at what a shabby state your idea was in back then. What would your friends and associates have thought of you if that spark fizzled out? Now you are ready to profit from a little showing off. You've made it this far, and you're going all the way. It's time for them to bother you at the party.

We initiate our sales chain by taking that literary work of art you created in the previous chapter and getting it published. Call two local newspapers and tell them what you're up to - "Local Citizen Makes Good." Every paper has a space for that kind of material. Send them or if possible, present in person your paragraphs about your widget, but NO PICTURES, PLEASE! of you or especially of your product. All you're aiming to do with these particular P.R. announcements is to create curiosity – a tease. This valuable publicity should not cost you one red cent to run in your local papers.

And make extensive use of both email and the Internet. There are a number of press release websites relevant to your product and most of them require no fee to post your announcement. Remember, your opportunities for publicity and networking are only limited by both your imagination and enthusiasm.

FREE ENTERPRISE

There's no reason to worry whether your writing is good enough for the paper. If they need to, they'll perfect your writeup for you, free of charge. Then you'll have professional copy to adapt for future use.

Local Magazines and Ezines

Plan these few releases in the papers at one-week intervals. Locate a local magazine and online newsletter or ezine, and see if you can arrange publication of your release. If you know of a local trade magazine relevant to your idea then send your copy to them. Otherwise, just one or two local neighborhood or regional magazines will work just fine. We'll learn how to utilize those trade magazines in upcoming chapters.

Not every publication or website will accommodate your needs, but many will. The magazine releases should appear about three to five weeks after your newspaper releases. But generally, the Internet postings are almost immediate. That will give you more rewrite time, if needed. And always try to include some form of professional picture or diagram because they help to catch attention and more effectively deliver your message.

Radio and TV

What about radio or TV? Is there a local radio station or two that your friends listen to? Radio and TV stations have spots called P.S.A.'s (Public Service Announcements). You can learn more about the potential magic of PSA's in the special segment of this book.

Cable TV and Community Television are giving the small towns a stronger voice with regard to local media happenings. We're not asking you to put your face on TV yet, but a lot of these small town cable stations have TV bulletin boards. Get your announcement on TV if applicable.

Don't stare at your email box expecting miracles to happen. Some of you may get two responses. Some of you may get 20. Be patient. This is feedback and refinement time.

Do *YouTube*?

New technologies often first appear as confusing novelties. YouTube suffered this fate during its inception. So what if anyone could post any video on line? Today of course, YouTube is a corporate Billion-Dollar sensation because it allows anyone to post or look at anything in living video form.

Now, when a technology is new, most people assume it will be too confusing or complicated to figure out or incorporate into their lifestyle or business model. But often

Often but not always, the Internet can transform our media efforts from 'write for print' to 'right now' and in your lifetime, you will actually witness the slow and painful death of many great print publications.

the opposite is true because new technologies can make our lives or business aims easier and more accessible. Such is the case with YouTube.

Imagine having a product that you want to demonstrate to someone across the country or, across the globe. You can fly to that prospect, demonstrate your concept and then, hope they will commit OR, you can post it on YouTube for free, direct many prospects in many parts of the globe to it, for the same effort. Which makes more sense to you?

Sending someone a YouTube demonstration is as simple as emailing them the URL (www. etc) where the video is located on YouTube. You is a tremendous advance is free media technology.

Take a little time to familiarize yourself with YouTube so you understand how it works. Think of it a free means of delivering or presenting your message to distant prospects and with the cost of fuel and travel these days, increased use of electronic communication where applicable makes perfect sense. Now, as I stated earlier, never pass up a face-to-face meeting when possible but when you can't do that feasible, YouTube.

Positive Blog Ratio

Some of you will build your concept through blogging. Having a blog site can produce many benefits. It can grow a swirl of interest and momentum, you can learn so much about your concept and its possibilities and, it can establish you as an authority, in a similar fashion that articles can. In addition, the interactivity with your audience can greatly increase credibility and public trust.

For the most part, you will discover that your blogs, feedback, articles and general comments will be met with support and enhancement. Most of you will scarcely encounter a single serious detractor. However some of you may encounter a 'flamer' or detractor.

There is nothing wrong with that and do not be put off or discouraged by these individuals. In fact, as you resolve an issue with them, other sideliners will be impressed with your ability to both stand up and, resolve problems.

This section is for those very few who may encounter negative feedback in their blog or online. I urge you not to let these kinds of generally worthless attacks stop you for your worthy aims. If, however, you've written a lot of books as I have or, if you find yourself in the public spotlight, invariably someone is going to say something negative about you. The vast majority of these will be obvious pranksters who are simply seeking to attack and create trouble for the fund of it. Most of your customers and colleagues are well aware of this. But there are cyber-stalkers out there and they are a fact of life, especially, if you've grown substantially.

Keep watching and thinking about where and how your concept can fit into the media pipeline.

FREE ENTERPRISE

Generally, these are petty people who slink around anonymously and deliver their attacks. This is nothing new; these are usually cowardly individuals who have discovered the wonder of the internet and most decent people see them this way. So don't take it too personally if you are the victim of this form of slander. And for the most part, you can ignore them but if it gets out of hand, you'll need to pay attention and set the record straight.

For the most part, you can simply ignore these childish or petty attacks and the perpetrators will simply fade away. If you don't fuel them, they will generally move on. However, on occasion, someone might blog something that could be harmful to your efforts.

Tips for Protecting your Good Name

1) **Determine what is worth responding to and, what should simply be ignored..** Sometimes, we'll hear something bad about ourselves and feel very insulted. However, it isn't of much consequence to our cause. These kinds of comments can include personal insults, sarcastic remarks or ridiculous personal attacks.

What they all have it common is an air of juvenility and thoughtlessness. For these, simply put yourself in the place of your loyal and supportive readers who will most likely see the comments as vacuous. You are best off by ignoring these and they will fade away. In addition, you will notice that most attacks are from anonymous sources. Your supporters will notice this as well. Generally. Worthless attacks come from an anonymous source.

Then there's the other kind of attack that will appear to contain substance and targeted vitriol specifically designed to cause harm to your image or enterprise. They will be accusatory in nature and may often refer to something in your past. True of not, this kind of attack must not be ignored. Otherwise, people will simply assume that it's the truth. For these, you need to do the following:

a) If the allegations are untrue. State as much in a simple denial (These unfortunate statements are not true and are simply designed to cause harm by deliberate distortion of the facts. The facts are...) Next, insist that the attacker identify themselves. Generally, that will be the end of it but if not, armed with the truth, you will prevail and these individuals will be exposed a petty and malicious.

b) If the allegations have a thread of truth to them but have been blown out of proportion, gracefully and stalwartly own up to the truth, with an explanation. This does two things. It shows that you can admit your mistakes and learn from them and it takes the destructive power away from the attacker and places you

The best dilemma in the world is suddenly receiving a LARGE Purchase Order and wondering how you're going to fill it.

in control of the situation and then, you can direct the thread back to the topic at hand.

Dilution

If the attacks are severe and ongoing, you should still politely respond as described above. But you can dilute the attacks by
encouraging your supporters to become profits of truth, To do this, they will visit any and all relevant blog and websites, wherever there is an open forum and very subtly, sing your praises. Their submissions must be subtly positive or they won't be viewed as credible. You can also construct your own web or blogsite and coalesce your positive elements and filter out the bad ones.

What this does is create a far higher ratio of positive things about you versus negative. And when it comes to slander and gossip, the majority rules so if the majority are positive about you, this situation will turn out as a positive publicity opportunity and you will be better established than before.

In my thirty years in and out of the public spotlight, I've been lucky that most of my reviews have been fairly positive but you do get the negative ones popping up. I usually thank those people for taking the time to enlighten me on my short-comings and that's usually all I need to do. I also point out the nature and intention of my eleven books which all center around healing and empowerment. They are positive and supportive of people.

Most importantly, I'm not injured nor affected by people exercising their right to free speech. Differing opinions help to enrich our culture and broaden our thinking. Imagine being a baseball player in a stadium with 50,000 people. You are the visiting team and most of the fans hate you. What are you going to do, feel upset from each of the thousands of insulting diatribes being hurled against you? Of course not. You're going to focus on your mission and hit a home run.

What about Lawsuits? Slander, stalking, harassment or any other form of criminal mischief, are criminal acts, whether in the real world or, the virtual one.. More and more laws are being amended to include all electronic media. So if you feel you've genuinely been harmed by a vicious attack, and can track down your attacker, you may have a case and good cause for action. You can seek out an attorney for a consult but he will probably pay far more attention if you can track down the perpetrator. In addition, you will have to clearly demonstrate that harm was done to you or your business and that the accused was not merely exercising freedom of speech

The pursuit of Free Enterprise really should be largely free.

FREE ENTERPRISE

Turn Respondents Into Sales

Okay, you have gotten your initial P.R. going and your releases will all be appearing within the next month or two. You shall be looking for just a small handful of credible responses. You should correspond or preferably meet face to face with at least five inquiries.

Why did they respond to your announcement? Find out what their specific interest might be in your gem. Build a file of each contact and their talents. Don't eliminate anyone as a possible participant at some future date unless he or she is dishonest or is simply trying to make money off of you.

All these people should be teaching you how to perfect your product. With every productive meeting, your product should improve, as will your own value as an authority. It's a good thing you held out through this chapter because this is when the big business breakthroughs begin to happen.

Many of you will clearly see how to move ahead with all the energy in the world. Many of you will actually get offers of employment or capital to make your product go. Some of you will begin to create potential distribution avenues. This is a good time to court distributors and reps because they can give you an idea of what how your product or service might best be shaped before you finalize it all.

If these releases don't catapult you into stardom, that's perfectly all right. The point is you have learned to develop a good idea without selling out or losing your shirt. Depending on your situation, you have saved anywhere from several hundred — to several thousand — dollars. And every time you do this, you'll get better at it.

The Second Round

After a few weeks or months, you may want to repeat this P.R. query process. To get a release in the same periodical again, announce a new development in your work. Do not do more than two of these preliminary release programs because we want to get on to our production phase.

Party Time!

Now you can throw a party. Invite your friends as well as some of the new business contacts you made to celebrate the birth of your idea. The party should help create momentum and support. In a positive social environment where people are feeling their best, you'll get some very good advice and feedback. Just be dutiful about following up on the promises people make. That's your only way of finding out if the promises are real or not.

If your group is in a really giving mood, give them some Post-it® notes, have them write their ideas down (one per Post-it®) and stick them up on the wall. Create a com-

Purpose, peace of mind and profit can all go hand in hand.

petition to see who can get the most ideas up on the wall. When the flow of ideas slows, have the group move the ideas around on the wall to put similar ideas into groupings. When most of the movement has stopped, then have the group create several word titles for each grouping. As the party closes down, thank everyone for their input, and then get to work.

First-Timers Beware

Let the ideas flow. If your product requires any degree of assembly, you are looking for those components. For first-timers, we have two bits of advice about components.

1) Beware of the high cost of buying too cheaply. Why buy sub-standard or lower quality parts that could destroy your entire project, not to mention your business credibility. Components like that aren't bargains at any price.

Whenever we trade stories with electronics marketers, we always seem to have a new battery-story to laugh about. When first-timers have a product that requires pre-installation of household-type batteries, they always head across the border or overseas where they buy batteries for next to nothing. These foreign specials generally last just until the consumer gets the failed product. After all recalls for replacement with quality batteries plus repair of damage from their leaking predecessors, it's a bit difficult to view those cheap batteries as any kind of bargain.

2) Make every effort to buy locally. If price is your problem here, negotiate. It's often better to keep it all local where you can have control.

If you're in the U.S., you've heard though that your basic assembly labor costs are much lower overseas, but added to your overseas costs are the costs of shipping, insurance, travel, etc. And international patent protection from such assembly plants is a real nightmare.

There are many able labor/assembly outlets throughout the U.S. whose owners want to work out a cost-effective arrangement. Give them a chance. If your product requires simple assembly, why not consider the mentally or physically disabled or institutionalized people who could do an excellent job for similar costs? If your product is more sophisticated, explore various senior citizens or veterans organizations before you go trading overseas, and what about a local trade or business school? There are always options as long as you manage quality and safety. You'll be more than just pleasantly surprised, as you explore these options in fact, your efforts could make you a community benefactor if you create new jobs.

So for now, you have this wealth of knowledge and excitement that you have generated. How far you have come, yet don't be tempted to rest on a gratified ego. You can play those games after you succeed otherwise you'll kill your progress.

"Free' + asking for your credit card number = unexpected charges or, even fraud.

FREE ENTERPRISE

You must organize all this data to give you fuel for progress. A danger point here is weak follow-up. Keep a planning calendar or PDA handy and be responsible about all your prospects. Keep your development meetings to the point and don't let them stray. This is a time for good ideas and not for gambling.

How to Create More Contacts

How many people or situations did you miss today that could have made a major difference in your venture? Often times, there is someone you already know who could really help you out but you're not sure how to approach them. Here are four simple ways just by using you email:

1) Go through your email and pick out people you've simply lost contact with for no particular reason. Send them a brief note re-introducing yourself. " I just wanted to say hello and find out what you're up to." Or, I wanted to make sure I have your updated contact information. (www.Plaxo.com and www.linkedin.com are also two effective tools you can use but I like the personal note.
2) Let stale contacts know about a new project you're working on and, ask them if they have any ideas.
3) As a particular question relative to someone's particular area of expertise. "I was wonder if I could ask your advice..etc" This can be very flattering and, open the door for deeper business contact.
4) This is a tough one and it doesn't work if you parted because of
an old financial dispute. But if you had a friend or business associate where you had some minor differences, consider

Contacting them and asking for forgiveness. "I'm sorry we had those differences before. I'd like to see if we could work things out and perhaps, work together again. What can I do to make it right..etc" This approach can really impress a former associate and often inspire them to want to try again with you.

POWERPOINTER SEVENTEEN
Building from Feedback

Earlier on as your idea was just being born; we collected vital opinions to improve your idea. Now is the time to gain feedback on the improvements you made. Use the logs on this and the following page to gage responses from the newer, professional critics and consultants that you'll be dealing with, during this and especially the next chapter.

When prospects are searching directories or Yellow Pages, they are not simply browsing, but are usually ready to commit. So be ready to deliver.

Professional People You Know
Name, Opinion

___

Your Reaction

___

Name, Opinion

___

Your Reaction

___

Professionals and Relevant People Developed Through all New Contacts, Press Releases, Networking, etc.
Name, Opinion

___

Your Reaction

All you need to do is create a thoughtful positive impression for your idea.

FREE ENTERPRISE

Name, Opinion

Your Reaction

ACTIVATOR SEVENTEEN
How to Overcome Burnout

Gordon Bronson

It's one thing to simply be tired or frustrated where some simple tips can help you bounce back but burnout is a more serious matter that suggests a loss of healthy productive energy.

Putting any concept into action requires full enthusiasm. You work relentlessly, striving for excellence. Time and ordinary routine succumb to the laser-like focus on the vision, causing the brain to be stuck in the 'on' position.

As you have by this time created a vision in which you truly believe, invariably you'll also reach certain points of mental hyper-drive where your mind and creativity are functioning at an explosive pace. That's wonderful; that's often how great ideas become something even greater. However, as with everything in this life, for every intoxicating experience, there also exists the morning after - the creativity hangover. Both of us are

Sensible solutions to widespread problems merit widespread media attention.

INITIAL SALES

intense workers and players, and sometimes we don't listen to what our bodies are telling us because we become so enthusiastic about our work. As a result, we both have experienced serious bouts of adrenal exhaustion, and both have finally learned that you can indeed 'sprain your brain,' and get so involved in the vision that you become its prisoner instead of its beneficiary. Hence, part of reaching your vision entails appropriate pacing. Following are some important tips for preventing burnout and insuring progress:

1) **Give It Your Best** - You want to make your project work and that means you have to give it your best. Identify your best attributes and contribute accordingly. Don't get bogged down in an area where you have no proficiency. You'll waste valuable time and increase frustration.

2) **"Can't we all just get along?"** (No, not yet.) When building teams, you certainly want the finest human resources possible. It's also important to note that the whole idea of team entails mutual cooperation. No venture is ever any better than the sum total of the personalities behind it. Make sure you have people around who:
- will be responsible and dedicated about their work.
- will be good ego-free listeners and contributors.
- are neither greedy nor inflexible.
- can manage anger and frustration in a mature manner.

3) **Honor Your 'Cycle'** - Even God rested on the seventh day. Work productively and efficiently, but don't merely labor without grander visions. As with overeating, know when enough is enough, when you have done all you planned for that given day or week and when it's time to rest. Don't over-indulge in your own enthusiasm. Train yourself to rest with a clear mind no matter what happens that day.

4) **Allow Things to Flow According to Chaos and Stumble Theory** - Many of the things we experience in daily life operate according to Chaos Theory principles including our projects. Chaos Theory says that even in the midst of chaos is order. So, don't sweat it. If your project seems a little out of control, it will all come together in ways you can't foresee. We can also learn from Chaos Theory that the period directly preceding a breakthrough is often the most chaotic and frustrating. So, push on through until something manifests in your favor.

5) **Keep Your Sense of Humor** or — Now is a Great Time to Get One if you've Never Had One.

6) **Declare Your Aims and Intention to Get There** - You've set your sites on a good idea and you're making it through but there comes a point in every venture where you don't know were to turn next. You still know this idea is good and the right one for you but, you're not certain how to really make the breakthrough

FREE ENTERPRISE

that will help you make it through all of the current headaches and challenges. What do you do?

While the answer is simple, it is no shortcut for the work. What you need to do is identify where you want to take your idea and then, *declare* that you will get there. You may not know how at present but make the declaration anyway. This serves as a means to help you to maintain your focus and will.

What Can We Actually Learn From Hulk Hogan

The tens of millions of dedicated wrestling fans know that it's pure and contrived choreography. Still they watch and cheer feverishly and relentlessly for their favorites. Certainly, the Hulkster has wrestled with severe reputational turmoil since his retirement (and my heart goes out to the Graziano family) but in his day in that magic rink, Hulk Hogan was one of the great inspirer.

The story was always the same. He would face insurmountable foes and take a horrible beating. Fans would be left breathless, jaws dropping, as they wondered each time, "Would he get up again or...was this the end for the Hulkster? Then more pummeling and somewhere in every spectator, disbelief was totally suspended as something in us pained for him. He's already defeated. He can't take anymore. He's a beaten man; it's time for him to surrender. There he is, motionless on the mat. Is he in fact really hurt? He must be. Is he dead?

Seconds feel like hours when suddenly, the camera finds an index-finger moving slightly as his opponent climbs to the top of the rope and readies yet another crushing blow. Next we see a hand move and his breathing seems to be getting stronger. But it's too late as his mighty opponent readies his final deadly assault, perched to leap down on Hulkster's head at any moment. The opponent leaps. It's the end. Or is it?

In a model of the most prurient of timing, at the last nano-second, the Hulkster rolls out the way of a certain end and his mighty opponent crushes to the mat in sheer agony. The crowd roars and with each crescendo, the Hulk seems to find strength from nowhere.

Now, he's up, his hand cocked to his ear, showing more strength with each increased level of the crowd's noise. The more he hears, the stronger he gets, until the crowd has readily fueled his spirit with ample strength to effortlessly pjn his opponent.

This isn't just a big fairy tale anymore than a great film that awakens something in us. Like the scene in classic film *Perfect Storm* where doomed Captain Billy Kine is laughing at every wave the Andrea Gale triumphs through successfully. One more bridge to a possibility of hope.

And where do hope and strength come from, vitamins, cheer leaders, reinforcement by success? No. Strength is a decision and a power that you find when it seems like there's nothing left. You start moving that little finger, you start breathing more steadily

If someone can successfully promote themselves for no reason, imagine what you could do with those same tools.

and you get up again. And as long as you are willing to get up again, you will always find a way through.

Success comes more easily than others but if you have a good concept and, refuse to give up, if you stay strong but also flexible and adjustable, you can always find something within you to make it through.

I have to note that my editor chastised me for using the doomed crew of the Perfect Storm as a model. "They died so what's the point?" The point is that they fought to the end and because they did, the drove forward right up to the end. That's the point of all we do, to drive forward in any way you can. And if you do no matter what happens, you'll have some measure of success and satisfaction.

ACTIVATOR EIGHTEEN
Practical Tips for Getting through the Tough Times

The songs have been around from the beginning of time. When you're low and feeling overwhelmed, have faith, walk on, get up and try it again. But we know that. We know what we're supposed to do when we're feeling overcome with every business challenge imaginable. What we are generally lacking are specific and tangible instructions that we can apply right now.

This is a time that any daring entrepreneur has been through more than once. It's a time when you start to actually miss your old day job because it afforded reliability and security. That's a natural plausible posture. As human beings, we want to feel safe and secure. We don't want to have to worry about payroll or, how we're going to make it through the next month.

Starting your own venture can challenge you in every way imaginable. Cash may not flow as expected in the beginning; payables may flow in at twice the expected rate. Your product or service may not deliver as originally envisioned, at least not in the beginning. So what do you do?

First of all, don't panic. If your idea was good to begin with, remain faithful to that good idea but step back for a second and consider these points:

1. **Did you budget properly for the development of your concept?** Even with all of the free systems to test, promote and develop your idea, there are costs involved. Some people automatically hire a staff before there is any demand for service, thereby draining cash before any is generated. Others will over-manufacture a product before gauging consumer response.
2. **Did you identify and pursue customers?** The sad news about advertising and publicity agencies is that you can do most of what *they* do for little or no money.

The impressive advances in electronic media are no big deal if our message is unimpressive.

FREE ENTERPRISE

3. **Have you worked to accommodate your customers?** You may have one vision fore your business but what do your customers really want?
4. **Have you created a proper pricing schedule that allows you make a fair profit and pay your bills?**
5. **If you haven't followed these basic criteria, are you prepared to make the appropriate corrections? You may have to:**
   a. **Cut back on salaries or staff.** Did you over-promise new workers? Do you really need them for as many hours as originally stated? Could part of their salary be as a commission?
   b. **Review general operating costs.** Did you rent an office when a home office would suffice for now, s your location accessible to customers?
   c. **Review pricing and fees to ensure you're making a profit while remaining competitive.**
6. **Talk to people.** One of the most vital elements to success or, to lead you to success, is to talk with people. We have become such an email-and text-message addicted society that we are forgetting how important a face-to face or, telephone conversation is.

Business survival is a choice to be both adaptive and inventive.

Go through your list of sales targets and ask anyone if they are ready to commit with you. The key driver of any business is sales or patronage so make sure you haven't become too electronic and hence, too remote from your prospects. You'll notice at the end of this book, even with the great volumes of sales, I am personally accessible to my readers.

The key is to survive in preparation to thrive. Even if you have to make cut-backs or any major modifications, as long as you can keep the idea alive, your business prospects have possibilities. It's important to have a consciousness of hope and momentum. To do that, you need to continually have a new vision for growth and sales.

For example, you may be a baker who wants to get your cakes into a fancy local hotel. Think of ways you can make a better product for them at a better price. Or, you may have a brilliant idea to make computer keyboards work more efficiently. Have you learned the steps to get your concept into the right and trusted hands?

Where there is any momentum, even if just in your imagination, there is hope and where there is hope for a good idea, there is a way to make it happen.

If two out of ten people respond favorably to your idea, why not Two-million out of Ten-Million?

The Price of Success

What is the price of success?

What does it really take to get there?

If we all believed everything we heard about how easy it was to live longer, stay in shape, look younger and, make more money, every home in America would be flooded with roomfuls of books, DVD's and exercise machines.

You'll notice that the one element missing from most infomercials and advertising campaigns is the 'W' word. Work. The reasoning is simple: Most products and books are promising to make your life easier in some way so they skip over the work element. So let's get real.

Nothing worth having will come easily but there are books and products that will make your goals more accessible. Most people believe that the purchase of a book, product or system is the first big step. A few years back, there was a diet-food supplement that sold over $100 Million worth of product which promised five to ten pounds of weight-loss in a matter of weeks. Follow-up studies showed that many people did indeed lose weight with this slickly-marketing product. Only problem was, it was later discovered that this product had no effect on weight-loss whatsoever. However, many of the people who bought the product were *ready* to lose weight and it was their dedication and commitment alone that precipitated their weight-loss.

Now there are many tried and true weight-loss products and exercise devices. But they won't work without a personal commitment from the user. This book contains everything you need to make your venturer successful but you are the catalyst to make it work.

So what is this price we have to pay for success? For those who have tried and failed to make a venture successful in the past, they may have only known discouragement, often because they find themselves in the same dilemma each time they make the effort. For some, that means, they can't get their venture to the market place or, they don't know how to promote or sell it. Often times, they place these things in the hands of someone else and when that fails, they give up as well.

When we fail at something, there is a little voice telling us why. We know subconsciously that we are holding ourselves back for any number of reasons. But it's often far too painful to listen to that little voice even if that voice holds the essential secret to the gap that is holding us back. And then we discover that is is actually not all that painful to fill in that gap. Learning to fill that gap is our personal price for success. The hope and promise of this book is to show you specific ways to fill those gaps that you never knew existed before.

No it won't be easy. It never is; there's always a price to pay for real personal success. But if you utilize this book properly, you'll find that there are more paths to success that you previously thought and that means if you are willing to dedicate yourself to making your venture successful, this book will help you make that success more accessible.

FREE ENTERPRISE

So that leaves only one question: Are you ready and willing to be successful? Don't you need to be more successful right now?

The other thing that so many small businesspeople or garage or basement entrepreneurs don't often realize is that one positive event may not produce a full upturn. For example, you may secure a strong sale or account and think, "Great, my worries are over and I'm going to be okay." People are conditioned to think this way because that is the instant-gratification miracle that has been sold to them in the media. We are conditioned to want everything now and often view one positive step up for our business as a big step. Be careful. In reality, it is probably just one of several steps you will need to make. First of all, the money may not come in for some time and what if that account falters, where will you be?

Real success for the small businessperson is not a one-shot deal where you will all the money and can now go home, like a lottery-Winner. Real success is determined by a diversity of accounts or opportunities that you create. The point is not to sit back just because you have one victory. Be proud, celebrate it for sure but understand that it is just a piece of your success.

The core of a successful business is growth so as soon as you see the indicators of that growth, look around:

* How did that first sale or account happen?
*Can you duplicate that success with a prospect with a similar profile?
* Are there completely different revenue streams you can create for your business?

Don't use the first hint of your success as an excuse to slow down. Continue on as if that first success doesn't exist. As in the movie *Perfect Storm*, they made it over many tough waves but finally, a giant wave came along and overwhelmed them. See those waves as metaphors for challenges and opportunities that make you stronger with each wave. With each success, see what you've learned and how your capabilities and confidence have expanded. You can do more now than you could just a little while ago so use that new level of competency to not just overcome new and bigger waves but to explore new oceans of opportunities.

Summary
Create initial target linkage.
- Submit your press releases for publication.
- Follow up with phone calls, when necessary.
- Seek out additional areas for media release, if applicable (radio, T.V, all over the Internet.)

Turn respondents into sales.
- Evaluate responses.
- Send out a second round of press releases.
- Throw a party and get some feedback.
- Determine how respondents helped you to make a better product.
- If your product involves manufacturing and assembly, see if you can keep it local.
- Don't get burnout. Keep up the good work.

Potential Challenges and Solutions

Challenge: Fear of using the media.
Solution: Admittedly, it can seem like a scary prospect but once you've done it, it becomes easy and fun. That local media is there to reflect news in your community. Your venture is news. Find the angle and spread the word to the best of your abilities.

Challenge: No responses to your media blitz.
Solution: It is extremely rare for no one to talk to you about your release. First, make sure your releases have been mailed, received and published. Your release may be unclear, especially if this is your first venture. Did you get all the help you needed to get your message out in an understandable fashion? If readers are at all confused they'll pass it by.

Submit revised and corrected releases to the same publications. Explain what you think happened the first time around and ask for a second chance.

If everything checks out yet you still receive no responses, call some of your friends and pick their brains. Send clippings of your write-ups to potential manufacturers, distributors, etc. and follow-up with phone calls.

Success isn't realized by some marketing guy's glitzy promise, it is a decision to do whatever it takes to achieve your worthy vision.

Challenge: Everyone's saying it's impossible for the little guy to make it against the big guys.

Solution: We have books and successful careers that prove them wrong Identify those factors that will make your idea possible.

Impossible can often be a stupid word. There is always some way to address the issue. Ridiculous, however, is a word you may want to listen to if you hear it a lot. If your venture is heading in the wrong direction, seek out the best advice you can muster and straighten it out and put those big guys in their place. Be persistent with a good idea but don't be stubborn about making a necessary change.

Challenge: Production and/or implementation seem too complicated.

Solution: Vendors and suppliers want to make money. If you can work with them to develop a marketable product, their heightened interest will help keep the assembly phase alive.

Challenge: Can't put it together in the U.S.

Solution: You probably haven't shopped around enough. U.S. suppliers go bankrupt daily because they lack sufficient financial creativity to keep making their goods in this country. How can you and a U.S. manufacturer team up to put your concept together in a cost-effective manner? Profit sharing? Other incentives?

Don't head overseas unless you've really exhausted all the possibilities, or unless yours is a task that might best benefit a developing country far more than the U.S. But be sensitive to the labor needs of your local business community.

Before You Continue . . .

- Have you made a real effort to coordinate and evaluate feedback?
- In development, are you solving the challenges by potential buyers?
- Are you building a workable team of cooperative resources?

POWERPOINTER EIGHTEEN
The Ages-Old Secret of an Attitude of Gratitude

In this developmental process, have you experienced times when you felt that your venture or you life for that matter, are going nowhere. This is a specific, quantifiable feeling where you begin to question the overall value of everything, and you wonder if you have anything of real value.

This is a normal part of the developmental process. It's the natural part that tests your resolve. What would cause you to give up? Finances? We've taken every step pos-

---

If you can find things to be grateful about your life right now, you can grow that list.

sible to protect you in that regard. Mountains of failure? That's usually part of the process which shapes your venture into something truly useful. And speaking of useful, you are useful. Have you forgotten?

The best way to be assured of success is to try to write a rational plan of attack every evening and then, wake up finding some things in your life that you are truly lucky to have. Being grateful for all that you have is a sure way to stay in a place that will foster success. Those individuals who are focused on the good in their lives are much more likely to attract others with the same attitude, which means that you'll have the greatest opportunity to attract success.

Don't be pulled into the swamp of the naysayers; you can afford that, especially in these times. They just want company for their lonely, isolating thoughts. These individuals will not encourage your growth and development. It is your job to stay in this place of gratitude if you are to succeed. Success breeds success.

Each evening, write down two things to be grateful for, and two positive things you are going to achieve. As you wake up, look at your list and think thankful thoughts. Say thank you for the simple things that you may have been overlooking. This will dissolve anxiety and negativity.

Once you feel the flow of gratitude, begin your day's journey. Occasionally, do some small unexpected act of kindness. It will come back to you. Remember, those little things that you fail to appreciate will be taken away. Then you'll wish you had been more grateful. You cannot imagine how this simple practice of appreciation will change your overall attitude.

ACTIVATOR NINETEEN
Giving Life to Your Best Idea

You've come up with an idea that excites and motivates you. It's a feeling that only comes from the prospect of something new. It's almost a sense of invincibility as you imagine how successful you will be when you get there. This excitement can last for days or weeks, as you talk about it with family and friends. Then, when it comes to taking that very first step, crash, it all drops like a stone. You want to get there, but when it really comes to taking the right steps, reality seems to rear its ugly head.

You just don't know what to do. So who do you turn to? Oh sure, there are consultants and companies more than anxious to match your excitement with promises to help you, some with good intentions and some with only the intention to take your money, and eventually your enthusiasm.

These guidelines are not about philosophy, but about doing it, and making it happen so that your concept takes shape without having to pay ridiculous fees to anyone. Yes, you have heard us state that before and will hear it again. We want to protect your dream, which leads us to the next steps:

Everything you do, right or wrong, can teach you how to do it better and make it all work together as a marketing team.

FREE ENTERPRISE

A. What Are The Most Promising Features of Your Idea?
This should be a relatively simple process. Many people should now be able to reply clearly based on all the lessons leaned exclusively through the process of advancing your concept.

_____

_____

_____

_____

_____

An important rule here is to *stay within the realm of your own capabilities, and the capabilities of your team.* To have an idea about how to make a better cell phone with no skills to engineer it, might make such a notion unattainable no matter how much faith you possess unless you have the right team to make it happen. At the same time, especially in a challenging economy, each of us is called upon to reach deeper into our talents, drive and capabilities.

As team leader, keep challenging your team to reach beyond themselves. What else can you all do together to grow this enterprise? Remember that your concepts must be relevant to your particular skill level, or reasonably attainable level. Yes, your idea will help you to grow beyond your present capabilities but keep your idea relevant so it becomes attainable. The next activator segment will prove helpful.

ACTIVATOR TWENTY
Making the Impossible Possible

There is always a way to make things work. Just look at the word always which is derived from *all ways*. If you think there isn't a way, you just haven't looked at all the possibilities or all the ways. You may not see it at the moment so you panic or stop progressing. But it's there and when you crash that drive into a frustrating obstacle, that drive can deteriorate into an unhealthy obsession. So step away from it all and allow your calmest state of mind to prevail and allow the following process to render the impossible into the very possible:

Think of this book as simply a series of innovative but easy-to-follow recipes for making your idea successful.

INITIAL SALES

1) What is your true personal goal aside from material success?

_____

_____

2) Why does it now seem obstructed?

_____

_____

_____

3) What will happen if this particular goal is not reached the way you envision it?

_____

_____

_____

4) Name five other ways that you can reach you stated goal or something similar:

_____

_____

_____

5) What will the consequences be if your goal is delayed?

_____

_____

_____

No worthy idea ever dies but it can get postponed until you have both the confidence and competence to really make it happen.

FREE ENTERPRISE

6) Will you learn new things about your idea if it's delayed and if so, how might that give you and advantage that you don't currently have?

_____

_____

7) If you are dependent upon other people to achieve your goal, how could you achieve a similar goal without them?

_____

_____

_____

8) How will this new-found independence affect your work and life in general?

_____

_____

_____

_____

_____

_____

_____

"Genius, that power which dazzles mortal eyes is oft perseverance in disguise." ~ Henry Austin

INITIAL SALES

CORE STRATEGIES AND TACTICS NUMBER TWENTY-NINE
Surprise Your Customer.
Always focus on what you can do to exceed the expectations of your customers. Excellent service will build customer loyalty through the toughest times. Do all you can to accommodate them and they will begin to rely upon you and tell their friends. Get to know your customer on a personal level. Learn something special about each prospect (dog's name, favorite activity) and make a note on their account file.

HOW TO SUPERCHARGE THIS TACTIC: Give a thoughtful gift to your key customers for the holidays. Also, send birthday cards to your customers. Consider coupons and special offers. Do all you can do to be easy to do business with, while maintaining a good profit structure!

HOW CAN YOU ENGAGE THIS RIGHT NOW FOR YOUR VENTURE?

_____

_____

_____

CORE STRATEGIES AND TACTICS NUMBER THIRTY
Send a Weekly or Monthly Email Update to Your Customer.
Include your latest services and online specials that they will only see if they read their emails. This is also an ideal way to update all addresses. In some communities, up to 15 percent of all residents relocate without informing their vendors. Send these even if you receive no response for several months. You never know when a customer might need you.

HOW TO SUPERCHARGE THIS TACTIC: Be the first with anything new about your industry. Also, be sure to update your contact information whenever possible. Many sales are lost simply due to the lack of current contact information. Also, when you're not immediately available, use your email Auto Responder. That's the free service that replies automatically when you're not able to. Use it to remind recipients of some new service or offering

HOW CAN YOU ENGAGE THIS RIGHT NOW FOR YOUR VENTURE?

_____

_____

_____

FREE ENTERPRISE

CORE STRATEGIES AND TACTICS NUMBER THIRTY-ONE
Renew Old Customers. Call old customers you haven't heard from and create a new trial/sample offer to bring them back in.

HOW TO SUPERCHARGE THIS TACTIC: *Encourage Comebacks.* Don't just ask your customers to come back, give them a reason (a free dessert, free consultation, free delivery on their next order, new and improved service..etc).

HOW CAN YOU ENGAGE THIS RIGHT NOW FOR YOUR VENTURE?

___

___

___

___

CORE STRATEGIES AND TACTICS NUMBER THIRTY-TWO
Have a Contest for Customers...But Be Creative. Customers love the idea of special service, positive surprise and, getting a little something for nothing. "Blizzard of Odds. *Guess when the next snowfall will be at Brianhead Ski Resort, Win a Ticket, Guess the Depth Too and Win a Season Pass."* Be creative and promote it well.

HOW TO SUPERCHARGE THIS TACTIC: If the contest is novel enough, you can often get free news coverage about it. What a great way to get a little extra free advertising!

HOW CAN YOU ENGAGE THIS RIGHT NOW FOR YOUR VENTURE?

___

___

___

___

___

Sustained self-employment is your best job security so don't hide your talents.

INITIAL SALES

Progress Journal: (please feel free to copy or scan this page only)

_____
_____
_____
_____
_____
_____
_____
_____
_____
_____
_____
_____
_____
_____
_____
_____
_____
_____
_____

Your Signature_____Date_____

CHAPTER EIGHT

PRICING, SALES AND DISTRIBUTION

Converting Dreams to Dollars

"Recipe for Success: One Part Need. Two Parts Heart, Shake Well."

Overview

If your idea is advancing appropriately, this becomes one of the turning-point chapters. Listen carefully to potential prospects. In roundabout ways, are any of them saying, "I might buy if you . ."?

> **Activator Steps for this Chapter**
> **1) Transition from concept to commodity.**
> **2) Get to market effectively.**
> **3) Track and Follow-up for success.**

Transition from Concept to Market

For those of you with some sales background, this is an excellent period for you. You can finally ply your trade with more product knowledge and enthusiasm than you have ever had.

A lot of you however, are chronic "sales how-to-aphobics." You're not just afraid of sales, you're twice as fearful about believing any advice regarding how you can become an able salesperson.

Pricing, sales and distribution are highly complex areas, and there are thousands of books dealing with these areas in particular. The only intention of this chapter is to make it relevant to your venture. Through this chapter, you'll get enough of a briefing to get things headed toward the results you need.

Much to your surprise, we are not going to cure you with a host of appropriate platitudes (though a few good ones come to mind). You can read every good authority and get a million good ideas. The real trick is to make it all relate to your venture.

Up until now, no book has ever proven to you that you can actually put all that good advice to work for you. If only one of these references could prove to you that you really can sell, then you would have the sufficient reinforcement to make sales happen.

Finally, you have invested in a book that's going to have you prove to yourself once and for all that you can sell, no matter what your background or fears.

"Imagination is more important than knowledge" Albert Einstein

It wasn't very difficult for most of you to engage those test subjects in the last two chapters. Did any of them really love your product or in fact express an interest in buying one? Very nice, you just made your first sale, and it didn't hurt much, did it?

Some of your test subjects have suggested refinements. Now that you have made those refinements, those subjects could also get very interested in your improved version. After all, you have improved life somehow with your idea. Everybody wants improvement in their day-to- day lives. From the simplest, most direct and most important level of sales, person to person, your final testing phase has given you more sales experience than you ever realized. Your testers have worked hard for you and now they want to buy the perfected version. To show your gratitude for their help, you will sell it to them at a greatly discounted price.

What about price?

How do you know what to charge for your goods and services? There are a few givens. In theory, merchandise must be competitively priced as perceived by the customer, but you also must make a profit. There are excellent pens for well under a dollar and there are pens priced at several hundred dollars. Therefore, competitive pricing also refers to the class and quality of the product.

Our ears ring daily from the barrage of special value sales that in essence suggest, "Get the same quality at a lower price. " Quality wars are better than price wars. Your efforts thus far should permit you to be competitive if your product represents a realistic improvement. Price wars can cheapen the public image of your product and then wipe you out.

There's a lot more involved in the pricing process than the mere comparison of a final selling (retail) price. Somehow, you have to eventually absorb all start-up and research costs. A competent tax accountant will help you to realize any legitimate deductions for your efforts, as well as all tax obligations.

After deductions, you must determine what your actual expenditures are. From inception to production, you can't miss a penny. And it doesn't stop there. What about shipping, distribution, advertising? Who pays for it all? Every step, right up to the end-user, shaves a little of your profit away. Still, there are ways to keep those costs down to a bare minimum.

The adage of cutting out the middleman is more of a gimmick than anything else. You may need legitimate middlemen to insure that your product sells on a large scale.

We had previously suggested that you could consider controlling the manufacture of your idea. If you have done that, you can now potentially earn a bigger piece of the pie for your efforts. It is critical in pricing to be market-sensitive, competitive, quality and value oriented and never arrogant.

Instead of approaching a manufacturer, you could make a similar deal with a competent distributor, although there are excellent ways to begin as your own distributor, as you will soon see.

Get to Market Effectively

Unless born from a merger of two big companies, most businesses began as small mom and pop garage ventures. Distribution may have meant driving around in the old jalopy and dropping off the goods at a few homes for a certain retail price which for this example we'll set at $5 each.

Then a couple of local stores wanted to buy the product. Our little manufacturer/distributor sells his product to them at the wholesale price of $2.50. In time, hundreds of stores want to sell this product, far more than the jalopy can cover. Enter the distributor who buys each item for $2 and then distributes it to the stores for the wholesale cost of $2.50.

How do you connect with all these distributors and retailers? That's one of the gems of sales success; locating the unlimited sales avenues to select the one that's right for you.

Trade Shows, Flea Markets, Fairs and Publicity Coups

If feasible, try to introduce your product or service at (or at least attend) a relevant trade show, carnival, flea market or fair. These can all be excellent avenues for building your sales knowledge and confidence.

You can find so much valuable sales, pricing and distribution data during a day or two at the right event. Generally, all the heavies in your field will be there and you can see just where you and your product stand.

Of greater interest is that you could make some great sales at the right event. Seven pieces of advice for trade shows:

1) In all the excitement, you'll hear a lot of empty promises. Try to sort them out then find and cash in on those few real leads.

2) With every interaction, collect a business card and on the back of that card note intentions with that prospect.
3) Work to create some form of kinship with prospects. Try to find something you have in common. Then you can draw on that when you reconnect.
4) Follow up on every prospect. Definitely send an email and a bite-sized sampling, if feasible. Absolutely call each prospect to keep the flow on an interpersonal level. Don't get in the habit of hiding behind email and snail-mail.

FREE ENTERPRISE

5) Ask for the sale. You'll hear this advice from me often. If there's the prospect of a sale, just ask for it. And if they say no, find out why and then re-approach them.
6) Attend as many relevant shows and events as you possibly can. People like to see the people behind the concepts.
7) Remain friendly, gracious and accommodating throughout the process. No matter the outcome, people prefer to deal with friendly people. Give them a reason to come back. To make this financially feasible, we are looking for broad scale success. One show is just a speck in your overall sales plan.

An Event of Your Own

Another option to consider is staging your own event. This of course depends on the nature of your venture but if your concept involves something that you could develop a tasteful theme around, it's worth considering. If possible and relevant, make an event that the whole family will want to attend. Offer free food or music or, even product samples; whatever might appeal to your target audience and, give them a good reason to show up.

Events can run as simple as a basic home or park event, all the way to creating a special benefit or tribute dinner. The key for staging any event is to plan and promote well. Look around your community. What types of events are more successful than others, how can you convert attention to interest and sales commitment, how are they promoted?

Another option is to partner up with a worthy cause that you could sponsor. The advantage of this is that you will be perceived as doing something genuinely supportive for your community and you'll generally have a host of volunteers at your disposal to help plan, set-up, run and promote it to all of their colleagues.

The key is to never do anything halfway. Promotion shortcuts are not lazy shortcuts. I hate seeing people hold up business signs on morning TV shows. Those chincy signs obnoxiously placed in front of the cameras in an attempt to gain exposure probably create more of a negative effect than anything else. That kind of cheap promotion is never what we're talking about. Think of how much more credibility is attained by being a guest on a talk-show or, by having your product featured as a prize on the David Letterman show. We're not out to hijack someone else's media; we're just using the free media to communicate effectively and tastefully. Even if you have a great idea, if you communicate about it poorly, you'll put prospects off. Get attention but with credibility.

PRICING, SALES AND DISTRIBUTION

Going Internuts without Going Nuts

We all went 'Internuts' and we have learned much. The key lesson is that there is no substitute for the wisdom of experience. And through the gains and losses, communication has been enhanced.

Via the birth and evolution of the Web, Trillions of dollars evaporated into thin air, leaving behind choleric investors and dazed 28-year-olds, surrendering their Jaguar leases at record rates. But these investor dollars reflected the great faith in progress and the lessons have been well learned. But now, that's all settled and the revenue potential of the Internet is virtually horizon-less.

The World Wide Web and the Internet are indeed amazing. On one hand, the elderly are safer, the handicapped can market to the world, the single mom can sell her creations worldwide in between carpooling and attending soccer games. Information is now available far more efficiently.

On the other hand, who hasn't received a scam letter promising them millions for doing nothing? Selling and con-artistry have become so rampant, that most people know what to watch for. Even in research, the user has to be careful not to fall into some sales-trap. But indeed, the library of the world is at our finger tips. It's really as if a whole new planet has been discovered. Because in this library, in skilled, ethical and discerning hands, information is interactive – it comes to life. You can blog on what you discover anywhere in the world. And you can learn at a pace never imagined before.

We still, however, have a very long way to go to learn how to manage this library. It can fool us, lie to us, steal from us; it can grow hate groups and seduce or children into dark and even deadly places. It will one day be a key factor in war tactics. It could even become a pivotal battle ground.

Imagine a war General being replaced by General Bill Gates. It's all about human evolution. And when you talk about evolution, you talk about education and commerce.

So once the web was able to become a center for commerce, it also became an opportunity for a new human evolution. That happened in the early-1990's, when html code was developed, allowing for credit card and e-commerce. From that point, the e-commerce gold-rush began. Who would have the next Billion Dollar idea?

Most readers at all levels understand the importance of a basic Web presence and in this book, you will learn how easy it is to get free and credible listings in Directories, Classified Ads, relevant websites and much much more. In fact, even if you've never done it before, it is often as simple as just doing it and remembering the good 'f' word: Free. From now on, whenever you are seeking out a paid service on the internet, first see if that service is available for free by simply typing in "free" before your search phrase.

Never before has a new communications technology created such excitement or over-commitment of resources. Not film, television, not the telephone – nothing. Even

FREE ENTERPRISE

the magic of radio – so elite and misunderstood in its infancy, it gradually found its way. Television? In the beginning, RCA could barely give away its stock. What about the automobile, or satellite relays? They were all revolutionary, indeed but never before has one single technology been capable of tying all the great technological advancements together.

More than ever, success use of the internet requires that you pay attention and use good common sense before committing to anything on line. Use pre-loaded disposable smart cards to avoid being perpetually charged without your knowledge or under-standing. (We talk more about on line financial cautions later on).

The Internet has become the great integrator. And through the immeasurable gazillions of wires and fingertip electronics, we have created a genie.

We rub its bottle with a stroke of the keys. And the electronic Genie says; "Sure, I'll grant you three wishes. I'll grant you 3,000 wishes. But you still have to do the work." The roadways will be provided. But we each have to figure out which to travel and how.

So make a wish, any wish. "Where Do You Want To Go Today?" as Microsoft used to ask. What do you want for your life and your career? Who are the people and organizations you need to find to really rocket your venture to success? These were the promises of the World Wide Web. And with each new day, you become the beneficiary of this process. But the old principles still apply. The Internet and World Wide Web are like shoes. They help everybody. But we still have to take care of our feet. There is no substitute for a personal encounter. The web can spread a message further and more cost-effectively than ever before but it cannot look a prospect in the eye. And through its billions of pages, there is no guarantee that even a good concept will deliver the promised goods or services.

We all need websites that can serve as both content sources that link us with the world. And if we're entrepreneurial, we need a brochure element of our site that sells while we sleep. But the best way to garner the most effective use of your website is to use other media to call attention to it.

Are there other basic ways you may need to integrate into your marketing? Yes, delivery of information has become far more streamlined. But you must never look at a single medium or technology as a panacea. And the hundreds of thousands of investors who sacrificed billions and billions of dollars in the first two year in the Internet 'Gold-Rush' know well, the wisdom of balanced use of all media.

If you're not net-savvy, you do need to get in line by getting online. In truth, after just a few hours of test-driving, the web can become a strong resource in almost every area of your life. One of the founding principles of this book was to make a wish and in effect, choose the idea that would best suit you. Then you were both challenged and guided to take that wish forward on a high-integrity level, by the most cost-effective means possible.

Most readers are astonished at how far they have taken their concepts. This is also the true challenge of the Internet – how far can you coalesce resources and genuinely advance you ideas.

Test yourself

At any age, at any stage, any concept, make a wish or two or three or even four, then jump on the web and see how many new resources you can amass without leaving your desk. But at the same time, remember that nothing takes the place of people sitting face to face with other people, looking in their eyes and hearts, and discussing their ideas – touching a product – watching a service in action.

Internet Sales

Because the Internet evolved from a grass roots level, it has also developed initially as a series of subcultures that are unique to its historical development. Where most people get in trouble advertising on the Internet is when they assume that it can become a less expensive form of junk mail, but spam is in fact an overt invasion of privacy. Instead picture Internet advertising as an extension of the personal, word-of-mouth advertising that you do all the time outside of cyberspace.

If you treat people with respect on "the net," they will refer others to you. The Internet is constantly evolving. We could discuss specific advertising trends that are effective for this moment, but would be completely obsolete a few months from now. Surf the Internet and learn all you can and as you do, practice separating truth from scams.

Learn the very latest advertising trends; learn the basic and newest ways to bring the most traffic to your site. Use your site as a strong interactive sales brochure. What is paramount is to sell with integrity.

Information from a Moving Target

If we recommended web directory sources today, they may be obsolete by the day this printing is released. Never before in our history has resourcing and research been such a moving target. That means that you not only have to keep up with the latest developments in your area of endeavor, you have to make sure that the directories you use are the most helpful in your pursuit. You need to be a good detective. You need to anticipate where new information might be, and you need to determine where your competition might be. That means you need to think with a lot of imagination and creativity. What might your competition try next and how can you be there with a more credible presentation.

FREE ENTERPRISE

Getting It Out There

Some of you are planning to open up a specialty retail store, or utilize flea markets, malls, direct-response radio, TV to sell your product directly to the public. Some of you will be depending heavily on Internet sales.

Any of these can be a good and sensible way to start if you can manage the capital appropriately. You may, however, want to first try out your wares in an already existing store, if feasible. That way you can get an intimate sense of how people actually react to your concept. What is their initial reaction? What makes them explore further or pass on it?

There are as many ways to get your goods or services to market as there are products. The key is finding where you and your concept best fit in the consumer/end-user arena. You must learn to test on a small scale, to be able to plan for success on a larger scale. Throughout this book, we have explored the most cost-effective means to achieve our successes. Be aware that you must learn solidly and build from every single failure or obstacle. That will be critical to your success.

Distribution and Sales

There is a great temptation to want to celebrate once a concept has been brought to reality, before any actual sales are made. Yet too much excitement before a sales network and demand have been created will only result in excessive impatience and disappointment. The best-made and best-priced product or service in the world still has to be properly distributed and promoted. On the following page are some tips to either get your initial sales going or to bolster existing sales.

Direct-Response ads can be cheap to produce and can get your idea out to the public quickly and convincingly.

PRICING, SALES AND DISTRIBUTION

Best Ways to Sell

The Wasteful Approach	The Sensible Approach
Pay advance salaries to	A qualified sales rep will sales reps.not charge to present your your untested concept to market providing your concept is of sufficient quality, relevancy and price.
Rent your own store or office space before there is any appreciable demand	Seek to gain a P.O. or service contract from home before you run up the expense of an office. When the time is right, maybe an existing establishment will sublet or share space with you with rent based on earnings.
Salary reps before trying to determine or commission standard to the trade.	Could you be your own rep in the beginning?
Concentrate on only one way of selling.	
Send out untargeted emails to the general public.	Build a targeted email and sales list to maximize sales possibilities.
Set a strict sales quota deadline after which time, you fire reps or just give up.	Learn, observe, adjust until you figure out how to get the sale.
Pay for expensive ads and other listings.	Get similar and more extensive listing for free.
Limit your approach to selling	Use as many of the free Enterprise Marketing Systems as you can

POWERPOINTER NINETEEN
The Keys to Successful Selling

1) **Self-Belief.** Yes, you've heard it in so many 'you-can-do-it' manuals, but sufficient belief in one's self can't simply be commanded. So try reason; if you have chosen your concept correctly, it should be something that is somehow a part of you and should then encourage you to represent yourself honestly with relaxed confidence. Some people complain that they are not salespeople but in fact, we all have to represent ourselves to survive. Courage is a choice. Cowardice is a choice. And there will be no growth and no opportunity for financial gain without some self-belief.

2) **Don't draw conclusions for the prospect** - If you're doing your job correctly, your prospects will draw the appropriate conclusions. It is your task to explain the function of your concept and its specific features and benefits.

3) **The Truth** - Don't fool yourself by seeking to hear what you want to hear, as opposed to what you need to hear. As early as possible in the development of your concept learn the truth about your product. What will you need to do to make your product marketable? The sooner you find out - the sooner your chances for success.

4) **Politeness vs. Charm** - Courtesy is always important no matter what you hear about your concept from prospects. Perhaps if you listen to them and evaluate their feedback properly, they might become your best customer one day.

5) **Don't push, don't beg** — You resent being forced into something. Your prospects are human, too. If you try too hard to make a sale by begging for a trial, offering a ridiculously low price or by lying, your prospect is not going to have too much faith in your concept.

6) **However . . . Don't let an opportunity pass you by**. Sometimes you may try something that requires flexibility in order to get a sale rolling.

7) **Follow-up for success.** The sale may be there but the timing might be off. If you know there's a real need, try again later.

Follow-up and Growth - Turning the Promise into Payment

It is one of the more gratifying experiences to have built up a concept to the point of sales. This can also be a time of great danger and frustration for a new business. You now know that you're concept is viable. You have seen ever-growing and ever-promising test-results, but then how do you bring it to the point where it becomes a viable, profit-making enterprise?

What most people learn about sales is that there is no limit to what they themselves can do, but on the other hand, anxious would-be entrepreneurs learn that nothing is an automatic process.

Even after you've completed your various test phases, you're still going to be testing. What did you do right that won the sale, and what did you do wrong that limited or prevented a sale? Successful follow-up is a willingness to learn, to evaluate, to admit mistakes and faults; then, you must convert those mistakes into profit-making lessons.

So..

If a prospect expresses interest, find out...

Prospect's Needs . . .

- How your product or service will be used or resold?
- What is their marketing program?
- What modifications could you feasibly make to accommodate client?
- Would these modifications serve other clients more effectively as well?
- Would these modifications help you to diversify and create a new product?

Prospect's Sincerity . . .

- Attempt to either close (complete) a sale or send a proposal and then follow-up within one week.
- If prospect continues to call and seek free advice, set a limit. Get proposal out and set your fee.
- Have you set up specific and mutually agreeable payment terms?
- If re-negotiation is necessary, get your money, but make sure you get paid.
- If the goods were delivered and accepted in good faith, then it's your money that's owed to you.
- Do not let receivables lag behind. Suspend further delivery of goods until account is rectified.

FREE ENTERPRISE

Your Approach . . .

-No matter the situation, have you handled it politely? Remember that today's headache could be tomorrow's bonanza.

The following exercise is provided to help you monitor and develop sales progress all the way to a successful sale.

Finding Hidden Markets

This is not a very impressive story regarding this author but if it teaches something meaningful, it won't be the first time I made a fool of myself. At this writing, my office is in Kanab, Utah, exactly four miles from my home and I spend long hours there, mostly for you. So my exercise routine entails mostly riding my mountain bike to and from work.

One cold Wintry day, I rode to the bank to withdraw some cash for an upcoming tour. I put the money in my wallet and, rode on to my office. When I got to my office, I reached for my wallet to get my credit card and, you guessed it, no wallet. Somewhere along my route from the bank to work, I had dropped it. A big chunk of cash and all my credit cards, just lying there somewhere for anyone to pick up.

Despite all of the coping advice I have offered and, tried to follow in this book, I admit to panicking a bit. I jumped on my bike and began riding as fast as I could with one thing in mind. As I rode, I worried that someone might pick it up and my cash would be gone. My eyes and brain were on double high-alert as I scanned the roadside. One mile, nothing, two miles, nothing. Finally, I reached the bank and there, right by the door, was my wallet. I rushed over to it, picked it up and, everything was there.

There it was in plain sight and no one had seen it. I had even called the bank to ask them to look around and they couldn't see it. This, of course, is the perfect story about finding sales and revenue where no one else is looking. No matter what shape the economy is in, if we work to uncover customers and markets that no one else sees, we get the sale, we get the money.

For your market, where is your hidden revenue, where are the sales that no one else is seeing?

A Simple Secret for Giving Your Prospect What They Really Want

You've decided to make a brand new treat that no one's ever had before. And it's really awesome. It's an all natural fruit-sweetened chocolate-chip flavored lollipop that that has only 50 calories. Your recipe is perfect and your manufacturing and packaging, slick and beyond reproach. So you put it all together and built your business hopes around this idea. You decide to start locally in supermarkets and mini-marts with a handsome space-sensitive hanging display at the check-out counter. The perfect impulse item. You set them all in place and just wait. How could the tens of thousands of shoppers resist this low-calorie treat?

A week later, nothing is happening so you give it more time. But still, no real sales, anywhere. Hmm, what's going on? You've checked over everything. You've followed the best manufacturing counsel available and gone by the book; by this book for that matter. Your product is beautiful, logical and it doesn't taste too bad at all. You did everything right. Except one thing: You forgot to ask the customer what they wanted.

You didn't test the idea; you didn't offer free samples or ask any individuals or informal focus groups what they wanted. You just said, "Here's my low-calorie chocolate-chip flavored lolly-pop. Now, buy it." What you didn't know was that most (not all) low-calorie replacements for the chocolate-chip cookie have been tried many times before and they fall flat as a well...a, cookie.

For most people, if they are going to indulge in a chocolate-chip cookie, they want the full experience. They want the real thing to really be emotionally satisfied. Before you try to finesse a sale that a prospect doesn't really want, listen to the needs of your customer first and test to see if you're close to the mark. In most cases, this book shows you how to save bundles of money and disappointment by testing for free.

When you carry out the sales process properly, there is virtually no sense of trepidation or fear of rejection because you are genuinely offering something helpful. So don't automatically assume that you can't represent yourself to a prospect. It's human nature to offer.

FREE ENTERPRISE

Sales Tracking Form
Please feel free to duplicate for computer use
Check One: [ ] YES [ ] MAYBE [ ] NO
Date _____ Business _____
Name _____
Contact _____ Phone _____
Email _____
Best time to call: _____
Address _____

Response to your concept: _____

The prospect would buy if you: _____

NO - If prospect is not going to be viable, check 'no' at top of page and then use a new page for another target.
MAYBE - If future sale is possible, check 'maybe 'at top of page and save this and the next page for continued sales tracking of this prospect until a definitive response is achieved.
YES - If a successful sale is made, check 'yes' at top of page and fill in the next page.
Payment Terms
Sold To: _____ Address _____

Amount Sold: _____
List Purchase Order Number: _____
Ship by: _____
- How do you know if you'll get paid?
- Can you ship C.O.D.?
- Can you ask for even a partial down-payment?
- What are your liabilities?
Do Not Ship until you have worked out mutually agreeable payment terms.
List terms:

PRICING, SALES AND DISTRIBUTION

Summary

Transition from concept to commodity.
- Establish fair and competitive pricing.
- Try to avoid using price as the main selling point.
- Emphasize quality of goods or services.

Get to market effectively.
- Go back and sell your product to your test-market. Offer these individuals a generous reduced rate.
- Determine most appropriate distribution avenues.
- Talk to major retailers.
- Talk to distributors relevant to your market.
- Try trade shows, flea markets and fairs.
- Check out the Internet
- Review "All the Right Moves" in this chapter to brush up on your selling techniques.

Follow-up for success.
- Use the **Best Ways to Sell** Table for every prospect which shows interest.
- Use the **Sales Tracking Form** to keep track of your prospects and ensure that you will get paid.

Potential Challenges and Solutions

Challenge: No confidence in selling your concept.
Solution: You have defined your goals and now must become comfortable with your project. You must believe in what you're doing, or no one else will.

Be flexible and don't expect to make every sale you attempt. Learn from each prospect as to increase your chances for success with your next prospect. Some of your best experiences will emanate from your sales experiences as you discover first hand what distributors and/or general public will and will not buy from you.

Challenge: Can't come up with a competitive price.
Solution: Some products or services command higher prices than others in a similar category. Price can be measured by what a willing buyer will pay to a willing seller. If you have a superior concept, price won't be the major issue.

If your product is similar to existing ones except yours costs more, why should people pay more for almost the exact same thing? Take a careful look at your competition and determine what features you could create to stand out and thereby merit a higher price tag.

FREE ENTERPRISE

Re-examine your manufacturing and distributing costs. These entities don't want to overprice themselves out of business. If necessary, get them to bend at least for the first six months of production.

Challenge: Can't find a distributor.

Solution: All goods are distributed somehow. A call to a couple of disinterested distributors means nothing. There are thousands of distributors and an equal number of creative distribution options.

You have to attract, persist and sell them at a price that must guarantee a profit for yourself. Consider all cost factors carefully.

Your first ad campaign can create a number of options that could build some sales volume, after which time you could be in a stronger position to approach a distributor.

Before You Continue . . .

- Have you developed a sense of pricing or general worth of your concept that is all market and no ego?

- Are you developing commitments that advance or imprison you?

POWERPOINTER TWENTY
Waking Up To Your True Potential

Many of us have become unconscious to the fact that we have slowly slipped into a deep conscious sleep. We wake up as normal and functioning but we failed to realize that we have gradually fallen into a deep and self-suppressive rut. Soon it seems normal that we are trudging through our lives without noticing the things that used to keep us inspired and learning new things.

We blame the economy, we blame our responsibilities. We blame our boss; anything but ourselves. Then one day, it all just seems too deep to even think about climbing out. We know we're at that point when we begin making brilliant almost inarguable excuses about how we got there and why we're stuck.

Once we realize that it is in this moment that we have the opportunity to create, we wake up to the fact that we can create change and be who we want to be, and do what we want to do in each moment. This realization is an awakening from years of unconscious conditioning created by unconscious thought. Most of us miss the fruit of life by getting caught up in daily tasks and chores as if these exercises are to fulfill us in some way.

ACTIVATOR TWENTY-ONE
Simple Research and Development

Let's suppose you've come up with an idea to create the greatest general household cleaner, but you don't have the hundreds of Thousands of dollars for research. Will it work? Will it sell? What do you do? How do you compete? The answer is simple and free.

This is when we figure out how to actually bring your concept to life. There are specific things you must address in order to do this successfully. The following questions will help to ensure that you are proceeding with your development in the most intelligent manner:

a) Is there either scientific or business evidence that your concept has merit?

___

b) If you are developing a competitive product or business, what are you doing to make your concept better than the competition?

___

c) On what basis do you think your enhancements will work?

___

FREE ENTERPRISE

d) What steps are you planning on taking to convince people that you concept will be more effective?

_____

_____

_____

e) Are you willing to learn everything you can to pursue your venture in the best way possible? How will you do this?

_____

_____

_____

_____

f) Have your researched the local competition, national if applicable? What are they doing wrong and how will you do it better?

_____

_____

_____

g) Have you researched the internet and yellow Pages to learn what everyone else is doing?

_____

_____

_____

_____

PRICING, SALES AND DISTRIBUTION

h) Do you have a committed team who are able to understand the research and help you to make something new or better?

i) Have you identified resources for developing your concept? List them here with contact info (phone and email address):

Research and Development is not simply a process you carry out in the beginning. You do use it, combined with your natural instincts to give your unique touch to your concept. But it is also an ongoing process. The greatest benefit of developing your own enterprise, aside from profit, is that you are always learning new things about what you're doing. And as you learn something new, you will find a better way to do it. Life is never boring for those willing to struggle to make it better.

If you were able at this point to answer the questions sufficiently, you should have a lot of foundation to really advance your venture. Look at the answers you have provided above and ask yourself how you can assemble these resources today and make something new happen today.

POWERPOINTER TWENTY-ONE
Turning Your Worst Traits into Your Best

"Don't beat yourself up," You've heard that said a million times and for each of those million times, it doesn't seem to help. That's because when we're down, we not only tend to let bad thoughts pig-pile us, we believe them to be true so down we sink ever further.

The principal reason for this is that we exaggerate our negatives and feel that we somehow deserve to be punished for all the mistakes we've made in this life for faults we were never willing to correct.

So here it comes, our financial and spiritual day of reckoning. If we've been too careless all our lives, we feel that there will come a magical moment where we will have to atone for our business mistakes.

For those of us who accept that we are each imperfect, there is some very good news: Just by shifting our perspective we can turn our worst traits into our best one. If we've been a clown all of our lives perhaps that can be conveyed as charm for effective sales. If we've been that careless soul, we can learn to use that trait to take calculated business risks. And so forth.

The key is to accept yourself and figure out how you can make your quirks work to your advantage. So the next time you find yourself getting down on yourself, stop and thing about how you might use those traits to enhance your business. You'll be amazed.

POWERPOINTER TWENTY-TWO
Turn Your Weakest Business Elements Into Your Strongest

The title of this Powerpointer seems to give this one away. Of course, we want to fix the most broken aspect of our business, or do we? For example, if prospects encounter partners yelling and screaming at one another, how inspired are they going to be to do business with you if they don't have to? Too many ventures tend to accept their business operations flaws as something they just have to live with but it's these very flaws that can erode a business from the inside out.

At the same time, addressing these points can create a long elusive break-through. Often when a business is in trouble, principals fail to identify what steps to take next but these simple steps can make all the difference.

1) Hold a fact-finding meeting with the goal of improving general operations.

PRICING, SALES AND DISTRIBUTION

2) Have everyone identify the biggest problems with the business. Do not list any individual as the problem as often well-intentioned people simply need to be redirected or repositioned. This exercise can also help ensure that team members are keeping their responsibilities well-monitored.
3) Develop a consensus of what everyone believes to be your company's single worst problem.
4) Declare that you are all going to turn it into your best opportunity. Have everyone spend a day or so developing ideas on their own.
5) In the next meeting, coalesce everyone's input and then, agree to a repair plan and assign tasks to each party.

Often, an effort like this can not just 'stop the bleeding', but can also improve a business dramatically and, solve many of the other smaller organizational problems.

ACTIVATOR TWENTY-TWO
Could We Run Out Of Money?

A lot of people wonder if there is only so much money and credit to go around, especially if sales aren't going that well and others are telling you that the market is simply depressed.

We hear about the majority of money being in the hands of the wealthy and many of us remember 'trickle-down' economics where it was believed that the money tax breaks and incentives we provided to the to the wealthiest Americans, the more money would flow like water, to the rest of us.

Well, first of all, let's address the concept of 'trickling'. Money doesn't flow, as if from one container to another or, from a great government well, so any water analogy is senseless. Money or compensation is a reflection of productivity.

If you create a way to retrofit lawnmowers to save fuel, and your neighbor pays you for it, your personal economy grows because you have created a useful service to your neighbor. If your neighbor shows you how to irrigate your lawn with only half the required water, you pay him for that service and his personal economy grows. The problem is, we only have so many neighbors. So eventually, some services require expansion to other neighborhoods, town and states. Not as true for consumables like food or plant products.

Now, let's suppose you want to buy a new car or a bigger home. That all depends on the shape of your personal economy. The point of exploring these various economic theories is to understand that their rate of growth is not hinged upon the state or spending habits of the government or, even, the home-credit crunch. Your rate of growth depends largely on your ability to develop your idea in such a way that it grows your personal economy.

FREE ENTERPRISE

It is not as if there is only so much money to go around. If you watch the financial reports, nobody says we're simply running out of money. What they are saying is that money cannot be found in the same places where it used to be. The river doesn't run dry so the good news here is that your economic future depends far more on what you are willing to do and, how well you are willing to learn all of the free systems to help promote and generate revenue for your personal economy.

Pundits argue that we can and have run out of money and cite the great Depression as sound evidence. But we pulled out of that period because we became industrious, largely through the coming of the Second World War.

In today's global economy where millions of ideas great and small, flow from brains like yours everyday, there are also millions of new opportunities everyday. You just have to learn how to access them. The internet plays a major role in this process but unfortunately, most people do not know how to access the awesome power of the web and they do not realize that this power is generally *free of cost*.

To really make the Internet useful, you have to focus on an idea that's both relevant and inspiring for you.

This is a lesson that successful writers and other creative folk often learn early. When they come up with a marketable book or song, the ideas in their brains flow to the world and money flows back. What could flow from your brain to grow your personal economy?

There's plenty of money out there. Go find it and, go make it.

CORE STRATEGIES AND TACTICS NUMBER THIRTY-THREE
Get it All on Paper and Online. Stationary, both on paper.. And via online graphics which include envelopes, business cards, and letterhead is a must. Consider using fold-over business cards with your picture, and marketing-based letterhead styles that give you room to list your services and credentials or benefits. That way you'll get maximum exposure every time you hand out a business card or send a letter. Have a Catchy tag line of slogan but make sure it's not stupid, humorous only to some or, insulting. Your stationary system is part of your internal marketing strategies so always include your tagline or slogan.

HOW TO SUPERCHARGE THIS TACTIC: Use That Stationery System to Write Personal Thank-You Notes. Let your customers know in a sincere way, how much you value them with a simple thank you and a special call-to-action available only to them.

HOW CAN YOU ENGAGE THIS RIGHT NOW FOR YOUR VENTURE?

CORE STRATEGIES AND TACTICS NUMBER THIRTY-FOUR
Create a Reception Room Resume. This is an important internal strategy designed to create trust and confidence in your target audience. It enhances the likelihood of a higher acceptance and eliminates *buyer's remorse* and questions like "have I come to the right place?" and "have I committed to the right product or service?" Resumes are both emotional and promotional. Tell the readers how you got your education and how you gain continuing education "for them and from them." Use "right quotes" to make personal statements that show your customers or clients that you care, are qualified, experienced, and that they made an excellent choice with you company. Mail them out to clients who have set an appointment prior to their visit.

HOW TO SUPERCHARGE THIS TACTIC: Put these resumes in your reception room and in new promotional packets. Hand them out at talks. A well-done resume will help increase your conversions. This is one of the strong initial means to help build your image with customers. Also, waiting in your reception area will provide them with the opportunity to read it carefully.

HOW CAN YOU ENGAGE THIS RIGHT NOW FOR YOUR VENTURE?

FREE ENTERPRISE

CORE STRATEGIES AND TACTICS NUMBER THIRTY-FIVE
Create a Marketing Brochure that Sells. If you want your business to appear professional and polished, have your brochure created professionally. If your budget is limited, create a two-color brochure instead of a three or four-color piece. The purpose of the brochure is to convince and motivate, in other words, to sell and/or to call to action.

HOW TO SUPERCHARGE THIS TACTIC: If the contest is novel Does your brochure have a motivation or incentive like a free trial or coupon offer that gets prospects contacting you to learn more?

HOW CAN YOU ENGAGE THIS RIGHT NOW FOR YOUR VENTURE?

_____
_____
_____
_____

CORE STRATEGIES AND TACTICS NUMBER THIRTY-SIX
Simple Classified Ads In many markets, a simple offer can work really well. "LOSE WEIGHT OR DON'T PAY," or "SAVE 30% ON UTILITIES OR DON'T PAY". These can be placed in large metropolitan papers or, in multiple small-town papers. All you need is one ad that works which you can then replicate in other papers. The numbers will guide this modest experiment for your venture.

HOW TO SUPERCHARGE THIS TACTIC: There Thousands of classified ads online where you can run your ads for free.

HOW CAN YOU ENGAGE THIS RIGHT NOW FOR YOUR VENTURE?

_____
_____
_____
_____

CORE STRATEGIES AND TACTICS NUMBER THIRTY-SEVEN
Say it with Posters. Professionally produced posters really sell customers and help increase business. Prospects associate professional posters with a professional operation.

HOW TO SUPERCHARGE THIS TACTIC: Posters can also serve as up-to-the-minute signs upon which you can post special offers or new announcements.

HOW CAN YOU ENGAGE THIS RIGHT NOW FOR YOUR VENTURE?

CORE STRATEGIES AND TACTICS NUMBER THIRTY-EIGHT
Study Economically-Challenged Business Arenas. When I lived in Iowa, there were two hair-stylists; one in a more upscale part of the community and another in more economically challenged area. When business was down, the latter shop immediately posted specials to attract walk-in customers or, even cut prices just to get people in the door. This also gave them a chance to win over new customers. Sometimes, those in areas where they have to work harder for each retail customer, have the most to teach us.

HOW TO SUPERCHARGE THIS TACTIC: Spend a day in an economically-challenged mall and see how many marketing tactics that you might apply to you business.

HOW CAN YOU ENGAGE THIS RIGHT NOW FOR YOUR VENTURE?

FREE ENTERPRISE

Progress Journal: (please feel free to copy or scan this page only)

_____

_____

_____

_____

_____

_____

_____

_____

_____

_____

_____

_____

_____

_____

_____

_____

_____

_____

_____

Your Signature_____Date_____

CHAPTER NINE

CREDIBLE, MOSTLY-FREE ADVERTISING THAT WORKS

"Hey boss, look at this."

"The world can't welcome you if they don't know you exist."

Howard Bronson

Overview

In advertising, you can get a lot of reassurances. Unfortunately, they're generally from advertising salespeople. There are no promises from maximum exposure, so in this chapter, we offer you maximum insight to minimize risk.

> **Activator Steps for this Chapter**
> 1) **Understand how advertising really works.**
> 2) **Identify media targets.**
> 3) **Create a professional image.**
> 4) **Get your message placed.**
> 5) **Focus on your audience.**

Understand How Advertising Really Works

Advertising - Madison Avenue; those creative geniuses who have the power to make you buy or do anything. There seems to be a buyer (market) for everything and anything. All you have to do is find it and influence it. We are told that obnoxious, repetitive TV commercials actually make us remember to buy those products. Are we really all that stupid or is what we generally see as advertising simply the best we are capable of?

As advertising and consulting professionals (or persons, depending on your point of view), we watch the TV commercials more than we watch conventional shows. It's like watching twelve little shows every half hour.

Commercials seem to be getting more glitzy and creative all the time. But is the increasingly shrewd consumer really buying all this new vaudeville?

Are we looking for reflections of trends? Not especially. Technique? Very often. Do we believe the claims we see? Very rarely. In fact, the TV is our lantern looking for an honest commercial.

FREE ENTERPRISE

Credibility - that's what you're after. How can you ever really be sure that people who buy their own commercials are telling you the unbiased truth? Some present what they call hard facts and statistics only to be rebutted by a competitor's contradictory claims.

Very often, paid ads lie, and that seems to be acceptable because people have traditionally responded by purchasing those goods or services. All the answers can be realized by understanding R.O.I. (return on investment) and tracking. As glitzy as advertising may seem, it works best when it's brought as close to a science as possible, with progressive steps, based specifically on tracking results.

Tracking is one of the key ways we have to learn about both product and marketing trends to which people really respond. We watch and read the news, everything we can get our hands on. We study net-trends and watch stock yields very carefully.

We don't believe what people or ads tell us unless we can really prove it for ourselves.. Try this: Go out and buy one of our favorite magazines (or visit their website): Consumer Reports. Pick out a couple of products that you believe to be the best available, and then see what Consumer Reports has to say about it. Generally, you'll be surprised and sometimes, disappointed.

The Credibility Factor

If an advertising agency has already tried to get their hooks into you, they have most likely told you that paid advertising is the only way to succeed. Since selling and producing ads is probably the only way they can stay in business, what on earth else are they going to tell you?

Well now you know differently. First of all, you have a leg up on most ad agencies because of the mountains of research you have already carried out. Research and homework are where any real advertising campaign actually begins. Ironically enough, it is often the weakest area for agencies. They'll give you a ton of ideas on how to spend your money but not much actual research.

That's why anyone who creates an ad without doing some simple homework, gets so frustrated; they spend a wad of money on a couple of ads against our recommendations, and then they tell us advertising doesn't work.

Just because a salesman tells you to buy an ad doesn't mean that you just bought a ticket to guaranteed success. Challenge those salesmen. How many of them would only take a fee only if their ads worked? Witness credibility succumbing to mere greed.

When we're given a budget to make a product successful, we consider that money to be a loan that we aim to pay back tenfold. We spend very little of our client's money until we can make that client's business grow.

A no-response ad campaign does more than make a client mad, it's a dream-killer, and we have promised to protect your dreams. Put those advertising agency and salespeople on hold for now. Don't join the hundreds of thousands of people who waste

CREDIBLE, MOSTLY-FREE ADVERTISING THAT WORKS

billions on incorrect advertising procedures. If the masses want to keep wasting their money, that's their problem.

Identify Media Targets

The World is divided not by Geography but by Multimedia. For your debut, we have a far more credible procedure that will cost you next to nothing. Most of you are more than halfway there already. We have often asked audiences to guess how many magazines are printed in the world today. We hear numbers like a hundred or a few thousand but never the actual number which easily exceeds several hundred thousand. And then there are the millions of websites, ezines and other electronic newsletters. Name a topic, any topic whatsoever. There's a magazine or ezine that covers that subject. Ever heard of Ballet News, or Bow and Arrow Monthly, or Totally Housewares? How about Poultry Digest magazine or Plastics Business magazine? And they are always available on the Internet, and when the Internet does a better job of delivering information on a particular subject, many but not all of the print versions will fall by the wayside.

There are literally Thousands of subcultures represented both by publications and the ever burgeoning Internet. One of the best examples of how this is happening is to listen to the various radio or television political shows, plus related websites, blogsites and chatrooms.

Hosts always used to ask where callers were from, but now they want to know more about their political allegiance or core belief system. It's no longer about physical geography but by one's identity. The virtual world is becoming real and this impacts how you promote your venture.

Each month, over thirty thousand people read Ballet News Over one hundred thousand read Bow and Arrow each month. Far more visited the relevant websites at lightning speed, gobbling up the best information they can find. Any topic, no matter how bizarre or mundane, has a relevant magazine, newsletter, Internet resource, and a world of people whose livelihood and or lifestyle is affected by it. Are you aware of the publications, websites, and other Internet groups that pertain to your product? Here's how you find them.

FREE ENTERPRISE

Target Newspaper, Magazines, Television/Radio Shows, Websites and E-Directories

Your assignment is to track down 10 outlets in each of the three categories if that many exist. For our purposes, the three categories of outlets are:

1) Newspapers, local and possibly national.
2) Consumer magazines together with relevant trade, technical and professional magazines targeted to product manufacturing, distribution, retailers, and all other pre-consumer areas.
3) Broadcast and cable TV programs, each with their own production staff to pitch.
4) Websites and chatrooms devoted to your type of product or service.

Newspapers and Their Accompanying Websites

The newspapers should be your every day papers on a local, regional and national level. Check out the various sections where your story could appear.

Consumer Magazines and Newsletters and their associated ezines.

For the consumer magazines, if possible, at least five should be relevant to your product's industry. The other five require a little brainstorming on your part. They should be general or broad topic magazines where an audience for your product or service may be available.

What's newsworthy about your venture?

For example, if you've invented a pair of scissors, you may pick up a hardware journal or cutlery news but you should also pick up a magazine about paper products, textiles or maybe, school supplies. You're seeking out related industries.

Use the five and five rule for the trade technical or professional magazine category as well. Now, how do we know these publications exist and where on earth do you find them? The easiest place to start is at the manufacturers that you've dealt with. They'll generally have the trade magazines of your industry lying around somewhere.

Next is the Internet. Think of the web as a living directory that can always give you new publication leads. If you know of a local ad agency, see if they will lend you these directory books for a few hours. If that's not possible, check your local library for any of the writer's market books.

Two of the prevalent directories are:
 - Standard Rate and Data Service www.srds.com

CREDIBLE, MOSTLY-FREE ADVERTISING THAT WORKS

- Writer's Market www.writersmarket.com

But always double-check every market by googling the topics we're covering because something new pops up every day and every time we search, we all learn something new.

Some are expensive to buy but collectively, their data books or websites list everything ever published. You can always go to your local library (we've sent you there before). And of course, there are countless magazine directories on the web, too changeable and too numerous to list. These are handy because you can generally transfer that contact info into your own database.

It is very important to learn how to conduct thorough searches on the Internet. The key is to enter the relevant key words into any Internet search engine. The more accurate your keywords, the more on target you will be with your results. Then it's vital to learn how to decipher fact from fiction. This requires training and instinct. In time, you learn how to become a good Internet detective, and that should become one of your most valuable skills. For the publications you have picked, get copies of as many of them as possible. Take some time to get familiar with each one. Especially in the trade magazines, study the ads, some of which may one day be your competition.

How do manufacturers and distributors keep an eye on the competition? There are many sophisticated ways. One way is to stay well read. Keeping an ongoing monitor on the market means all manufacturing costs and technological developments are up to date.

"Hey boss, look at this!"

You could watch or read ads, but you already know that ads aren't your most credible source of information. Let us tell you about a holiday that occurs at nearly every manufacturer or distributor just about every few weeks. It's called, "Hey boss, look-at-this" day.

On any morning when trade magazines arrive, salespeople rush to grab copies, of which there are generally several. Do they quickly skim through the ads? No. Do they sit down to read a nice long article? Not at this time.

You will see them turn to one place first and study it intently. That section is known as the "New Product," "Product News," "Industry News" or a number of other similar headings. Their eyes feverishly scan this section looking for what the industry is up to, studying the competition. The moment they see something that may affect their own product line, they dash into the main man's office and say, "Hey boss, look at this!" Then there's also that deluge of daily Internet discoveries, rushing to every relevant email target.

After years of advertising and scores of accounts, we have seen more things happen from the New Product sections than any other area of advertising.

Aim is the name of the game

FREE ENTERPRISE

How to Boost Traffic to Your Website or Press Release through Supercharged Keywords.

When the television infomercial was being tested for this book, I placed a two minute snippet of a rough-cut of the show for about five of my backers to see. In a very short time, there were over 300 hits for that little snippet. I didn't promote it or email anyone else about it but simply gave the sampling an interesting title. 'Bailout Alternative'. And why not? Since my book empowers individuals to bail themselves out of the respective financial challenges, it fits.

Many people when faced with the task of listing keywords look at this as a shot in the dark because they don't understand how to make this system work effectively for them. If you're under-utilizing your key-words or key phrases, you're missing the opportunity to attract a substantial number of visitors.

What is truly newsworthy about your venture?

Key words and phrases are critical for so many of the free initiatives you have learned in this book. Aside from increasing web traffic and search engine listings, they can help to sub- stantially boost the response to articles you post, classified ads, cross links to other sites and, the ever important generation of new visitors and new business.

Here is the recipe to maximize the power of your keywords and phrases:

1. Simply think about all the ways your site, article, etc benefits your intended audiences.
2. Think about how your site may be relevant to news or a general news trend. To see how one enterprise does an excellent job at this type of trend tie-in, visit: The Radio and TV Interview Report. www.rtir.com Every week, they email all registrants about how their publications connect to current news and general trends.

This exercise may take some time and thought to discover the relevancy of your concept. It is a process of imagining what your audience may be thinking about and how your concept can meet those needs.

3. Visit the Google Trends Lab/ Zeitgeist at http://www.google.com/trends or, you may go directly to the top 100 currently visited at http://www.google.com/trends/hottrends if you want to make a more detailed study of trends and compare or cross-reference lists, there are many listings you can review. Also, you may use (for free of course) the Google Ad Words Keyword Tool where you

CREDIBLE, MOSTLY-FREE ADVERTISING THAT WORKS

simply enter a term or terms, and you can then see the popularity of the term at the present time.

In addition to Google Trends, here are some more trend sites. These sites are not in any particular ranking or order. Don't be overwhelmed by this list; all you need to start is to find a few popular keywords that are relevant to your venture. You can always build on and adjust that list over time.

AOL Hot Searches: See up to the minutes most popular searches on AOL.

Ask IQ: See top searches at Ask.

Dogpile SearchSpy: This will give you their current top search terms.

dWoz Search Phrase and Search Spies Lists

Lycos 50: Shows top searches at Lycos each week.

MetaCrawler and MetaCrawler MetaSpy **Service**.

MSN Search Insider: Top 200 current searches on MSN Search

Yahoo Buzz and Keyword Selector Tool: This free service is primarily designed to help advertisers who wish to select terms to target with ads on the Yahoo network. But you can use it to see how popular particular terms are.

Some of the top trends may seem unfamiliar because they represent news that may be happening right at the moment. What you are seeking is twofold: More enduring topics like *how to heal a broken heart* or *how to save money of groceries*. The other element of using keywords that will be seen embodies the trends. What some hot celebrity's latest break-up or drug arrest can teach you about real love…etc. You can also use this system to help you write press releases that build off of those current events or trends like Radio and TV Report (noted earlier)

The final step of course, is to choose keywords that are relevant to current topics, trends or general keyword searches. As you generate your lists of how your business can benefit keyword searchers, see how that list can expand as you study what the most popular searches are and, how your site relates to that. If you have truly made a relevant connection for a prospect, they will be appreciative and you could very well earn a new customer that you never would have attracted had you not used your imagination.

Keyword utilization is a true 'increase business in your sleep' effort. It's easy to learn, it costs nothing but your time to set up and the more you do it, the better you get at it. Just think in terms of how many ways you can be the solution and answer to what a prospect is looking for. What problem does your service resolve, what need does your

What's newsworthy about your venture?

FREE ENTERPRISE

service fill? Your customers are looking for you but they may not know they are looking for you.

There's an age-old adage in advertising: *You need to fish where the fish are.* The simple process of mastering keywords will allow you to place your hook in the precise parts of the water where those fish truly are.

SCAMGUARD WARNING
Key word Abuse and Misuse

It's happened to all of us. You're researching a subject and submit relevant keywords, expecting to be led to helpful resources but instead, you find yourself looking at listings or sites that have nothing to do with your search.

There's nothing more annoying in this time-jealous world than to be deliberately mislead to a site that has no relevance to your search. So those who misuse keywords create more resentment for their site than sales. At the same time, some clever folk will use some of the most ongoing keywords just to draw prospects to their sites, like key sex-topic words. The lesson: Be creative but not deceptive. Make sure your site has real and sincere relevance to the keywords you list. If any free and/or successful system is abused, it will eventually lose it effectiveness and disappear.

Those who followed the procedure we've outlined in this chapter have loved the money we have saved for them while giving their product a chance to prove itself.

Everyone benefits from proper use of the media. That's what you're learning here. Your first big media lesson will be through the magic of these New Product sections. If you receive tremendous results from a particular magazine or web posting, that may be the place to go for future paid advertising. This initial campaign is not a P.R. tactic.

Public Relations involves using the media to showcase civic interests of an individual or organization. Proper public relations will play a very powerful role for your cause as you will see shortly.

For now, we are going to promote your concept on a very wide and powerful scale for almost no money and certainly a savings of several Thousand dollars in advertising expense. We can do this because the cost to run a blurb and photo of your product in either print or online is generally nothing. Though some magazines and websites do charge a space fee for their New Product sections, most do not. Those that do not charge a fee are the smart ones because they invite and encourage the growth and prosperity of the free enterprise system. They invest a pittance in giving this space and if that helps to make your product a success, it could pave the way for a mutually profitable relationship.

There's an even more significant reason that they should give you free press. The introduction of your product or service is news and it's their job to report the news. For a magazine to run one or two releases over a few months for you is usually no problem. Any more than that for the same new product is taking unfair advantage of the media system.

Why You Should Root for 'Woot'

There are literally millions of specialty websites that we could talk about but one of the best natural extrapolations of the original print and on line media releases has to be www.woot.com Starting at midnight every night, Woot features one either new or simply unique product every day, they describe it ala 'New Product Style' and then, it's available for on line sale right then and there.

This of course advances two vital elements.
- It either introduces or features one interesting product with excellent promotional copy.
- It offers the product for instant sale.

Woot is of course, not the only site that does this but at this writing, it stands as an excellent example of what many readers need to pursue.

Make Sure Your Respondents Experience a Credible Image

You're either in or, nearing the process of presenting to the public so it's a good time to either build or refine your image and substance in the corporate world. To start, we would like you merely switch on your computer and create any basic letterhead that you need. Even if you're a small business, identifying yourself as 'vice-president' will carry more respect with prospects. But sometimes, you'll need to be production manager, or comptroller. You should develop a simple logo from allowable software or through any website graphic art sites.

If you need a title under your name and your item is a product, consider using the following label: "Product Research and Development." If your enterprise is service oriented, try "Manager" for blue collar or "Program Director" if it's white collar in nature.

With respect to letterhead, be sure to include your contact information, including your email and website address, if you have one.

As with business cards and even envelopes, letterhead can also serve as a mini-resume, where you can state your company's purpose and some brief credentials.

Print at least 250 envelopes, cards and letter stock. You also have the option to print as you go, allowing you to modify headings as necessary. If you have become affiliated with a prestigious company, get permission to use their letterhead and have them print business cards with your name on them, or at least get clearance to imprint their logo on your card. And make those cards disappear.

FREE ENTERPRISE

Even when we're relaxing at home for a weekend, we'll each give out 20 to 30 business cards just to inventors and craftspeople we meet at garage sales, hardware stores, wherever we go. And always give out at least two business cards to each prospect. That way, they can give one to a friend.

If you need to class-up your letterhead a bit, another alternative to consider using is high quality, specialty papers and a good laser printer to build a complete business look at a fraction of the cost of a custom print job. This is a rapidly growing industry as many people are leaving the corporate world to strike out on their own. Especially now and most especially since the recessional post-horrors of 9/11/01 have inspired a new and critically-important entrepreneurial age.

A note on specialty papers: Be careful not to choose a well-known design paper. They have become so wide spread in use that now people can usually quick-print recognize specialty papers from custom designs. This may not be good for your enterprise especially if you want to be remembered as being unique and upscale.

If you're stuck for a good name for your company, don't settle for anything sarcastic. Cute or clever names are fine as long as they clearly indicate what the business is all about and they must not offend. You don't want to turn off any of your prospects. Or you can use your last name followed by the publicly known name of your product. Example: "Boatner Laser Systems" or "Our Family's Homemade Ice Cream."

If you think you can get away without using letterhead, remember you will already be saving a considerable amount of money in advertising costs by using this book. But we urge you never to take a shortcut, if it can be publicly perceived as a shortcut. From an established image and credibility standpoint, create appropriate letterhead.

To take the next steps for both our goods and service readers, we are going to create two fictional businesses. Our first business will be a service company and we'll call it: "Betterway, Inc."

Two young women, one a single mother with no educational background and the other, a two year business student with a knack for successfully solving small business sales challenges. They have formed a management company to help keep small businesses on a profitable track.

We'll call our product company "Auto Solutions" (Inc. if applicable). Retired chemist Fred Adams has developed a substance that not only cleans windshields, it removes scratches from the glass. During his little product debut party, a friend suggested he call his formula, "Windshield Swiper." The name stuck. From that, he developed a scratch-remover/ polish and fuel-injector cleaner.

CREDIBLE, MOSTLY-FREE ADVERTISING THAT WORKS

Picture Perfect

What is the very first thing a company should do? A lawyer might suggest registering the business or establishing patents. But we believe that the first thing that makes a business a real business is...business, as in sales!

The generation of revenue that turns the dream into something financially viable. So that's where we're starting

The first step for both companies is to take a photo. It must be a professional looking shot so if you can't do a proper job, find a professional who will do it at a reasonable cost. There are photo deals available everywhere but the best way to go is digital. Check out local film-processors, or even department stores. This is when it pays to have a friend who is a photo buff who can take an excellent photo for no charge.

To photograph the Auto Solutions producers, Mr. Adams had his local artist friend make up some labels and attached them to a couple of dummy bottles. He took a two-foot by three-foot sheet of clear white art paper. Since the bottles are a little dark, the white background will help to show up the product. His photographer curved the art paper against a corner of the wall and floor to create a seamless background. When the photo is processed, all the viewer sees is the product on a white background.

Generally, this will be done with digital camera, making it immediately ready for print and online use.

Mr. Adams knows that he needs to show the superiority of his product in action, so he also takes a picture of his product in action, perhaps showing half of a scratch removed. Some products mandate a demonstration photo 3-D imaging or PowerPoint to make their function clear to the reader. Another advantage of the "Image Approach" is that it can get the message across more immediately. Remember, prospects need to understand the function of a product as immediately as possible.

For Betterway, the two women are currently working out of their homes. So of course, we need a different image shot, which will be an elegant shot of these women in an office setting, well-dressed.

They don't know any photographers and did not want to send unprofessional images, but they found an easy way around that one. One of the local papers who agreed to do a story on them, had assigned a photographer to take a picture of them in their client's office. He has agreed to give them the full use of this excellent photo if they will promise to engage his services when they produce a major ad for a client or themselves. And they promised to recommend him to their own clients. In addition, these women got a few of their clients to write short testimonials that they could feature in write-ups.

You'll want high-grade images that publications can enlarge or decrease. If digital, make sure it's high resolution — at least 10 megapixels or more to meet the requirement of publishers and webmasters. (Check requirements first). That way, you can print out

FREE ENTERPRISE

copies of 8" x 10" size that are comparable in quality to photo prints, for much lower cost per copy.

Generally your release will entail a few inches in a single column, but sometimes, you'll get lucky and get much more space. And depending on the level of interest you generate and the time you're willing to put in, you can gain placements in hundreds of Internet sites, in a very short time-frame.

And as you learn to negotiate and create viable story angles, you'll even gain some nice articles.

For your print campaign, you will need 50 clear copies for our initial phase and they must be quality photos, or the magazines won't run them. Most printers today can print quality photos photo paper. We are aiming to save money but we never want to look sloppy or disorganized.

Aside from these photos to mail, you'll want to scan your photo, so you can instantly send them to hundreds of magazines, ezines, websites and directories.

Don't Overlook the Basics

Since we know to fish where those fish are, when it comes to seemingly outdated communications technologies, why change equipment if the fish are biting? Many businesses have given up on snailmail and faxing altogether believing that the Internet is all they need but if faxes are working for you, don't stop unless and until you know a replacement strategy is proving effective, especially since blast faxing can rise above the fray because it's not generally done these days (and always, you have to adhere to the strict 'do not call' or 'do not email' guidelines.)

We are living in an age where YouTube, Facebook, MySpace and Linked-In are fighting for your attention along with the myriad forms of advertising. And consumers, especially, the eletro-savvy under-thirty market rush to populate them but most new media does not replace existing media. Media is getting very personal. In effect, they work to compliment and enhance each other. The key is striking the proper balance by testing and tracking the various media forms. If distributing ten-Thousand brochures each week to surrounding hotels works for you, don't assume the Internet or radio will reach those people just as readily.

Thirty years ago, when I first began developing and sharing my PR systems, I submitted a simple press release for a skeptical client for his new product. He had been spending thousands for his print ads and was getting nowhere. But that first simple (and free) press release got him his first $100,000 order. This same system works just as well today so don't overlook the basics.

And remember, each of the scores of communication and social networking sites will involve your time. Be jealous of your time; make sure that these sites help to make

CREDIBLE, MOSTLY-FREE ADVERTISING THAT WORKS

your life more efficient or enjoyable but if you have a venture to promote, make sure you're not getting overly fascinated to the point where you are forgetting to use them to grow your overall venture.

And now for this 'Bulletin'

Those who know me know of my great penchant for animals and Olde English Sheepdogs (I've had six). So you can imagine my shock and sadness when one early July evening, my

six-month old puppy (the one that climbed that ledge and defied gravity) just vanished into thin air. One minute I was playing with her in the fenced in back deck; I turned my back for a moment and she was gone.

I panicked like a parent suddenly separated from her child imagining the very worst and in that despair, I did nothing to help find her. So in a very short time, I thought about every tactic I ever knew. I scoured the Internet and registered her in every lost dog site. I posted an ad of Craigslist.com. Then I thought that I should also aggressively apply the basics so, just as I'm certain you've seen in your neighborhood, I posted notices at every phone pole, I knocked on every neighbor's dog, I posted a notice on my car window. For one final touch, I posted a notice on every bulletin board I could find.

Finally when that fateful call came, the lady who found her, she had seen my notice not on line or, via anything electronic but buried amongst a morass of notes and ads in the local supermarket bulletin board.

That good only community bulletin board, community calendar or, even the local coffee klatch; they are sometimes the only place that people get news or information. So whenever you're engaged in a campaign, remember you principal goal is to reach the people.

All in a Word

Next, you'll need to tell your readers what you're talking about. Dig out those original releases you submitted during your initial test phase. They can be in the form of print clippings, or printouts from the Internet. You can see that the various publications and sites have usually modified and cleaned up your original literary gem.

Get an idea of their style and layout. Get out your pen or tape recorder and rework that release. Our fictional Mr. Adams has chosen his action photo to work with. Though he received some positive feedback from his original releases, he wasn't very pleased with how they were rewritten by the publications. Here's what they did: "Auto Solutions, Inc., of Malibu, CA, claims to have developed a series of supposedly unique car maintenance products. For further information, write Auto Solutions, P.O. Box 75, Malibu, CA."

FREE ENTERPRISE

"Claims?" "Supposedly?" What kind of help is that! The first time, most publications gave him only a couple of inches of space, at most. But he learned some lessons, one being to demonstrate the product's effectiveness, and then spread that information around. The more to-the-point, supportive information you can supply, the better chance of a credible write-up.

This time around, his releases are playing much better. Here's how most of them now read. He's even getting some interviews and articles: "Auto Solutions, Inc. of Malibu, CA, has come up with an inventive new line of auto-care products. One of their products, which we tested, is called WINDSHIELD SWIPER.

This product is one of the first ever to completely remove deep windshield scratches in just minutes. After the scratch is removed, the glass is left completely clear and intact. They also have an equally polish and injector-cleaner. For further information, visit their website at www.autosolutions.com or call…

He did five things differently this time:
1) He sent photos by mail and electronically, and via his website.
2) He learned how to sharpen his description of his products.
3) How did he get the magazine to eliminate the cynical wording? Very simple. He sent them a professional sample. The magazine had the time to try it out and see it work. As an added bonus, they also gave him a reader-response card number just for the asking.
4) In addition, he discovered that the magazine had a toll-free number so he called them to discuss his product. This personal call kept him from getting lost in the email fray. Generally, you won't have to go through all these steps to insure a good release. Still, it's nice to have these means available to you.
5) He arranged to get his website posted on the release and he arranged for a link between the publisher's website to his own.

That's how you maximize a publicity opportunity. It's not going to be feasible for many of you to send a sample of your product. Instead you can send any performance tests or even testimonials from credible sources. For a service entity like Betterway, they have only three clients but they have boosted that client's profits by and average of 19 percent. The women asked their client to write a brief letter attesting to this increase and included copies with each release-request. Don't worry if you have no samples or testimonials to send. For the most part, unless your claims seem ridiculous, your release will run in a positive light.

CREDIBLE, MOSTLY-FREE ADVERTISING THAT WORKS

Whatever you do, you should include with your release a cover letter on your letterhead. We recommend the following format:

Your Professional Logo Here
Date (Important)
(Addressee)
Dear (name of press release person, if available):

My company is pursuing viable avenues of results oriented advertising and your **(magazine, website, ezine, directory, blog site etc)** was recommended to us. I would appreciate if you would run this press release and photo in your upcoming issue. If you have any questions regarding the information I have sent you, please call me at your earliest convenience.

Thank you very much for your prompt and courteous attention.
Respectfully yours,

Get Your Message Placed In Thousands of Free Media Sources

You should now be well on your way to assembling your complete packages for your target publications. Your new packages should pack a lot more punch than your initial queries. Some of the magazines will still chop and modify, but that's perfectly okay. If, however, they inform you that they charge a small service fee to place your release, cross them off your list for now. You are offering these magazines an opportunity to grow with your venture. If they're not perceptive enough to comprehend that, then their business acumen is highly limited.

"Why Should They Run Your Release?"

Everyone grows by investing resources. We'll often lend free time to certain prospects as a means to help them advance their ideas.

As ideas advance, they ultimately become high-performance clients, and everyone makes money.

Similarly, a magazine generally has a new-product section as a means of investing in viable concepts. Then, if the product grows as a result of the publicity, that individual will select that magazine in which to purchase ads, because they have already seen the potential for positive Return On Investment.

This is another fine example of bringing marketing as close to a science as possible.

FREE ENTERPRISE

Sending Out Your Package

In keeping with our theme of "Move Forward or Rot," let's begin our advertising campaign. You've lined up your print and electronic media venues for placement. Don't shortchange yourself on the number. The first fifty are just a test to work out the e-bugs.

In the pre e-days, when I distributed press releases for the 84 Olympic products, we had product releases in over 800 magazines.

The downside was that we had to send out Thousands of releases and this was before the advent of the public Internet or email. And we had a lot of competition for tight media space. Today, most people are so used to just doing it all electronically so when publications receive media info the 'old-fashioned way, sometimes it garners more attention that all of the electronic transmission of info that people are so used to sending. You'll see this theme constantly throughout the book.

If you're targeting 50 print publications, then you want to target at least three times as many websites or free directories. Also, consider sending out faxes; they can get more attention than any mail. **Remember, that when it comes to advertising anything for free, always include Craigslist.** Here's the best way to start your media distribution matrix with the first fifty:

List #1

Go over your list of publications and websites and choose six of each that you feel will have the greatest impact. With the balance of magazines and websites, choose three within your concept's particular field, and general newspaper publications and websites, nine of each in total. Of these nine, one should be from your high impact list. Label this as list #1.

List #2

Repeat this procedure with another nine magazines and websites, except this time, choose two others from your high impact list. This is list #2.

List #3

You should have 32 publications and Websites remaining, which include the remaining three from the high impact column. NOTE:

Most images and copy will of course be transmitted electronically but you may also send them by snail mail if your electronic access is limited. Also, if you're including a sample, then snail mail is definitely warranted.

The e-revolution can mean that instead of months from now, often you can begin reaching customers and testing concepts today. But the best results are realized from a skillful blending of the new with the old. Whenever you

CREDIBLE, MOSTLY-FREE ADVERTISING THAT WORKS

We don't want any reader to be left out of the process. Buy thirty 5" x 7" (approx.) top-folding envelopes. The larger size is used for more than just the purpose of accommodating your photo. Of course, you will cover a lot more territory and save most of the expense by doing all of this electronically.

Within each envelope, or email attachment, be sure to include:

1) Your cover letter and news release on your business letter-head. Each cover letter may be a photocopy or offset printed but you should affix your original signature on each one.
2) Your Product Photo, with your business card taped to the back.
3) Any additional supporting documentation, with your business card attached to each document.

If you're able to mail an actual sample, be sure to include the above package in your sample mailing. Don't send your sample unless it appears completely professional and refined. Get help from your local starving artist or printer, or both.

If your product looks and photographs sloppily, that's tantamount to the guest of honor attending a formal gathering in a torn shirt and old blue jeans. Don't under-value the impact of properly-engineered snail-mail. Even though it can be more costly and time-consuming, under certain circumstances, it can stand above the fray of emails and actually gain you more attention. You just have to experiment.

If your product presents itself well, but you haven't developed a container yet, at least seal it in a sealed plastic bag. When we first began shipping out product samples, we didn't have a plastic bag sealer, so we used to go to the local meat market. For a few bucks, they would professionally heat seal all of our wares and never did anything smell of sirloin.

Don't let anything arrive damaged. Protect it well. Mail a couple of test shipments to yourself to see how your package holds up. Address each package or envelope and always use a specific name, if available. To the lower left of the address, write the word, "PERSONAL" as shown below

– space and underline each letter.
Your Name
Your Address
Name
Address
P E R S O N A L

If a specific name is unavailable, head the address with: Attention: News Release Department. Off to the lower left of this address, write: "DATED

FREE ENTERPRISE

MATERIAL ENCLOSED. PLEASE OPEN IMMEDIATELY."
Your Name
Your Address
Attention: News Release Department
Address
DATED MATERIAL ENCLOSED.
PLEASE OPEN IMMEDIATELY

Gather up your mailings from list #1 only, march down to the post office and send them off regular postage. The post office should be adequate for most items unless your parcel weighs enough so that a parcel service could ship it cheaper.

If you can afford an extra few dollars, send each mailing Priority Mail or a competitive ground service. Though not mandatory, this type of mail can often command more immediate attention and response. Overnight and Priority mail is also highly effective if your budget allows. The key is creativity, not doing what everyone else does.

Those first nine mailings should be fairly inexpensive. If you've followed our instructions your initial releases should to appear within two months.

After two weeks from your first mailings, send off your mailings from list #2. Five weeks after that, mail off to all your addressees on list #3.

Now, send or email a duplicate mailing, electronically – cover email and the photos. There's an alternative way to create more of an effect for snailmail: You can first send a brief email announcing that you have a new product or service that you want them to review, and that the information will be arriving in the next few days. You can also ask in the email if they want to see an actual sample of your product.

Of course, you want to use mailing judiciously at this point. If you can do this electronically complete with either a product image, moving virtual image or bite-sized electronic sampler of your concept, that is the way to go.

Back to your first emailing and mailings which are now hurrying off to their respective destinations. When we carry out publicity programs like these, nearly everything we send gets published. That's what happens with a few years of experience. When we started out, less than half of our items were published. If we had known all of the things we've shown you in this chapter, our response rate would have been much higher.

After your first mailings, wait about one week for replies. On the following week, email those magazines or even better, call those that have a public access toll-free number or use any of the free or low-cost phone services.

To find most toll-free numbers, simply visit the client's website and insert 'toll-free' in their search box. 1-800-555-1212 is the old free standard for land-lines but for cell phones, many information calls can run several dollars. Try googling for a free, sponsored 411 like 1-800-FREE411. Remember that if you call, most media folks are very busy and may not have the time for you, so an email can be far more efficient.

CREDIBLE, MOSTLY-FREE ADVERTISING THAT WORKS

Most toll-free and general directories are available on the Internet. If you can't reach the decision-makers by phone, send them an email.

Follow-up for Success

Email is of course, the most efficient means of creating correspondence. When you call these publications, ask them if they have received your news release and then find out when it might be published. If they need something else from you, do what you can to accommodate them, outside of paying any fees for your releases. Through these phone calls or of emails, they may find you and/or your product interesting enough to write a small article. Generally, each magazine will have a schedule outlining when they will be publishing various topics. Find out if there is a specific issue that may be ideal for the release of your product.

Another Helpful Tactic

Keeping in mind that the personal approach can place you light years above the fray, if at all possible, if you can either visit a editor or publisher personally, you may create several additional possibilities for promoting your venture. Maybe they'll give you more prominence in their new product section or maybe they'll see fit to write a short article about your enterprise. The downside of this is that if you don't approach them properly and politely, you could close off all your chances. So if you can make an appointment, take them to lunch, that's great but don't stalk and media prospect. Persistence has its place but if someone is put off with either you or, your idea, or just doesn't see the relevance, just back off; there are plenty of editors in the sea. On the other hand, if an editor likes your concept, listen to their ideas and then determine how you might work together. Some publishers may even allow you to run a print ad on a 'Pay per Sale' basis.

Why so much emphasis on the personal approach?

Often, especially these days, when I walk into a client's home, I often see more of one particular thing: More bills lying around; more than ever before. As is human nature, when we receive something negative, we tend to develop an aversion to it. So we get all these bills, we know we need to pay attention to them and be responsible but many cannot right now so they pile up and often end up getting ignored. But when a creditor is able to get you on the phone, you can often become 'inspired' to pay more attention to that bill.

Same with the positive use of voice contact. Direct and immediate human interaction can often prompt the most immediate and best outcomes. So whenever you can use the phone or, meet with someone in person, do not hesitate to do so. Too often people actually distance themselves from their desired outcome by overuse of email or, other forms of indirect contact. Have enough faith and pride in your product to meet with people on a face-to-face basis whenever possible.

Directories, E-Directories and Classified Ads

Many publications produce industry-related directories in print and online. These directories list all sources relevant to that industry. Often, you can get your product or service listed in these directories for free, and under many different cross-referenced sub-headings.

And don't forget to prospect catalogs. The best way is via search engines and websites, where you can contact them directly to learn their submission process. Generally, these directories and catalogs are free for the asking, especially if a publisher is trying to promote it to the industry or the general public.

If that's not possible, sometimes they will send you a previously published issue for free and you can generally find what you need about them online.

It is important to note however that some publishers frown upon sending out old issues because some of the information may be obsolete. What have you got to lose by asking?

Your other option is to simply check with your local library. They generally have all of the latest publications unless yours is highly specialized.

Remember, all of these gratuities are really not mere giveaways. They represent an investment on the part of the various publishers in your venture as well as the future of their industry. Such investments are the kind of premiums that can really pay off for a publisher as your endeavor grows. There is always the other side to contend with. Some of you will be told flatly that no releases are accepted or that your release will be subject to a several month waiting period.

The waiting period is no problem because these efforts are being layered with your Internet efforts and many of those are instantaneous. Just try to get an idea of your publication date and then change over the name of this publication onto list #3. Then pull another publication off of list #3 and send it off immediately. If they seem negative on any free news releases, be very courteous and thank them for their time. And always be courteous, no matter what you hear because you never know when your paths may cross under very different and far more profitable circumstances.

If the outcome isn't positive at first, if all parties involved deal with the problem responsibly and with good character, the result can pave the way to very strong future friendships and positive business relationships.

Keep that friendship factor in mind but remember that we always try to find alternate routes leading toward our intended goal. If a publisher initially gives you the cold shoulder, wait a few days or a week and then call back. This time, ask to speak to the

CREDIBLE, MOSTLY-FREE ADVERTISING THAT WORKS

advertising salesperson. Tell this person why you sent your information to the magazine and what it could mean if your press release is successful.

Often times, a perceptive ad salesperson will invest a few column inches in your idea to pave the way for positive paid dealings with you in the future.

If all else fails, find out what type of editorial material they will accept and submit a small article. You'll notice more and more that magazines and online articles are filled with lists and tips because people need information quickly. So if you can create a similar type of article, you increase your chances of getting published. In the meantime, some of you may have received notes or phone calls from the various magazines. These first nine releases will give you some excellent experience on how to get your best releases out there.

It is advisable to have a few extra release packages handy in case a magazine misplaces it or if you find additional publications that you want to be in. As you get ready for your next mailing, there may have been some changes in your product. Modify your news release accordingly and send them away.

Your third mailing/emailing at the end of your last five-week interval should be your best. Some of your first releases should have appeared by now and you can use those releases to further perfect your presentation.

Most of you will enjoy a good degree of success with this major kick-off of your advertising campaign. Your net result is actually a cornucopia of benefits generally reserved for publicity campaigns costing several Thousands of dollars.

With the help of the next chapter, you will learn how to deal with questions that can really make your jaw drop. What if a company wants to buy ten gross of your product? Who do you send samples to? What about quantity discounts and payments? What about brochures? And most importantly, how do you close the sale?

The above questions are known as "Demand Problems" and they are the best problems in the world to have. For thousands less than what is conventionally spent in advertising today, you could be on your way to a real fortune.

What ever happens now, at the very least, you know that you can feasibly take any good idea and give yourself a chance to profit handsomely without having to gamble away large sums of money.

The price of making a good dream happen is good thinking, not big money! Things might happen with money but things always happen with productivity. In simplest terms, you are all seeking to develop a concept of the highest integrity and then connect with the right seller, distributor, etc. and the right buyer. Yet, most people don't even stop to think about who their best prospective audience might be. And for concept success,

FREE ENTERPRISE

so much depends not just on the concept, but the correct delivery of information to the proper source.

Focus on Your Audience

As you progress through this process of making yourself known, you will gain invaluable data about where and how to find your best customers or end users. As you develop and refine those targets, keep a log as you hit your target market.

Most people are only familiar with the term 'target' as it pertains to shooting something. We don't just shoot an arrow in the air, we aim for the bulls-eye and we concentrate our energies on reaching that target. Yet in product or service marketing, too many people don't even look for their target market. Instead they try to sell to just about anybody without even aiming and of course usually run out of arrows before they hit their target. We've all experienced that uncomfortable feeling of someone trying to sell us something we have absolutely no interest in. At the same time, as you learn to identify your prospect, they will start to look for you as well.

Identify Your Target (this section may be duplicated or scanned)

Where are they? Who are they?

Prospect Profile
Describe Concept:_____

_____

_____

What will the concept be used for? _____

_____

_____

Where are similar concepts used and sold?

_____

_____

CREDIBLE, MOSTLY-FREE ADVERTISING THAT WORKS

What places might my relevant audiences visit for recreation?

_____

_____

_____

_____

For Education?

_____

_____

_____

For Commerce? _____

_____

_____

_____

What types of relevant newspapers, magazines, newsletters, Websites, search engines and directories might my prospects read?

_____

_____

_____

_____

FREE ENTERPRISE

TV or Radio? _____
_____
_____
_____

Now you have a target - something to aim for and hone in on, and suddenly your world of prospects seems far less over-whelming because you have a fairly good idea of what you're aiming for.

"But Where Do I Get My Bow & Arrow?"

While we may be closer to reaching our target, knowledge of where you want to go doesn't get us there. You have to learn the tricks of your particular trade - the inroads to your market. Remember to track down mentors who can teach and guide you.

Why not just hire a Distributor?

Engaging the correct distributor or sales representative (a distributor generally buys then distributes your product to specific retail markets, a sales representative may generally act as a broker for many different companies) can be a componental part of your plan but certainly doesn't guarantee mass sales. And the wrong distributor can lock you in to a distribution deal even if they can't deliver for you. Proceed cautiously by interviewing several prospects.

There are plenty of distributors and representatives out there, but many serve only a fraction of a particular market. You have to find the one who can reach your market. And they have to prove their worth before getting a permanent commitment from you. Then you still have to call attention to your concept.

Support

Assuming you go with a distributor, you still have to figure out how people are going to know your product is available. Maybe you'll need several distributors. It's all part of the search. But to reach a market successfully, you have to address several aspects of marketing and each aspect should work in concert with the other.

Just as we have undertaken everything else in a progressive test-step format, this will be most important when it comes to advertising. Most people have a very narrow vision on what advertising is. They think it means buying space in a publication or some

CREDIBLE, MOSTLY-FREE ADVERTISING THAT WORKS

other form of media, after which time, people flood to the stores and buy like crazy. Well if that were true, every venturer would simply buy ads and just cash in.

Of course, successful exposure is a very different story. You have to focus, then your production has to make the right impression and you have to be careful to protect your investment and maximize your return potential.

A Multi-Million-Dollar Campaign for under $5,000?

This is one of the coolest ways to propagate your venture state-wide, nationally or even, internationally and, achieve the same results as if you spent millions. You see television ads all the time everywhere via a plethora of media but how does a typical well-produced television ad become a television ad? It of course starts with the client who wants to drawn attention and patronage to his business. Wanting to do it in the most professional fashion, he engages an advertising agency who concludes that television would yield the client his best R.O.I (Return on Investment).

The ad agency then researches the business and develops a series of campaign proposals and if the client likes one of them, they establish a budget. Even for a regional campaign, fees can range in the Tens of Thousands of dollars so sometimes smaller companies will attempt to produce the ad themselves but if the quality and call-to-action isn't up to par, they could actually scare away customers.

But spending too much of a state-wide or national campaign could send a company into bankruptcy. Most ad agencies are more than happy to spend your money but they will make no guarantees about results. If their campaign is successful, they will grab all the credit; if they fail, it's all your fault.

So just like the manifold ways of tapping into the Internet Freeways, what if you could create a Multimillion-Dollar television campaign for your venture for under $5,000, and sometimes, well under that? Of course you'd do it but you'd have to see it to believe it.

If you know who Smokey Bear, the Crying Indian, *Nothing But Nets*, Anti-Smoking Ads or Michael Martin Murphey's Wildfire Foundation are, you know what a PSA is. It is a Public Service Announcement created generally as an appeal for a topic related to the well-being of the public. Most but not all of these causes are non-profit and, have a 501(c) 3 tax-exempt status, meaning that your contributions are tax-deductible.

In addition, while you can indeed use your non-profit to raise money, it must be a legitimate cause and it absolutely must be completely detached from your commercial enterprise. In other words, you can't use a PSA as a cover to promote a commercial venture. However, if the PSA grows your non-profit, some recognition will naturally spill over to your for-profit side.

FREE ENTERPRISE

While local television air time can run in the Thousands of dollars, running a national ad just once can easily run in the Hundreds of Thousands of Dollars. But the placement cost paid to a station or network by the client for a PSA is free, because it serves a social benefit to the public.

Stations and networks run a certain amount of PSA's for free to comply with FCC regulations regarding community and social service obligations. Often, you will see bus banners and even billboards with public service ads warning us about email scams, or dangerous driving, etc. And in the corner, you'll notice a little insignia from the Ad Council. The United States Ad Council is largely responsible for many of the beautifully-produced PSA's and that's where a vast majority of causes turn to develop and distribute their public service ads for their charitable concern.

The Ad Council does a highly professional job of researching, writing, producing, duplicating and distributing your PSA and their list of clients-in-waiting is both long and impressive. All you have to do is pay them around $700,000. (SEVEN-HUNDRED-THOUSAND DOLLARS) and commit to a minimum of three years with them. Oops..$700,000. a bit pricey for you? Well then, let's take a look at doing the same thing for under $5,000.

Here's the recipe which we'll compare to the higher-priced process:

Then you can decide which one you can afford. I will walk you though this while citing an actual example that I did last year for the Wild Mountain Fire and Forestry Foundation in Utah.

Recipe for Your Very Own PSA

STEP ONE: What is your aim? What do you want your PSA to accomplish for you? Do you want to raise money, awareness; are you looking for someone to donate their used airplane?

STEP TWO: Do you qualify? If you are raising money as a charitable concern, you need to be a certified non-profit, generally what is known as a **501(c)3**. While you can apply for a 501(c)3 on

your own, you will probably need some help. There are many legitimate companies on line who offer this service for a fee ranging between $400. to $800. This can take several months so be prepared. However, once awarded, the exempt status is retro-active for a year or longer.

Also, you will generally be better working with a more localized company with a real office so you can check up on their progress.

CREDIBLE, MOSTLY-FREE ADVERTISING THAT WORKS

SCAM ALERT – When you need to raise money, there are tons or companies out there offering to help you… for a fee. For that fee, which can range between 2,500. and $20,000., they will aggressively try to convince you that they can secure your tax-exempt status on an expedited basis. Be very leery about engaging these services. They will promise to not only secure your 501(c)3 quickly but, for an extra fee, will tell you they can raise the grant-money you are seeking through their professional grant-writing process. When you're desperate for money, this can seem as tempting as Pumpkin Chocolate-Chip Cookies but you should view them with the same scorn as those unsolicited foreign emails promising you millions. These 'Grant-Scams' are similar to the Inventions-Wanted scams. Instead, study any offer carefully and explore how to do most of the work on your own.

STEP THREE: Design Your PSA. For the wildfire prevention PSA, we wanted a recognizable spokesperson. Our first choice was the composer and singer of the 80's song 'Wildfire' Michael Martin Murphey.

After some simple Internet sleuthing through his website, we were able to contact him and learned to our surprise, that not only did he write that song but was already a staunch supporter of wildlands preservation and prairie restoration. He readily agreed to do it. Now all we had to do was arrange the shoot.

STEP FOUR: Prepare Your Production. Not only was it easy to write the PSA and our appeal for support, 'Murph' helped us every step of the way. To ensure the ads fit his style and delivery. He even gave us the rights to use the 'Wildfire' song in our ads at no cost.

STEP FIVE: Accrue Your Crew. Unless you have some training, you should not try to shoot this ad yourself. There are exceptions. "The beautifully-produced 'Nothing But Nets' campaign included many basic DV-cam shots and the effect worked but you cannot take shortcuts on production values like shooting and editing.

For the Wildfire campaign, several things fell into place. First of all, we asked Murph to provide us with a tour schedule and determined that we could coordinate some hours before a per-formance in Moab, Utah. Next, we needed a competent video crew, preferably, in the area. In a matter of hours, we found Jim Mattingly of Omni Video who agreed to work within our pro- duction budget which was under $2,000. This included editing. Jim came highly recommended as a local field reporter who had produced a lot of tourist ads and, had even done some work for CNN.

FREE ENTERPRISE

STEP SIX: Shoot Your Ad. Murph was running two hours behind so feared we might not complete the shoot with good daylight. But we did; two PSA's plus a 90-second streaming video for our website. We got some great footage and the editing was precise and professional. If you haven't seen the ads on TV yet, they can be seen under Michael Martin Murphey's name on YouTube.

STEP SIX: Distribute Your Ads. If you google PSA Distri-bution, you will notice some companies will offer to do it for you…for just $50,000. Or, you can always go back to the Ad Council with a check for just $700,000. OR…you can follow this amazing process as follows:

a) Test: First, you need to test your PSA locally to ensure that it's delivering the message. This can take some time so you need to be patient. PSA's may be free but they do not run very often each week on any station.

How to Get Your PSA's on local television or radio

Just call the stations and ask what they need to review your PSA for placement on their station. Most stations will accept a DVD but some prefer a Beta sp format. Neither is expensive to duplicate and with the right home computer, you may be able to burn DVD copies yourself.

b) Adjust: If necessary, make adjustments on edits. Is your phone-number promi-nently displayed, is your website easy to see and remember? Is your call-to-action really calling people to act?

c) Retest: Then, if your ads are now formatted and ready for larger distribution, including national distribution, how do you do that? Just the copies alone to reach hun-dreds of stations would place you well over budget. But I promised you a National PSA all-inclusive for under $5,000. (or, well under that). So here's the coolest part:

Real National Distribution for Your PSA

My distribution 'secret' is really not a secret at all to most insiders, no matter what they may charge you for distribution of your PSA.

The simple secret is …'NAB.' That's it's. What's NAB? It's the National Associa-tion of Broadcasters. On the third Friday of every month, NAB distributes qualifying PSA's to well over 1,000 key stations nationwide for download via Satellite feed.

Stations then update and refresh their PSA inventory by cycling in the new and rel-evant PSA's. The cost for this service is not $700,000. It isn't even $50,000. It is FREE. All you have to do is meet their basic criteria for a bona fide PSA and away you go.

CREDIBLE, MOSTLY-FREE ADVERTISING THAT WORKS

So there it is: A real and genuine national campaign for under $5,000. And all you have to do is have a worthy cause that is structured as a non-profit. And it doesn't stop there.

You can do the same thing with CNN and the Weather Channel and there are many more subsets but these are key and these are FREE. The national Public Service Announcement criteria are fairly reasonable so use your imagination. Is there a way that you can create your own Multi-Million Dollar campaign for next to nothing? Is there a cause that you could serve or, affiliate with?

My cool secret for promoting your interests nationally or even internationally is now your secret.

The Best Ad That Never Ran

Did you know that back in 2009, one of the most successful television commercials during the Super Bowl never made it on the air? How can that be?

The now-famous ad, produced for the People for the Ethical Treatment of Animals (PETA), was a rather racy ad showing scantily-clad women interacting with vegetables; not in an obscene way but it was certainly suggestive. The tagline: *Vegetarians Make Better Lovers*.

The network determined that the ad crossed the line and it was pulled from the line-up. Now the moment that happened, the ad became one of the most talked about issues of the Super Bowl. Millions eventually flooded YouTube or anyplace else that they could see the ad. By the end of the 'controversy', nearly 50 Million people were at least aware of the ad. So without spending Millions to distribute their ad, PETA plotted an extremely brilliant strategy and not only got their ad out there, even more people paid real attention. They figured out how to stand way above the fray and compete in a Multi-Million dollar advertising arena simply contriving a controversy.

Now here you are, perhaps with a modest business aim. Or maybe in fact, you have a much larger vision for your concept. How do you accomplish that? We've already established that it looks cheesy to hold up your ad in a crowd of a morning news show. But what if your ad created a polite and legitimate controversy? It could happen but your ad would need to:

   a) represent a very worthy cause.
   b) be masterfully produced.
   c) embrace a legitimate controversy both in its production values and its subject matter.

Of course, this is not an easy task to accomplish. Essentially, the aim is to get your ad to make the evening news because of a legitimate controversy which ends up depriv-

Little guys like you work their way up the media food-chain everyday; what's stopping you?

FREE ENTERPRISE

ing the public of your message. But studying what PETA did and how this became an international story may provide yet another means to make your concept into something newsworthy.

The little guy withy a big and worthy idea doesn't generally get the needs breaks to get the word out. And sometimes those messages are highly beneficial. What PETA did was 100% original and can never be repeated but this is simply another example of media pathways that may be open to you, if you can figure out how to plug into them and, do so in a non-offensive manner.

Give Birth to a Direct-Response Television Campaign, even if you don't own a TV

You see them everywhere and, more than ever before, especially in this economy. The Pasta-Makers, Pet Nail Trimmers, Magic Switches; things that seem amazing and that promise to make your life just a little more convenient, as long as you call that good-old toll-free number. Some of these items are indeed effective; I test them all the time.

Some of them don't really work as promised, if at all but you bought the 'sizzle' (the promise) without knowing about the steak (the product). If the ad is clever and convincing, you call. But if see a product that you could really use, what an ideal way to sell and buy whereby you could benefit from this product in the shortest time frame, directly as a result of watching the ad. The use of Direct-Response ads is expected to grow as the economy struggles to maintain.

Direct Response is a way of jumping off the virtual sales shelf and calling more attention to itself. So imagine how cool it would be if you could sell your product in this manner but how? How could you possibly assemble the resources, the production crew, the editing? And even if you do all that, how could you possibly get you ad on the air? All of this costs Thousands of Dollars at the very least.

You know what's coming next; I'm going to claim that there is a way to put this together for little or no money. First of all, take a second look at the title of this section: How to Give *Birth*… I can show you a way to actually get the campaign started. I am only the Gynecologist; you'll have to be your own Pediatrician.

As with the Internet, many technologies and general social services have accidentally converged to create truly amazing and broad-reaching growth opportunities not just for the little guy or growing entrepreneur but, for most small businesses. One that we've alluded to briefly is Community Television stations. These are usually local, limited band stations that generally broadcast just to your immediate community. Virtually anyone can create a show and have their very own *Wayne's World*. Sometimes, participants pay a very nominal fee to use the equipment or, to purchase recording materials but often, the whole process is free. And this can spell two interesting media opportunities for you: You

CREDIBLE, MOSTLY-FREE ADVERTISING THAT WORKS

may be able to produce your own 60-second Direct-Response Ad or, you may be able to produce an Infomercial for little or no cost.

Recipe for Your Very Own Direct Response Television Ad:

STEP ONE: Find A Community Television Station. Is there one in your community that you will be able to use? If not, see if there is one in a neighboring community. Any town-hall should be able to direct you accordingly or simply flip the channels until you find it.

STEP TWO: What Will They Provide? Find out their specific parameters. Some may want you to take a brief class to teach you how to use the camera and, the editing. Sometimes the equipment may be a bit antiquated as it is often donated. But as long as you know how to use it and the end-result is achieved, you should be fine. The training is usually brief and sometimes, there will be someone to actually assist you for no charge.

STEP THREE: Plan Your Media Project. You will need to write your ad and even though the ads you see are fairly simple, copywriting for television is not as simple as it looks. Because the entire message and call to action must be conveyed within 60 seconds, the words and images must be chosen very carefully. If you can't afford to hire a copywriter, see if anyone at the community station has any copywriting experience.

Also, it can be helpful to watch a number of direct response ads and try to mimic their style. It can also be helpful to get as many eyes on the copy as possible. People often think they are better writers than they really are so it's important to collaborate here if you can. Be sure to show your product in action in varied situations. The images will tell the story, the writing supports that story.

STEP FOUR: Call To Action. How do viewers order your product? In the beginning, you may have to start modestly since you may not have the means to secure a toll-free number but, maybe you could set up a second phone line in your home-office until you can. And what about accepting credit cards? There are programs on line or through your bank but be sure to research this carefully. There are also fulfillment companies you can engage to process and ship orders when you've graduated to that point. In

STEP FIVE: Begin in Anyway You Can. The key is getting started and since your resources may be limited in the beginning, for ordering your product in the beginning, you may only be able to have viewers send a check to an address on the screen. Or, maybe the community station has a number you can use, with voice mail.

Reach the U.S.A. with your PSA.

FREE ENTERPRISE

STEP SIX: Getting Your Ad On-Air. Assuming, your ad is sufficiently professional, it's of no good to anyone unless it's running on television somewhere. But how do you do that without paying the Hundreds, Thousands or even Millions of Dollars to do so? The best place to start is that same community television station where you produced your ad. They may simply let you run it occasionally for no charge or, they may have strong restrictions against running anything of a commercial nature on their station.

Then, you have second option: Assuming your ad has some legitimate widespread commercial appeal, you can go to small local commercial television stations and ask them if you can run your ad on a 'Per-Sale' basis. This means that for every one of your product you sell through their station, you will pay that station a pre-agreed-to percentage of that sale.

STEP SEVEN: Refine Your Ad and Grow! If you begin to achieve some success with your free television campaign, you should consider pouring some profits into professionalizing your ads and, continue your per-sale campaign. Also, be sure to place your ad on YouTube and similar free-post sites. But you may have to soften the message a bit to meet their guidelines.

Getting on television or streaming online (like YouTube) in a credible, non-embarrassing manner is a challenging and competitive affair. Producing an ad, even of the highest quality, is no guarantee of success. At the same time, many direct-response television ads began with little more than a video camera, the will to succeed and, an idea with genuine appeal.

No matter what your budget may be, even if it's non-existent, always proceed as if you're producing the finest production ever to meet the small screen. The crazy thing about products and commerce, especially as pertains to direct response, you could have the worst product ever but it could sell well for a while because you have a quality direct response ad. Conversely, you could have the best product ever but without public awareness and distribution, it could be the one to fail. Aim to both have a quality product and aggressive distribution and you'll afford yourself the best opportunity for success.

Affiliate, co-op and crossover marketing are not new but their applications have changed markedly, To learn more about this process as it applies to online applications, please visit www.pepperjam.com. Then, try to secure some trial affiliates on your own, who would help promote your website for a small per-sale (not per-click) fee.

Negotiate

The idea of television advertising, especially when resources are limited, seems like a far-fetched prospect. But something interesting happens in an economic downturn: Television stations and networks have a harder time selling media which means the

CREDIBLE, MOSTLY-FREE ADVERTISING THAT WORKS

amount of 'unsold inventory' (ad minutes) increases. As a result, most television stations, especially local stations become more receptive to creative liquidation of their ad space.

Ad services want to grow with their clients so it's well worth a conversation to see how flexible they might be.

Summary

Understand how advertising really works.
- Be credible.
- If you are going to use an advertising agency, do your homework so agencies can't prey on your ignorance.

Identify media targets.
- Identify appropriate publications for your news releases.

Create a professional image.
- Create a business name if you haven't already.
- Create a complete business correspondence look; i.e. business cards, letterhead and envelopes.
- Acquire a good photograph.
- Write a credible product or service description.

- **Get your message placed.**

- Submit news release packages and e-releases according to the prescribed timetable.

_Explore the possibility of producing either a Public Service Announcement or and Direct Response Ad.

- Make sure you follow-up so your efforts aren't wasted.

- Be sure all your basic data is readily available on your website.

-Explore the possibility of utilizing a PSA for your venture.

Focus on your audience.
- Make sure you are focused on the right target audience -

Potential Challenges and Solutions

Challenge: Can't locate the right special interest publications, websites, ezines, Directories, Electronic Classified ad sources, Community Television Stations or Distribution resources.

Solution: If this process were simple and dumped in your lap, everyone would be doing it. This is both a 'learn-by-doing' and detective operation but if you stick with it, you can identify free or low-cost resources everywhere.

CREDIBLE, MOSTLY-FREE ADVERTISING THAT WORKS

I've never known of a product or concept that didn't have a related publication or some website resource. The answers are there. You just have to know where and how to look. Make google your best friend. You may also need to spend some time learning how to search the Internet and, how to ask those key questions that deliver the answers you are truly looking for to advance your concept.

If your Internet access is limited, go to your local library. Your local librarian should at least be able to point you in the right direction and help you access the e-world.. Librarians are also highly-trained researchers whose services are usually available just for the asking. Make certain you have checked out any related industries or retail businesses. Try the Yellow Pages.

Don't merely rely on the Internet to resource key publications in which you can place free news, check the newsstands and ask the magazine stores if they can look up your related topics in their order books. Often, no matter what you find on line, a newsstand can teach you a lot about what people are actually reading about your topic.

Challenge: Can't get any of your material published or placed on line.

Solution: This would be very unusual unless your concept violates certain ethical or general publishing guidelines. Seek out additional magazine sources. Find out why your items have been rejected and make the proper corrections. For any aspect of our society, there's a form of media that represents it. Stretch your imagination. Get your news out there.

Before You Continue . . .

- Have you researched potential publications, websites, registries and directories for free exposure?

- Have you written energetic press-releases that clearly communicate the advantage of your concept? Do you have visual support and streaming videos, if necessary to convey the efficacy of your concept?

- Have you followed our procedures for submission and placement?

POWERPOINTER TWENTY-THREE
Let Your Concept Guide Your Future

It's an odd paradox. We are admonished to plan our lives but if we plan too tightly, we may go in the wrong direction. What is the solution? The simple answer: It's in the doing.

Our actions both shape and direct us, and sometimes tell us which way to go. This is the process of creating the ever changing story of why, what, where and when. What it is you want to do, why, where do you see it going, and when do you want to get there?

These are critical questions but they cannot be answered by standing still. So you think you need to create a sophisticated marketing plan and not stray. That's partly true.

You need Instructions and a Vision about where you want to go, and how to get there, but it's your actions you take and the inherent results that matter.

Every success has a story behind it, a story we can all learn from. Like the Ken-Mark Boys in the tiny Cape Cod town of Centerville, Massachusetts. Years ago, this office-technology supplier was interviewed by a local journal and asked about the secret for their success. The interviewer, a staunch and traditional business journalist, asked this highly successful team about the details of their business plan. The boys laughed. They had no detailed plan, just a formula that worked.

They commented that while others were busy creating detailed plans, raising untold amounts of money and having countless meetings, they were out there selling and making money. Your story is going to happen when you take the chance to find your best formula for success. And that story will reveal that map. Without the story, you have no map to follow along the road to success. As you begin your venture, one important word of advice:

Begin..

And pay attention to:

...The reasons WHY you must make a change and check to see if you are doing it for the right reasons.

... What do you want to get up every morning and rush out to do, and where you want to end up? How will that feel?

...When do you see this happening? hilanthropic activities, friendships, family relationships, personal well-being

Little guys like work their way up the media food-chain everyday; what's stopping you?

What is your vision? Can you see it? Can you see yourself being successful? How will that look? Write a paragraph or two about what you see. Then try to transfix that story into your mind and see it everywhere.

POWERPOINTER TWENTY-FOUR
Selecting the Best Marketing Systems for Your Concept

Before reading this book, most people could only name a few ways to market a product or service but now you see that there are hundreds of mere basic systems and then each one of those systems has several adaptations. And of course, there are an unlim-

Little extras can add up to a lot of profit.

CREDIBLE, MOSTLY-FREE ADVERTISING THAT WORKS

ited number of combinations. As a young inventor and entrepreneur, I basically took over the family garage at an early age in fact, from the point when I turned eleven years-old, our family car never saw the inside of a garage until I left for college. As a result of my inventive curiosities, I would constantly find myself in the little local hardware store. Every small town had one. The smell of paint, lumber and the old wood floors. And shopping was easy because they usually only had one brand. In, out and back to work.

As a young adult almost immediately after Home Depot opened their doors in Massachusetts, I had occasion to need a power drill After driving around for ten minutes just to find a parking space, I remember the exact feeling I had when I finally walk in the door: Sheer amazement. This was hardware store heaven. After meandering around her vast aisles, I came upon the drill corridor and my joy transmogrified to sheer MELT-DOWN. How was I going to choose among 100 drills? Who would have the time to do that?

Perhaps you're feeling the same way right now. You're excited because you now know that your idea is possible and attainable. But which direction should you ultimately take your concept and how much is this all going to cost?

The answers are simple and the cost is either minimal or, nothing at all but be certain to pay attention to the steps for evaluating and evolving your concept so you don't end up with a warehouse of broken dreams: Here are those steps:

1) Agree firmly on either one concept, idea or product to test.
2) Determine what your concept's best and superior features are.
3) Determine your contact information.
4) Start by developing a free and simple press release and distribute it for free through just one or two of the simple press services.
5) Observe the results. Where are they coming from, what industry or field of interest?
6) Develop a Press Release or New Product Release and aim to place it in relevant web sites and their accompanying print publications.
7) If relevant, test a direct-response ad and carefully evaluate the response.
8) Determine which media is delivering the strongest results.
9) Aim to either get more editorial mention in the strongest websites or publications or create a paid test and measure your Return on Investment. As you determine what promotional tactics work for you, keep expanding the process remembering that every situation is different. For example, if you have a storefront that sells souvenirs in a tourist town, two of the most important sales elements are both your sign and some visibility of your product. Then you'll want to distribute a brochure in all connecting towns and gas stations and web directories. You build out from your original media foundation.

FREE ENTERPRISE

The key is to determine what is going to be the most visible to your customer on an initial basis. But how do you determine that? The answers are surprisingly simple:

1) If you have an existing business, simply observe who your most frequent customers are. Where do they come from, are they a particular age group, do they have certain interests in common?

2) What do they read, what radio stations do they listen to? If you were one of your customers, what route would lead you to your business? A sign, business cards or brochures in all local businesses. Think about the pathway that would lead your customers to you and never settle for just one pathway.

Then go through the *'Core Strategies'* list and pick out just one or two strategies at a time to test. And remember to try to do as much as you can for no cost and if you do have to commit any money, make sure the system will contribute to your profit.

I finally ended up not only getting used to the Home Depot but now I can't live without it because I can choose those tools that will precisely meet my needs and you can choose the marketing tools that will precisely grow your dreams.

The Great Big-Bird Exercise

Here's one of my favorite ways to help readers get some excellent power-boosters for your concept. Providing you feel that your concept or process is sufficiently protected, do the following:

1) Create a gathering of as many people as possible. If you belong to some organization, ask if they will participate. Try to have at least 25-50 participants.
2. Hand out a few post-it not sheets to each participant.
3. Explain to them what you're up. Describe your venture in sufficient detail for them to understand it .
4. Let them know of any specific challenges you are facing.Tell the group that you're trying to resolve those problems but are facing roadblocks.
5. Ask the group for their specific answers or solutions to your roadblocks. Have them write down their suggestions and then, bring them up and stick the notes to you.
6. The more you look like Big Bird at the end of this exercise, the more successful the exercise.

You can and should legally use a PSA to support or grow your legitimate non-profit, educational, socially-beneficial venture.

CREDIBLE, MOSTLY-FREE ADVERTISING THAT WORKS

ACTIVATOR TWENTY-THREE
Hitting Home Runs

There are many ways to get to home plate. You can hit a single or double etc and then be driven home by your teammates, you can walk around the bases or, you can hit a home run. It's fun to think about how Babe Ruth struck out over 3,000 times. And then he had his home runs. There are millions of active and budding entrepreneurs who embrace this technology as their primary mode of operation.

Imagine if a hitter could really trigger a computer program embedded in his brain to determine whether or not his swing would deliver a home run. That's why this book was created. Once you learn the techniques and they become a part of your business framework, you can stand at home plate and determine which pitches might have a greater chance of hitting a home.

You can now test any number of directions that you might want to go in for free or very little money and when you see the one that starts to garner the response you're seeking, swing!

Home runs or no swings; this is how I live my life along with millions of savvy business people who really want to drive their best ideas forward. I develop ideas and test them with press releases, blogs and websites nearly every day. From these responses, I learn how to formulate far better marketing approaches because I learn what my end-user wants first.

There are some excellent direct response ads out there touting some excellent products that reflect truckloads of sensible research, and we have all seen some terrible ideas that don't work but, that sell quite well simply because they are sold quite well.

If somebody is trying to hard to sell you something instead of offering you something that is truly relevant to your life, be suspicious.

If somebody is trying to hard to sell you something instead of offering you something that is truly relevant to your life, be suspicious. Why do those someones have to shout so loudly?

It's because the product or service cannot stand alone on its own merits.

Because I listen as intently as possible to the needs of my prospects and then create the best possible product based on their needs, I don't have to force my ideas on people. My strike outs at the plate only affect me and not my end user. I use those strike outs to teach me what direction not to go in so that when I'm ready, I stand at that plate and there it is, my home run.

FREE ENTERPRISE

POWERPOINTER TWENTY-FIVE
When Things Don't Go As Planned

Humans love the sense of security that a plan affords them. We love to see that everything is laid out and clear and we feel so much more secure when everything planned out. We plan our day, our houses, our business. And when things don't quite go as planned, we feel very insecure.

For a successful entrepreneur, planning is largely an illusion because as we've shown, it changes so often so as you develop your idea you'll see your plan both unwind and then unfold.

This is not to say that you shouldn't have a plan but a *flexplan*, as we call them. Hold fast to your ideals but be willing to bend, learn and restrategize when the path to success presents many and varied twists and turns. Success is never as easy as the fancy infomercials plan but it does happen to the persistent and adaptive.

CREDIBLE, MOSTLY-FREE ADVERTISING THAT WORKS

CORE STRATEGIES AND TACTICS NUMBER THIRTY-NINE
Write Conversion Scripts for Front-Liners (Receptionist, Sales Associates, etc). Identify common needs, questions, and obstacles to appointment setting. Write responses to answer questions and overcome objections. Train your staff to use these scripts. Evaluate, upgrade, and even test staff skills as needed.

HOW TO SUPERCHARGE THIS TACTIC: Have the script posted by the phone, right next to the internal incentive plan for those staffers who bring in the most new customers, or existing customer Upsells. Be sure to train customers as sales are a necessary skill for any job?

HOW CAN YOU ENGAGE THIS RIGHT NOW FOR YOUR VENTURE?

_____

_____

_____

_____

CORE STRATEGIES AND TACTICS NUMBER FORTY
Create a New Customer Orientation Kit. Give every new customer an orientation kit that includes your brochure, business card, resume, a warm welcome letter, and discount certificates. Think of this as a sort-of operations/owner's manual. Giving these items out as a kit instills a sense of reassurance and confidence.

HOW TO SUPERCHARGE THIS TACTIC: In the kit, provide an appointment or service/maintenance calendar with you so they can more readily keep to their schedule.

HOW CAN YOU ENGAGE THIS RIGHT NOW FOR YOUR VENTURE?

_____

_____

_____

_____

CORE STRATEGIES AND TACTICS NUMBER FORTY-ONE
Create Customer Satisfaction Surveys. Mail out a multiple-choice checklist to every customer and leave room for comments. Ask for permission to use their survey as a testimonial and ask for referrals. Allow for anonymous response, and include self-addressed, stamped envelopes for reply.

HOW TO SUPERCHARGE THIS TACTIC: Create incentives for those who respond, especially for those who offer valuable testimonials. Also, consider doing the survey by email or phone making responses easy for the customer.

HOW CAN YOU ENGAGE THIS RIGHT NOW FOR YOUR VENTURE?

_____

_____

_____

CORE STRATEGIES AND TACTICS NUMBER FORTY-TWO
Create Effective Professional Signage. External signs provide valuable repetition. "It is the gift that keeps on giving." It is usually a one-time purchase that doesn't require you to keep on paying for your investment. Effective signage is the only external marketing piece that is a "pay once" investment. Make sure your sign tells your prospects what you do, why you should be contacted, and how. Make it easy to read at a distance and use bullets to list your benefits. The challenge is to be professional, informative, and enticing without causing car accidents. And remember, signs should not stop outside. Make your office or waiting room takes advantage of an opportunity to see with the appropriate media or signage.

HOW TO SUPERCHARGE THIS TACTIC:
Temporary Sign or Banner. Create a special offer and fly a temporary banner. Be sure to respect zoning restrictions. Put impressive statistics in numbers such as "Over 10 Years of Experience," or "Highest Ratings in Industry." Readers like numbers because it gives them confidence in you. Add a call to action and use large, easy to read fonts ("Call today and find out why we're the right choice."). A simple rule is: "The more effectively you tell without crowding your space, the more you sell, if you tell it well."

HOW CAN YOU ENGAGE THIS RIGHT NOW FOR YOUR VENTURE?

_____

_____

CORE STRATEGIES AND TACTICS NUMBER FORTY-THREE

Have lots of special offers. From discounts to new programs or product modifications, clients love new ideas that may serve to improve their results with you.

HOW TO SUPERCHARGE THIS TACTIC: Prospects also love to hear about new things; the element of positive surprise gives them new reasons to keep coming back.

HOW CAN YOU ENGAGE THIS RIGHT NOW FOR YOUR VENTURE?

CORE STRATEGIES AND TACTICS NUMBER FORTY-FOUR

Make Your Print Ads Work. If they're done intelligently, print ads do work but don't expect people to come flocking to your door if your ad isn't structured properly. With print ads, well-researched content and placement are critical. Test your ads by placing them in different publications, on different days and in different sections (i.e. if you're targeting athletes, try your ads on the Sports pages). If you run an ad series, make them look similar, but advertise different services. Use testimonials. Establish a need; tell the reader your solution and why they should choose your service. Give them motivation to call by listing a terrific offer, and use a deadline in your offer to create the incentive to "Call today!"

HOW TO SUPERCHARGE THIS TACTIC: Remember, your reader will be asking: "So what?" "Who cares?" and "What's in it for me?" Answer these and you've got a sale! Also, as mentioned earlier, always seek out and test free online classified to see which works best for you, especially if you can achieve the same or better result for free.

HOW CAN YOU ENGAGE THIS RIGHT NOW FOR YOUR VENTURE?

FREE ENTERPRISE

CORE STRATEGIES AND TACTICS NUMBER FORTY-FIVE

Press Releases Pull. As we've shown throughout this book, getting free write-ups and even photos in various new product or general sections of relevant magazines can initiate distribution for a product. Become the authority and resource in your field by reporting to your ever-growing email list, everything that's new or important for your customers to know about via blast email, RSS feed, txt messaging or even blast faxing.

HOW TO SUPERCHARGE THIS TACTIC: And always, whenever communicating with your client, have a call to action that incentivizes them to buy. *Ski Area's New CrossOver Promotion A Big Success…Get Your Free Coupon Here…etc*

HOW CAN YOU ENGAGE THIS RIGHT NOW FOR YOUR VENTURE?

_____

_____

_____

_____

Identify your audience and communicate to them clearly.

CREDIBLE, MOSTLY-FREE ADVERTISING THAT WORKS

Progress Journal: (please feel free to copy or scan this page only)

Your Signature_____Date_____

CHAPTER TEN

CREDIBLE, NO-RISK PAID ADVERTISING

Maximizing 'Return On Investment'
"He who has a thing to sell and goes and whispers in a well, is not so apt to get the dollars, as he who climbs a tree and hollers."

From the back of a sugar packet from Kraft Foods, at the former D'Olympio's Deli in Hyannis, Massachusetts

Overview

We are going to explore further how to transform advertising from an out-right risk into a viable investment. There are unlimited free or low-cost means to gain high-integrity exposure for your efforts.

Activator Steps for this Chapter
1) See advertising as an investment.
2) Place media creatively.
3) Put it all together.

See Advertising as an Investment

It used to be, you'd grab your snailmail and there it is - a windowed envelope with a check for five-thousand dollars in your name.

Completely surprised, you drop everything to open it. This money's really going to come in handy. Hopes immediately fade as you behold the entire document which says,

Imagine if you saw the following in the mail." This is followed by the now obvious dummy check but it's too late. You fell for it. You opened the envelope before throwing it away.

Today, look at what people around the world do on the Internet just to try to get in front of your eyes for a moment. Look how hard they try to know you and cookie you. If just a fraction of a percent of the recipients respond, the effort pays off.

One Dollar at a Time

Everywhere you look, you see ads promising to make you Thousands or even Millions of Dollars, even in this economy. Let's take a look at those promises for a moment: Let's suppose it was indeed true that everyone reading or hearing those ads could make

Technical or Professional Magazines, and Websites

FREE ENTERPRISE

Millions or even Hundreds of Thousands of Dollars. Well, isn't that what just recently destroyed both the stock market and housing markets, the idea that anyone could make inflated sums of money? And notice how most of those over-promising ads generally use the term *make* money, instead of earning money. To me, the idea of making money, as these ads refer to it, implies the artificial creation of a wealth that either won't sustain or, was never there in the first place.

The heart of this book is to show you that you can create real revenue from a worthwhile idea and as a result, earn extra income. As you grow and refine your idea and, the means to communicate about it, that income should increase. And since the book teaches you how to adapt and adjust your concept to keep it relevant and valuable to your prospects, the chances of growing your revenue on a sustainable basis increase.

Did you know that there are millions of people who earn a good living dollar by dollar? In fact, it's often how the greatest grassroots fortunes were realized, one burger at a time, one slinky, one pack of Juicy Fruit gum...the list is as large as the foundation of this economy but we don't see it because far too often, we only see this big fortune that we're sure is just lurking over the horizon. In fact, sometimes we become so transfixed on a phony horizon, that we forget all the steps to get there. And suddenly, as with so many programs, the concept stops just almost as quickly as it starts.

Use this book to develop a sustainable and growing relationship with your venture. Learn from it, evolve with it. If you do, you chances of a sustainable relationship with improved earnings will increase as well. Dollar by dollar by dollar. That's the foundation.

The problem is that the deceit makes us very bitter and mistrusting. We feel invaded, and an increasing percentage of us are growing so numb, we are probably throwing away some real checks and some important emails.

Enter the new SPAM age, and suddenly, the effective and efficient electronic delivery of unsolicited information has hit such a lightening pace, that it becomes much more difficult to be fooled. For the average Internet user, SPAM promises so many free things, that nothing becomes enticing anymore. And that's good because that compels legitimate advertisers to use better integrity in their efforts. That's *Free Enterprise*. And it challenges deceitful advertisers to become even more deceitful.

There are ways you can do mailings, extensive Internet ads and other media placement, with little or no money up-front, but even once you learn what they are and how to do it, how can you determine the ones your audience will respond to? The primary answer is to test with as minimal financial risk as possible. We've already worked on getting an understanding as to how to profile our prospective target. Now you have to take one-step further and develop a solid sense of your audience. So the first rule of thumb is: know your audience and then find them.

CREDIBLE, NO-RISK PAID ADVERTISING

What are they watching, reading or listening to? If you're close to your target, you'll create the potential for a mutually profitable formula between your enterprise and that media.

One way is to seek out relevant publications and websites, and links, especially the ones with heaviest traffic. But also seek out specialty sites, ezines and specialty print newsletters.

Next, based upon the logic of the profit potential, you'll need to convince that website, ezine, magazine editor, radio or TV station or network sales-manager, etc., that your enterprise represents at the very least, a good bet for a market-test. Very often, especially the smaller stations or publications will want to work with you and will even help you to develop a no-risk test, since they know that their real profits are based upon sustainable client relationships.

They will also often help you write and produce your ad for no charge because they know that if the ad is produced properly, your concept will have the best chance of selling. There are always innocent victims for every form of outright media deceit. It's enough to make the average entrepreneur wonder about media credibility in general. So how do you get people to respond without having to mislead them to gain their attention? The positive avenues available could fill volumes.

We discuss more about copy writing in Chapter 12. Be clever, witty, bright and effective and always, always get expert opinions on your writing. Be substantive. Be anything. But tell the truth, or it will come back to haunt you.

The underlying premise must be honesty. You can give away gifts, specials and discounts. You can advertise this to a limited extent on the envelope of a direct-mail package. But never orient your copy so it seems to promise something that you can't really deliver. First of all, it's generally illegal and secondly, your quick fix can erode your credibility. Go for the efficient buck but not the quick one.

Placing Media Creatively
Mass Mailing Blues?

If you ever carry out a direct-mail campaign or mass-email or blast fax, text message, pop up, viral, etc and receive a similarly low response rate, don't let anyone convince you that you should be satisfied with a low response rate. What you should be considering is that you're not focusing sufficiently on your audience.

Perhaps you have a good retail-use product or service and you're convinced that an honest mass-mailing campaign is the way to go. Should you invest several thousands to undertake a direct-mail campaign? You could wind up spending a lot of money just to turn sour on advertising.

FREE ENTERPRISE

Proceed with caution and don't expect any miracles from a mass-mailing, unless your target has either previously purchased from you or is given great incentives. If you really think a direct or mass mailing/emailing will best serve your cause, try utilizing the following two money-saving tips:

Instead of laying out the cost of all that postage, if applicable, see if your local newspaper will distribute your brochure as an insert. Include a discount coupon just to introduce yourself.

Direct mailing always has a better chance when you give people a real incentive to respond. Be aware that the one criteria not to use when choosing a particular advertising media, is popularity.

Think about the flood of SPAM-related mail you receive. Most email boxes are so flooded with ads, that prospects often avoid the legitimate ones as well.

After a while, it all looks like the same waste of valuable time. The rule of thumb – if everybody's thinking the same way, how can you think differently. If everyone is betting heavily on email ads, consider blastfax or snailmail coupons.

Ad Specialty Items

There is a fantastic multi-billion dollar industry known as the "Ad Specialty Industry" or "Remembrance Advertising." The beauty of this industry is that it creates, manufactures and sells gifts of virtually any product with the name, address or slogan of a business firm imprinted on it.

Since specialty items are generally sold in large quantities, they are usually low-dollar products but there can be exceptions. Maybe you could approach corporations to utilize your product as an ad specialty.

Crossovers

Crossovers, specials or premium offers essentially permit you to hitch a ride on a widely distributed product. You see these offers everywhere, everyday - "Special Offer," "Free Offer." - on cereal boxes or any product.

Relevancy is the key. Seek out widely distributed products that might already be attracting your potential customers. Your product or service must somehow compliment but not compete with your piggyback targets.

Suppose you produce a video, CD or DVD tour-guide of Cape Cod. Ocean Spray® juices are largely a Cape Cod product. You could approach them to make a special offer of your product on some of their products, perhaps to buy your DVD at a special discount; the customer must include two proof-of purchase seals from two different bottles of juice.

In theory, Ocean Spray® should love it because it increases consumer interest for their product. You really love it because your product is advertised in millions of homes

CREDIBLE, NO-RISK PAID ADVERTISING

for a longer period than your direct mail or our electronic ad, might have been, all at tremendous savings. You could develop reciprocal coupons, website cross-links, or discount agreements where the two products each offer a discount for the other.

The options are as extensive as there are products and services and then, multiplied by each other in all combinations. What an opportunity to get you offering out there, if you just follow the steps and take the time to do it!

Maybe a travel website or magazine would co-op with you and offer your CD to every new subscriber. There's no limit to whom you could approach, Win-Win. Everyone benefits and once again, you've carried out exposure for your goods or services for little or no money or risk.

Game Show Prizes

Some popular TV game shows are seeking out particular consumer products as prizes. For little or no fee, your product could get national exposure. What have you got to lose by simply asking?

What about fulfillment and supply? What if you get Thousands of orders for your product? We maintain that demand problems are the best problems to have. Don't prepare by overstocking, but instead have resources ready should you need to switch into high gear. You'll find the fulfillment solutions. Just be sure to always work within the time frames and commerce laws governing shipping and response times.

Putting it All Together

You don't need a degree or license to employ these techniques as your own just like you don't need to waste money on marketing techniques that do nothing but leave you with less money. We want you to have the success without having to spend to excess.

If you've followed our advice up to this point, you have given your idea a chance without wasting a lot of money. You can see that our greatest emphasis has been on three basic aims:

1) Free news and new product releases through print sources including wire services.
2) Free distribution and exposure through crossover promotions and 'per-sale' arrangements.
3) Free exposure through Strategic placement as per the Core Strategies list.

There are many marketing books available, all packed with an encyclopedia of advertising techniques. We went much further than that. We feel that you will best benefit by utilizing the specific techniques outlined as a general format. Advertising that does not promote sustainability and long-term sales-growth may profit a station, magazine or website in the short-run but will not build the important profitable long-term relationships that all vested parties need for viable growth.

FREE ENTERPRISE

Look around you. There's advertising everywhere. You see glimpses of products on TV shows, movies, local bike-races, fund-raisers; all promoting name-recognition, good-will, and hopefully that appropriate spark to motivate the consumer or end-user to act. And as many ways as there are to advertise, there are twice as many arrangements to pay for that exposure; many of which cost either nothing up front or nothing at all.

How does your idea fit in the world? Where are the exposure possibilities that you can create when you're not there to sell it first hand or to the masses? How can you create arrangements that will profit your enterprise, especially in the beginning when it's most needed?

Virtually every venture needs to be marketed and advertised, and in advertising, it's generally an accepted prospect that you risk money for possible return, especially with new ventures.

Hopefully, through this chapter, you should begin to see that you don't have to do it that way and that advertising and general exposure can become the viable investment that it was meant to be.

CREDIBLE, NO-RISK PAID ADVERTISING

Summary

See Advertising as an Investment but invest wisely.
- Know your audience.
- Develop your ad.
- Be honest.

Place Media Creatively
- Be creative about mass mailing.
- Investigate newspaper fliers.
- Provide a coupon with your offer.
- Approach relevant businesses about ad specialty items.
- Find a related product you can approach for a piggyback mailing.
- Explore all exposure and distribution avenues that can display your product without draining your bank account.
- Try direct response TV ads especially if you can share profits with the station in lieu of an ad fee.
- Investigate placing your product as a game show prize.
- Be prepared to respond to a rush.

Put it All Together
- Try all of the approaches we have laid out for you.
- Look at what others are doing and learn.

Potential Challenges and Solutions

Challenge: Getting discouraged about making a good piggyback (crossover) distribution contact.

Solution: Never pin your hopes on just one or two possibilities or you'll be a slave to their goals and you may have to sacrifice too many of your own. Try to create ten viable options for each program. Even if a company rejects your idea at first, find out what changes you could make and resubmit.

Challenge: Can't find any piggyback-distribution possibilities.

Solution: Finding the right one can take some time. This chapter tries to scratch the surface of crossover options available to you. New systems pop up every day.

Before You Continue . . .

- Are you now exploring ways to make advertising work for you by means of free exposure?
- Have you identified specific exposure ideas that best suit your venture?
- Have you tracked your media results to determine your best return on investment?
- Have you followed through sufficiently to enact your campaign?

FREE ENTERPRISE

POWERPOINTER TWENTY-SIX
Learning To Lead

As your venture develops you may find yourself in a role that you formerly left up to others: Leadership. That means you'll have to make decisions that will not only affect your life, but the lives of others. And that means you have to have a strong vision that not only makes sense to you, but to others as well. You may be called upon to trust your decisions more than ever before. Trusting yourself is exactly that. What is your self? The inner voice and the calm feeling of knowing that accompanies it. It will guide you to your goals. This trust will allow you the freedom to be who you want be and go do what you want to do in life.

To get to that place, create a process that you are comfortable with. Don't make any decisions out of emotion or frustration. Take all the time you need to weigh all sides

Aligning Yourself for Success

What is success to you? Your vision may be different from what everyone else sees as your calling. But you may certainly use your calling to support your vision.

Your Vision

Where does your vision come from? Is it driven by fear, anger or vengeance? Are you creating your vision as a result of subliminal messages from: advertising, television, obsession with an individual or celebrity, greed, selfishness or feeling of scarcity?

Or is your vision a result of what you truly believe? And will it: bring about a better world, serve others, help those less fortunate, and provide comfort and security for your friends, family and those you care greatly about, universal safety and security, be a great role model, or help you to find peace within yourself?

1) Make a list of things that you would love to do because they would bring about a better world for the higher good of all humanity.
2) Make another list of the things you are currently doing in your life right now.
3) Go down both lists and check off the items that only result in bringing about a better world.
4) Compare both lists and move the appropriate items from list 2 to list 1.
5) Begin to focus your attention each day on the items in list 1. You may find that your list 1 contains answers for you that you may never have considered. Allow list 1 to resonate with you and get very quiet about it. Insights will come to you about list 1. Write them down.

ACTIVATOR TWENTY-FOUR
Creating a Flexplan

FOR YEARS, I've received marketing and business plans often between 50 and 100 pages long and have often been hired to answer one simple question: Why isn't the 'plan' working. So I would admittedly deposit their ridiculously generous checks and sit by my pool and suffer through every word.

Generally, at the end, I would ask myself if this grand plan solved the marketing needs of the business in question. Of course, that was hard for me because I didn't understand much of what I was reading. Now, I've written fluid and successful marketing plans for years for a living but I didn't understand these wordy missives, all prettied up and packed with statistical analysis. So if I didn't understand these reports that were allegedly and specifically engineered to produce sales, how was middle management going to be able to follow these directives? Of course, they couldn't so sales would just stumble along and everyone would simply pretend that they knew what they were doing.

Marketing and business plans may have some clever and seemingly complicated elements to them or, they may be designed to market as in 'sell' but in essence they should be no more complicated to follow than driving directions or a simple recipe.

Who needs this product, business or service and why?

Marketing for the production of sales results entails various forms of communicating a need, want or desire. There are literally hundreds of ways in which we can communicate and that's the trick but once we identify those strategies and the tactics to make those strategies work, it's an easy path and the directions should be easy.

I know this to be true because I generally take those 50+ page marketing plans and consolidate them into 10 to 15 pages that become far more effective. I do this by identifying the following elements:

Targeting: How do we reach these people?

That brings us to Strategies. Of the hundreds of means available to communicate effectively for the purpose of sales, which are the best for your venture and what tactics will make it possible? Then, as we outlined in the guide, you have to look at each required strategy to determine whether you can do it effectively for free or, if there will be a necessary expense. Remember that if you can get to the same or better place without cost, why waste the money?

As you shape your marketing plan, there are certain points of action that every successful business needs to become competitive. Review these nineteen basic points and measure your progress with each:

FREE ENTERPRISE

1. Are you doing everything to maximize visibility on search engines? You must do this because you need to 'fish where the fish are' and the Internet is what most people rely on. If you do not do this, your competition will do this to and will slowly siphon away your business no matter your location, or physical presence in the market. This includes all banners and reciprocal links.

What Are You Doing_____

_____

_____

_____

_____

_____

_____

What Are You Missing?_____

_____

_____

_____

_____

_____

_____

_____

_____

_____

CREDIBLE, NO-RISK PAID ADVERTISING

2. **Are your service people building or losing customers?** There's no advertising like personal recommendations made between friends and family. The best way to encourage this type of positive "viral marketing" is to provide excellent customer service, not just with free coffee, TV or Shuttle service but with genuinely friendly people – working hard to solve customer's problems and, make them feel valued. Take the time to properly train and motivate your sales people and do what is necessary to satisfy your customers' needs.

What Are You Doing _____

_____

_____

_____

_____

_____

_____

What Are You Missing _____

_____

_____

_____

_____

_____

_____

_____

_____

FREE ENTERPRISE

3. **Is your URL prominently displayed?** You maximize your advertising efforts by listing your Web site address on everything you do. Print the URL on your company's letterhead, on your business cards, on the front of your building or the door to your office suite. Use the URL in your email signature. List the URL on any print advertising that you do, including phone books, brochures, fliers, and direct mail pieces.

What Are You Doing?_____

_____
_____
_____
_____
_____
_____
_____
_____

What Are You Missing?_____

_____
_____
_____
_____
_____
_____
_____
_____

4. What shape is your personal referral network in? Channel the energy of your most enthusiastic staff and encourage them to promote your company's product as they surf the Web.

What Are You Doing?

What Are You Missing?

FREE ENTERPRISE

5. Are you blogging regularly? People like to complain about everything and blogging creates direct access. If you ignore blog trends and dialogue in your industry, the public will eventually assume that all negative comments are true and valid. A Weblog, or *blog*, is a collection of short articles, essays, or loosely-formatted thoughts, usually written by one individual. Since the 2004 U.S. presidential election and genius e-strategist and campaign manager for Howard Dean's primal scream, blogs have become extremely popular as both a medium to get your message out and a vehicle for paid advertising. Blogs also encourage reader comments, making them a valuable tool for gathering customer feedback. Companies such as Blogger (www.blogger.com) will host your blog for free. You can also install a blog on your own Web site with free software such as MediaWiki (http://wikipedia.sourceforge.net).

What Are You Doing?

What Are You Missing?

6. Are you podcasting? Podcasts are audio files recorded in a radio talk show format. By posting podcasts on your Web site and other sites like Apple's iTunes (www.itunes.com), customers can subscribe to your podcasts, download them as soon as they are available, and then listen to them on their computers or portable MP3 devices. The software to create podcasts is free; for more information visit www.podcastingnews.com.

What Are You Doing?

What Are You Missing?

FREE ENTERPRISE

7. Do you participate in relevant online communities? No matter what the topic, there are thousands of people discussing it passionately on the Internet. By contributing to these discussion groups, you can inform your customers and advertise your business..

What Are You Doing

What Are You Missing

CREDIBLE, NO-RISK PAID ADVERTISING

8. **Are you growing your email list?** Your loyal customers want to know what's new about your services, and what specials you're offering. Building this list will help you to build your business.

What Are You Doing?

What Are You Missing?

FREE ENTERPRISE

9. Are you securing relevant reviews and ratings? If you're at the top of your game with your business, why not get on some of the great rating lists. Look how well it works for the hotel industry. People look for the stars and then, make a nearly immediate decision.

What Are You Doing

What Are You Missing?

CREDIBLE, NO-RISK PAID ADVERTISING

10. Have you selected a relevant charity or community cause? From sponsoring a local little league to donating a portion of your earnings to fight global warming, charitable giving helps to shape your company's character but it goes much further than that. Many budding entrepreneurs suddenly find themselves with a few extra dollars in their pocket and more than a few temptations. However, the first and wisest step should be to look around your life and how your community has helped you and give something back to that source first. It's not only a positive logical move, it's good karma. Aside from all of that, genuine charitable giving can often deliver a great deal a credible publicity.

What Are You Doing?

What Are You Missing?

FREE ENTERPRISE

11. Are you publishing updates about your industry? Whether you present high-visibility reports or regular newsletter updates about trends in your field, Authority Advertising is a great way to both build customer loyalty and create new prospects.

What Are You Doing?

What Are You Missing?

CREDIBLE, NO-RISK PAID ADVERTISING

12. Have you earned special recognition? What have you achieved that advances your industry?

What Are You Doing?

What Are You Missing?

FREE ENTERPRISE

13. Are you offering a limited free trial? You will have your market share if you follow the guidelines in this book but customers won't simply be handed to you. Often a great way to secure customer loyalty is to provide a small sampling of your service for free or, for a limited cost.

What Are You Doing?

What Are You Missing?

CREDIBLE, NO-RISK PAID ADVERTISING

14. **Is Your Internet Coupon Really an Effective Lure and do you email them to existing customers?** Give prospects a reason to try your services and, to keep coming back. Unlike a free sample, a coupon should be a discounted incentive.

What Are You Doing?

What Are You Missing?

FREE ENTERPRISE

15. Are you finding free press opportunities relevant to your venture? These media opportunities crop up by the hundreds each day. Identify the ones that produce real results and continue to test new ones each week but make sure your information fresh and interesting.

What Are You Doing?_____

_____
_____
_____
_____
_____
_____
_____
_____

What Are You Missing?_____

_____
_____
_____
_____
_____
_____

CREDIBLE, NO-RISK PAID ADVERTISING

16. Are you using FREE classified ads? You need to because your prospects often look to them and if you're not there, your competition will be. Use services like Yahoo! Classifieds (http://classieds.yahoo.com) to post free ads for your products and services. Also consider posting offers for free samples of your products, sweepstakes, and other giveaways.

What Are You Doing?

What Are You Missing?

FREE ENTERPRISE

17. Are your service people building or losing customers? There's no advertising like personal recommendations made between friends and family. The best way to encourage this type of "viral marketing" is to provide excellent customer service, not just with free coffee, TV or Shuttle service but with genuinely friendly people - no better way to keep customer than to make them feel welcomed and valued. Take the time to properly train and motivate your sales people and do what is necessary to satisfy your customers' needs.

What Are You Doing?

What Are You Missing?

18. What is the state of your critical business alliances and partnerships: Build partnerships with businesses that offer complementary products and services, and then promote each other. Make joint press statements about your industry, your partnership, and your products and services. Make sure your partners provide links from their Web sites to yours.

What Are You Doing?

What Are You Missing?

FREE ENTERPRISE

19. What kind of ezine are you publishing for prospects? Without an email newsletter ezine, about your industry, products and services, and related news of interest to your customers, you are losing customers and prospects.

What Are You Doing?

What Are You Missing?

POWERPOINTER TWENTY-SEVEN
Protecting Your Credit Card and Direct bank expenses

One of my editors suggested that I was being repetitive regarding consumer protection issues. It's very hard to win fights with editors and publishers. Aside from simple redundancy, they were concerned about both making the reader unnecessarily paranoid about tricks and scams. I countered that as the economy gets tougher, the crooks and scams become even more deceitful and that consumers today need to have a greater consciousness about protecting their financial interests. So this time, I triumphed over my editors and as a result, you benefit.

When we talk about free sites with free services for Search engine optimization or, press release distribution, or anything, *that means free*. So if a site is advertising a free trial of their service, you need to make sure it stays that way.

For example, if a site has promised you free press release distribution but asks for your credit card information, how can it still be free? The answer is both simple and deceptive. Every site (including yours, I hope) wants you to be a loyal subscriber so they will typically offer you a free trial month and then, will record you credit card information. What they bank on *literally* is that you, as with over one-third of their subscribers, will simply forget to cancel your subscription and suddenly your free trial begins to chip away at your credit card bill or bank account. So, unless you keep careful account and cancel on time, here are the steps you must take:

1) Aim to work with and test only free sites where no credit card information is required.
2) If the service or site seems especially appealing, find out if you can pay by postal money order or by funds other than from your bank or credit card accounts. How to protect and ensure your growth
3) Use preloaded gift or 'smart' cards that have a very small amount loaded onto them. For example, if you're exploring a press service that costs $21.00, get a $25.00 gift card so additional funds can't be extracted.
4) For anyone out there doing online commerce, automatic or online bill-pay, change all of your credit card numbers and bank account numbers at least every three months.

FREE ENTERPRISE

SCAMGUARD
The Giant Difference between Free Services and THEFT

Before you jump on line and endeavor to write to us about all the truckloads of software you can grab for free, all the books, movies, music and general business operating programs, STOP. These are not the kind of free systems that we are ever suggesting or endorsing. Yes, you can access programs (often stolen) from the Far East and, even in this country but, we want to make it clear that we are never endorsing this kind of behavior.

This is outright theft of intellectual property and if that's not enough to ward you off of the behavior, many of these pirated or programs have any number of bugs in them just waiting to not just gum up your software but they can eat your hard-drive alive.

Not long ago, against my advice, two friends of mine went inter nuts about grabbing things on-line; one tapped into endless music sites for free and the other: Every business site and book he could find. For weeks, both bragged to me about the free world they discovered and often wanted to share it with me.

I never took the bait. In fact, for me to download any attachment requires a series of extraordinary filters. Well, you can guess the ending. First, my little music pirate began to complain that her laptop kept crashing. She was lucky though, once she broomed the programs out of her system; everything worked fine. My business pirate was not as fortunate. He not only lost all of the programs he stole, his entire hard drive locked up and he lost all of his legitimate software and hardware. It cost him nearly Two-Thousand dollars and many frustrating hours to make things right again.

This book is a chronicle of the free idea development and media revolution. As with any new freedom, you need to handle these new media freedoms responsibly or you'll self-destruct both your own credibility and user rights. It is vital that we all respect its boundaries and that's not so difficult to do: *If you have to steal software, it's stolen.* There, that was easy.

SCAMGUARD
Crumbling Cookies

Most of the terms you find related to the Internet make sense and are often remembered by word or image association. I like cookies to eat but often not in my computer. For most of the free systems that I have taught you, you will not have a problem with cookies but some offer trial services just so they can in fact, plant a cookie in your computer which stores information about you relative to that site. Still, for the most part, your gains will far outweigh any problem with cookies. But sometimes, these cookies not only contain information you provided but occasional and mysterious ads that you can't seem to track down.

CREDIBLE, NO-RISK PAID ADVERTISING

Some people like cookies or, are at least comfortable with them. I am not a big fan because I fear computer viruses or other simple and unwanted incursions on my time. And even if one cookie keeps sneaking in annoying media; that can waste your time and energy so I generally crumble my cookies.

You can crumble your cookies with any number of free software and anti-virus or anti-spyware programs. But you can also broom them out of your computer yourself by taking the following steps:

NOTE: This process is relatively easy but if for any reason, you are not comfortable with it, either consult an expert or, refer to one of the free systems available to eliminate cookies. Also, deleting cookies can mean that some sites you use regularly may no longer recognize you but I easily address that by just reacquainting myself to only those sites I'm interested in.

Here's how to get rid of all the cookies in your computer:

1. Open Windows Explorer by right-clicking the Start button, Explore.
2. Open your Temporary Internet Files folder.
3. Look at the top of the right section where all your temporary Internet files are. There is a column labeled **Type** (along with Name, Internet Address, etc). Move your cursor to the word 'Type' and, click on it. This will place all of your cookies in one folder or 'cookie jar.'.
4. Bring your cursor to your **cookie file**s (any file with '.cookie' in it.)
5. Then, all you do is highlight and delete every cookie file. NOTE: Be sure you are only deleting cookie files. Also, always be careful about the validity and safety of anything you download or open on line.

FREE ENTERPRISE

CORE STRATEGIES AND TACTICS NUMBER FORTY-SIX
Target Prospects for Sales.
Create a 'wish-list' of target prospects and clients you most want to connect with, then call and request a meeting to discuss how you can help them. Take the time to figure out what significant prospects could benefit from your service and approach them.

HOW TO SUPERCHARGE THIS TACTIC: Use your imagination. There are people looking for your business right now. The more you figure out how to adapt your product or services to them, the more possibilities for your business.

HOW CAN YOU ENGAGE THIS RIGHT NOW FOR YOUR VENTURE?

___

CORE STRATEGIES AND TACTICS NUMBER FORTY-SEVEN
Create a Club or Special Membership.
Customers love the idea of belonging to a special group that provides them with special discounts, gifts and other advantages.

HOW TO SUPERCHARGE THIS TACTIC: Give out a personally imprinted Card to customers with a special discount or elite web services Code.

HOW CAN YOU ENGAGE THIS RIGHT NOW FOR YOUR VENTURE?

CORE STRATEGIES AND TACTICS NUMBER FORTY-EIGHT
Consignments or Space-Sharing. If you have a product for retail, arrange to place it in relevant local stores on consignment for a test.

HOW TO SUPERCHARGE THIS TACTIC: If results are positive, you can use those results to increase your shelf-space, get into their other stores. This is like giving prospects a bite-sized sample to prove that your business will benefit them. Aim for a prominent retail section in a store relevant to your service.

HOW CAN YOU ENGAGE THIS RIGHT NOW FOR YOUR VENTURE?

_____

_____

_____

_____

CORE STRATEGIES AND TACTICS NUMBER FORTY-NINE
Fliers, Val-Pak & Co-op Coupons. Some businesses mistakenly think this type of advertising is cheesy. Get over it! Your fliers and coupons won't look cheesy unless your marketing materials look that way. You can control the image you project by the way you deliver your image. Other potential items are cash-register ribbons, or minor/major premiums (Magnets, matches, stickers, t-shirts, pins, etc). The use of coupons and fliers are a very cost-effective way to market.

HOW TO SUPERCHARGE THIS TACTIC: Remember, in this media, you have only one second to get your reader's attention so you must create an emotional trust connection immediately. If the response to these items generates a measured sales ratio far beyond the cost of these products, then you have a positive return on investment and should continue utilizing it.

HOW CAN YOU ENGAGE THIS RIGHT NOW FOR YOUR VENTURE?

_____

_____

_____

CORE STRATEGIES AND TACTICS NUMBER FIFTY
Professional Service Directories. Often these listings are free and can get you all over the Internet delivering you that distant customer who never before knew you existed.

HOW TO SUPERCHARGE THIS TACTIC: Sometimes you can be cross-referenced in the same directory so you'll have more chances to be sought after.

HOW CAN YOU ENGAGE THIS RIGHT NOW FOR YOUR VENTURE?

CREDIBLE, NO-RISK PAID ADVERTISING

Progress Journal: (please feel free to copy or scan this page only)

_____
_____
_____
_____
_____
_____
_____
_____
_____
_____
_____
_____
_____
_____
_____
_____
_____
_____
_____

Your Signature_____Date_____

CHAPTER ELEVEN

PUBLICITY

Developing Good Sales 'Karma'
"The best form of marketing is truth well-told."

Overview

If you could achieve more credibility and results with a virtually free, well mapped-out publicity campaign, wouldn't that be the wisest way to begin? As an added plus, the benefits often extend far beyond your original concept.

> **Activator Steps for this Chapter**
> **1) Understand the importance of genuine good-will.**
> **2) Build an image from the beginning.**
> **3) Make the good will mutually profitable.**
> **Understand the Importance of Genuine Good-Will**

"Full Spectrum Marketing," "Saturation", "Market Penetration" and "layering" are just a few of the terms used for the art and science of successfully getting a message out. You must do more than reach a target (intended) audience. You have to motivate them to act positively on your message. Think of how many billions of dollars large corporations spend just to get you to like them, even if you sometimes want to hate them. "Corporate image." A company's cigarettes can kill hundreds of thousands of our citizens, yet they want you to see how they're protecting women and children here and abroad. Huh? This is marketing at its worst as it attempts to use a goodwill message to deflect the viewer from the truth.

The negative long-term net result is that it makes it harder for those with a genuine goodwill message to get through. However, there is way to reach your prospects through sincere cause marketing on a grassroots level.

How unfortunate that that small handful of corporations overtly aim to deceive the public but how fortunate that you won't ever have to stoop to that. You're going to prove that you really care about your community and the worthy causes that your potential customers care about not just on the surface but deep down and consistently, so choose your causes, products and services wisely.

FREE ENTERPRISE

The Truth about Advertising

In general, the advertising professionals will cut one another's throat to win you over. Take a moment to think how much advertising has affected your own life. You can't be too fat, thin, ugly or handicapped unless an advertising campaign develops ethics of convenience for profit's sake. It can be hard to remember who you really are! It doesn't have to be that way and you can still create successful, very low-cost publicity campaigns that work just as well. Advertising should and can be much more of a credible force in our society. The post 9/11/01 pro-America campaigns are a prime example of advertising being used to awaken the hopeful spirits of our embattled country.

You begin with a quality product or service. Then you tell the truth well. Prove your compassion: Become a credible force for your product or service.

The Full Spectrum

Of course, you have to deliver that honest message through many different sources (spectra). That is why you will incorporate the various spectra or layers we outline and integrate, and therefore, you will increase your chances of motivating your prospects. In short, never assume that one ad, one letter or any single spectrum will achieve your desired results.

Advertising is much bigger than most of us realize. Virtually every facet of our lives is affected by it. We are just beginning to realize the great evil and great good various advertising and public relations campaigns can create. The news events and people in our day-to-day lives don't just tell us what's going on, they can change the way we look at ourselves.

So what do publicity campaigns do? They work to win your heart, claiming to be part of this fabric as well. They win your heart; they may earn your trust and loyalty.

There are no shortages of heroes in this world. The problem is that most of us don't know where to look for them, and our quest is somewhat blinded by the business of terrorism which not only holds individuals hostage but international television as well. When a handful of terrorists strike, these murderers hijack a global audience for their cause.

Broadcasters will argue that they have an expressed responsibility to deliver the news. But what happens when they inadvertently promote and enhance terrorism and related acts of horror by making TV celebrities out of the perpetrators?

In the late eighties there was an interesting trend in national news-casting: tears. There were many teary-eyed newscasters after a sad or horrible story. That trend worked for a while but they're not crying any more. This is not because there are any fewer heart-wrenching stories; it's because you're not crying anymore. You've heard it all before. You're more focused, not on others' whining but on what you can do at various levels to maintain greater global and or regional well-being.

You are more solution-oriented, and savvy advertisers realize this because they know that the real differences are made by you. That's right — you. You're going to show the world where the media coverage really belongs; not with acts of horror, but with the little personal civic efforts that you can do to attack these problems. After all, who likes to see grown newscasters cry? Shouldn't the press play a more active role in reporting a solution? There used to be an interesting news-show called 'The Crusaders'. It differed in that it not only sought out hard copy and human-interest stories but also engaged in viable and tangible actions, leading to solution. That's media at its best.

Build an Image from the Beginning

You are going to be part of the world's real force of heroes and as a legitimate reward, your venture will profit. You've already proven that the individual who seeks out intelligent solutions can always find a way upward. For Example . . . Betterway, Inc. wanted to incorporate their civic concerns into a viable business function. They also would love to spend twenty thousand dollars on a modest print, radio and television campaign. The problem is they only have $941 in their company bank account budgeted for the next two months of marketing.

They watch the news and read all the local papers. After a few weeks of "town-watching," they have come upon a community problem that they want to do something about — child abuse. Their town is small, somewhat isolated and economically-challenged so there is a slightly higher than normal rate of teenage pregnancy, drug and alcohol abuse.

After some soul-searching, they realize that they can utilize their business-empowerment skills to help teens with self-esteem issues. They make arrangements through the local high school to run a two-evening self-esteem workshop. But they package it like a Tony Robbins seminar for teens.

The school, as well as the two local newspapers, provided ample publicity for the workshop. And the turnout is enormous. After all, the kids get to miss a few nights of homework. In addition, many parents who have brought their children end up staying for the workshop as well.

The program is a hit right from the start. Their style and delivery is talented and unique but the theory behind the program is as old as humankind: Raise the sense of self-value and you reduce the proclivity to self-harm. The message also played well to the parents, concerning their responsibilities to their children. The women become civic heroes and through this, they develop a healthy flow of new prospects and clientele. All that horrible, rotten news out there. Betterway, Inc. had one solution, and they wanted equal time. And they were able to get the support of local media.

FREE ENTERPRISE

In your own situation, you could garner the free support of print, county websites, radio and local television. The key is to have a genuine cause and to become knowledgeable about that cause. After that, it will naturally tie in to your enterprise.

One positive news story can equal scores of paid ads from the believability standpoint. Betterway, Inc. saved thousands of dollars in advertising costs and business became so good that they will have to hire more help.

Everyone has benefited. The community is a safer place and many teens have a brighter view of the future. The company realized a success it might never have had the chance to and heightened productivity has created more new jobs. The TV and radio stations have a civic duty anyway but now their image is enhanced because they've shown their concern for the needs of the community. That's going to help their business interests.

When good solutions get equal time with the bad news, what was once a problem now becomes an opportunity. This is not just mere public relations good will stuff as the term is generally viewed. Our community heroes have made a viable and active contribution to their community and through the way they proceeded, profitable results were immediate and tangible for all concerned.

What's the Goal?

These teen seminars were the ideal choice for their business, and there are thousands of other community needs. The goal is to find and address a timely topic in a manner that compels participants to depend on your office and have a potential interest in your business. The issues of good will or community involvement surround us. It isn't enough that donations are tax-deductible. Someone has to channel those funds and create the proper programs for recipients. If you knew just how beneficial the right involvements were, you'd take another, far more positive view of community service.

Another Example . . .

Those who know of the young Joe Kennedy, aspiring politician and son of the late R.F.K., are familiar with his efforts as head of the Citizen's Energy Corp., an organization that helps the poor keep their homes warm during the cold Massachusetts winter months. His efforts have actually saved scores of lives of elderly people whose only fault was poverty.

You have to respect this man for the genuine good he is doing. Genuine good deeds transcend all political party lines. Since his organization is nonprofit and deeply essential to the community, he deserves and gets a lot of free TV, print and radio press. He has laid a foundation of good will and action and if he plays his cards right, he'll become a very bright star in the Kennedy legacy.

In case you're wondering sometime, there is nobody who is smarter than you, only others who had the willingness to discover their gifts before you discovered yours.

PUBLICITY

You Can Even Save the World

Here's another and very different example: Rock-n-Roll music had never really been able to shake the devil image that began in the paranoid fifties. Then, along came Bob Geldof and his production of "Feed the World." Suddenly, the music assumed focus and a conscience that raised millions of dollars and saved hundreds of thousands of lives in Africa. And now more than ever before in our history, look at the unification in our country, and around the world, as good and decent people everywhere raise their voices and causes, as towers of strength and hope.

Giving of ourselves has never been more important. Sharing goodwill in your small town and on a global scale has never been more important. And it is incumbent upon each of us ensure that this energy grows stronger, especially in these challenging times.

(Okay, we'll take a breath.) No one's asking you to take on the world, just the part that's somehow relevant to your venture. Give the principles in this chapter a chance to work for you. Take a good hard look at your project and put this chapter to work.

You'll not only enjoy a credibility that will help build your product, you could earn enormous exposure for thousands less than it might normally cost you. And you'll deserve it. When the people draw positive conclusions about you through your good deeds, they will in turn, trust you and support your business. It's almost as if there is a kind of sales 'karma.'

We could all stand to hear a little more good news. Think how grateful your community, state or even country will be to you for making some good news.

Currently, and sadly, we're primarily served by the news media only in that we are relieved that the horrors aren't happening to us, as we sit safely in front of the TV, entertained, secure, informed and that ugly 90's concept: NON-ATTACHMENT. How easily the distancing afforded us via the electronic age has made us forget that each one of us can make a difference, but we each have to once again learn to mix with the world. We all have means to communicate, but what is the message?

Two decades ago, we saw a continued trend of deposed dictators who used to be able to run their countries at will until television exposed them to angry masses. The former Philippine dictator Marcos really met his downfall the moment he lost control of his TV station to his courageous successor. The American military overthrow of Saddam Hussein was largely a TV war, backed by brave soldiers and 'embedded' reporters.

Sometimes all news seems bad and leaves us feeling helpless, but one small step to attack those problems can make all the difference in the world, especially when millions of dream-makers out there each try to do their share. Among the great fringe benefits of your own small but significant contribution is growth for your venture.

Global visions begin in a single home and even more than that, in a single heart.

FREE ENTERPRISE

Make the Good Will Mutually Profitable

In the world of professional endorsements, major athletes or other celebrities push products and causes because their elevated social status creates some degree of credibility. The irony of it all is that you can do the same thing (especially now) without having to be a superhero. Just do a good deed in your community, get the media to work with you, and you'll enjoy all the hero-credibility you'll ever need. Don't be afraid to approach the media with your ideas. They are in business to serve the full spectrum information and entertainment needs of the community. Enormous, result-oriented, positive exposure can be achieved by sensible use of the media. Now you know how to build that relationship.

Camera-Shy?

That's fine. Stay that way. Shyness or excessive modesty can become a great credibility tactic. Sometimes, you can remain behind the scenes all the time and let the newscasters do the work. If you do happen to get in front of a camera, be yourself and quell your fears by remembering that you have something to teach people. After a few minor experiences, you'll get used to it. As we've said all along, give yourself a chance to discover and grow with your assets. The emphasis is on the civic event so find a cause that you can push and use it to your advantage. Your efforts will serve as another dimension of your overall campaign.

Who says you have to be rotten and heartless to be successful. Rotten and heartless people who happen to do well financially are not successful human beings and usually wind up spreading unhappiness wherever they go. When we refer to full-spectrum marketing (intelligent saturation), we must always monitor the real needs of our community.

Something about Nothing?

Two decades ago, one of the many classic Jerry Seinfeld's sub-plots was Jerry and George's creation of a 'show about nothing'. The multi-episodic theme drew raves and further established Seinfeld as one of the greatest comics of our age – for creating a show about nothing, within a show about – nothing.

What does this teach us? Who knows, who cares and who can possibly draws any corollary to any aspect of our social evolution? Perhaps the answer can be found in Julia Allison, the beautiful young lady who, without any appreciable or acknowledged talent, successfully promoted her name and image to millions. What did she do to deserve such fame, praise, admiration and adoration? The answer is a Seinfeldian *nothing*. Truly nothing. She just lived here life as the rest of us do, but with one big difference: She promoted herself, brilliantly and, in a way that could teach anyone struggling to keep their finger on the pulse of the latest and greatest promotional tricks and tactics. Using gossip and, 'follow-me' sites like Gawker.com, Twitter.com and Radar Online, coupled with the construction of a 'hear I am' website, Julia has become well known by tens of Thousands of loyal followers who make daily visits to her website. She is by all definitions, a celebrity, well-promoted and well-known, but, for no reason other than she made herself known.

Now since she has a following, she could easily monetize her efforts with sponsors seeking to reach her genre of audience. Let's review: Someone does nothing but promote themselves and, can now transform that into a profitable personal industry. So is there something, anything in my devoting a valuable page of my book to the substance of nothing? You bet because if you've studied all the things that Julia Allison has done to get herself out there to promote 'no thing,' and you think like most of my readers, you can only come to one conclusion.

If Seinfeld and Allison can use the media to create a real success over nothing, imagine the possibilities for you and your *something*. Imagine it and do it, it's real, it's completely possible and you have hundreds of helpful pages to get you there!

About that Sales Karma

The lesson of this chapter is to find out how you and your venture can both benefit and profit by finding your free avenues of service-oriented exposure. If you're genuinely doing something worthwhile for your community, let the world know.

It's a big world with millions of possibilities. Still there is nothing more powerful than a message well delivered. Make it your message. As your venture grows, you may find legitimate uses for various forms of conventional advertising. But make sure it works for you. If it's not profitable, even after tweaks and adjustments, then it's time to consider all the other alternatives.

FREE ENTERPRISE

Summary
Understand the importance of genuine goodwill.
Build an image from the beginning.
- Seek out examples in the media of promoted community services, charities, etc.
- Determine the best community cause you can best champion with your product.
- Develop a plan which clearly shows you and your product aiding that cause.
Make the good will mutually profitable.
- Develop all free media avenues to publicize your interwoven cause.
Potential Challenges and Solutions
Challenge: Can't find a relevant civic project.
Solution: There are always issues that need desperate attention. Just ask your clergy, social worker or police officer.

Indeed, you want people to buy your goods or services on its own merits. Somehow your product improves somebody's life. If it's something for a handicapped person, that is ideal media material in its own right. If your idea is a better widget with no civic relevancy, that doesn't prevent you from doing something to increase your prospects' impression of you. As the respect increases, more people will believe in what you're selling. Consider a well-publicized donation of your product to a needy group. It's important that you are genuine with your endeavor so find a cause you can be sincere about.

Before You Continue . . .
- Have you looked at your project from either a community or global enhancement perspective?
- Have you thought of ways to create positive imaging for your concept that would lead to free publicity?
–Have you developed some initial steps to help achieve your plan.

POWERPOINTER TWENTY-EIGHT
Book Many Mini-Vacations

During the process of building your idea into something great, you'll often feel bouts of seemingly boundless energy. You'll go on for days, often one too many and not realize that your best thinking is beginning to grow a bit stale.

That's why it's so important to take a day here and there to do the things you love to do because it will inspire you to think more creatively and allow your spirit to be feel fresh, childlike and creative once again.

Simply taking a little time, even just taking a walk will help to substantially reduce frustration. For me, a walk in the forest always helps o recharge my batteries and clarify my thinking.

Mini-vacation days are extremely important during this process as it is the reason you are doing what you are doing in the first place, freeing yourself to enjoy you life more. Here are some tips to help you to make time for the life you love:

1) Set both a day every week and a few hours each week (not including weekends) to do the things that you love to do.
2) Don't depend on weather or friends to keep your plan.
3) While on your mini-vacation, leave your office worries behind you. Let it go! Accept everything as it is and don't stress about a thing. Remember, you're on vacation!
4) Don't make any business calls.
5) Allow thoughts to come and go, but do not stress about a thing. You will receive insights about life in general which you should cherish.
6) Look at your vacation as the mini-reward for your efforts thus far.
7) The only tools permitted are a pen and paper. Cell-phones for emergencies and friends only.

Keep Hobbies or Mini-Escapes Close and Frequent

Whatever hobbies you love to do, have them accessible at a moment's notice or when the urge arises but remember that your hobbies may change should your own hobbies actually become your business. Spend time doing things that empower you and keep the floodgates of fun and adventure open. If you love music and play the guitar, have the instrument by your desk while you work and when the urge to play arises, do it. There is a reason the urge is there. Your inner voice is saying – I've worked enough for the moment and would like to do something I love to do to break up the monotony. Go with it and have fun! Then return back to what you were doing. You will feel refreshed, alive and free. This idea feeds your need to feel independent and at the same time creates a great feeling inside you that satisfies a certain need.

ACTIVATOR TWENTY-FIVE
The Power of Personal Rebooting

We've all done it, watched our PC's lock up and melt down for no good reason, shut 'em down and then restarted them, and everything started working normally again. But what about a personal rebooting to help refine of approach to marketing and sales of what we've created?

Not very long ago as I was completing this book, I rented a home in Vermont for the summer where I would have peace and quiet to put the final touches on my work. It

FREE ENTERPRISE

was a pleasant enough property nestled in the woods of Wilmington, Vermont and it took no time to settle in and begin work. It also took no time for the wireless system to break down and then, both the land-line and my cell phone stopped working.

At first I considered this to be a real communications emergency. How would my clients reach me, how would I be able to continue conducting my business on a global scale? I was surprised at how quickly I got used to having no phone service having spent so much time on the phone of late. But no email, that would be a disaster. So I headed down valley to the local Wilmington Library. But it turned out the entire valley would be without Internet service for several days. I thought we would have to leave the valley but then I decided to use this situation as a bit of an experiment.

How important are the various elements of communication, what do people find most credible? Here was my perfect opportunity to review my communications protocol so I decided to turn my situation into an experiment of sorts. I randomly designated ten of my e-consult clients as unwitting participants. These are clients that I have worked with very effectively for several months to many years almost exclusively by email. Then I selected ten of my clients whom I largely worked with by phone.

Three painful days later when both phone and Internet services were back up, I swapped these clients so those I was dealing with by phone, I would deal with by email and vice versa. The results both taught me valuable lessons and reminded me of principals that I had long neglected.

In a nutshell, my former phone clients were very pleased by my added detail of providing more specific instructions in writing. In general, they appreciated how my written 'recipes' helped to guide them forward far more efficiently. After this experience, several upgraded their service to include e-consults.

What about my email clients who were suddenly receiving personal phone calls? In general, they were very pleased by this personal touch and even though I could provide them with far more specifics and guidelines by email consult, they felt far more attended to by the personal calls.

While it's important to understand how every form of media matters and has its specific place and effect; My Space YouTube, Facebook, Twitter viral text messaging, email, phone, e-communities, blogging, print, snail-mail, fax, leaflets, e-cards and e-card discs, books and the hundreds of variations therein, it is more important to know that each media form is not a substitute your direct clear verbal communication to another individual. But if you tried to communicate intimately with just one prospect at a time, you would get nowhere without reaching the masses. You need *mass*-media but we often need to reach prospects one at a time. Now you can do both.

The key is to know the communications 'wavelength' your prospect is using. During key elections, our data on this comes in at a highly accelerated rate. For example, in the '08 presidential election, President Obama made consistent use of cell phone text-messaging to his constituents. Since more young people use text messaging regularly, Obama was able to get an early edge with young voters, largely because he gained early access to them.

Media is somewhat diluted these days so that means that you may have to use several media options to reach your best number of prospects. Get familiar with them. A while back, when I wasn't able to reach one of my daughters by phone, motivated by exacerbated parental concern, I finally had the motivation to send her an urgent text message, asking if she was okay. Within minutes she called me and praised me for "using the language of her generation." I got the wavelength and you should to. Don't be afraid to at least learn about technology that could make a difference for your business. It's not as difficult as it seems.

What I discovered was while many of us seem on the surface to be utilizing media forms properly; too many of us are actually hiding behind media because we're afraid of direct communications. Most everyone has become annoyed at someone and shot of an angry email that they later regretted but how vitriolic would they be to their victim in person. Email can create the illusion of effective communication but can in fact be a means from hiding from clients.

As a writer, I have crafted many speeches and position papers for some notable individuals and a few comedians. Sometimes I wondered why I didn't have the courage to get up front and of the audiences as these people commanded. They got the glory and the big money; I was stuck with a meager paycheck and the sublime satisfaction of having 'sold' my wisdom to another more courageous soul.

Use electronics as needed but never use them as a substitute for direct communication when possible. When I was electronically unplugged for those few days, I became far more aware of how I had been using electronic gadgetry and 'McMarketing' to distance myself from my clients. Me, the guy who has been in more basements, garages, kitchens and homemade laboratories and made his name by helping each individual with a custom program designed exclusively for his or her needs. Face to face. Direct contact.

Becoming unplugged reminded me of what my foundation is and helped keep my services genuine. As you get involved in all of the various genres of communications marketing that serve your needs, always remember that at the core of any plan, at the top of it is you and your prospect; you speaking to your prospect.

Many people make fun of infomercials and direct-response advertising in general but chances are, you are one of millions of honorable people who purchased this book as a result of seeing me in a direct-response infomercial or ad. I did my best to make use of the electronic mass media to appeal to you as an individual. You must hone in and then find the best way to speak directly to your individual prospects. If you are making a cor-

FREE ENTERPRISE

porate appeal, the rules are basically the same but you are often appealing to a committee and must speak directly to several individuals on a personal level.

Go ahead and reboot yourself. Take a look at all the media you're working with or intending to work with and imagine that you can't access it. How would you proceed? This is important to do so you'll look at all of your media options with a fresh perspective.

PUBLICITY

CORE STRATEGIES AND TACTICS NUMBER FIFTY-ONE
Radio Advertising and Supplemental Interviews.

Radio ads can create major impact if they are written and produced well. Your radio copy must provoke an emotional trust connection and prompt the listener to make telephone contact with you. Use professionals for your voice-overs. Radio stations will usually have available voice-over professionals. Make your copy compelling. Tell a story, but grab your listener's attention in the first sentence ("If your energy costs are going through the roof, we have a number you need to call"). Let the station help you. They will generally include this for free. Buy sensibly. Don't fall for specials from a station none of your prospects listen to. Sometimes, your local cable station will produce your ad and run it on major networks in your local area, for very little money.

HOW TO SUPERCHARGE THIS TACTIC: Many local access cable companies have free audio and video production training programs, where you can use their equipment for free. The only drawback is that you must be aware of the problems associated with buying too cheaply. If you sacrifice production values to save money, it will also cost you quality customers.

HOW CAN YOU ENGAGE THIS RIGHT NOW FOR YOUR VENTURE?

_____

_____

_____

_____

_____

CORE STRATEGIES AND TACTICS NUMBER FIFTY-TWO
Television Advertising.

Advertising on local television allows you to take advantage of niche markets and audiences through loyalty and attraction of niche-related programming. It gives you exposure to a wider audience, audiovisual impact, credibility, and enhances the effectiveness of your other media promotion networks in your local area, often, for very little money.

HOW TO SUPERCHARGE THIS TACTIC: As with radio, many community access cable companies have free video production training programs, where you can use their equipment for free but with the same potential benefits and drawbacks as free radio production.

HOW CAN YOU ENGAGE THIS RIGHT NOW FOR YOUR VENTURE?

CORE STRATEGIES AND TACTICS NUMBER FIFTY-THREE

Crossover Promotions. Contact other businesses and establish a mutually beneficial referral relationship with their products or services. Design 'buck slips' or coupons to give to your customers and cross-referral coupons for them to hand out to their clients. Locate a product of theirs that you could use to promote and sell your product, make sure you could also sell their product. Suddenly, you've immediately increased the size of your prospects. For example, if you make a special chili sauce, find a canned bean manufacturer who would let you place an ad on the back of their can in return the manufacturer could do the same on your product. Use your imagination. The crossover possibilities are endless.

HOW TO SUPERCHARGE THIS TACTIC: One of the keys to doing successful cross-promotions is to seek out opportunities that can benefit you. After you find some promising prospects, come up with ways in which your services can benefit them and approach them with your opportunities for their growth not your opportunity for your growth. Once you get one in motion, seek to get other crossover deals in the works and then, promote them through your other advertising media.

HOW CAN YOU ENGAGE THIS RIGHT NOW FOR YOUR VENTURE?

CORE STRATEGIES AND TACTICS NUMBER FIFTY-FOUR

Gifts and Samples. Oddly enough people do not always value a product or service that is given away for free, but they love samples that are relevant to the things they are looking for.

A great example of doing this right are the mini-meals customers get at Costco. As a result, happy customers buy more on impulse. Samples also represent a smaller investment of resources. The exception is when you send a customer a thank you gift for their loyalty.

HOW TO SUPERCHARGE THIS TACTIC: If relevant, think about giving away some of your product or service as gifts or prizes on radio or television shows.

HOW CAN YOU ENGAGE THIS RIGHT NOW FOR YOUR VENTURE?

_____

_____

_____

_____

_____

CORE STRATEGIES AND TACTICS NUMBER FIFTY-FIVE

Frequent Buyer Program. Some vendors hand out punch cards and punch a hole for every purchase. This can be done for almost any retail service. You benefit most from rewarding loyalty.

HOW TO SUPERCHARGE THIS TACTIC: You can send a private email invitation to special patrons and possibly include a temporary password that entitles them to special services or discounts.

HOW CAN YOU ENGAGE THIS RIGHT NOW FOR YOUR VENTURE?

_____

_____

_____

_____

_____

FREE ENTERPRISE

CORE STRATEGIES AND TACTICS NUMBER FIFTY-SIX
Community Service. Sponsor a drug awareness, or child safety day and get free media coverage and the opportunity to hand out business cards.

HOW TO SUPERCHARGE THIS TACTIC: Personally volunteer to a worthy cause or, donate goods or services and get media exposure for it, if done in a tasteful manner.

HOW CAN YOU ENGAGE THIS RIGHT NOW FOR YOUR VENTURE?

_____

_____

_____

_____

_____

CORE STRATEGIES AND TACTICS NUMBER FIFTY-SEVEN
Pro-Active Event Marketing. Do you have a better sports drink or muscle analgesic? Why not prove it by sponsoring a local sports team? Are you a master at helping other deal with human or financial loss? Seek out, organize a breakfast for a group where your concept is relevant and offer samples, sales or both. Be sure to have prominent signage.

HOW CAN YOU ENGAGE THIS RIGHT NOW FOR YOUR VENTURE?

_____

_____

_____

_____

_____

PUBLICITY

Progress Journal: (please feel free to copy or scan this page only)

Your Signature_____ Date_____

CHAPTER TWELVE

CONVENTIONAL ADVERTISING

If It Doesn't Pay, You Don't Play
"Money is nothing more than a by-product of how you see yourself at any given time."

Howard Bronson

Overview

You may be savvy, but when it comes to advertising, we all tend to be gullible. We want to believe in miracles and shortcuts. When promoting a concept, it all comes down not to ego-gratification, but to the bottom line. Remember that the prettiest lies are always worse than the ugly truth.

Activator Steps for this Chapter
1) Create honest success.
2) Hire help as a last resort.
3) Structure a realistic campaign.
Create Honest Success

For us, advertising is an exercise of telling the truth very well. People complain about what they've purchased to the tune of billions of dollars each year. And it's not enough. The number should be much higher. That's because too many people stray from that truth just to make a sale.

Every consumer has experienced this. You buy something, only to become disenchanted because the item did not deliver on the promise implied in marketing or advertising. It's too easy to be fooled, not because ads are so tricky or deceptive but because too many people want to believe in miracles. We love to shop; we love to buy into the miracles, if just for that momentary rush that we've made our lives a bit better than the rest.

Ad execs, marketers, salespeople, etc. can be a very pushy, manipulative lot. After all, sales are the lifeblood for all of us and we have to survive with whatever techniques are available to us. Obviously, the bigger the package a salesman sells, the more money they make. Yet how many ad agencies are willing to talk about the big money campaigns that didn't succeed?

FREE ENTERPRISE

Obviously, the bigger the package a salesman sells, the more money they make. Yet how many ad agencies are willing to talk about the big money campaigns that didn't succeed? That side of it is not a very glorious experience. There are many brilliant advertising people out there. Still the only guarantees they can make are to give you their best efforts within the constraints of their own capabilities, willingness to learn and most importantly, their integrity.

We can't merely ask the media to be more responsible, but we can be more responsible about our choices. Even successful tycoons must constantly rethink the massive advertising expenditures that they formerly favored simply because it seemed to work.

Even for a successful campaign that costs ten million dollars, what if the same powerful results could be realized for a fraction of that fee?

Then companies would have more profit to spend on research, development and other high-growth areas. This would also mean that the smallest venture can also have access to those same marketing and advertising techniques.

And they do. We're going to help you level the playing field, so that your venture has the same or better chance at success. That's what progress is all about; that's why the Internet is such an advent; it places more information and possibilities into each individual and hence, empowers them. That's how true progress is made, when the measurable results are a better, more efficient way that creates more opportunities and growth for everyone.

We're still after great success; in fact, we're after even greater successes and we are bringing that power to you. From that littlest inventor looking for a chance, to the great CEO's seeking a better use of communications and sales technology, it's reorientation time and the revolution begins with each and every one of you. From now on, you control your advertising expenditures, so more profit goes to you instead of people like us. There's an added bonus; what you learn from this book about marketing will help you to become a far savvier shopper.

Your Full Spectrum marketing will cover all the angles, to assure the success of your venture. Major agencies may push this marketing concept under many different names and their definitions can be very limited.

Full Spectrum Marketing

Full Spectrum Marketing, or 'layering' has a different meaning for every venture. But for each one, you must make legitimate use of every free or economical marketing technique available to you, in order to reach every facet of your buying public (market).

CONVENTIONAL ADVERTISING

You must also seek out useful and relevant community themes that effectively bond the various forms of media with the side benefit being the growth and development of your venture. This chapter will give you enough of a base to understand how to separate the snake-oil salesmen from the legitimate sales and marketing people.

Some marketing people will use this book to enhance and compliment their already-good techniques so the numbers of competent advertising people are increasing daily.

As the advertising industry tells the public all the time, "Why pay more?" You can ask them the same question. Why should you ever pay more for advertising that will not achieve any better results than you may now be enjoying. Even for the least expensive venture, we have saved thousands of dollars in the birth stages during that critical first year. Still once you've reached some semblance of cruising speed, don't feel compelled to run to the first conventional ad agency that woos you. No matter what has happened to your concept in its first year, the ad execs would have taken the profits that should have belonged to you. Even if you lost money and went down in debt and defeat, they would have made money and excuses.

There are extremely valid advertising services and agencies out there, but you must never approach them as hopeless and helpless. Our systems give thousands more ventures a chance to happen. That's better for you and your increased successes are better for our economy. There's nothing stronger than personal excitement and incentive. No one has taken your money, spent it and left you hanging.

You're too smart for that now. By employing our systems, you've given your venture a great running start but suppose your project now mandates massive paid exposure. Though not necessarily inevitable, sometimes agency services are needed.

Barter for Ads

You may also be able to trade your goods and services for advertising time, either directly or through a third party who would accept your item and, in turn, provide the advertiser with a needed service.

In exchange for receiving that product or service directly from you or from another provider whom you paid with your goods or services, you will receive advertising space or time. There are people who will make just such an investment in you but generally, most agencies don't have that kind of faith in their results.

Now there are definite exceptions to this type of contingency program. For example, bigger agencies that maintain a staff to serve large concerns can't afford to take such risks no matter how good they are. However, there's nothing stopping that agency from trying some spot contingency programs as indicators of what could happen on a larger scale.

FREE ENTERPRISE

Hire Help as a Last Resort

Before you choose an agency, be certain you have gone as far as you can go using our techniques because they do work. After several months of positive growth indicators, try recycling some of our publicity techniques.

Are you continuing to build your image as a source and authority in your field? You could attempt a different angle with the magazine program or submit articles or editorials explaining (or be interviewed about) how your concept has improved things. Have you exhausted the piggyback possibilities?

Our first rule about ad agencies: Use them intelligently, only when you need them. Use wisdom in determining your advertising plans and not the expenditure of high dollars as the key ingredient. You should immediately be suspicious if an ad agency:

- Insists that arbitrarily buying a large number of ads is the best way to go
- Does not start out with comprehensive research
- Is not willing to create a "test" relationship.
-Attempts to immediately place you on a retainer.

If an agency specializes in only one form of advertising, like just newspaper, for example, what do you think they're going to tell you to do?

Similarly, many radio, magazine, or newspaper advertising salespeople could approach you with the same pretense about the form of media they represent. That's a lot of what today's sales are all about.

Be careful, don't believe everything you see and hear- but you already knew that. But don't ever believe the statistics they show you unless you can verify that they are unbiased. Agencies should serve you when you need them to fulfill a specific task and should not create a steady draw against your profits. Larger long-term campaigns could mean an exception but still, watch how your money is spent.

Look Closely to Tell Them Apart

If you're even considering a relationship with an ad agency, chances are you're making some money and want to make more. As you begin to realize significant profits, you'll run into two categories of business people. The first type will protect and enhance your earnings. The second type will take your money and do very little else. Keep your eyes open. I have labeled much of today's advertising as ineffective and overweight.

You, and thousands like you, are using this guide to render the dinosaurs obsolete. Agencies currently employing the systems we have laid out will love this book but the antiques who must now make major changes will scream loudly. That screaming is a good sign of an agency unwilling to learn and grow. Eventually and collectively, you will render this book obsolete. And then you know what will happen? With your help and feedback, we'll write a new version.

Know Your Risks and Share Them

Advertising implies risk although some agencies and systems have better track records than others. Some call this risk an investment but how many agencies will guarantee a return on that investment?

Yes, you often have to take a chance to succeed but sometimes agencies will take the risk with you. We generally will do so with clients as a statement of faith in our work.

If an agency or ad exec really believes his ads will succeed, ask that person to give you a month's worth of free ads to test his promises. If those free ads work and you make money, you could consider a limited test run for a similar period of time.

Maintain the Last Word

Agencies receive fees in the form of commissions, retainers and/or salaries. Their systems of compensation vary. You also have the option of setting up an in-house agency. Or maybe you've become so proficient at your marketing, that you are all the agency you'll ever need. You hire an ad agency for one thing only — results. How they go about achieving those results varies and can make the difference between your success and failure.

That's why you should have an authoritative hand in how they spend every penny. Most importantly, if they have not read this book, you may find yourself talking way over their heads. Make sure they get a copy. Those few dollars they spend on it could make all the difference in the world for a successful profitable relationship with you and other successes-to-be like you. Once they have read the book, you still must shop carefully. If you're seeking out a certain specific form of the media, still make sure you're only paying for what you need. Let's say you want to develop a TV ad to run on a local station, do you really need an entire agency for that? Maybe you just need a video production company or a top student from a communications college. Or maybe that local TV station can produce what you need for free or at a discounted rate since you're already buying time.

If you do break down and buy ads in any form of media, make sure that particular medium gives you a healthy share of free additional P.R., news, article space, whatever is relevant to your situation.

If your product does something for someone or something else anywhere, there's also a news event hiding in there somewhere.

Cut Out the Fat

When seeking out advertising services, cut out all unnecessary middlemen. Don't pay for a chain of services you don't need. A clever advertising man can advertise himself much deeper into your wallet than you really want. Shop around. As you've already seen, the exact same or better results can be realized for less if you just learn how to shop.

Structure a Realistic Campaign

Research and tracking make all the difference in the world. Once you've selected an outside agency or yourself as your in-house agency, begin with research. If the agency is smart they'll ask you all kinds of questions about you and your product, your dream. Some of the queries will seem very sophisticated, some will seem very stupid. Be patient and answer each question with respect. As they research, they are developing a proposal, for which you should not have to pay for unless you execute it.

The formation of a proposal or marketing plan can take a few days or a couple of months, depending on the size and scope of your venture.

Assembling a marketing proposal or plan is not a burden for a professional. The plan will also demonstrate how well that agency understands Full Spectrum Marketing. You'll know very quickly whether they've read this book or not. Study the plan. Spend a day or even a week evaluating it.

Never make decisions right at the presentation when emotions may cloud your ability to make rational, cost-effective determinations. Look at their fees and project what they could cost you over a year's time. Will you be locked into them even if the relationship falters? Are they taking on some of the work that you are already proficient at yourself? They may show you some artwork, slogans or body copy (the writing that comprises the ad). As you review all this material, you have to keep asking yourself, "How will this all work to sell my product?" If you're reading a lot of cute copy or medium-funny jokes, a warning-flag should go up.

Beware of Humor

We've noted earlier in the book about using humor to cope, process and manage your venture. But this is different. Being outwardly funny or comical is a special talent and unless you're really clever, you must be very careful here. One person's joke is another's slander.

Humor and cuteness can work extremely well but require a very special talent. Intended humor could be taken as cruel by certain groups. You can be sure that reprimands are often handed out or follies are abashedly exposed by any number of regulatory or special interest groups. Be careful with cute stuff.

Be Careful How You Say It

Headlines and slogans and art are what initially attract your reader or listener. Don't lose them. As we get into copy writing, remember; don't offend people or even your competition.

Yes, you see it done all the time from major competitors, which is perplexing because offensive tactics are remembered long after the product or message have been forgotten. If you knowingly insult people's intelligence, they'll ultimately seek revenge by losing faith in what you say. Even if they depend on your product, they'll seek an alternative if one ever comes up. In sum, blatant offenses in any manner ultimately create new competition

Good copywriting tells the truth in such an appealing, credible and informative manner, that the readers are motivated to buy. It's easy to stray away from that ideal since advertising and creative writing are so interrelated and multi-dimensional.

Try writing some ad copy yourself. You could be very pleasantly surprised. After all, you've already done some writing. Your magazine releases are an excellent place to draw ideas from. You can also draw from your experiences in making sales presentations. What did you say to win them over? You know your audience. Begin by writing to them just as you talk to them. Grab that old trusted friend and persuade him to believe what you're selling. Get it down on paper. A good friend will not be afraid to give you harsh criticism if you deserve it and that could prove very helpful.

Whoever writes the copy, here are some additional standard pointers that he or she may want to integrate.

More than Academics

When new advertising students come to us they always blurt out the word, "AIDA" or "AIBA" or "AIDCM." These strange-looking words are actually letter groupings that roughly spell out the following advertising formulas:

Attention
Interest
Desire
Action

AIDA = Same sequence with the B of Believability; or AIDCA = Same sequence with a C for Credibility; or AIDCM, with M for Motivation. In turn, we're supposed to be impressed that they can pick that up from a textbook. But can they write? Can they live with and sensitize themselves to a product and make me understand and believe what they're saying?

FREE ENTERPRISE

Most importantly, can they enhance their writing from valid criticism and mistakes? If yes to all of the above, and most importantly, if their work makes money, then we don't care what formula they can recite. We are only interested in ethical, cost-effective results. Formulate a plan. Incorporate only the professionals you really need for only the time you need them. Rework and revise that plan as you progress and discover better paths.

Pay. Or No Pay

The table on the next page covers many of the concepts which we have discussed in detail throughout Chapters 9, 10, 11 and 12. Use it to review and to build a consolidated advertising, marketing and publicity strategy for your inspirations. Have fun, take your time and never hesitate to re-read any element that you're unclear about.

Blueprint for Free Advertising

CONVENTIONAL ADVERTISING

	Pay	**No Pay**
Publicity, Co-ops and Crossovers	Agency	Contact Sources Yourself
M a g a z i n e s, Releases	Buy Ads	Free Articles/Press
Newspapers and Newsletters	Buy Ads	Submit Articles
		Start Your Own
Radio, Television	Buy Ads	Free Interviews or product giveaway
Internet and other On-line Services	Buy Services	Access over 50,000 free classifieds, directories search engines and blogs
Consultants	Hire someone to do what you what you already learned how to do in this book	Put experts on your team in exchange for a share of profits.
		Become your own spokesperson.
		Be a presenter at a show or seminar
		Sponsor a community service activity by providing free space or relevant product in exchange in exchange for free media exposure.
		Seek out unsold advertising inventory (billboards, radio television, print).
		Produce and distribute a national Public Service announcement, if relevant.

Summary

Build an Honest Success Story
- Stick to what we have taught.
- Barter for ads as a way to save money.

Hire help as a last resort.
- If using any aspect of a conventional ad agency, make sure you know what you're buying. Pay for only the services you need.
- Begin your relationship by having the agency read this book.
- Don't hire without reasonable assurance or a strong return on investment.

Structure a realistic campaign.
- Attempt to structure a results-oriented contingency program.
- Be sure the writing serves the need to sell the product. Beware of humor.

Potential Challenges and Solutions

Challenge: The ad people insist that the programs in this book don't work.

Solution: I would say the same thing if my livelihood were threatened.

Asking an ad exec to substantiate his discontent is not an unreasonable request. If they can give your product the same momentum and credibility in the first six months as cheaply and effectively as we can, then give them $300 for the full six months to prove it. By the way, prepare to say good-bye to that $300 and much more. Please don't spend more than you have to, as opposed to what they say you have to spend.

New and better ideas integrate with the old to enhance them. You can't begin to imagine what people will promise when it comes to selling an advertising account. Let their hype roll off your shoulders and keep your perspective. A promise is not a promise unless it is in writing and signed by the authorized and participating parties.

The advertising profession consists of persons from every imaginable background. The only experts are those whose cost-effective techniques work for you.

If you've never met advertising people, you may be enthralled by the first one you meet. That's why you should meet several to gain the best perspective. This kind of experience is a great way to test your ability to decipher charm and enticement from pragmatic advice.

Before You Continue . . .

- Do you understand the realities of conventional advertising?
- Do you now understand how to utilize conventional advertising in a more cost effective manner?
- Could you design an equally effective advertising campaign for little or no money?

POWERPOINTER TWENTY-NINE
Growth at Multiple Levels

How is the growth of your venture growing you? At the end of each chapter we not only review items that are learned from a "to do" standpoint, but also from an alignment standpoint.

To make sure your are keeping aligned with your overall progress, you must continually ask yourself: Is everything you did today, thought today, felt today, aligned with the values and philosophies of my true nature? Or have any of your accomplishments been tainted by motives counter to your vision and ideals?

Ask yourself the following questions to ensure you continue on a productive, contributive path:

1) Do I find the phone calls and contacts made today light and easy or filled with a sense of fear and pressure?
2) Do I feel that I have helped others in some way by my contact or did I cause them to feel uncomfortable and burdened?
3) Can I see that because of my accomplishments today I have taken one step further to ultimately making the world a better place or has it been only self serving?
4) Will the result of my actions ultimately move me to a place where I can feel that, as I've grown my venture, it's made a positive difference in the lives of others as well?
5) Can I feel good about today's accomplishment? If you feel good about what you have accomplished today, then you have already succeeded in reaching your most essential goals.

ACTIVATOR TWENTY-SIX
Getting Inspired when you're Tired (or even Fired)

There are completely different levels of both capabilities and results between an individual who choose to have confidence and those who choose to find any excuse not to.

Why is it so important to have personal confidence as a core principal as opposed to a response to psychobabble cheer leading? The answer is clear: If we merely tell ourselves that we can achieve something, we may be lying unless and until we achieve it. The other key challenge is to find the wherewithal to apply logic just when you feel emotional, illogical or defeated.

In business development, things are never going to work turn-key and anyone who is looking for an easy way out today will pay a tough price tomorrow. We need to be guided by a passion where we are willing to learn vital lessons but, where we refuse to accept failure as an option.

The fun of building an enterprise is best realized in overcoming what may seem to be impossible obstacles that leave you drained, defeated and unable to take the next step. Yet, you still find the way to take a breath and take that step and climb out of any challenge. Successful enterprise is a victory over challenge, not complacency. Your success will keep you alive, challenged and growing, even if you've never had a real business success before. Success often reflects enthusiasm, drive (and some dumb luck) and the fact that you chose to believe in your success this time will yield rewards far beyond your expectations.

Yes, there will be times when you'll want to give up and when you'll see things about yourself that really seem to get in your way. But if you maintain a reasonable degree of confidence and persistence and you're willing not to cave in, then you'll find a way to turn paralyzing worries, doubt, frustration and anger into positive high energy. Just use the systems in this book to drive your idea forward and believe that you can do it. If you have enough faith in your idea, even what used to be the most dreaded of days can become something new and exciting. People who choose to believe in their value and potential have a distinct advantage. Choose to be one of them.

Climbing the Steps

You'll find big dreams hidden within the smallest companies in fact, the reason so many business remain small is they don't find the way to reach those big dreams. What makes matters worse is the millions of business-ads out there promising often instant riches "$8,000. in the first month, $43,000. in the first week. So when many of you (and you know who you are) bought into those programs and success, wealth and the big house in Beverly Hills didn't magically appear (Did I forget the new Mercedes?), you determined that success was not for you.

I don't know of any short-cuts and I'm not selling any. What I am teaching are better, cheaper (often free) and more effective ways to do things. To even suggest that you don't need to work and work hard to achieve your aims is a ridiculous notion and meaning no respect to any of my readers, selling get-rich schemes to lazy people is the ultimate scam.

After all, they'll be readily tempted by the notion that they can keep on doing nothin' and of course, they'll buy those schemes and, do nothing. Then when nothing happens for them, they'll still do nothing about. Perfect for the schemer.

If you really want a bigger success, you must first picture it as a point at the top of a large stairway. You can't leap right to the top of those stairs; success and growth are a process. They have to be if you really want to both own and keep your success.

It's only natural that reaching that top step should seem impossible in the beginning. How on Earth could you possibly get there? You don't have the money, strategy or influence but what you do have is your present place, and you need to view that pleasant place as a proving ground, a dress-rehearsal for your climb upward. The better you refine and perfect your concept, the sooner you take the next step upward but that's not all that happens. As you climb, your concept improves as well. You also begin making important friends, associations and potential strategic partnerships. As you foment these connections, understand how each one might help you in the future. Keep them in your good stead.

There's another big factor as well: Rising above objections and rejections. Children crumble under criticism and rejection. Have you ever seen a small child after you tell them can't do something they want to do? They fall apart. Adults need to do a little better than that if they really want to mature and evolve. One of the fundamental functions of a business is to solve problems. The more you learn how to overcome rejection by solving problems more effectively, the more courage you grow because you now know how to do more. You're climbing the steps. Competence begets confidence begets competence.

As your venture grows, you actually need more confidence at first because that's what you'll need to make that magic sales call or, visit that impossible prospect. Armed with your growing base of knowledge, you now know that you'll find a way to meet the needs of that new more challenging prospect.

A client of mine came to me in essential ruination. A political purge robbed him of his upper-level corporate job, topped with an unexpected and brutal divorce that robbed him of his confidence. As a proud vet, what he did indeed know was that he would eventually heal, providing he was committed to healing.

When we started, he was cash-poor but rich in talent and extensive connections in his particular industry. As I carefully assessed his situation, I ascertained that he was a tremendous asset to his industry. He had invented several processes for clients over the years but never claimed any ownership or rights. So one day, a company he used to consult for approached him to secure his signature of a patent process he developed. "Sure," he said, "how much do you want to pay me?"

"How about….nothing," was their reply.

So we negotiated. He had created this multi-million-dollar process and he knew it was time to reach that top step. We proved that he invented and owned this and cited both the intermittent windshield wiper and the Blackberry settlements, both of which settled heavily in the favor of their individual inventors.

"...so sue us," they replied.

My client did something even better. In the process of my interrogating him for every nuance of information, he remembered another associate who very much wanted this technology and, who had a massive worldwide distribution program already in place through another product serving the same industry. My client had known this associate for over 25 years and trusted him both as a friend and businessman. He made an exceedingly generous deal with his friend. When the first company learned that they lost the patent rights due to their own arrogance and greed, they were outraged.

":So sue me," my friend replied. My client reached that top step, with a few stumbles right at the last moment. But he was ready, trained, networked and prepared so that top step was just waiting for him. No, it isn't easy at the top step and it shouldn't be. And when you're starting out, it all seems unattainable. So if I were to write one of those over-promising get-rich quick ads, it would be more like a get-rich slowly ad.
If you take it step-by-step, you'll really be able to see your greatest success and fulfillment in the horizon. You'll be encouraged as that horizon broadens and, how it broadens your capabilities and possibilities. Think of it all as if you're assembling a giant jig-saw
puzzle. The more pieces you fit into place, the more the picture becomes clear.

POWERPOINTER TWENTY-THIRTY
State of Mind = State of Income

I have no reservations in telling you that there are times in my life when I have struggled financially and I'm okay with that. I share that history with some of the greatest and most dedicated minds in history. No one handed me a chunk of money and said, "Go have fun." Whatever I made in this world came from my own creativity. And after all, it's always important to remember that any money you're handed is not money earned but any money generated by your idea, that's money to be proud of.

While many people and businesses that use the techniques in this book are extremely wealthy and financially successful, if you do not fall into that category, I very much want to speak to you for a moment to assure you that you can elevate your life and rise above your current situation.

My earlier financial struggles create an advantage for me over other 'entrepreneurial writers' and others who invite you to become "rich like them." I was there, where many of you are now. I've been through the struggles and frustrations of working to create cash-flow, large or small. I've worked with nothing and made it into something. Your struggles are my struggles. I understand. I have been poor and at the same time, I never was poor. Even after my divorce when my support obligations were often more than double my monthly income and I was three months behind in rent, I never ever viewed myself as impoverished. The concept was just not part of my vocabulary. I would read about people barely making it or, living out of their cares or mired in a sea of debt and would think, "Those poor people." Even thought my situation was not all that different, I never thought of myself as being in that same place. Then one day, I took a hard look at my debt-to-earnings ration and realized that by definition, I was indeed poor at the time.

So then, why wasn't I struggling or despairing? Why wasn't I scared? I had no safety net and could have been tossed out on the street at any moment. Years later, I realized the reason: I never accepted my penury as my fate. I always accepted my visions and aspirations far more in my focus than my immediate and temporary inconveniences. Like a camera that focused on the main subject while blurring out the background. Then I looked around and discovered something remarkable: There were poor rich people,people who had either financial stability, home, cars, steady income or even great wealth, people who didn't look like they were poor or struggling and certainly didn't fit the definition of poor, but were poor nonetheless.

I began to see poverty as an acceptance or resignation that the material or emotional suffering in your life will be permanent. I started seeing it as more of a way of thinking than a condition. "Outrageous", "How dare you even make such a starry-eyed insensitive statement when thousands of children starve to death every day on this planet." These were just a few of the comments that were publishable from my editors whose primary contention that due to global politics and geographical deprivation, there were Hundreds of millions of people destined to be born poor and, to die poor.

Well, I suppose I could have responded by deleting this entire section as most writers would do when a point seems to go irrecoverably awry. I could say "Oops, sorry." Or I could absolutely acknowledge the real suffering and inequities in this world and that's what I elect to do. Yes, there are many poor and suffering people in the United States but when I look at the starving and still largely ignored children in Darfur and similar, I say, "Now, that is real poverty." And I hope that my readers do what they can to help improve the lot of people in those situations.

What I'm addressing here is self-imposed deprivation and limitation by labeling oneself as poor and unable to break through.

There are so many ways to make a real and ongoing improvement in your financial situation but that becomes impossible if you think of yourself as systemically poor. At the very least, think of yourself as struggling upward and think of your current situation as temporary.

FREE ENTERPRISE

CORE STRATEGIES AND TACTICS NUMBER FIFTY-EIGHT
Market Marketing. As with Costco, if you have a household invention, often your local supermarket will allow you to display and offer either approved food samples or coupons for your product. Demo Marketing - Sponsor an event, contest, or race - something that allows you to gain high exposure for the effectiveness of your product. NOTE: Be sure your product has met all food or relevant product safety requirements.

HOW TO SUPERCHARGE THIS TACTIC: When you do this for a product, have the item available for sale right next to your display.

HOW CAN YOU ENGAGE THIS RIGHT NOW FOR YOUR VENTURE?

_____

_____

_____

_____

CORE STRATEGIES AND TACTICS NUMBER FIFTY-NINE
Quickie Sponsor. Print up color decals or stickers with your artistically rendered logo and ask relevant companies, race car owners, or anyone you can think of if they will display your decal. Be sure to have something to offer them from your service or product to make it worth their while. Don't simply look for favors but seek out ways you and another business person can help each other.

HOW TO SUPERCHARGE THIS TACTIC: The more hip and cool your logo, the more you can get prospects to take you up on this quickie sponsor offer.

HOW CAN YOU ENGAGE THIS RIGHT NOW FOR YOUR VENTURE?

_____

_____

_____

_____

CORE STRATEGIES AND TACTICS NUMBER SIXTY

Get Sponsored. Yes, you've heard me mention all of the countless causes you can sponsor but what about the other way around? If in fact, any company or organization could benefit from the work you do, why not contact them and see if they have a grant or sponsorship possibility to help both support and promote your project.

HOW TO SUPERCHARGE THIS TACTIC: Google potential sponsors and grants and try to figure out how your cause may be sufficiently relevant for you to sponsor. For example, if you work in forestry, you might consider approaching Nokia who depend on wood for their furniture.

HOW CAN YOU ENGAGE THIS RIGHT NOW FOR YOUR VENTURE?

CORE STRATEGIES AND TACTICS NUMBER SIXTY-ONE

Make Yourself Known. Suppose you're attending a speech relevant to your concept. Aside from asking the speaker the right question at the right venue, how can you be seen using and benefiting from your own product?

How to supercharge this tactic: Wear a clever t-shirt or button that tastefully describes your service. Give out coupons for samples of your service, if relevant.

how can you engage this right now for your venture?

FREE ENTERPRISE

CORE STRATEGIES AND TACTICS NUMBER SIXTY-TWO
Develop Professional Referrer Strategies. These are marketing strategies designed to promote and retain referrals from colleagues and other business professionals. One of the strongest referral bases you can build is with colleagues who are impressed with your skill level. It's critical to foster professional relationships with those who believe in you. Each week, take a potential referrer to lunch or implement a 'Key Referrer Program.'

HOW TO SUPERCHARGE THIS TACTIC: When a professional referrer consistently refers customers to you, take the time to thank them for their efforts with a personal letter. Another way to encourage your key referrers is to identify their hobbies and interests and send discounts and thank you gifts that pertain to their special interests.

LEGAL NOTE: Sometimes it is unethical or illegal to compensate certain professionals, customers, or colleagues for a referral. Before proceeding, have a clear understanding of your state's guidelines (with websites the concern may be national or even global).

HOW CAN YOU ENGAGE THIS RIGHT NOW FOR YOUR VENTURE?

_____

_____

_____

_____

CORE STRATEGIES AND TACTICS NUMBER SIXTY-THREE
Become the Authority with Professional Alert Newsletters. The purpose of an alert newsletter is to stimulate professional and customer referrals by establishing your expertise. Unlike general newsletters, alerts provide reinforcing communication with your professional target audience by establishing your value to the readers. They can be the result of your specialized knowledge and research, providing readers with advantageous information that might not be available elsewhere. They are written in an authoritative style from one professional to another.

Since they are mailed out every three to four months, they give you an excuse for continuing to mail to your target audience or professionals. They also allow you to continue to tell them what new things you can do for them. It sets you up as an expert in your specialty and keeps your name in the forefront of your audience's mind.

HOW TO SUPERCHARGE THIS TACTIC: Some people get so proficient at this, readers become almost dependent on you as a key information source and that means more sales opportunities.

HOW CAN YOU ENGAGE THIS RIGHT NOW FOR YOUR VENTURE?

_____

_____

_____

_____

CORE STRATEGIES AND TACTICS NUMBER SIXTY-FOUR
Attend a Weekly Lunch Group. Besides your private weekly lunch, meet colleagues for a meal and bring information to them directly and in a memorable way by making a personal contact. Face-to-face contact protects your existing referrers, helps troubleshoot any problems, and gives your colleagues a better understanding of who you are and what your expertise entails.

HOW TO SUPERCHARGE THIS TACTIC: Host a monthly 'Growth Luncheon' and invite different target customers. Be sure to always be generous with your alert newsletter and business card.

HOW CAN YOU ENGAGE THIS RIGHT NOW FOR YOUR VENTURE?

_____

_____

_____

_____

CORE STRATEGIES AND TACTICS NUMBER SIXTY-FIVE
Court Reception Room Staff of Referrers. Be sure to send food, flowers, gifts and goodies occasionally to your key referrers, at the front desk, reception, and phone staff or any source who refers prospects to you. You want to establish a good relationship and to have them remember your name. These first impressions are key influences for any business.

FREE ENTERPRISE

HOW TO SUPERCHARGE THIS TACTIC: Identify and reward the people who actually do the work to make the referral happen. This will perpetuate the referrals and encourage others to make referrals.

HOW CAN YOU ENGAGE THIS RIGHT NOW FOR YOUR VENTURE?

___

CORE STRATEGIES AND TACTICS NUMBER SIXTY-SIX

Reverse Sales Engineering. When you get a professional referral, be sure to call that professional referrer and report the outcome of that customer's experience. Give the referrer periodic progress reports. Whenever you receive a referral, track it down. Be sure to thank the referring party, and as noted in the previous tip, if permissible, within legal constraints, create some form of gift thank-you even if only in the form of a skillfully crafted letter.

HOW TO SUPERCHARGE THIS TACTIC: What is key is that the referring colleague knows that they made the right decision in referring a prospect to you. If you succeed in making the referrer feel this way, you've assured repeat business for yourself. It's important to know where each good lead comes from.

HOW CAN YOU ENGAGE THIS RIGHT NOW FOR YOUR VENTURE?

___

CORE STRATEGIES AND TACTICS NUMBER SIXTY-SEVEN

Cards on the Counter. Print up a special business card that offers a special trial of your product or service. Place these cards on the main counters of every office or relevant business within five miles. Be sure to ask permission of the human resources director. When they agree, kindly request that they send an email announcement to their company about your cards.

HOW TO SUPERCHARGE THIS TACTIC: Offer the receptionist or the 'keeper of the cards' and even greater discount as long as they make sure the cards remain available on his or her counter.

HOW CAN YOU ENGAGE THIS RIGHT NOW FOR YOUR VENTURE?

___

___

___

___

___

Strategies and Tactics number sixty-EIGHT ***Reconnect Innocently.*** Simply email all of your old contacts, requesting an update of contact information. This can open the door to potential new business with dormant clients. How have their needs changed. How have your offerings changed?

HOW TO SUPERCHARGE THIS TACTIC: Ask old contacts what they're up to and how you might be able to help them with any new venture.

HOW CAN YOU ENGAGE THIS RIGHT NOW FOR YOUR VENTURE?

___

___

___

___

___

CORE STRATEGIES AND TACTICS NUMBER SIXTY-NINE
Revisit Your Rejects. Have you ever bid on or, proposed a project that was rejected without finding out why? Sometimes, it could have just been a matter of a few Thousand-Dollars or, some minor informality. Try to reconnect; common business aims can turn rejection into teamwork.

FREE ENTERPRISE

HOW TO SO SUPERCHARGE THIS TACTIC: Create a brand-new approach for one of these rejectors; this can also help to open a long-closed door.

MOVING GOODS & SERVICES TO MARKET

Progress Journal: (please feel free to copy or scan this page only)

Your Signature_____Date_____

CHAPTER THIRTEEN

MOVING GOODS & SERVICES TO MARKET

The Joy of Demand
"Retail sales are like a train rolling around a meandering track. The trick is to know exactly when to get on board."

Overview

This is what you've worked for — your purpose, your path and hopefully your bread and butter. It's response time! You've cast your net. Now it's time to reel in the prospects.

> **Activator Steps for this Chapter**
> 1) Evaluate responses by tracking sales from each effort.
> 2) Be prepared with supportive date when making any sales presentations.
> 3) Sound professional and confident. Listen well so you understand your market and always tell the truth.

Evaluate Responses

When we mentioned earlier that productivity of goods and services makes money and not the reverse, we really couldn't prove that until this chapter. Your first advertising campaign is in motion and people are beginning to ask you some challenging questions. You don't want to appear ignorant because you'll be embarrassed and you'll create doubts about the integrity of your product. Letting your own doubts cause you to give up transcends foolishness. You have something that people want. That's the bottom line. Everything else between trading their money in exchange for goods and services is secondary. You'll solve all the little headaches as necessary.

Generally, you'll not hear from the dry goods stores or the major retail distributors. They have a purchase and distribution system that's complex enough to write another book about. We have seen these big guys buy a small guy's products, but that's rare. Generally, they have to be approached.

Your initial advertising campaign is capable of cutting through some of these complexities because perceptive buyers will keep their eye on certain new product sections.

FREE ENTERPRISE

You should be hearing from a number of smaller distributors and retail dealers. They will ask you about shipping, availability, pricing, quantities, etc. and you should be ready with the answers. Make a list of your distributor, wholesale and retail pricing information, shipping dates, everything you can think of.

There are specific terms and systems that distributors use for their specific industries. Try to learn as much about your area as you can before you make or receive your first phone call. If you are confronted with something you're not sure about, tell the truth. But tell it in such a way that won't turn off the customer. Inform your customers that you will get back to them within the week with the information.

Be Prepared with Support Material and Clear Contact Info

Many will ask for price lists or brochures. Have it ready at the touch of a button via your website,, but if you're making a live presentation, have hard copies ready to present. Don't become too reliant on all the electronics, especially when they detract and sidetrack from the message.

Though these are generally necessary tools of the trade, aim to keep your data exchanges down to a minimum. We have written, designed and printed hundreds of brochures and as your enterprise develops you can do a lot of fancy things. For now, just think in terms of the "PDP" or

Product Data Pages and Sites

This will consist of either a minimum two-page website, attachment, or a single sheet with a black and white photograph or a very good line drawing or illustration, under which you will clearly list all of your product features and benefits. This list should include product advantages over competition, features and benefits, without revealing any trade secrets. Dimensions, shipping weight and quantities should also be included.

If making hard copies, print only 100 product data sheets to begin with. Build up some profit and make corrections via these first hundred before you print more. You'll also need to photocopy or quick print price lists, one for distributors, one for dealers, and one for retail customers.

Sound Professional

Most inquiries will come by email. But when you receive calls, if you're a home-grown business, you can get away with simply saying "hello," but consider some alternatives. To enhance your image you can engage an answering service who will answer with your company name, or you could use voicemail.

MOVING GOODS & SERVICES TO MARKET

The first time you saw your idea as something that you could touch or see function, it seemed like no excitement could ever top that. Compare that to the present as you actually respond to the demand you created.

What began as a mere notion is now well on its way to improving your life and the lives of many others. Hard work is a nice principle. We've worked hard to develop our promotional systems. No doubt that hard work has helped many people realize certain degrees of success. But so your efforts are not wasted, be sure you've worked the hardest on your strategies. Nothing beats good thinking.

You have seen the beginnings of various routes to the future. There are many more exposure techniques available to you. All you need is more of that good thinking and a willingness to not limit yourself.

FREE ENTERPRISE

Summary
Evaluate Responses
- Answer all inquiries honestly. Pledge to research what you do not know.
- Learn as much as you can about distribution in your product's industry.

Be Prepared with Data
- Have basic product data sheets available
- Print price lists for three different audiences:
- Distributors
- Dealers
- Retail customers

Sound Professional
- Answer your phone with your company name.
- Consider an answering service or an answering machine.

Potential Challenges and Solutions

Challenge: No responses to your promotional campaign.
Solution: Some responses can take months, others will contact you right away. If most of your releases have been published and you still have received no inquiries, there may be something in your photo or your text that's turning them off. Have you been careful to clearly portray your product as an improvement over the competition?

Give each element of your campaign a chance to integrate and deliver.

After all three phases of your release mailings, if things aren't at least beginning to click, review chapters 1 and 2. You may have missed something in concept development. Were you honest about the test results? Did you make the appropriate corrections or was your mind already made up before you began testing. Bad listening makes for weak conclusions.

Challenge: Good responses, but unsure how to handle them.
Solution: The delightful dilemma. Chances are you'll make some money under these circumstances. If just to close those first few crucial deals, hire an expert in your field on a temporary basis, but only as a last resort.

Essentially, your prospects will be more concerned about your ability to follow-up than on a wealth of knowledge and experience. Whatever you do, don't lose the sale.

Challenge: Overwhelmed with too many orders.
Solution: First of all, congratulations. Now don't blow it. Run to that local manufacturer and/or distributor and show them your flood of orders. Or...many successful ventures used a garage or living room as the first office or production plant. You could de-

velop your own fulfillment (product delivery) system and hire local high school students to help with the process.

Those orders mean money is waiting out there with your name on it. Find the means to go out and collect what you've worked so hard for.

Before You Continue . . .

Can you respond to leads with an appropriate brochure or sample?
Can you follow up properly to close the sale?

POWERPOINTER THIRTY-ONE
Conditioning Yourself for Success

This is a great book for bringing any concept to life. It is most probably the most definitive source for making and marketing a product. But then the question is: will your venture make a difference?

We designed this book for people who will use their success to serve the higher good. We believe that anyone can make money on an idea. That's the easy part. But the big question comes after your success. What will you do with your success?

This is a hurting world. Everywhere you turn, someone is in need, someone is hurting. As a consequence, we are often forced to wear tighter and tighter blinders and 'burrow' or cocoon ourselves into an insular world. What we don't realize is that this behavior eventually 'forces' us to mix with the world, sometimes in a very uncomfortable way.

The book is written and designed to take the reader on a journey inward to a place where true success lay dormant, waiting in eager anticipation to be revealed. We realize that every human being operates from a perspective that is unique only to that particular person, and while we would love the reader to glean all we are saying right away, and produce exacting results, we understand that it will take time for this process to resonate with the individual.

Having said that, it's important to respect time. Too many people pretend that time never passes. It is our challenge to help the reader get closer to the level of understanding where real change can take place, where one's true purpose in life reveals itself. Until this happens, we must look together for ways to uncover what lies beneath the veil that has eluded us from what we are truly seeking in life.

Before we began to write the allegedly ethereal aspect of this book, we had been admonished by so-called experts not to get

too philosophical or theoretical because readers may feel they are being preached to instead of specifically supported. There is a very fine line.

So let's agree for now to take the experts advice in keeping the language as clear and instructional as possible, but please keep in mind that in order to create the change

FREE ENTERPRISE

you may be looking for, you must be open to allow your mind to consider new and unlimited possibilities you may not have realized before. The toughest, most pragmatic problem often requires a vivid imagination.

Throughout the book you will find that some points that are made may not have a clear answer and may appear to be somewhat vague. We do this purposely to let readers find their own answers.

Be prepared to let go of what you think you know, because where we are going, you are not going to need the baggage. From time to time you may be asked to recall some knowledge from the past that will serve you only to allow important insights to flourish. Other than that, your memory will not be needed as it contains the residue of past negativity that will prevent the flow for which you will need along your journey.

Once you arrive at a certain level of understanding, you will find that you can apply these principles not only to marketing, but to any other aspects of life you wish to be successful at.

POWERPOINTER THIRTY-TWO
Create Worthy Aims

Wanting money in and of itself is not a worthy goal. Wanting your idea to succeed and prosper is a far better goal. "The money will follow," as the old expression goes.

With the exception of basic food, clothing, shelter and love, need becomes the compulsive illusion of want. Need is not a choice, want is a choice. For example, you don't need a bigger house, fancier car or more jewelry. You may want those things but you certainly do not need them.

Remember, human beings have survived for thousands of years without cars, jewelry or expensive summer homes. You only feel that you need those things because you think you do.

Your thoughts have determined that in order for you to be happy or complete you must have more things in your life. Letting go of this type of thinking will allow you to begin to move forward, otherwise you will remain trapped in the illusion of believing that wanting is a need to survive. It is not. Without letting this belief go, you will be unable to begin the journey. We are always one thought away from departing for the journey and one thought away from arriving. Enjoy the adventure and the success you can have. You are the Captain.

ACTIVATOR TWENTY-SEVEN
Protect and Ensure Your Growth

We've come far, you and I and it's essential that we continue taking the steps to maintain a healthy business. Often, entrepreneurs are thrilled by how easy their success can arrive and, how quickly it can leave if they fail to pay attention to some of the basic ground rules. Here's a god checklist to help guide you:

a. Say "No Thanks" to Investors and Banks. As we've said, productivity makes money. Especially in the beginning, try to make your venture income-producing, not debt producing. After all you started it to make more money. When the time comes to borrow money, first make sure that your venture is showing financial promise. That way, when you do turn to banks or investors, you will be a healthier prospect for them.

b) Say No to Most Internet Offers of Foreign Money. Unless you've been in a coma, internet scams involving phony checks, reverse wiring theft are at an all-time high, suggesting that many people are indeed in a coma. As the internet has grown and now offers countless free services, visitors have generally grown more scrutinizing. Exercise old-fashioned savvy and never send any fees to anyone over the internet to secure financing. The internet advances everything but sometimes you just have to meet people face to face to know if they're real.

c) Begin Modestly. Don't set up an expensive fancy office in the beginning, and don't over-hire. In fact, most of your team should be sharing the risk with you and, doing all they can to ensure productivity.

c) Choose the Right Idea. Make sure that this is a service or product that you truly want to provide. It needs to be something that you will grow with and that will motivate you to get up every morning, and go that extra mile to ensure profit.

d) Fill A Need. You can work and grow with passion but don't simply go by instinct. Do people need what you're doing? How can you prove that on a small test-basis? Where are these people?

FREE ENTERPRISE

e) Look Like Your Well-Established. While it's dishonest to pretend to look big, it is important to project a sense of competency and organization. Have a clean office where everyone knows what they are doing.

f) Think About Solutions. All the time. How can you serve your customer better? How can you serve and compete for the same clients that big companies are going after? This will train your creative 'muscle' and better ensure your growth.

g) Pay Attention To Your Competition. Watch them, learn from them and imagine ways you can serve their customers better.

CORE STRATEGIES AND TACTICS NUMBER SEVENTY
Propose a Use for Dormant Resources. Whether human or mechanical, down business cycles have one common thread: Idle Resources. But instead of laying off anyone, see if there's a way get resources; human and otherwise, working on any project at a reduced rate; or even a spec project. Sometimes the keys out of a down business-cycle are invention, initiative and simple cost-reduction. Remember that 60% of something is better than 100% of nothing!

HOW TO SUPERCHARGE THIS TACTIC: Consider creating a second company and give out generous ownership shares for those willing to contribute their time and expertise to any given venture.

HOW CAN YOU ENGAGE THIS RIGHT NOW FOR YOUR VENTURE?

CORE STRATEGIES AND TACTICS NUMBER SEVENTY-ONE
Choose a Great Company Name. Your company needs a name that's descriptive and easily recognizable such as "Jones Public Relations."

HOW TO SUPERCHARGE THIS TACTIC: If the name you currently have isn't helping to convey and sell, change it and then, announce that change is a free press release.

HOW CAN YOU ENGAGE THIS RIGHT NOW FOR YOUR VENTURE?

FREE ENTERPRISE

CORE STRATEGIES AND TACTICS NUMBER SEVENTY-TWO
Pay careful attention to the latest forms of communication technologies, especially if your target audience is younger. Text messaging, blogging, Twitter, Facebook, Myspace; where is your audience getting most of their information. Where there is information flowing to your targets, you need to be part of that flow.

HOW TO SUPERCHARGE THIS TACTIC: Don't ever look like you're obviously prospecting. Instead, simply communicate your expertise.

HOW CAN YOU ENGAGE THIS RIGHT NOW FOR YOUR VENTURE?

MOVING GOODS & SERVICES TO MARKET

Progress Journal: (please feel free to copy or scan this page only)

_____
_____
_____
_____
_____
_____
_____
_____
_____
_____
_____
_____
_____
_____
_____
_____
_____
_____
_____

Your Signature_____Date_____

CHAPTER FOURTEEN

THE INTERNET 'WORKS' SYSTEM

How to Become a 'PAMPS' Champ

You've made it this far and you'll be glad you did. We've been showing you all along that there are specific alternatives for pressing your venture into action and onto the market and you've seen how these principals work at each step. But we've saved the very best for last. It's the step and issue that stands as the main reason that 90% of all good ideas fail. **P**romotion – **A**dvertising – **M**arketing – **PR** and Sales. **'PAMPS'** Most folks are no champs when it comes to 'PAMPS'. But that has all changed in an amazing way.

Due largely to internet competition, especially over the past year, you can sample such a significant quantity of free media and promotion services, that you can reach thousands, even hundreds of thousands of prospects, ONGOING, on a quality level for FREE. Why not compare and decide for yourself. At then end of these three pages, we know you not only be convinced but, will become far more hopeful about your access to the media. Finally, you'll see the possibilities for real success are literally at your fingertips. At this very moment, not one some*one* but *hundreds of thousands* of someones are spending approximately $80 Million each day to market their business or inventions. They're paying:

$10,000 - $200,000 for print or radio ads

$5,000-$10,000 each month to retain a 'marketing expert'

$10,000 to $100,000 of a video production.

$1,000 – to $20,000 to build an e-commerce website

$20,000 to promote their website and exchange banners or to have someone maintain blog or internet communities.

$1,000 to $5000 to rent office space they don't need.

$5,000 for excessive patent or copyright protection that they do not need.

FREE ENTERPRISE

Also, at this very moment, a few clever someones:

...are getting in magazines, ezines, e-directories, websites, search engines on radio, television for FREE or for very little expense.

...are successfully serving as their own marketing expert

...are both getting videos produced and seen by millions of relevant viewers for very little money.

...built their website for FREE.

...network by visiting blogsites and relevant communities for FREE.

...have attracted measurable website traffic to their site that generates sales for FREE or very little money through FREE press releases, FREE website optimization, FREE keyword placement and banner exchange.

...work in their kitchens, basements, home offices or, share office or manufacturing space for FREE or very little money.

...have ample legal protection for their product or service at a cost of $200. or, far less.

Our second someone:

...has a quality positive image

...has secured the shortest distance to a sale.

...has the means to deliver their product or service.

...is making a profit.

Our second someone isn't cheap, they are wise. The careful way that they have approached their venture has protected their assets and allowed them to test the sales waters without laying out any great expense. Most importantly, they learned how to use the internet effectively by asking the right questions.

For example, you can hire a PR firm to write a press release and distribute it and pay $5,000. each month. That firm will write your press release and distribute it with no

THE INTERNET 'WORKS' SYSTEM

guarantees that the word will get out. Very few contingency deals in the PR world. Or you can usually learn how to write a reasonably-effective press release yourself and then distribute it for FREE to at *least* hundreds of thousands of *relevant* readers.

ACTIVATOR TWENTY-EIGHT
Proving to Yourself That This Really Works
If you're still wondering if this really can work for free

Put this guide down and go to your computer and Google *Free Press Release Distribution*. Then, only test the ones that are free or that offer a free trial with no credit card requirements. Even if they ask for your credit card and promise one free trial month, that usually means that they will automatically charge your card for the next months. The free sites will only ask that you register so make certain you always have a second email address to collect junk mail. Also, make up a name so you can track each site.

> We could list Thousands of effective and FREE sites for:
> Press Release Distribution
> Banner Exchange
> Placement on Thousands of Key Search Engines
> Optimization of Placement
> Free Placement in Directories
> Classified Ads

...but the sites and their offers change constantly so you need to shop and build and modify your own list. Just remember to ask the right FREE question and keep your credit card, bank account and PayPal account to yourself! Which someone are you, the one who spends a fortune and gets nothing but discouraged or the other someone who is taking just a few simple steps to master the media and reach your intended target.

Be the second someone for just one week. Try accessing FREE media as instructed here and then, decide for yourself. Savvy second someones get their media up and running and then, spend just a few hours each week evaluating responses, making adjustments and expanding their reach. And remember, you always have your free e-consult with us if you need it.

FREE ENTERPRISE

Travel Free? These Days?

You bet, if you qualify. *Let's suppose you've developed a new plumbing technique or anything new and novel in your field. Your goal is to get to a convention or seminar but you don't have any money. But if you can prove to the sponsors that you have something special to contribute, they may pay you to travel to them. So there's your free travel. It's real and it happens all the time, even in this economy.*

There's also another way to travel for almost free. These days, many airlines have discovered the basis for a growing trend that may apply across the board. For flight services sometimes, just 10 to 20% of customers pay for most of the costs. That means if you fly off-hours and search out amazing specials, you become one of those 80 to 90% of the rest of the customers who simply fill seats.

Call on us and we'll help make sure your concept is traveling in the right direction. This final step is the catalyst that will make sense of the entire spirit of both the book and guidebook because it will make everything else work fluidly. Follow the steps, especially the ones described in this last phase and go make your concept happen.

Making Your Message Work

Writing a press release, free ad or new venture description is not as hard as most people think. You don't need to be a writer; you just need to express yourself clearly and simply. And when they hit the right nerve, amazing things can happen. I've seen some incredibly simplistic paragraphs launch companies. I've also seen some people fall flat and not achieve what they were aiming. Where people generally fall down is on the assumption factor. Most people assume that if they write something and send it out there through any number of techniques outlined in the book, the message is getting through. Then, if there's no response, they assume their idea or litmus test was not as good as they thought it was, they abandon it.

Before you do that, you need to make sure your message is getting through. You need to make sure that your description is working. First and foremost, keep it simple and clear. Save the fancy terms for those directly in your field.

When you write a press release, litmus test, general description or ad, consider these points:

THE INTERNET 'WORKS' SYSTEM

1) Is your message clear? Will the reader understand what you have done or are trying to do? Great ideas fail because sometimes great minds cannot communicate in understandable terms. As I've said, most ideas can be understood in ten seconds of less, and not just understood, but also *appreciated*.

Virtually every time I've seen a release that doesn't work, it was because I couldn't understand it. Whether it was a simple concept or intensely complicated, the challenge is to make the language understandable. Think about this:

a) What is your goal in your press release, ad, litmus test or general description?
b) Who are you trying to reach?
c) What do you want the readers of your release to do? What is your call to action?

The best way to test a press release is to read it out loud to a few people. You will immediately see their level of understanding and receptivity on their faces.

2) Keep the Promise Real. When writing, do not make exaggerated claims. I'm one of those millions of should who actually buys things from direct response and infomercials. Aside from commercial curiosity, I like to see the ingenious ideas really work. Sometimes it's like a roll of the dice. I once bought this amazing razor from an infomercial and it is truly the best one I've ever seen. I've used it for years. Their promise was real. Recently, I saw advertised a razor that supposedly stayed sharp for life. Okay, here's my money. It did not work at all and I was mad. This second razor was a piece of junk that didn't work but was aggressively sold on a direct-response ad.

Be real. Be clear about what your concept delivers or, intends to deliver. That's the best way to build a growing response. After a little practice, you'll be amazed at how effectively you can communicate to your intended targets.

ACTIVATOR TWENTY-NINE
Cata-'List'

As you read this book and wonder if you can make a better chocolate-chip, or micro-chip, along with that wonder is a nearly automatic sense of doubt. Essentially, the almost universal sentiment is "Can I really do this, can I really make a difference in my own life, let alone others?" This is even true for people who actually read and follow directions to assemble their kid's toys or, who actually know how to set the clock on their ancient VCR's. They followed every step in this book and the systems worked. But still, they wonder if they too can make a difference in their household income and can then maybe have a positive influence somehow on the world?

FREE ENTERPRISE

The short answer is yes, everyone can make some positive difference but the BIG question is how? When you set up the dominoes, nothing happens, at least not until you give that first domino a little tap.

You can follow the directions and directives in this book and get everything in place. But every venture needs that extra push that makes it all go as far and wide as it truly can go. That's the catalyst. Chemistry defines a catalyst as a substance that causes or accelerates a chemical reaction. The term has also evolved to a secondary definition involving people. So the second definition is: something that causes *activity* between two or more persons or forces. Then a third definition was born: "a person or thing that precipitates an event or change. But it's the *fourth* level or evolution of this term with which most of us are familiar:

"A person whose talk, enthusiasm, wisdom, efforts or energy serves to cause other people or circumstances to press into action."

So how do you create or locate a catalyst? You've set your own dominoes in place and your program is most likely working and making some money. But how do you find that magic trigger who can really take your venture to a sustainably higher place?

The short answer is simply to talk to the right people. Now before some media outlet or irate critic mocks me for offering glib advice, let me give you the nitty-gritty: Creating a business can define us and set a beacon of metaphoric light that attracts amazing people who could make a major difference in our lives. But we can't simply exist with that in mind, hoping that these people will be drawn to us like a moth to a flame.

As shy as some of us may be or as discouraged as we may feel at times, a business affords us an opportunity to expand our world through the people we meet. As you have been building your business and both attracting and seeking out customers, you have created a foundation which is the product or putting certain pieces and sometimes, people together all to work as an effective team. You already created and catalyzed something functional at some level. So now comes the second level: Engaging those people and resources that can take your venture to a higher place.

Make Sure Your Efforts include these elements:

1. **Review your triage lists for your business.** Where do you want your business to go or, not to go? If you're happy with your rate of growth, you may want it to become more self-sufficient. The point is to have some specific goals or intentions in mind and on a simple cata-'list', so that your antennae are up and looking for that right fit or opportunity.

2. Pay attention to what similar businesses are doing. Is there a relevant association you can join that can help you gain an increased skill-base and, new customers or clientele that you truly want to work with?

3. Take a second look at people you've known for a while. Because of your new or evolved venture, do they, or the interests they represent, now have more relevance.

4. Pledge to hand out at least five business cards each day to any new friends or potential contacts that you make...and be sure that your business card at least defines who you are and if relevant, offers some bite-sized free sample of your service. Also, remember to always give anyone two cards so they can hand one to their friend or associate

5. Meet, email or write to both old associates and, brand new prospects each day. Have a sense each day of a new group of prospects you might be able to serve and just start the ball rolling with a suggestion of how your business might serve their interests.

6. Remember your most important catalysts are always...each and every customer.

7. Think about who might help take your business or idea to a higher level, but as you do so, always update your self-assessment. Prospects are far more interested in backing momentum than, being responsible for same.

8. Create new possibilities every day..even if it means sending out emails or, calling former prospects just to update and, to learn why they went elsewhere. Knowledge about how to improve something in your venture is always an awesome catalyst

In essence, a catalyst can help you to accelerate in the direction you're already heading so the stronger you're moving in that direction, the better your chances for success will be. The great thing about business catalysts is that no matter how things are going or not going, a catalyst can really make a difference.

Too many people trying to run a business let fear and worries run them instead of allowing themselves to run their business. It can feel rather overwhelming to wake up and wonder how you're going to make it all work. Or you can wake up and say. "Wow, maybe today, I'll meet that magic prospect who will really make a difference." But you won't know that unless you get out of bed and make something, anything happen. And if you do, I promise you that anything good can happen. This is how people and events catalyze each other.

CORE STRATEGIES AND TACTICS NUMBER SEVENTY-THREE

Hunt for Business. If the business isn't coming to you, you need to engage every resource to go to the business; that's what your sales force is for but there's a third alternative as well: Seek out the often hidden or buried prospects.

HOW TO SUPERCHARGE THIS TACTIC: Often, there are people actively seeking your services but they're on a different media or sales-plain. For example, your state or Federal government need goods and services just like everyone else. This includes the military. However, they generally don't make their needs know using conventional means. So you have to find them by seeking our *RFP*'s – Request For Proposals., or Request for Bids. Often, as with grants, this potentially available revenue is given away with very little competition. The bidding process is many and varied and does require time and practice but think about it, whether you're selling psychological services or soap and the military needs soap, why shouldn't you go after their request? The same is true with any state, Federal or even local community. What needs of theirs can you meet and how can you find them and make the bid?

HOW CAN YOU ENGAGE THIS RIGHT NOW FOR YOUR VENTURE?

_____

_____

_____

CORE STRATEGIES AND TACTICS NUMBER SEVENTY-FOUR

Book Speaking Engagements. Speaking to local clubs can be an effective prospecting tool-also meetings that are full of member professionals that you may want to get referrals from. Choose a hot topic that is meaningful to your audience. Distribute a great handout on your topic, and don't forget your appointment book, your actual product, or your marketing literature (brochure, promotional flier, and resume). As you close your speech, offer a free sales or service consultation as a professional courtesy to discuss any special needs a customer or client might have. Mention that you have your appointment book available for anyone who would like to book a free consultation.

HOW TO SUPERCHARGE THIS TACTIC: Shoot a video of some of your best speeches and then distribute that video to some target speaking associations with a strong cover letter. If it's good enough (as they should always be), you can even record some of your more informative speeches and sell the tape through small magazine ads or free press release write-ups. Or, you can send the DVD to a speakers Bureau.

THE INTERNET 'WORKS' SYSTEM

Many people are terrified of speaking in public and prefer to hide behind the internet or, their general advertising media. But as a test and testimony to your faith in your own work, learning to simply communicate comfortably in public is a good tool to have.

Start by talking with a few friends and then, a small group and so on. *Toastmasters* is also an outstanding organization for honing your speaking skills.

HOW CAN YOU ENGAGE THIS RIGHT NOW FOR YOUR VENTURE?

_____

_____

_____

CORE STRATEGIES AND TACTICS NUMBER SEVENTY-SIX

Go to School. Here's the scenario: You desperately need extra skilled help and can't budget for it. A local high school or college student needs work experience but can't find it. All the two of you need to do is get together and that's usually a matter of posting a free ad in your local school's paper, website and especially, good old-fashioned bulletin boards. You can often create arrangements with interns, externs on many levels. The key is to find qualified participants with at least a basic understanding of your field and, a willingness to work. Make sure that all work parameters (insurance, general liability) are spelled out clearly in a written agreement.

HOW TO SUPERCHARGE THIS TACTIC: Create a contest at the local school. These can be especially beneficial when seeking creative solutions outside of your own organization.

_____

_____

_____

_____

Educated' is not a worthy credential until that education becomes activated.

FREE ENTERPRISE

Progress Journal: (please feel free to copy or scan this page only)

_____

_____

_____

_____

_____

_____

_____

_____

_____

_____

_____

_____

_____

_____

_____

_____

_____

_____

_____

_____

Your Signature_____Date_____

CHAPTER FIFTEEN

BUSINESS SUCCESS

The Elements of Sustained Profitability

"When you create, close your eyes and dream, but when you market, open your mind and listen."

Overview

It has often been said that more than 90 percent of all good ideas go undeveloped to the graves with their creators. To reverse those odds and bring an idea to life is the core theme of this book, but bringing an idea to life does not guarantee the survival and perpetuity of that idea.

What is needed in the long run are sound business management practices and a focus on the needs and expectations of your customers.

> **Activator Steps for this Chapter**
> 1) Assess your business management needs constantly.
> 2) Take action to build management practices which will sustain your business.
> 3) Always listen to your customers and take action on their input.

Down in the Engine Room

Once you've created something from your heart and mind and completed the various aspects that bring it to your market, you have to engage in a major changing of hats, from creator to manager. Only children play with things for a while and then lose interest, but if your concept has truly become a part of you, and you've sustained it to this point, now is the time to take the appropriate steps to eventually allow the idea to sustain you. It's time to go down into the engine room, assess the equipment you have in place to cruise your flagship and continuously monitor and upgrade engine performance to meet the demands of your market.

Most businesses tend to form themselves. Scant and casual orders for goods or services become more regulated and increased.

Eventually, business-growth can become like a herd of wild horses that must have the right 'head of horsehold.

Then one day, the house or small office-space cannot possibly accommodate the calls, the flood of mail or the necessary impression required for visiting prospects. Suddenly, what was just an idea now becomes taxable income.

The Turning Point

Now that your dream has become reality, it's time to become increasingly realistic about building the appropriate business structure. Switching more into 'business mode' essentially becomes a function of numbers.

When to set up your own office basically becomes an issue of both when space and staff are necessary and when it becomes cost-effective to obtain these resources. To be premature in building an office infrastructure can drain precious financial assets and threaten an otherwise promising idea.

One of the keys to appropriate business management is to apply all logic and intuition with minimal emotion (with the exception of a positive attitude) to your managerial decisions. Don't be seduced by the trappings of a successful business until you are a successful business. Do not over-commit to space, human resources or raw materials.

As this book has evolved into your marketing plan, many of you are now formulating business plans, which generally focus on management and growth. If seeking funding or other forms of participation, don't create exaggerated promise of potential return. From the investor / participator vantage point, logical investing also begins with emotion; a sense of comfort and appeal for the idea. Sky-high projections are not the key appeal. Dreaming is safe; spending is risky. Do all you can to make sound decisions to reduce risk and increase profitability while always respecting your team.

Finance and Accounting Savvy

You like your concept; they like your concept. They're buying; you're proud, but are you heading toward profit or mere ego-gratification? Using your computer or traditional ledger it is advisable at this point to log all costs of doing business, all costs of providing goods or services, as well as gross and net profits.

If you are computer-wise, there are plenty of excellent computer-based applications for under $50 which can help you stay on top of you finances with the smallest of effort.

If you want to free up your time for what you feel are more important matters, it is perfectly acceptable to retain professionals to assist in basic accounting tasks. However, choose wisely and be sure that you really want to spend your resources for this type of support. At some point, your venture will hopefully grow to the size that you are essentially forced into hiring professional support. At this point, assess your situation and make a prudent decision as to your course of action.

Being a true leader requires a willingness to be more wise than vain and, more correct than popular.

BUSINESS SUCCESS

Steering the Ship

If you are in fact running the business end of your concept, the goal is to create an operation where over time net or actual profit after all expenses, shows growth indicators after a period of two to six months in most cases. Of course, this number will vary with each venture. In that the design of this book has been to create a value-chain for your concept, many readers have enjoyed slight revenue increases right from their initial contacts with prospective buyers.

To get to this point, many readers have become something they never have experienced in their entire lives — a leader. The issues of leadership primarily involve good ego-free listening for sound decision-making, and good team building. Some of the most critical positive decisions of our time have been made by leaders who had surrounded themselves with outstanding advisors. This optimal form of decision-making is called consensus; getting the best advice to then invoke the most effective and appropriate decision.

ACTIVATOR THIRTY
All the Resources you'll Ever Need

I've mentioned Rustic Mountain Furniture earlier in this book and I know there are hundreds of thousands of similar stories and excellent examples. But I feel a real kinship with this company and its creator Clayton Cox.

Years ago when Clayton was wandering though the Aspen and Pine thickets of Cedar Mountain near his home in Southern Utah, he did not see the twisted scraps of Aspen and Pine as merely the dead pieces of the forest, he saw furniture and from those scraps, he went on to build a million-dollar furniture business that sells some of the strongest, longest-lasting and most beautiful furniture.

When he first saw these random logs in a different way, he took a chance and began shaping them into bed frames and low and behold, people began lining up to buy them. This inspired Clayton to try to go in new directions and today, he has over 80 unique creations for any home or office.

Moe Dixon is one of the great folk musicians of our time who travels the world and shares his joy with his ever-growing list of great music that reflects the best of all of us. As a side benefit to doing what he was born to do, Moe makes an excellent living through his concerts and, through the sale of his CD's on line.

Whenever you visit Moe, the first thing he will do is take you up a ski life in winter or, to the water in summer to windsurf or kayak. Once out in the wilderness, his first words are always "WELCOME TO MY OFFICE."

You've been told that you need to rent an office, hire an accountant and a lawyer and designer and purchase an excess of inventory. You've been told to perhaps even

Managed Growth is Sustained Growth

FREE ENTERPRISE

borrow the money so you can purchase advertising to promote your business or, to hire a consultant to develop your business plan and guide you along the way. Then perhaps you were told to just sit there and wait to see if the people responded. In the meantime, people everywhere are simple walking through their own metaphorical forest and finding their fortunes from little more than an inspiration.

When I lost everything in my divorce and I mean everything, that included my three computers and laptop computer. How would I survive? At the time, I couldn't afford to replace all of that technology but I could afford pads of yellow lined-paper. That reminded me that I had always done my best writing first on paper and often, while walking through the forest where I'd bump into people like Clayton. Then when I really needed the use of a computer, I would simply stop into any of the thousands of libraries throughout the country, often in very small towns. This also gave me a chance to tell the libraries about my other books and, to arrange to get those books placed in those libraries.

If you're waiting for all these great supportive resources to magically appear, what do you already have to start breathing life into your concept? For many successful businesses, with very little, they discovered that they had all of the resources they would ever need.

The qualifications you now possess as a leader is that you have guided your concept to this point, so you've evolved into this position. Now you have a good degree of substance behind you.

The following are the key points for business success:

1) Keep the idea viable both attitudinally and financially.

2) An effective listener makes an effective leader.

3) Don't over-commit on your venture without realistic possibility of return.

4) Watch and learn from your competition

5) Work to create business partnerships who might make use of your services or, trade referrals with you.

6) Remember that whatever you're starting with, you always have something and many free resources to get you going.

7) Continually reassess all aspects of your venture to ensure excellence and a growing market-share.

8) Never ask for anything from anyone but instead, offer the benefits of your concept. When you create value for who you are and, what you're doing, people will eventually pay for that value.

9) Never react to major economic news except to calculate how you can turn the news into an advantage. Many new millionaires are being made right now simply because of the toy recalls from foreign suppliers. Imagine how well makers of non-toxic toys are doing.

10) Remember that some days will be stronger than other days but this is generally your choice.

11) Options and Opportunities. So what if you tried hard and lost an option. What about the hundred or so options you **haven't** *yet tried. There are always many ways to achieve your goal. Keep your options and eyes open.*

12) Treat Your Teammates Well. Even if you enterprise has fallen on hard financial times do all you can to be fair to your colleagues. They won't mind sharing a reasonable across-the-board cut but you may have many other options. Before taking any action, discuss matters with them and listen well to all of their suggestions.

POWERPOINTER
You Can Always Do More

If I tell you there are 300,000 free distribution avenues for your press release that would seem very hard to believe. But it's true. If I tell you that they will trip over each other to get you to use their service for free, that seems very to believe unless you've seen it it for yourself.

You should be able to identify hundreds of free press sites that are specific for your venture. And if I tell you there are 11,371 sponsored sites available for repeated free media service, you will let me know of thousands more. And if I told you that you'll save two to twenty-thousand dollars using these sites, you can prove that to yourself anytime you want.

Free Enterprise has never been more free. We are truly in the midst free media revolution and it has placed the power of broad-sweeping advertising sales that used to be the domain of the wealthy, big business directly into your hands. That means that the

FREE ENTERPRISE

smallest business can have the largest success if they are willing to learn this very simple system and, if they are willing to put the time in.

I don't know why it sticks in my mind but years ago after conducting a seminar, someone asked how many times you need to submit a press release to make it successful. I thought I'd have some fun with the audience so I asked for random guesses. "Five", "Eleven" "Twenty-Six" Everyone had a different number in mind and this went on for sometime as if there was some magic number. Nobody got it right because the simple answer is; *It takes as many as is required to achieve the success you desire.* That could mean three, that could mean thirty.

Most readers know that I have written several books in many fields. Several of them from some time ago still move off the shelves here and there. A few of my earlier marketing books continued to grow for years after their life cycle but none grew as steadily as my Random House book How To *Heal A Broken Heart In 30 Days*. The title of this book reveals its promise and clearly it was well-delivered by co-writer Michael Riley and myself.

When its sales cycle dissipated a few years ago, I decided to experiment with only free media and search engine optimization. Suddenly a book that should have been near 600,000 to 800,000 rating began climbing steadily. Just for fun, I kept up the process and the numbers continued to improve.

Today, the book has enjoyed Amazon ratings of under 1,000 and still remains close to that ranking. The more I use these free systems found in this book, the better it does. And if I have the time, I could always do more.

So now that you have explored the free systems in this book, what can you go and when you've done all you feel you can do, what more can you do? You can always do more to keep your concept alive and growing. So don't stop until you've hit your magic number.

ACTIVATOR THIRTY-ONE
Don't Let You Stop You

Guilt is not an emotion, it is a weapon that is sometimes used against but for the most part, we choose to use it against ourselves and there isn't a person alive that can't find a reason to feel guilty.

Guilt can be described to having peanut-butter stuck in your blood. It slows down and distracts positive thinking. Centuries ago, it was the primary weapon to keep the masses in check. Even today, how many people do you know who function out of guilt instead of kindness and love.

For my readers who are either starting out or seeking to greatly enhance their existing business, they know a guilt that centers around money, bills and family. It's all centered around a fear of letting people down. If that becomes too overwhelming a force, we are back in the same place where worry used to put us. Our conscience begins to hover over us like a great dark cloud with a reprimanding tone saying, "Why aren't you doing more, why aren't making more money, why are you letting everyone down?" Even strangers at the bank can trigger these negative feeling in you.

Instead of being ruled by your conscience, you need to reshape your consciousness to where you attitude and forward momentum are so strong, that your spirit becomes infectious and will then, attract all you need to become successful.

The other element of forward momentum is communication. Even if you're just beginning to take baby steps to heal your life, people will see it and will generally want to work with you because you will both be moving in the same direction. If you look at your business community as a group of people all roped together climbing a wall, sometimes one of you will need a little help climbing. It's the person that completely gives up and lets go of the rock that really drags everyone down.

Steer your momentum upward, talk to people and prospects, and let them see your intention and aims. One break, one sale, one contract can turn everything brighter and allow you to take your guilt and, place it in a small box somewhere.

How This Applies To Your Marketing Efforts

What good are any marketing techniques, plans or advice if they don't work? The truth is, most of the things you hear about that flood the Internet and Infomercial world do not in fact, work. The ads that proliferate the airwaves promise you quick and instant riches but if most of those promises were true, think of how rich the approximately 50 million people, who bought one promise of another, would actually be. The reason they aren't rich is they were fooled by one money-making scheme or another.

Now, here you are having purchased and now, largely completed a book touting literally hundreds of ways and means to make your idea profitable, even if you don't have the financial or technical means to do so. So if I'm doing smack downs on schemes out there, I had better make sure that my systems really work. And they do and I test, evaluate and upgrade them with each printing. So then, what if you've tried a number of my techniques and they haven't worked for you? Should you come running to me or, simply write a diatribe of bad reviews? I hope not. Instead, consider the vital element that makes any of my systems work: *Enforcement*. What that means is you have to learn, adapt and adjust any of my techniques so that they are enforced and actually start working for you. Do not expect your first press release to perform miracles and allow you to fire your advertising or PR guy. Each of these techniques requires some time until they begin working for you in concert. The key is that you experiment with each of the systems until they begin working for you or, until you are able to enforce them. Remember that success of your venture is more a decision to stick with it until it all works.

FREE ENTERPRISE

FINAL CORE STRATEGY
The Rule That Rules All Rules..

Track! Track, It's All About Feedback. Track Everything! Track every time a contact is made as a result of a marketing strategy. Use this information to calculate your ROI, or Return On Investment, *so you can learn what's working and do more of it.* and, so you can learn from your mistakes..

How to Determine Your Return On Investment (ROI):

Let's suppose you ran a print ad that cost you $100 each week to run. Let's assume you paid someone $500 to design and produce it and that you ran the ad for eight weeks. So your initial expenditure for the ad was $1,300. Now let's suppose you got $5,200 in gross sales from the eight weeks of running the ad. Your ROI is 4:1. That means that for every dollar you spend, you're getting four dollars back. Do you need to know how well your marketing investments are working for you? Code your ads, fliers, coupons, and letters, everything, and track the contacts each source provides you. Make tracking sheets for your front office staff and insist they track every call. What brought in the call? How did they hear about you, from what media and/or person? Did they book an appointment? If not, why not? List their objections so that you can overcome them in the future. Provide your staff with a telephone script to help them learn how to convert incoming inquiries and marketing responses into appointments. You cannot compute your ROI unless you track. If you cannot compute your ROI for each strategy, you will not know which strategies are working and which are draining your marketing budget. Make tracking your mantra. At the same time, give a campaign sufficient time to work. A radio campaign can take weeks before you learn proper placement and ideal schedule.

The next step is to look at every sales and marketing tactic that's working for you and, figure out how to get them to work effectively together. For example, if your website works well to capture sales, be sure to mention that site on all of your other advertising, including your signage.

Love Your Contradictions! The strongest aspect of any of us are the inner contradictions which compel us to grow stronger, more courageous and more strategic. The harder we work to overcome our greatest weaknesses, the more capable we become at solving those issues not for ourselves, but for others

Progress Journal: (please feel free to copy or scan this page only)

Your Signature_____Date_____

AFTERWORD

OVERCOMING ANY BUSINESS CHALLENGE

With the 10 Solution Rule

Endings should be stronger than beginnings. After all, with all that you've learned from this book, you and your concept should be stronger so I like to close my books with strength and uplifting encouragement, instead of just fading into the last page.

For years, I studied what support would be helpful to my readers and what would be just a waste of their precious time. I know that for as much excellence and dedication we can find in any book, a book can only do so much. You must now use the materials to find the right solutions to make your business work to the maximum degree.

Still, you'll discover that as you aim big, the potential disappointments can be much bigger as well but that's no reason to not stay on your proper path. We've learned that when we have an overwhelming business challenge, we now know that is far better than not trying at all. I'd rather worry about a big business headache that could solve many problems than one or two or ten nagging bills.

We also know that when we worry, we tend to shut off our thinking. Many people mistakenly believe that our thinking shuts itself off but we do it to ourselves. Also, when we worry, it becomes psychologically impossible to hope. Further, once we shut our thinking off, it remains in the off position until we do something to either forget about it or, act upon it. Forgetting about it can involve going for a walk, sleeping it off, all the way to various addictive behaviors to sublimate anxiety. The bottom line is that as we've described before, worry makes a meal out of momentum but there is a simple way to turn that productivity and hope switch back on more powerfully than ever.

3 Steps for the 'Ten-Solution' Rule

1) *First, you have to admit that you're worried.* This is the hardest part because unlike panic which can hit you like a brick wall out of nowhere, worry creeps in little by little until you feel flooded and immobilized. So if you see the signs of being stuck, immobilized; you may even feel physically lethargic, you will often feel far too weak to take any effective action.

2) *Turn to Your Team*. Chances are they are not feeling the same symptoms. If you don't have a team, turn to your partner or friend. Tell them you dilemma but not in terms

Embrace the chaos in your path as necessary to your success.

FREE ENTERPRISE

of feelings. Instead, tell them about the problems that are making you feel this way and ask them for specific solutions that you can take action on right now.

Recently, a close friend had raised the money he needed to develop a simple children's website and TV pilot. His backer was going to give him $50,000 but to get this money, my friend had to work for this guy as a virtual indentured servant for six months. Still, he would be getting his money and to fulfill his dream and that's what mattered most.

Anticipating the arrival of the funds in his bank account, he began purchasing some of the basic resources to finalize his website. Then the day before the funding was to be transferred, the investor pulled out with no explanation.

At first, my friend saw his entire dream melting away and trudged to his office to deliver the bad news to his three teammates. While everyone felt badly, they decided to each contact other prospects. They developed both a solid phone script and a great form letter describing their situation.

As they began pursuing this new option, despair quickly turned to hope but after calling upon nearly sixty prospects between them, discouragement set in again. The convened once again to determine when they should just stop asking and then my friend said the exactly correct response. "We should stop after we get the funding.

When he finally got around to calling me and explained the entire situation, I showed him how he could reduce his financial requirements by about two-thirds. That was the easy part. Then I instructed him to go back and contact everyone he had previously contacted because now he was requiring far less. In less than a day, he not only, had his money, he had received commitments from several sites to do cross-promotions (cross-links and banner swaps, etc.)

So now he had a better deal with a far greater chance of success and by taking action and staying on that action until he succeeded, he realized that as long as he didn't quit, he would prevail. So you already know Step **Three:** Develop and pursue alternatives until you achieve your stated goal but be flexible about the many alternatives for achieving that exact same goal and generally you will yield far better results.

I call this my *ten solution rule* because for me personally, whenever I encounter a challenge, I make myself come up with ten alternatives. But your numbers could vary and as with my friend, you need to pursue your solution until your arrive at it. That is the exact number for you.

If you glean nothing else from this book, one of the most important things to know is that whenever you're in a bind and no matter how big it seems, if you simply start taking action to address it, you will instantly start to make that problem smaller. So get yourself so busy working on your hopes that you have no times for your problems or fears. Always argue for your own best optimism. What follows are a few fun brain exercises to further condition you for the success that I know you will have.

AFTERWORD

How many solutions to your impossible challenges could you and your colleagues list right now?

_____

August 17, 2008 – David Freeman, daring and inspiring adventurer who co-authored the outstanding book '100 Things To Do Before You Die,' died afterfalling in his house and, hitting his head on a glass door. He was 47. What are you going to do with whatever time you have remaining?

FREE ENTERPRISE

SURVIVE-R-CISES

Business Survival Exercises

Our thoughts are traitors and make us lose the good we oft might win by fearing to attempt. **William Shakespeare**

How true thy words. There is no gain without pain and if the gain is painless at first, there will be a price of some lesson to learn down the road. There are no rewards without risks. However, the down sides are much easier to deal with for those who are better prepared. You will never be completely able to predict or control how the market or business trends will occur or behave but, you can to a very great extent, control how you will deal with the unexpected. When you achieve that, you can turn problems into new opportunities, or at the very least, part of the educational process.

Following are four unusual exercises designed to help you think more creatively. There are no right nor wrong answers and you may try them over and over again as time goes on. The key is to relate them to some of the day-to-day issues you will face as you build the knowledge to build the courage to build your dreams. Here are the exercises and what they pertain to: One tip: Try to be as creative as possible.

1) COURSE CORRECTION – NEW DIRECTION
An Exercise in Going Backwards and Forwards in Time

Part One:

I receive a lot of questions about choosing the right idea. People want to know if they're on the right track and often claim to have no idea how to get anywhere near the right idea. For millions of people, the answer is staring them right in the face…in their email.

Most people keep a portion of the emails for quite some time, almost like keeping a record of their lives, like a mini e-bio. Those of us who do this wonder why on earth we do this. As with old junk in a closet, when you throw the stuff away, your rarely miss it. But old emails offer us something more. They can serve as an archive into our lives, state of thinking and evolution, or even lack of thinking.

I'm an email-keeper and my old emails provide me with a record of my thinking that goes back nearly ten years. In those years, I have evolved and perfected my free-enterprise marketing techniques. I can also observe the many paths I attempted that just weren't meant to be. Some of that process can be somewhat humbling and downright

AFTERWORD

embarrassing. Most people will see efforts and intentions and ideas just breeze on by unfulfilled, like being in a time-machine, and we'd rather not live them all over again. But if we're willing to push past that pain, there is a lot we can gain.

This book and the show concept have taken years to develop. Some of that process had been very discouraging. First, about six years ago, I set out to create a definitive marketing book but quickly realized that the internet had not sufficiently evolved to where it is today. Then I received funding to develop two different television show formats on the subject but the first group wanted to go in a different direction and the second never released the show. Finally, after seven years, three aggressive attempts, with all of my friends and advisors begging me to abandon all hope, I became inspired. How? Because I calmly reviewed my email history and could clearly see my procedural mistakes. I was also highly purpose-driven; I knew that my research and experience could facilitate the development of hundreds of thousands of new ideas and that without it, most of these ideas would never see the light of day and their creators would simply give up. I was not going to let that happen.

It's not pleasant to admit that you've made very big mistakes as I have often had to do. But it's really wonderful to bite your lip and take a good hard look and how you can learn from those mistakes and apply those critical lessons to your original vision.

Follow this rudimentary checklist:

1) How many years back does your email account go?

_____

2) How far back have you saved your emails?

_____

3) Why do you think you kept them?

_____

_____

_____

FREE ENTERPRISE

Next, go back to your earliest emails and, skim through six months of your history:
1) What was your general confidence level about your pursuits back then?

_____

_____

2) What were the biggest mistakes you made in your life back then?

_____

_____

_____

3) What do you wish you had done differently?

_____

_____

_____

4) What ideas or initiatives did you either fail to recognize or were afraid to apply?

_____

_____

_____

5) How will this process make you current concept more viable?

_____

_____

AFTERWORD

If you'll allow yourself to go though this process and really make some honest reassessments, even your staunchest opponents
will marvel in envy.

Part Two:

For the second part of this exercise, we need to travel in the future. This is designed to help you explore the things you really want to do. This takes a lot less time than part one. Here's your recipe for traveling into the future:

Step One: List all the things you really want to do professionally. For example, public speaking, think-tank consulting, etc:

_____

_____

_____

_____

Step Two: Why aren't you trying to do those things now?

_____

_____

_____

Step Three: Now, travel far into the future. Imagine that you're old and your time is drawing near. Are you there? Now, look back on your life. What things do you wish you had tried that you knew you could do, but never did?

_____

_____

FREE ENTERPRISE

Step Four: Look back at Step Two and ask yourself the same question, WHY AREN'T YOU TRYING HARDER TO DO THOSE THINGS NOW? What are you waiting for?

Most of us put off those vocational challenges that could really allow us to reach our potential. Regret is one of the most painful of all experiences so, while you're still alive and able, take some chances, dare yourself to know yourself and allow the best of yourself to bring out the best in your ideas.

Authors Note: Whenever I want to get re-inspired, I listen to James Taylor's song Look Up from your life from his Hourglass CD.

2) FINANCE . . . *The Burning House*
An exercise in finding hidden alternatives

You are in the attic of an old wooden house. You are the only one in the house, and in the attic are nothing but old bed sheets and some old standard household tools. There is no telephone, no rope, nothing else.

As smoke begins to seep through the floor, you realize that the house is fully engulfed in flames and that you will not be able to escape down the burning steps as everything below you inside the house is completely engulfed.

List at least five ways you can survive and escape:

_____

_____

_____

_____

_____

_____

_____

_____

_____

AFTERWORD

3) NEGOTIATIONS . . . *The Unplanned Meeting..*
An exercise in balancing finances

You are at home relaxing in your backyard. Your venture is starting to make a profit but you have still had to postpone certain bills and prioritize others to keep things going and growing. Suddenly, a car pulls up and three tough-looking men get out and ask to speak with you. You invite them to sit with you since they are not strangers, but you never expected to see them together. One is your banker, one is your manufacturer and the third is the advertising representative of a leading local radio station and newspaper that you have been advertising in on a financially rewarding part per-inquiry and part directly payable basis.

The banker states that he will not lend you any more money to pay the manufacturer. The manufacturer informs you that he will not extend anymore credit and will not continue manufacturing until past invoices are paid and then it's C.O.D. only. Your advertiser tells you that he will no longer advance you any free space and that it's cash up front or no more ads. Your product or service is selling and you need to not only maintain existing advertising, but you need to expand it.

List at least five ways you can continue the survival of your company while managing the relationships with these unexpected visitors:

FREE ENTERPRISE

4) DEDICATION . . . *The Family Squeeze*
An exercise in improving your supportive relationships

Your husband, wife, parent, whoever, is losing patience with you. Your dedication to your venture keeps you working tirelessly in the garage or living room most evenings and weekends.

But you are excited about what you're doing, and while you do agree that family comes first, you believe this venture could make a big and positive difference in your life as well as your family's. However, your spouse or friend is threatening to leave if you continue putting so much time in this. Quitting your regular job is not an option because your venture cannot possibly support you or your family at this point.

List at least five ways you can continue pursuing your concept while also not sacrificing as much family time:

_____

_____

_____

_____

_____

_____

_____

_____

_____

_____

Exercises are designed to stretch and condition muscles. For these brain exercises, we're shaping up the brain and the will. Do them diligently and at various stages of your own development and each time, you'll discover new possibilities and approaches.

AFTERWORD

Remember to:
- Assess your business management needs constantly.
- Take action to build management practices which will sustain your business.
- Always listen to your customers and take action on their input.

Potential Challenges and Solutions

Challenge: I don't have the skills to solve these exercises. These require lawyers, negtiators and maybe firefighters.

Solution: It is not about skills but wills; like the inventiveness that you applied to your concept. You need to learn how to work with many different types of professionals, so reach in that brain of yours and invent new solutions, using "re-solutions."

Before We Conclude . . .

- Have you survived each exercise in your most imaginative fashion?

- What uniquely special and creative steps did you take to insure your survival?

- When was the last time you reviewed your mission statement?

- Are you willing to make your dream a part of your bloodstream?

- Are you willing to find a way to persist with a good idea no matter what happens?

How Never Quitting Guarantees Success

A close friend of mine in the same field had a relentless dream whose only obstacle were a series of annoying realities. His plan was to create a television show for entrepreneurs and inventor to help both inspire and, make the American dream available to millions of people. He knew his subject like no one else and had been in the laboratories, and homes of literally hundreds of would-be entrepreneurs. Always, he took copious notes about everything and anything he could discover to support these individuals.

He knew that if he just had the right production team, he could make it work. He was already doing national television interviews and the response was overwhelming. In fact, one day following a remote interview from Washington, D.C., one of the world's leading infomercial producers at the time tracked him down and made him a multi-million-dollar offer; the show, everything. But this angel had a downside: He was facing a massive lawsuit which eventually paralyzed his entire business.

Talk about disappointment. My friend was literally a few months away from realizing his dream. Then nothing. Even still, my friend knew that as big as this disappointment was, it was not bigger than his dream and had nothing to do with the merits of his

FREE ENTERPRISE

idea. So he dusted himself off and, kept his eyes open. Perhaps someone would pick up the ball. Indeed, one year later, one of the largest direct-response radio organizations had heard about his first venture and offered to develop it on radio, to sell a series of C.D.'s for entrepreneurs.

This time, he was not going to let his idea get knocked down. In the contract, he negotiated a guarantee for completion, "as long as the company remained in business." Pretty good deal as this was a solid company. But no one could have predicted that one of the founders would fall ill and the company would dissolve. That's just what happened two months later. The company died and the deal died along with it. By this time, everyone who knew my friend and admired his efforts, felt that this was a dream that was just not meant to be. Even my friend himself seemed resigned. At least on the surface.

He went on to become a successful director of a large marketing concern and then, a few years later, left this comfortable post to yet again pursue his dream. He was invited to join a new company centered around helping individuals develop their ideas legitimately and soundly. They wanted him to develop an entire array of media, a television show and even a bus to visit inventors throughout America. This seemed like a dream come true; the backing, the people, everything was in place. But as with many dreams, he received a rude awakening when the primary backer and CEO decided to go off on his own and closed the company literally overnight, leaving everyone to twist in the wind.

So it now seemed definitely that this wind had finally dissipated his idea for good. No pulse, this concept was dead. But three months later, a noted Hollywood producer tracked him down and proposed not one show but an entire channel devoted to entrepreneurs, with my friend as the manager. Just when he thought the concept was on its last legs, a producer came a long and offers many feet moving in his direction. This producer talked about creating many TV channels, he talked about raising billions of dollars, and he talked about buying some powerful existing channels. He talked. And talked and talked. And talked. After a few months of this Hollywood "promise' land, my friend realized that all there was, was talk and no action.

It was as if every discouraging experience was conspiring against my friend. He wondered if he would ever get a break and if anyone would really appreciate his dream. He questioned his own competency and wondered if he was the problem. Maybe people didn't really like him but were afraid to tell him so.

He decided to go back to conventional consulting. On that same day, he received a call from a very successful businessman he met skiing a few months earlier. He owned several TV studios and offered my friend a studio, salary and one year to produce his show. The studio had an excellent staff. There they built a beautiful set for the show, the followed his script to the t and when the pilot was completed, he discovered that it was no longer his show. But during that productive year, my friend had developed many solid

For the entrepreneur, it's a brand-new day everyday. What do you choose to do with it?

relationships in the industry and a producer readily picked up the ball and the show was restructured under his parameters. Then that producer went bankrupt and my friend was back in familiar territory; each time, getting closer but never quite making it to the dance.

By this time, not only were all of his friends urging him to abandon this dream, he was telling himself that all indicators were against him. How much more foolish could he or anyone be to even think of continuing along these lines. Every sign said "This is not to be". Except the sign in his heart that knew his core idea was viable. Otherwise, why would so many people along the way try to become involved?

He decided that he needed to take more control and that it wasn't enough to have a dream or even receive an offer on that dream, you have to directly manage the development and growth of that dream every step of the way. He decided to try to sell his pilot to independent stations and the response was very strong. One of the calls led to a return call from ITV, the company that finally produced this show and he arranged to get the book published. Then, unbelievably, just when his shows was to be launched, ITV stopped distributing infomercials, but this guy never took any of these stumbles personally, and that's why you're reading and benefiting from this book today. Yes, that crazy dreamer who refused to give up is yours truly.

But wait…there's more…

No, I never gave up but you can't just tell readers that the secret to their success is simply to never give up. There has to be something deep inside each entrepreneur, there has to be some driving force. The stronger the force, the harder it becomes to give up under any circumstances. So now, the rest of the story…Twenty-five years ago, my extremely strong United States Marine (Semper Fidelis) father was cut down in the prime of health and strength at the youthful age of 60, not by an enemy bullet or some accident hiking in the wildness or, riding the rivers wild but by a simple mistake from a knee operation. After his death, I made a graveside promise to him that I would find the means to look after his lifetime bride. That has not always been an easy promise to keep, especially for a young entrepreneur with a family of his own to support and now, with five children, college loans and child support. But this was a promise to my father, not to simply send a few dollars to mom here and there but to ensure that she never had to worry about money.

This commitment took my motivation out of the standard 'you-can-do-it' coaching realm and into the sacredness of a promise. When you make a promise that is powerful enough to sustain your motivation, you transcend drive and even obsession and go straight to zeal and you stay there until you reach the plateau. Then you learn more about your subject and you jump to the next plateau.

This book has certainly been a grand success for me but look how deep the drive to succeed. If you simply try to do the same, your success will be no less powerful.

FREE ENTERPRISE

And the beneficiary of all that I've learned over ten years of rejection in trying to build this dream, is you. Instead of giving up, I knew my idea lived vibrantly inside my heart. I knew my idea could both benefit millions in a real and meaningful way and measurable way and, I knew it could make hundreds of millions of dollars for my readers. I knew I could help people to find real and credible ways to make extra money and I held that mission as sacred and at the utmost. Sooooo, when does commitment make sense and, when does a commitment indicate that you should be committed to a mental hospital? When is it foolish to continue, when you run out of money? That doesn't make sense. How can a dream run out of money?

Do you give up when your best friends, colleagues and advisers insist that you give up; do you drop your heart-felt idea when there are absolutely no indicators for success? No indicators except one - That knowing inside you that that promises you that if you can just commit to never quitting, your healthy unselfish obsession will prevail when the time is right.

When I first had the concept for the show, there were still just a handful of free and credible publicity techniques. Today there are thousands so my 'delays' in my dream actually helped my dream to become much more valuable for you, the end user. Sooooo, this is all well and good but how do you yourself find the personal willingness, dedication and drive to press on even when everyone's against you and, you're hanging on by a thread? A while back, an outstanding and dedicated company I was consulting for (www.wildfirefoundation.org) needed someone to staff a fire look out tower on Lookout Mountain in Eastern

Oregon. No one was available for the five-day commitment. So I volunteered. I needed a break from the intense office work and felt this might be an ideal way to reframe and refresh my thinking. Eleven hours later, there I was, atop this 7,100 foot peak in a little shack. Alone. No running water, no electricity, nothing but the shack and a short-wave radio to report on any fire activity.

The nights there were black and cold, dotted with lights miles away. I was really alone for the first time in years. My only company were the bears, mountain lions, rattlesnakes and the ceaseless howl of the wind. If anything happened to you up there; if you fell and couldn't get up, there was no life-line button to push. You were really on your own.

More than once, when I'd hear a strange banging or spooky growl that sounded too close by, I admit to being a bit afraid. Coupled with a powerful imagination, as the days progressed, I noticed that I was starting to use it against me to create fear and disarray instead of hope and logic.

Where am I going with this anecdote? Imagination can be a powerful resource for keeping our dreams alive or we can use it to indulge our fears and doubts and, turn it against ourselves. We can and often do, use it to defeat our own dreams. So how do you

AFTERWORD

know if you have a magnificent obsession or, a ridiculous one? How do you discern the real difference between justified persistence (as I have done for years) versus just plain foolishness?

Give Your Venture The Same Level of Passion

1) What is so special and unique about your idea?
2) What is so special and unique about you and your ability to accomplish this idea?
3) Why should you be the one to make this idea happen?
4) In your absence, would someone else be able to accomplish this as uniquely and effectively as you?

5) Can you clearly see and defend why you can succeed with this idea even when everyone else (including yourself, at times) is urging you to quit?

6) Even after multiple failures, are you willing to learn, persist and, find the ways to make your idea succeed?

7) Are you aware of the thousands of failures endured by Thomas Edison to try to find the correct filament to make the electric light bulb? Do you know how many times legendary home run-hitter Babe Ruth struck out?

If the greatest achievers among us failed constantly and hopelessly, what makes you think that you can avoid at least some setback? Failure is a crucial component of success. Clearly, from this story, you can see that the real secret to success is to be willing to fail all along the way. But the secret to achieving the secret is persistence, again, that willingness to get up again. Persistence must be part of your routine and elemental in your dreams.

One success after a thousand failures makes sense of it all.

FREE ENTERPRISE

Persis-10's

Whenever I ask a group to describe what causes the most number of business failures, the majority attribute the economy, followed by poor planning or weak marketing. Those sound like sensible assertions but unfortunately, they couldn't be more wrong. The greatest cause of business failure is *surrender*.

Business failure is not an end result but a decision, especially when it pertains to small start-ups. If you follow some of the most successful companies today, you'll often discover that their current products or services have nothing to do with their original offerings. This should be obvious since successful ventures adapt to current needs and climates. That's because successful companies must be as adaptive as they are driven and focused.

So my guarantee to you is this: If you find a way forward, you will find a way to succeed and a means to grow. But that takes persistence and you can't persist if you don't love what your doing. Fascination, excitement, hope; these are the elements which drive your forward.

Success also requires the right knowledge. That's the whole idea behind this book, to provide you with the easily accessible steps to ensure the advancement of your idea. And these solutions are largely simple. In fact, as you discover just how simple they are, you'll be amazed at how far you can take your idea with just a little effort. You'll be especially amazed to learn that most of these steps are free for you to use. This is also the time when many of you will kick yourself for having spent thousands of dollars to achieve less of a result than what you can now achieve for free.

All of the above is a solid argument for why you need to persist because if you're willing to get there, you will get there. Never let the heart of a good idea stop beating. What follows is my 'Persis- 10's – My David Letterman top-ten reasons why you must persist with a good idea. Refer to the Persis- 10's anytime you're feeling stuck.

Press on, with the Persis-10's

1) **Cut back on your expenses, not your vision**. Don't fall apart if you can't make or general expenses. You may have tried to grow to far too fast. Making the adjustments to allow you to press on is usually easier than you think. It's really just a matter of determining what you must have to move forward at this point.

What do you really need to make your idea successful?

_____

_____

_____

AFTERWORD

What do you not need at this time to make your idea successful?

_____

_____

_____

If you choose to keep the idea alive, you will find a way through.

2) **Simply refuse to quit**. If you've chosen the right idea, it lives inside of you. That which is a part of you cannot be taken from you. Be patient and hold fast.

3) **Believe relentlessly in the value of your idea**. Scrutiny is a healthy part of Refining an idea but self-doubt is an exercise in defeat. If you know your idea has value, then your only real challenge is to figure out how to communicate that value to those who will buy.

4) **Find another way to achieve it**. Human beings have only survived because they learned to adapt and change. The willingness to adapt is key to success. There is always another way that you are just not seeing at the moment. List three things you can do to make your concept more marketable:

_____

_____

_____

5) **Refuse to take no for an answer**. The concept of No is a fascinating one that we touch on several times in this book. No does not mean that you can't do something, it means that the person saying no can't do it. No means, "not me" or "not here" or not this way. But you thought that no meant the end. It simply means the beginning of a new direction.

6) **Move forward even if you have to stumble forward.** Human beings love to see people rise up above impossible odds but you know that it's not as hard as it seems. It's simply a choice and if you are determined to make it work somehow, you'll eventually have society cheering you on. In addition, you garner some great free press just by inspiring others with your hard-fought-for success story.

7) **Take a break**. Exhaustion diminishes brain energy and limited brain energy equals false pessimism. Sometimes we become so engulfed in our idea that we lose control of it, like Ahab riding his Great White Whale. But what if Ahab had strategized differently? Instead, he was driven by an extreme obsessiveness. Sometimes, you need to

just step away from your idea, and all the headaches and refresh your thinking. The, you can return to it all with a renewed energy and spirit.

8) **Ask for more support**. Just like some people don't realize that getting a sale is a simple as asking for it, most people are limited in their ability to ask for the right kind of support. This vital support is usually found in the form of information. Knowledge and Wisdom. And it's generally free of charge. If you can't find it on the internet, talk to your friends, interview experts in your field (something, I always advocate); Study. Learn the better ways that will drive your idea forward.

9) **Find a more effective way to communicate to prospects**. How can anyone buy from you or work with you if they don't know you exist? Your concept is a solution to some problem somewhere. This book spends a lot of time on the art of communication. Use the techniques well so you may effectively communicate. Your prospects are waiting, why aren't you talking to them, especially now, when most of the means to do so cost *nothing*?

10) **Identify how you may be holding yourself back**. It's been said in many ways: *That's which resists, persists*. If you keep making the same mistake and achieving the same limited result, what is it in you that you are not willing to address?

Do not intentionally hold yourself back. You deserve a success and you need to remove any obstacles that will lead you to that success. Make the decision to start doing that today. The techniques in this book will work for you if you are willing to let them work.

FINAL ACTIVATOR

Stay with it . . . Grow with it

"Why am I putting up with this! All I seem to get from customers is abuse and disrespect. They just don't seem to understand what my intentions are. Yet, I stay with it. No matter what I persist; I grow; I stay with it. My friends tell me I'm crazy, but I secretly think they're a little jealous."

Many of us have felt that many times. Yes, we persist because this idea is a part of who we are and we must find a way to share it with the world. And once you start, you'll encourage yourself piece by piece, brick by brick, word by word. If we don't jump the ship, we can most likely find a way to patch it up and make it work better than ever.

People often ask me why I do this and what sets me apart from other entrepreneurial support folk. To me, the answer is simple and, the only answer that matters. I've never been in it for the money but believe there is something within that drives me to inspire others to struggle to reach for their best.

All of my life from when I had my first profitable business at age eleven has been dedicated to the joy of personal development through personal enterprise because I know how

No matter what happens, no idea or venture dies unless you finally stop trying.

good it feels deep down in the soul. As we try to discover our gifts, we gain the privilege of discovering our truest selves and the joy of sharing that best part of ourselves with others.

Keep the Dream ALIVE
1) *The dreamer element in each of us is the most important part of us.*
2) *When we attempt to act upon our dreams, dreamers offer new ways to do everything. New ways to live, think, eat; new ways to survive and carry on.*
3) *Dreaming doesn't simply require courage. It grows courage in you that you thought you could never have.*
4) *Pay attention to your challenges but don't be afraid of them. You can do it. You can find a way.*

TIME TO MAKE YOUR BEST IDEAS COME TO LIFE!

Each of us is born with certain gifts. The trick is to find and develop those gifts. No matter the age, social status or previous track record, it's never too late or too early to find and grow with your real talents.

Percentage-wise, there are more unhappy rich than unhappy poor people. There's no greater wealth than one which stems from discovering and growing with your own natural gifts.

The first step is to discover your best ideas and then instead of reacting to life, you can act upon your dreams. Every idea, every proposal, every lead is completely worthless without sufficient follow-up and exploration that achieves each step of your plan. Without that follow-up, you may as well never have started in the first place.

During our formative years, most of us were continually reinforced for every effort we made. We were told that trying was more important than the results. That's fine for growing up and learning but not for real idea-builders.

In the real world, only results count and all the empty promises delay the success that's waiting for you. It's far better to say, "I have done," than "I am going to do." Otherwise we are merely fishing for childlike gratification.

Each of you has a separate and unique opportunity to profit greatly from your dream. The more you can focus your energies on completing each step, the more you will profit. If your concept requires meetings, make sure those meetings are creating profit. Proceed at your own pace and style but channel your energies toward achievement.

We live in a world where the right knowledge transforms any dream into a possibility. Take this book and make your best dreams happen. Make your best self happen.

FREE ENTERPRISE

Don't just wish or hope for a better world, make a better world. Let your strengths overcome your weaknesses and let yourself grow.

My intention has been to help make all good dreams possible. That's the ideal that built this country and it's a wonderful principle. Have I promised you instant riches like all those miracle ads that take advantage of your right to hope? Of course not! Profit motive does not forgive deceit.

Could these techniques make you rich or famous? Indeed, I do have some clients who have used our techniques and become millionaires but our goal has been to see you become more fulfillment-oriented than merely money-oriented. You could make a lot of money but why just have things of value if you haven't developed values?

Get out there and make things better in your own way. Have fun. You will make more money and you may indeed get rich. My wish for you, however, is that this book has helped your venture give you a more enriched life.

If you'll indulge just one more story from me, I think it will prove useful. In the early nineties, I used to be a very minor writer for Jay Leno and while I would get a joke on here and there, I wasn't really all that good at it; just one of thousands looking for a break.

Still I tried as hard as I could to learn the craft and even made efforts to speak to Jay himself. Imagine my surprise when he not only took the time to call me but spent nearly an hour on the phone two separate times, trying to help me realize my potential as much as he possibly could.

I learned that I needed to go in other creative directions but I also learned that a client can never be too small or unimportant. So as I crafted the support element for this book, I drew upon this important lesson: Always strive to interact personally with your clientele.

If you need additional support, I encourage you to contact my organization. I read and respond to every email consultation personally. Some are done by dictation but I work to ensure that each inquiry has my personal guidance.

If you're following the steps in the book, your idea should be advancing. But if you do indeed require some special guidance, there are three low-cost support services available to you as follow:

PLEASE NOTE: All consults are handled in the strictest confidence and security. We will also gladly sign a Non-disclosure agreement if you request. ALL FEES ARE NON-REFUNDABLE.

One-Month Trial Unlimited Email Correspondence

Just $99. (Per Concept)

AFTERWORD

Email your toughest challenges and we'll work with you until the problem is solved. Then we'll stay with you to ensure your success. The only limit is that you may only submit summary reports or illustrations not to exceed ten pages and this is only available through electronic submission.

Three Months Unlimited Email and SnailMail Correspondence Just $199. (Per Concept)

We'll be there for you for a full 90 days for just $299. In addition, this program allows you to send products or plans of any length for specific review and recommendations. (Return postage is required if you want materials returned).

Six Months Unlimited Email and Snail-Mail Correspondence Just $299. (Per Concept)

You'll receive our full program for a full six Months for just $499. This program also allows you to send products or plans of any length for specific review and recommendations. (Return postage is required if you want materials returned).

On-Site Consultations and Other Engagements

Mr. Bronson is available for speaking engagements, seminars and on site consultations as his schedule permits. Fees begin at $2000. per day plus travel expenses.

Help, Howard..we need you right now.

Many businesses find themselves in crisis, especially now. Competition is up and revenue is down. The result is often a blindsided shock that seems to happen in moments. Suddenly, you realize that diminished or evaporated revenue is telling you to close your doors. But what if you could save your business by opening your mind?

For most faltering businesses, there are generally more options that the small business venturer realizes. What often comes to mind are layoffs but there is a better way if your team is truly committed. The business is always out there but often the business has to adjust their sights or purview of services, which can be done in a moment. Twenty years ago when my publishing company was desperately looking for new ways to survive, I received a phone call out of the blue asking me if I could write and produce a television show. "Sure, I can do that," I replied without missing a beat. Then, after I hung up the phone, I asked myself the vital question: *How do I do that?* I already knew I could write the show. All I had to do was learn how to put it all together and found many willing and talented professionals to help me do that.

FREE ENTERPRISE

I digress and if you're reading this, you don't have the time to waste. If you're a small businesses with a good idea in a bad financial spot, this service is for you. Yes, if costs money but the investment of this little bit of capital could save your investment. And compared to what other turn-around specialist may charge, you may see this service as a fair bet.

What you Receive

Depending upon his schedule, Mr. Bronson and his top-level staff literally drop what they're doing and convene immediately regarding your venture. Providing they can schedule it, you will receive a response within five business days.

How to engage this service

Simply send an email directly to Mr. Bronson at howard_bronson@yahoo.com and put EMERGENCY in the subject header.

Include your name, phone number and the best time to reach you.

What does this cost?

The cost is $1,195. , is non-refundable and must be paid in full and, in advance.

What You Receive

Upon receipt of payment in full, you will receive an email form that you need to fill out and email back as soon as possible. Within five business days, you will receive a series of at least three specific courses of action to keep your business in motion to hopefully thrive. After our response, you are permitted one follow-up email to clarify any suggestion or, ask any additional questions. Only one follow-up email is permitted.

Guarantee

There is absolutely no guarantee expressed nor implied and no fees paid are refundable. In addition, purchaser must understand and acknowledge that we are in no way financially responsible, liable or accountable for any results, negative or positive.

General Acceptance Policy

AFTERWORD

While most concepts are within the realm of feasibility, we do reserve the right to refuse any product or venture which we feel would either not benefit from this program, or that we at our sole discretion, deem to not be ethically appropriate.

To order any of these consulting offering, simply email: howard_bronson@yahoo.com

In the Subject Heading, list the name of The Service along with your phone number and best times to call. You will then be contacted to arrange for secure payment.

For special onsite requests or speaking engagements, simply email the above address with the subject heading: SPECIAL REQUEST.

INDEX

Additional Support
    e-consults from the Author 428-431

Advertising
    conventional 353-374
    unconventional 271-318
    publicity 299-332
    self-promotion 253-332

Ad Specialties *302*

Alternatives for..
    development *and production 193*
    paid advertising 271-318
    prototypes 35, 149-150

Banners and Signs *230, 251, 294, 308, 389*

The Great Big Bird Exercise *290*

Boosting Core Marketing Strategies and Tactics *59-63, 88-89, 116-119, 141-144, 175-176, 198-199, 223-224, 249-251, 293-296, 330-332, 347-350, 368-374, 385-386, 396-397, 406*

Conceptualization
    finding your best idea 30-33, 41-63, 72

Coping
    Humor 159-162

Copyright
    How to Access Free Government Forms 78-79, 128-136, 139-140

Core Strategies and Tactics *59-63, 88-89, 116-119, 141-144, 175-176, 198-199, 223-224, 249-251, 293-296, 330-332, 347-350, 368-374, 385-386, 396-397, 406*

Coupons and E-Coupons *223, 302, 303, 331, 348, 368, 369*

Courage *236, 365, 406, 409-411*

Customer Service *4,6, 12, 14, 59, 60, 88, 97, 100, 101, 143, 154-155, 165, 178, 183, 184, 189, 198, 199, 214, 223, 224, 236, 309, 324, 426, 427*

Development *7, 36, 41-47, 65-89, 168, 236, 342-245, 257, 328, 354, 364, 421, 426*

Discouragement, Frustration
    (please see 'courage')

Distribuition
    Product 193, 206, 227-251
    Business Concept 258, 259, 299-232
    Radio or Television Ad 276-281

Direct Response Advertising
    Radio and Television 198, 285, 289, 291, 345, 347

Dreaming *7, 13-14, 19, 22, 25, 27, 28, 30, 33-35, 39, 41, 49, 65, 73-79, 86-87, 97, 114, 12-121, 124, 161-162, 219, 227,-251, 263, 273, 291, 339, 364, 399, 400, 419,-423, 427-428*

FREE ENTERPRISE

Do-it-Yourself.
    Press releases 196, 201, 258,-260, 265-285, 296, 301-302
    Product test 92-118, 123-145, 300-301
    Idea Litmus test 51, 52, 392, 393

Events Planning 118, 126, 229-230

Finding Money
    through simple invoice assessment 169
    Via sales of your venture 193

Fraud and Scam Protection 5,33,34, 57, 76,155, 207, 231, 233, 260, 278, 279,327, 328, 329, 364, 383

Free
    Advertising 253-318
    Free classified advertising 76, 231, 250, 258, 272-278, 391
    Directory listings 153, 208, 231-233, 256-262, 390, 391
    Media distribution 196, 201, 258,-260, 265-285, 296, 301-302
    Idea testing 19, 47, 68, 82, 90-93, 109-133
    Press releases 196, 201, 258,-260, 265-285, 296, 301-302
    Public Service Announcements (PSA's) 202, 277-285
    Publicity 299-332
    Sponsored sites 17,171, 270368, 369, 403
    travel 392
    Web Site Development (Google free or sponsored web sites)

Government
    USPTO site 34,130,

Grants 369, 396

How to
    build a team 11,25, 34, 53, 54, 69, 123, 130, 169, 401-403, 409, 410
    create free national or international publicity 202, 277-285
    promote your venture for free 299-332
    identify Free Resources 17, 153, 155, 258
    get and stay inspired 342-343, 363-366, 401-402, 413-415 assess and secure best protection, patent or copyright options 6, 33-37, 79, 93-109, 128-135
    overcome excuses 10-13
    price your concept 227-251
    test an idea for free 19, 47, 104-127, 160, 190-213
    write a press release 196, 201, 258,-260, 265-285, 296, 301-302

Inventions
    Development 7, 36, 41-47, 65-89, 168, 236, 342-245, 257, 328, 354, 364, 421, 426

Keywords, Metatags and Phrases
    How to Find the Most Impactful Words 7,199, 257, 258-261

Inspiration 342-343, 363-366, 401-402, 413-415

Litmus Test
    How to test and idea for free 19, 47, 104-127, 160, 190-213

Loan
    Alternatives 170, 189, 254

INDEX

...ts and Copyrights
Protection 6, 33-37, 79, 93-109, 128-135
Paranoia 98-99

Manufacturing
Low-Cost Alternatives 7,21,34,55,93,101,124-129, 149-150, 153, 179, 181,184,187, 190, 193,213,229,242,257,417

Marketing *59-63, 88-89, 116-119, 141-144, 175-176, 198-199, 223-224, 249-251, 293-296, 330-332, 347-350, 368-374, 385-386, 396-397, 406*

Models and Prototypes
How to Build at Lowest Cost 35, 149-150, 190

Media
Creating a media image for your concept 63, 100, 123, 124, 142, 143, 175, 249, 266
Overcoming negative media 203-205,

Money
Alternatives for 213, 262,264 , 271-318, 389-402, 271-318
Improved Budget Management 168-171

Michael Martin Murphey *277*

Negotiating *51, 118, 181, 185, 207,237, 264,284-285, 417*

Networking
Social Networking 26, 61, 155, 201, 209, 234, 264, 311, 366, 390

Persistence *14, 29, 45, 92, 172, 183,189, 271, 292, 364, 419, 426*

Poverty
Changing your mindset 342-343, 363-366, 401-402, 413-415

Public Service Announcements *202, 277-285*

Publicity *202, 277-285, 299-332*

Referrals
How to Get 294, 311, 348, 370, 372, 402

Resources *17, 153, 155, 258*

Reyka, the famous Sheepdog *47, 265*

Riley, Michael *148, 404, 435*

Rustic Mountain Furniture *25, 401*

Sales *210-224, 227-251*

Scam and Fraud Protection *5,33,34, 57, 76,155, 207, 231, 233, 260, 278, 279,327, 328, 329, 364, 383*

Seminars *337, 338, 361, 404, 429*

Shaw, John *161*

FREE ENTERPRISE

Shawshank Redemption *37*

Social Networking *26, 61, 155, 201, 209, 234, 264, 311, 366, 390*

Solutions *3, 4, 9, 18, 50, 81, 84, 108, 137, 162, 163, 210, 217, 241, 286, 305, 342, 362, 380, 384, 409-411*

Strategies *59-63, 88-89, 116-119, 141-144, 175-176, 198-199, 223-224, 249-251, 293-296, 330-332, 347-350, 368-374, 385-386, 396-397, 406*

Survival
  Exercises 412-418

Team Building *11, 25, 34, 53, 54, 69, 130, 169, 401-403, 409, 410*

Test *19, 47, 104-127, 160, 190-213*

Time *172-174*

Tracking *240, 254, 406*

Wild Mountain Fire and Forestry *278, 422*

Zero-Based Budgeting 59-63, 88-89, 116-119, 141-144, 175-176, 198-199, 213, 262, 264, 271-318, 389-402, 271-318, 223-224, 249-251, 293-296, 330-332, 347-350, 368-374, 385-386, 396-397, 406

Other Books By Howard Bronson

How To Heal A Broken Heart in 30 D[ays]
(Random House)

Early Winter, Learning To Li[ve]
Love and Laugh After a Painful L[oss]
(Bestsell Publications)

Dog Gone, *Coping With the Loss of A [Pet]*
(Bestsell Publications)

Sking Without Seeing, *A Talking Book w[ith]*
Raised Diagrams for Teaching Snow-Sking [to]
the Blind